7/18/21

MW01148631

To Lt.Col. Wm.A.Allanson USMC(RET)/my number
one pilot and friend for over 65 years.
The author of this book lost my interest
at beginning with all the technical info.
But since my stroke in 2017 my brain don't
function like it use to. But later in the book
is interesting. After the officials in

charge decided they had all the bodies
they stopped search and left but
farmers, contractors and others on the

island have found bodies even in the
21st century. Enjoy your reading.

Semper Fi my
Great friend
Adios
JJS

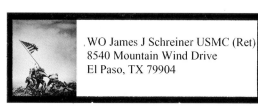

WO James J Schreiner USMC (Ret)
8540 Mountain Wind Drive
El Paso, TX 79904

LEAVING
MAC
BEHIND

LEAVING MAC BEHIND

THE LOST MARINES of GUADALCANAL

GEOFFREY W. ROECKER

FONTHILL

To those who fell,
and those who wait.

Fonthill Media Language Policy

Fonthill Media publishes in the international English language market. One language edition is published worldwide. As there are minor differences in spelling and presentation, especially with regard to American English and British English, a policy is necessary to define which form of English to use. The Fonthill Policy is to use the form of English native to the author. Geoffrey W. Roecker was born and educated in the United States; therefore American English has been adopted in this publication.

Fonthill Media Limited
Fonthill Media LLC
www.fonthillmedia.com
office@fonthillmedia.com

First published in the United Kingdom and the United States of America 2019

British Library Cataloguing in Publication Data:
A catalogue record for this book is available from the British Library

Copyright © Geoffrey W. Roecker 2019

ISBN 978-1-78155-734-1

Typeset in 10.5pt on 13pt Sabon
Printed and bound in England

Prologue:
The Last Day

He awoke early on the patrol's last day.

Everything hurt. He had long since stopped counting the blisters, the bites, and the bruises as the march went on; they were merely a collective ache. His skin, lashed by liana vines and sliced by knife-like *kunai* grass, was pruned and softened from ever-present moisture. When he was not wading a stream, he was pouring with sweat, and the weather cycled between raining, just about to rain, and just finished raining. Yesterday's punishing climb was the latest exertion of a month-long sojourn through the swamps and thickets, ridges, and valleys of a sweltering, stinking bump on the backside of the world. His officers called it Mount Austen; the native guides called it Mombula—their word for "rotting body." Whatever you called it, this mountaintop on Guadalcanal was just about as far from Coleraine, Minnesota, as a guy could get.

He lit a cigarette with the dawn, red-rimmed blue eyes staring out of a ruddy face turned jaundice yellow from atabrine. They were all dragging ass. Dysentery was the order of the day; the sudden liquefying of the bowels robbing men of strength and dignity as they scampered for the tree line or simply slit holes in the seat of their pants. Others shivered and sweated in the early stages of malaria, their perspiration irritating the weeping ringworm ulcers that covered their bodies. "Jungle rot," they said. "Got that creepin' crud." Blood ran down their legs and pooled into their boondockers, rotting their socks faster than they could wring them out. More than a quarter of them fell out, and many more should have. Tempers were short, but morale was still high. They were all volunteers.

He raised his hand and signed his name in 1939, two years out of high school and the Civilian Conservation Corps. His mother was dead, and his father was ailing, but his siblings always worked together and now he, the youngest by far, would do his part. In San Diego, he learned the new language of shitbirds and boots, of '03s and BARs, of pride in traditions dating back to the Revolution. He was intelligent, trustworthy, of good character, and took to the training like a fish to water. They presented him with an emblem, named him Marine, and shipped him to Hawaii. Two months later, he learned that his father had died.

He saw the meatball-marked aircraft swooping low over Ewa Field on one December Sunday in 1941, saw the smoke billowing from stricken ships in Battleship Row, saw the oil-blackened bodies of sailors pulled from the wrecks at Pearl Harbor. He made a personal vow of vengeance, but after the raid, aviation gasoline was more valuable than a PFC's crusade. So he took eight men to Damon's Island, posted guards, and watched for saboteurs.

Months passed. Wake fell, Bataan fell, Corregidor fell, and their Marine defenders disappeared into captivity or oblivion. Midway held by the skin of its teeth; some of the newly-minted hero pilots had flown or fueled from Ewa Field. The 1st and 2nd Marine Divisions boarded convoys and sailed west, their destinations classified but their intent unmistakable—revenge for Pearl Harbor. Soon, the word Guadalcanal was on everybody's lips. Marines and sailors were launching the first offensive against Japan. Meanwhile, defending Damon's Island required a daily phone call to the first sergeant at the barracks.

Pvt. Purcell approached him in August 1942. "Corporal, I'd like permission to put my name on the Carlson Raider list."

The 2nd Marine Raider Battalion was back from Makin. Newspapers blared the story of a daring commando raid carried out by hand-picked volunteers clad in black-dyed dungarees and published photos of the President's own son holding a captured Japanese flag. This first official recognition of the Raiders painted a picture of "hard-bitten veterans" ready to give "plenty of hot lead and cold steel to the Japs."[1] Col. Evans Carlson wanted more volunteers for his battalion, and Purcell wanted a piece of the action. The corporal gave his permission, with a condition: "I can't get away now, but will you put my name on the list, too?"[2]

Now he was here on Guadalcanal, one of the "Gung-Ho" Raiders. He had good leaders in Lt. Does and Cpl. Croft, and a trustworthy fire team in Privates Farrar and Van Buren. They called him "Whitey" for his fair hair. He could subsist on bacon and rice, communicate with Melanesian guides, and identify the distinctive prints of Japanese boots on a muddy trail. He had stood security at the base at Binu, walked point on patrols, and fought the Japanese in near total darkness. He knew how Barber from Company "C" was tortured and killed and scattered in pieces, and how his own company moved through a Japanese field hospital, bayonetting the wounded and sick where they lay. They had buried Marines along the way but none from his company; it did not seem to matter that he had left his lucky rabbit's foot in his bags at Espiritu Santo. It was almost over, the Old Man said, and they would return to the perimeter as conquerors of the Japanese, of the island, of the base human nature that sought the easy way out. Then Carlson himself led them in their hymn, "from the halls of Montezuma to the shores of Tripoli," and when the native boys joined in for "Onward Christian Soldiers," the melody blended in "a daring challenge to any enemy soldiers within [the] sound of our voices."[3] It was the proudest moment in many a young life.

And it was in this spirit that Cpl. Albert Laddce "Whitey" Hermiston was told that he would be the point man for the point squad, leading Carlson's Raiders down the final trail to safety, to a hero's welcome, to a hot meal. He had marched and fought for 150 miles. What was one more day?

They buried him beside Farrar and Matelski at noon.

Author's Note

I first learned about my family's role in World War II when Robert Ballard's *The Lost Ships of Guadalcanal* hit bookstore shelves.

I was nine or ten years old, and Dr. Ballard was who I wanted to be when I grew up. He had found the *Titanic* and the *Bismarck* and brought the stories of ships, passengers, and crew to vivid life. I had no idea where Guadalcanal was, but the book had Dr. Ballard's name on it and one of those great Ken Marshall paintings on the cover. That was enough for me. I sat right down on the bookstore floor, looking at the pictures, planning a future in maritime archaeology and wondering how to convince Mom to buy me a $40 book.

Like all of Ballard's books, *Lost Ships* is richly illustrated with photographs and paintings. There is a shot of an American cruiser flying a dozen signal flags, one of those rare color shots that reminds you that the past is not all just black and white. I was on this page when my grandmother wandered by and glanced over my shoulder. "Oh," she said, "that looks like the *Quincy*."

She was right. I was surprised. My grandmother is a wise woman, but identifying warships in a single glance was not a talent I knew she possessed.

She told me her uncle, Ned, whom the Navy called Lt. Cdr. Edmund Billings, was an officer on the USS *Quincy*. He had gone to sea and never returned. Missing in action and presumed dead. We looked through the book together and found a picture of the *Quincy* in her death throes at the Battle of Savo Island. She was lit up by searchlights and burning. Perhaps at that very moment, Billings was staggering out of the ruined pilothouse, muttering his last words to a frightened ensign: "Everything will be fine. The ship will go down fighting."

There were more pictures and paintings of the wreck site. Clearly, Dr. Ballard had done it again. I was in heaven; my grandmother was very quiet. I did not think to ask what she was thinking. If I remember right, she was the one who bought me the book. It is sitting on my desk as I am writing, and a photo of Great-Granduncle Ned Billings hangs on the wall. He never did come home. And he is not alone.

There is collective anguish preserved in our National Archives system, tucked in the personnel files of lost loved ones. Letters from families asking for news, for confirmation of a rumor, for personal effects, for photographs, for the return of the dead. Some are brief and businesslike, even formal, as if concluding an unpleasant but necessary transaction. Others last for pages, appealing to the humanity of the bureaucracy, invoking a child who never saw their father or an ailing parent who cannot accept their child is dead. From page to page, neat penmanship grows shaky and devolves into a scrawl as the writer's emotions take over. All are difficult to read, but those on behalf of the missing are doubly so. And there are so many of them.

"Missing in action" carries an awesome weight, even after several generations when the individuals concerned are long gone. They are missing not in the sense that they may still live, but in the sense that, to their families, they never really died. It is the difference between "killed in the war" and "never came home," between "Here lies" and "In memory of," between healed scars and open wounds. The trauma grows less with each generation until it is buried beneath the surface, but it is still there, dormant. The return of a long-lost family member has the potential to heal a hurt that was never fully realized. I have been to a few of these repatriation ceremonies and know this to be true.

This book is, by necessity, limited in scope. I chose to focus on Marine Corps ground units, partly because the evolution of doctrine is more evident in the records they left behind, and partly because history tends to blend the "grunts" into nameless statistics. Except for the infamous Goettge Patrol—which happened to fit the subject matter perfectly, and (to paraphrase another author) "no history of the campaign would dare omit"—I tried to bring lesser-known events to the forefront. I could not tell every story, and for that I am sorry. Marines, soldiers, sailors, Coast Guardsmen, pilots and tankers, artillerists and infantrymen—everyone who went to that island left a part of himself behind, and so this book is for them.

Many have helped along the way, and although some may not know it, I owe them a debt of gratitude. The professors of Norwich University's graduate program, especially Dr. David J. Ulbrich and Dr. Jonathan House, helped channel enthusiasm into scholarship. The patient, helpful staff of the National Archives in College Park answered repeated email requests and rewrote my illegible pull slips. I particularly wish to thank Nate Patch for his invaluable help with the Marine Corps muster rolls. Also, the archivists at the Marine Corps History Division in Quantico, who let me leaf through Col. Goettge's unit journal. Next time, I will bring a quieter scanner.

An incredible circle of colleagues and fellow researchers kept me on track, honest, and well-supplied with documents and information. Justin Taylan of PacificWrecks and Rob Rumsby are incredibly knowledgeable, and their years of dedication to Pacific War history and to non-recovered servicemen are both admirable and inspirational. Geoff Gentillini of Golden Arrow Research helped me acquire scores of records from the St. Louis archives, and has been a trusted sounding board for the past five years. Michael Bracey helped track down records in College Park. Marnie Weeks and Lisa Hirano keep an eye on all the boys in the Punchbowl and have provided pictures and information about the last resting places of Marines from across the Pacific. Jennifer S. Morrison has forgotten more about genealogy than I will ever know, and her ability to navigate the tangled roots of family trees is past compare. Jennifer also connected me to Katie Rasdorf, without whom I would probably still be struggling to find the front door of Archives II, let alone any of the useful information that made its way into this book.

The families of veterans provided invaluable insights, as well. I am particularly indebted to David Wollschlager, for sharing his interview with Charles "Monk" Arndt. To Trish Berne, Katie Wahrhaftig, Scott and Wayne Tompkins, Carl and Kevin Custer, Becky Ague, Drs. Jeffrey Panosian and Claire Panosian Dunavan, Dottie Pendleton, Anne Anderson, Tony Corriggio, David Stacey, Gordon Thompson, and many more: may your ancestors rest in peace and come home soon. My own family gave their love, lent their support, and occasionally let me escape to upstate New York for a bit of fresh air and some quiet writing time. My mom even bravely agreed to read—and proofread—the first draft, and if that is not a mother's love, I do not know what is.

To Gunga—a good Marine and a better friend—we will get MuMu back. Semper Fi.

And finally, my wonderful wife and best friend, Esther. Without your patience, perspective, love, and encouragement, I do not know where I would be. The best book is a done book, and this one is done. For now.

CONTENTS

1

The Exorbitant Bill

The price paid for victory by a nation ill-prepared to fight was apparent to all who studied the record. A single item of this exorbitant bill was the cost of deferring preparation for proper care of the dead in war until the outbreak of hostilities.

Edward Steere, *The Graves Registration Service in World War II*[1]

On a little embankment a few feet inland from the coast road, in what had once been a grove of trees, stood a crude cross marking the grave of a Marine.

After months of devastation, the land was beginning to heal. A thick carpet of new grass covered the grave, and communications wire hung from the branches of young shrubs. Tendrils of green vines snaked up the shattered stumps and crept along the ground. In time, they would climb the monument and pull it down. A bandolier draped casually over the crossbar, as if misplaced and awaiting the return of its owner. The shrapnel-pocked helmet atop the cross was beginning to rust, but the flattened mess tin bearing the name of Cpl. Robert Wallace still shone brightly in the February sun. The makeshift monument was visible to anyone headed west along the coast road; the name scratched on the tin could be read by anyone who cared to pause. However, those heading west along this road were heading for action, and there was nothing special about the grave of Cpl. Wallace. There were hundreds like his on Guadalcanal.

Gunner John F. Leopold was one who paused. As the assistant D-2 (intelligence officer) of the 2nd Marine Division, Leopold had a keen interest in observing the final stages of the campaign and was probably headed towards the front at Tassafaronga when he passed the lonely grave on February 2, 1943. The gunner pulled out his camera—he was also the Division's photographic officer—quickly composed his shot and moved on. Two weeks later, while touring the banks of the infamous Matanikau River, Leopold spotted another lonely grave just feet from the water. A rusted Garand rifle poked from a mound of rocks. Leopold read the inscription scrawled in childish capitals on the scrap wood cross. "RIP. HERE LIES A DEVIL DOG."

On February 18, shortly before leaving Guadalcanal, Leopold paid a visit to the island cemetery. He might have found the place unusually busy, as the first Graves Registration unit in the Solomon Islands was being commissioned there that very morning. The entire strength of the platoon—seven former quartermasters and one former artillery corporal—bustled back and forth with stacks of forms as native laborers sweated over their shovels, digging new graves. Army trucks unloaded a grim cargo; the bundles, wrapped in stained ponchos, quickly disappeared into the makeshift morgue. Leopold wandered over to the old section of the cemetery, where the Marines killed in the early days of the campaign were laid to rest. A poem adorning the grave of PFC William Cameron caught his eye:

> *And When He Goes To Heaven*
> *To St. Peter He'll Tell*
> *"Another Marine Reporting Sir*
> *I've Served My Time In Hell."*

It took several years to tabulate the butcher's bill exacted by the Guadalcanal campaign. The Army estimated some 550 fatal casualties from the American and 25th Divisions, though their history of the campaign questioned the numbers.[2] The Casualty Division Headquarters, US Marine Corps, arrived at a total of 954 leathernecks of all ranks killed in action, with a further 103 dead of wounds and 145 "missing, presumed dead."[3] Some 60,000 ground troops fought there between August 7, 1942, and February 9, 1943; hundreds fought in the air, and the United States Navy contributed thousands of sailors whose loss figures were never accurately compiled but easily numbered in the thousands. Historians writing in the late 1940s quibbled over the figures, but most agreed on one thing: "the cost of victory, though dear, had not been prohibitive."[4]

As these military chroniclers wrote of the dead in the past tense, the story was still unfolding. Between 1947 and 1949, American ships returned to the Solomon Islands for the express purpose of repatriating more than 3,000 fallen servicemen. While civilian crews labored to exhume the largest cemetery in the South Pacific, uniformed specialists climbed ridges and sloshed through rivers, retracing old battle lines with tired maps, searching for signs of those who had died or disappeared in the jungles of Guadalcanal. The passage of time frustrated their efforts; new growth, both natural and manmade, had transformed the battlefield so that even those who had fought for the island had trouble getting their bearings. They found a few dozen out of the hundreds that they sought.

The ships returned bearing caskets of bones for processing at a laboratory near Pearl Harbor. Here, anthropologists confirmed or rejected the identities attached to the dead of the Solomon Islands. The completion of their work triggered a multitude of forms to the deceased's next of kin. Some forms inquired about cemetery preferences. Others reported that a loved one thought forever lost had been found. And many carried the unwelcome news that the father, husband, brother, or son was not coming back at all. A board in Hawaii had examined his case and deemed him non-recoverable. The cases were closed, but the wounds remained open.

In April 1951, accomplished historian Edward Steere put the finishing touches on Volume 21 of the Quartermaster Corps' Historical Studies series. Entitled *The Graves Registration Service in World War II*, Steere's opus tracked the evolution of the administrative process by which the American military recovered, identified, buried, and eventually repatriated its war dead. This noble task, he opined, was necessary to satisfy the emotional and patriotic needs of a civilized nation. Invoking the words of Thucydides, Steere described the return of the dead from the Peloponnesian War, when the citizens of Athens turned out to publicly celebrate and mourn the departed and dress their bones with flowers. The "similarity of sentiment and method of expression accorded the warrior dead in ancient Athens and in modern America" led him to argue that the veneration of military dead was all but essential to the foundation of a democratic society. It was a "melancholy fact that only within the past hundred years has any government been willing or able to assume the obligation of identifying and burying in registered graves the remains of all who gave up their lives in war."[5] He told of the dedication of national cemeteries at Antietam and Gettysburg, and how Lincoln so movingly eulogized the dead to give meaning to their sacrifice, comfort to the bereaved, and motivation to a war-weary population. He recalled how the Quartermaster Burial Corps marked the graves of soldiers lost in the Spanish-American War, and the groundbreaking effort to bring the honored dead home as "probably the first attempt of a nation to disinter the remains of all its soldiers who ... had given up their lives on a foreign shore and bring them ... to their native land for return to their relatives and friends."[6] He remarked on the revolutionary evolution of the service between 1917 and 1921, as skilled technicians and trained administrators accounted for no less than 79,129 fatalities suffered in the Great War. To Steere, this was more than performing a service, it was carrying out the embodied will of the American people.

However, the progress made after World War I did not carry over into World War II. "Planning for the emergency of war was regarded in many intellectual circles as a base betrayal of the memory of those who had fallen in the recent conflict," Steere wrote of the interwar years. If the "war to end wars" had been fought, why continue the grim study of preparing to receive and bury an army of corpses? The question, foolish in hindsight, had been answered more than 400,000 times since December 7, 1941.[7] Steere's 200-page tome was an attempt to future-proof the burial process, and the experience had been a trying one. He gave vent to his frustration in a heated preface:

> The continuity of graves registration organization was broken during the peace, resulting in an arrest of the function and such a condition of atrophy that it could not be reinvigorated at will. Changes in tactical doctrine ... were paralleled only by revisions in the paper organization of the Quartermaster Graves Registration Company. Then, while some sixty manuals were prepared for the field forces during 1941 with a view to embodying lessons of the revolutionary form of mobile warfare that had destroyed the Polish and French armies in campaigns of a few weeks duration, the graves registration manual was written in reference to conditions of the war of position fought over two decades before in Western Europe.[8]

Steere is referring to Technical Manual Number 10-630: *Graves Registration*, the first War Department publication dedicated to the subject since 1924. Previously, the subject had been covered in the briefest possible terms by sections in other manuals, notably the December 1940 TM 10-100 *Field Service Regulations: Administration* (six paragraphs in the final chapter, titled "Miscellaneous") and the April 1941 TM 16-205 *The Chaplain* (two pages of a section entitled "The Chaplain at War.") Both volumes drew upon the 1924 manuals with minimal revisions.[9] The new manual (abbreviated to TM 10-630) provided a comprehensive overview of the quartermaster's duties relating to the collection, identification, burial, and eventual repatriation of wartime dead; it made no provisions for establishing a peacetime Graves Registration Service. The companies it described on paper would be called up in the event of war, and not before. Any plans for disseminating new information in advance of armed conflict were not to be. TM 10-630 entered publication on September 23, 1941, a scant ten weeks before the attack on Pearl Harbor. The Quartermaster

General had, as the saying goes, prepared to fight the last war instead of the next.

Naturally, a lack of preparedness led to confusion. The shipment home of remains from stations outside the United States was suspended immediately after Pearl Harbor, thus mandating the need for temporary overseas cemeteries and requiring commanders stationed abroad to address the problem as they saw fit. A February 1942 War Department circular required adherence to TM 10-630, but apparently provided little by way of instruction, and the manual itself "as a reference guide left much to be desired." The Army's Quartermaster Graves Registration Companies, duly called up at the outbreak of hostilities, were still being trained; eight of them were in existence in August of 1942, but none were ready for overseas duty. Until training programs could catch up with the demand—and no facilities for comprehensive training would exist until early 1943—the process would be defined by a lack of coordination, standardization, and cohesion, all of which would have a massive impact in the years to follow.[10]

Steere continued:

> In these circumstances, the establishment of a graves registration service for the field forces necessarily took the form of attempting to activate an obsolete paper scheme and then adapting it to situations alien to a doctrine that had consistently ignored existing conditions by looking fixedly to the past.... The lag imposed by an almost studious neglect of graves registration until the eve of Pearl Harbor was never completely overcome during the course of hostilities.[11]

At no time was this need for adaptation more glaringly apparent than during the first year of war in the Pacific—a frantic few months that Steere and other scholars have characterized as a "period of improvisation." There was no accumulated knowledge of how to handle massive casualties in an amphibious operation. The pre-war experience of South Pacific garrisons—"where deaths were few and problems of evacuation, identification, and burial were totally dissimilar to those encountered in the battle zone"—would be of little help.[12] Nor would the emergency methods devised on Wake Island or in the Philippines: the burial parties were either in Japanese prison camps or were themselves dead and buried. Troops in the Solomon Islands would have to figure out proper procedures on the spot. The results of their improvisations would last for decades.

In *Soldier Dead: How We Recover, Identify, Bury & Honor Our Military Fallen*, author Michael Sledge identifies five categories for the recovery of military fatalities: combat, post-combat, non-combat, area clearance, and historical.[13] Guadalcanal was (and still is) the scene of countless instances of these five categories, each of which has influenced, directly or indirectly, the recoverability of individual fighting men.

Combat recovery is, as the name implies, the act of collecting the dead while under fire. "It is a given that soldiers want to recover their fallen comrades," writes Sledge. "At the time of death, they are not thinking of identification and further handling, temporary burial or concurrent return. All they want is to bring the bodies of their friends to a safe place, and this entails great risks."[14] When two men from his company were killed in action at Point Cruz in November 1942, Plat. Sgt. Rhynette Spell took a patrol of volunteers into enemy territory to retrieve the bodies; failing that, he reportedly had them buried on the spot rather than leave them to the enemy. In another instance, PFC Richard J. Kelly and PFC Francis E. Drake, Jr., went to the aid of a wounded friend trapped between the lines. Drake was himself shot and killed on the return trip; Kelly managed to get the wounded man to safety and then went back out to retrieve Drake. These were individual acts of bravery, motivated not by any official policy but by the unspoken understanding of no man left behind. Only in the most extreme circumstances would a unit withdraw without making some attempt to recover its dead, or at the very least collect personal effects or identity tags that might help confirm the death. Unfortunately, these circumstances did exist, resulting in more than a few notations reading "due to battle conditions, body not recovered."

Post-combat recovery occurred immediately after the bullets stopped flying. Sledge divides this category into two phases. First was the removal of the dead from the battlefield or aid station to a collection point, a task usually accomplished by combat troops who were handling the bodies of their friends. In a by-the-book instance, this would have been a designated spot established by Graves Registration Service (GRS) personnel who were prepared to handle remains properly, check and confirm identification, and begin the rigorous administrative process that ensured the right name stayed connected to the right remains. However, few Marines possessed such training in 1942, and a Guadalcanal collection point was more likely to be a nearby trailhead or road—if one existed near their location. This point was chosen to facilitate Sledge's second phase of recovery: transport from the collection point to "areas where the next steps of disposition took place."[15] On Guadalcanal, this meant the cemetery near Henderson Field, initially called the First Marine Division Cemetery (FMC) and later expanded to the Army, Navy, and Marine Corps Cemetery, Guadalcanal (ANMC). The "next steps" involved collecting dog tags or other identifying media, fingerprinting the body (if possible), and taking a tooth chart (also if possible) before burial in a marked grave.

This system worked well enough for casualties sustained inside the perimeter or on defensive actions where Marines retained control of their position. In more remote areas or with units on patrol, the second phase was generally not possible. Firefights in the jungle usually resulted in more men wounded than killed outright; the necessity of evacuating those who were not yet dead outweighed the need to bring back a buddy who was past help. These patrols were frequently operating several miles from friendly lines, over rough terrain. Heat and humidity exhausted stretcher bearers—as many as six were needed to transport a single casualty—and an armed escort was needed for protection. In one event in September 1942, a combat patrol by the 1st Battalion, 7th Marines, had so many wounded that the battalion commander detailed two of his three companies to bring them back to the perimeter. In a fight atop Mount Austen on December 3, 1942, the 2nd Raider Battalion sustained three casualties, including a severely wounded platoon leader. Their need for medical attention dictated a faster pace the following day; as a result, the point walked into an ambush and suffered an additional three killed and four wounded. The three dead were buried near the ambush site; an hour later, the wounded officer succumbed and was interred in a lone grave beside the trail. (A fourth wounded man later died in the Division field hospital; the patrol's last casualty became their first to be buried in a Guadalcanal cemetery.) Neither unit was able to bring out their dead; thus field burial was a necessary expedient. In these cases, the collection point became more of a consolidation point. A group of graves standing together stood a better chance of being rediscovered than single graves scattered about an area. Consolidation was done in both preceding examples. The 7th Marines Battalion created two small cemeteries of five graves each—distance and terrain prevented further consolidation—while the Raiders carried the body of one ambush victim some distance up a steep slope to ensure his burial in a visible location. (The lone officer, 1Lt. Jack Miller, was the exception; unfortunately, his grave was later lost.)

It should be noted that these field burials, while hardly ideal, were performed with the understanding that they were only temporary. Most combat Marines believed that eventually "somebody" would be back to get their buddies and did their best to situate graves in visible locations—along trails or tree lines, on riverbanks or ridges—and to describe the location, either by map coordinates, measured distances, or other notable landmarks. One Marine's grave was, somewhat unhelpfully, described only as being the "only grave in the vicinity."[16] However, any number of mishaps could befall a marker: washed away by flooding, knocked over by a falling tree, uprooted by foraging animals, removed by vengeful enemy troops, or even destroyed in a subsequent battle. The time elapsed between burial and retrieval efforts was such that many markers were simply gone by the time anyone came looking, and by that point, rough coordinates or landmarks were usually not enough information.

Non-combat recoveries involve deaths of servicemen in incidents related to military operations, but not direct contact with the enemy—anything from an accidental drowning or vehicle collision to plane crashes or explosions while handling munitions. While the recovery conditions for non-combat fatalities were generally more favorable than combat situations and had a higher identification rate, they could still pose problems. A particularly nasty incident occurred on December 21, 1942. Two trucks collided; one happened to be carrying a cargo of land mines for the Army Corps of Engineers, and the resulting explosion obliterated the occupants of both vehicles. The dog tag of PFC Herman Dallas Avery (Weapons Company, 2nd Marines) was found near the site; this was the only clue that he had even been present. A luckless labor detail had the grim task of collecting the pieces, which were all buried together in a single grave as Unknowns X-42 through X-45. This grave was thought to contain only four remains, but post-war laboratory analysis identified parts of no less than seven men. Even then, the remains could not be segregated into individuals, so the men were given a group burial in Chattanooga National Cemetery.[17]

Sledge includes his final two categories—area clearance and historical—under the umbrella heading of "non-combat" operations, as these may only take place once an area is secure from threats that might impede the careful, thorough search for lost remains.

Area clearance involves "searching for those remains that have not been recovered in previous operations, and ... disinterring bodies from temporary gravesites established when it was impossible or impractical to remove them to major cemeteries."[18] On Guadalcanal, this operation began shortly before the island was formally secured and continued, in various iterations, through 1949. The first evidence of a mass reinterment occurred in January 1943, when the bodies of five soldiers from Company "I," 164th Infantry were reportedly interred in Row 94 of the FMC. All five had been killed in action the previous November; the fact that they were identified at the time of reburial suggests that they were in well-marked and well-preserved graves. The 164th retrieved most of their field burials before the battle ended. Immediately after Guadalcanal was declared secure, other Army units took to the field and searched out their dead, which led to a massive increase in the size of the recently established ANMC. Fortunately, by this time a rudimentary Graves Registration outfit was available to assist with cemetery operations. From that point on, although the units occasionally rotated, there was always a GRS presence on Guadalcanal.

These GRS teams handled area clearance when they could, although it does not seem to have been their primary duty. Guadalcanal grew into a major base, with supply depots, training areas, and hospitals all contributing their share of fatal incidents. Occasionally, when new construction turned up scattered bones or a curious sightseer unearthed a grave in the jungle, the GRS troops were dispatched to collect the remains. By this point, no recognizable physical traits remained; fingerprinting was impossible, bones were often eroded or fragmentary, and the GRS men, while better trained, were by no means forensic experts. Without identifying evidence—a tag, a grave marker, or marked personal effects— these remains were buried as "unknown."

After the war, two major area clearance tasks remained. The first was the closing of the ANMC, which had grown to include well over 3,000 graves. (Many of these men were initially buried on other islands; Guadalcanal served as a consolidation point for all cemeteries in the Solomon Islands.) Responsibility for exhuming these graves fell to the 9105th Technical Services Unit. The other was a search and recovery mission for isolated graves and missing personnel across the Pacific. The 604th Quartermaster Graves Registration Company (QMGRC), one of the more experienced units of its type in the theater, assumed responsibility for this complex task. The 604th made two such expeditions, visiting Guadalcanal in 1947 and 1949, but met with limited success. Only 178 remains—just under 2 percent of those thought to be missing in the entire theater—were found. Active searching officially halted in 1950. Those left behind were declared "permanently nonrecoverable" while hundreds of remains were "approved unidentifiable" and buried in national cemeteries as unknowns.

We are currently in the era of historical recovery. The Central Identification Laboratory, Hawaii (CILHI)—created to identify the remains of World War II Pacific theater dead—was reestablished in 1976 with "the mission to recover and identify all unrecovered United States service members from past wars."[19] Since then, an evolving array of government agencies have conducted active investigations into incidents involving non-recovered military personnel, and civilians lost in military operations, dating back to 1941.[20]

The Defense POW/MIA Accounting Agency (DPAA) is the current government entity charged with recovering, identifying, and repatriating the physical remains of American servicemen killed in action and buried overseas. In their terminology, individuals buried with honor as unknowns, lost at sea, or missing in action are classified as "unaccounted for."[21] This grammatically unwieldy yet surprisingly handy phrase, which frequently extends to include "those not repatriated or identified from isolated burials," is a blanket designation for servicemen whose identity or precise burial site is not confirmed. Determining the fate of the dead is personnel accounting. (Its companion term, personnel recovery, relates to "the recovery and reintegration of isolated personnel" who are still living and should not be confused with "remains recovery" as used in this book. There are no ongoing personnel recovery missions for World War II-era losses.)

When compelling evidence of an incident site (e.g., an airplane crash site, mass grave, or scattered bones with American military equipment) is found, the DPAA's Research and Investigation Team (RIT) generates leads from archival files and oral histories. An Investigative Team (IT) explores the most promising leads and conducts a survey, searching for evidence that may connect the site to an individual case. Sites are prioritized by factors such as terrain and accessibility, political and international relations, jeopardizing factors like urban development, and the likelihood of finding identifiable remains. If the IT recommends a site for further inspection, a Recovery Team (RT) is dispatched to conduct an archaeological dig, which hopefully results in the recovery of identifying media or human remains. The DPAA also oversees the exhumation of remains from national cemeteries, in conjunction with the Department of Veteran's Affairs.

Currently, the DPAA reports a total of 82,134 individuals unaccounted for in conflicts from World War II to the present day. Of these, 72,744 date to the World War II era, with 47,469—including nearly 3,000 Marines—in the Indo-Pacific area.[22] An imaginary DPAA field team deployed to the Guadalcanal in February 1943 would have had about 520 members of the United States Marine Corps on its priority list. This figure would include individuals missing in action on land, sea, and air—who might, conceivably, still be alive—and those who were known to be dead but whose remains lay buried or unburied in remote or unrecorded locations on Guadalcanal or the surrounding islands. First, the team would eliminate some thirty Marines buried at sea with the appropriate ceremony (not, technically, unaccounted for, as opposed to those missing as the result of ships sinking, aircraft losses over water, or drowning). As the years went by, they would gradually tick off 108 other names identified from unknown burials and field recoveries. By 2019, they would count a total of 386 Marine Corps personnel (including eight Navy corpsmen attached to Marine units) still unaccounted for from the Guadalcanal campaign. This number represents 28 percent of fatalities in Marine units during the campaign, and more than one in ten of all World War II-era Marines so classified today.

The National Memorial Cemetery of the Pacific in Honolulu (commonly called "the Punchbowl") holds the remains of more than 160 unidentified individuals who were exhumed from the ANMC or found in isolated graves on Guadalcanal. This number includes American soldiers, sailors, and

Coast Guardsmen from across the Solomon Islands; a few Japanese soldiers and Melanesian civilians are thought to occupy plots here, too. It is likely, therefore, that at least some of the 386 Guadalcanal Marines are not lost in the boondocks but buried as unknowns in Hawaii. And it is possible that additional research into their cases might reveal their identities.

While the DPAA is the only agency that can officially "account for" an individual, independent researchers and nonprofit groups have had a decided impact on increasing the visibility of non-recovered cases, and in influencing which sites are targeted by Recovery Teams. The MIA Recovery Network, Justin Taylan's Pacific Wrecks, Ted Darcy's WFI Research Group, and others spend countless hours working with original documentation and creating case files arguing for DPAA investigations. Pearl Harbor survivor Ray Emory spent twenty-five years researching the mass graves of USS *Oklahoma* crewmen at the Punchbowl and campaigned to have the remains exhumed for identification. A trial run on one mass grave was made in 2003. CILHI director John Byrd estimated that the site contained the commingled remains of nearly 100 individuals, of whom only five were tentatively identified.[23] Between 2008 and 2010, Emory's research helped identify those five sailors and return them to their families. Encouraged by this success, the Department of Defense ordered the exhumation of the remaining *Oklahoma* burials in 2015. Since then, more than 100 sailors and six Marines from the ship's company have been accounted for, and the investigation is still ongoing.

Other nonprofits send teams into the field. Usan Kurata's Kuuentai was formed in 2006 to search for Japanese soldiers in the Philippines and Mariana Islands. In 2014, when the Joint POW/MIA Accounting Command (JPAC, the predecessor of DPAA) dismissed a proposed cooperative effort on Saipan, Kurata created the subgroup KUENTAI-USA to handle any American remains found at his excavation site. With a minuscule budget and limited time—the area was slated for residential development—KUENTAI-USA recovered the remains of several American soldiers. Thanks to these efforts, four members of the 105th Infantry Regiment were returned to their families. The Bentprop Project sends a volunteer team to Palau every year; they claim to have located dozens of wrecked World War II-era aircraft, both American and Japanese. Their 2004 discovery of a B-24J Liberator, which they nicknamed "Number 453," led to the recovery and successful identification of eight of the eleven crew off the coast of Babeldaub Island. The search became the basis of Wil S. Hylton's book *Vanished: The Sixty-Year Search for the Missing Men of World War II.*

A Florida-based organization, History Flight, focuses their Pacific efforts on the island of Betio in the Tarawa atoll, where over one thousand

Americans fell during a three-day battle in November 1943. Several hundred Marines, sailors, and Army aviators were not recovered from the field after the war. When the organization's research into mass graves on Betio met criticism from JPAC, founder Mark Noah built a team including archaeologists, forensic odontologists, and a renowned cadaver dog named Buster. In 2015, History Flight conducted a dig at a shipping facility on Betio and discovered "Cemetery 27," one of the largest American field burial sites found to date. The remains of almost fifty Marines were handed over to the DPAA and CILH for identification; more than half—including a Medal of Honor recipient, 1Lt Alexander Bonnyman—have been returned to their families. History Flight's continuing work on Betio has resulted in the recovery of hundreds of partial remains, some of which are helping to resolve the identities of unknowns buried in Hawaii. These achievements have not only helped solve an enduring mystery of the Pacific war but brought closure to many families and increased public awareness of the "Tarawa Marines."

Guadalcanal has not been the subject of such scrutiny, but recent activity suggests that it may move up the priority list. Honiara, the capital city of the Solomon Islands, is built on the site of many bloody battles; many unaccounted for individuals, both American and Japanese, lie within its limits, and several have been discovered quite by accident. In 2013, a Honiara resident unearthed three sets of remains while working in his yard; two of these, PFCs Harry C. Morrissey and Francis E. Drake, Jr., were accounted for late in 2017.[24] A few miles away on the slopes of Mount Austen, another local man discovered the wreckage of an American F4-F Wildcat fighter. Bureau number 02095 was still visible on the fuselage. Researchers quickly identified the plane as one flown by 2Lt Elwood Ray Bailey, a fighter pilot with VMF-223, who went missing after a dogfight on August 24, 1942. Bailey was long thought to have parachuted from his plane over Iron Bottom Sound; the discovery of human remains and personal effects changed the story of his last moments completely. Bailey's identity was confirmed on September 27, 2017. Even more recent reports suggest the discovery of two more burial sites, reported to be the resting place of ten additional Marines. Army remains have been found as well; two pilots, Maj. Peyton Mathis and 1Lt Leonard Farron, were discovered near the remnants of their aircraft, while remains and a set of identification tags belonging to PFC Dale W. Ross of the 35th Infantry were turned over to American authorities in 2017. Ross has not yet been officially accounted for.

The difference between "recovered," "identified," and "accounted for" should be clarified. The first classification pertains to remains when retrieved from an isolated burial or location; these are, officially, still nameless individuals. The presence of media like issued equipment, identification tags, or personal effects is a valuable clue, but not enough to identify a recovered individual. Soldiers may borrow or salvage one another's equipment, personal belongings entrusted to a friend may be buried with them, and identification tags might wind up with the wrong body for any number of reasons. The body of an individual last seen in one place might turn up in another; one need only reference the case of Elwood Bailey for proof. Because the margin for potential error is tremendous, investigators err on the side of caution. According to period records, the third individual buried with PFCs Morrissey and Drake ought to be Pvt. Albert L. Bernes—their battalion lost three men killed in the same area, and primary sources indicate that they were buried at the same time and in the same location. However, the final pieces of the puzzle are still missing, and so Bernes—and whoever the 7th Marines buried in "Lunga Area, Grave #2"—are not, officially, one and the same.

The second classification indicates that sufficient evidence has been received to definitively state that a particular set of remains may be associated with an individual (or, in the case of commingled remains, multiple individuals). Proof of identification may be obtained through the comparison of dental and physical characteristics, much as it was in the 1940s. Enlistees at the time were screened for tuberculosis; some still have X-rays in their medical files, and these can be compared with recovered clavicles. Comparison of mitochondrial DNA (mDNA) with a living person is considered the most accurate indication of identity, but this can be an expensive process. Taking a sample from seventy-year-old bones that have been burned, blasted, or buried in acidic soil for years is a challenge; locating a matrilineal relative willing to submit their genetic information can be difficult as well. Most identifications are achieved through a combination of these factors.

The DPAA works closely with different Casualty Assistance Offices, which act as liaisons between the agency and the family of the deceased. Once identification is complete, a full report is sent to the Senior Casualty Officer for presentation to the Primary Next Of Kin. The PNOK is asked to accept the findings and assume the required responsibilities. Often, the question is just a formality: families are informed of developments in their case, which can span several years, and many are understandably anxious to settle the mystery. This is the penultimate step in the process; the DPAA issues a press release announcing that a missing serviceman is officially accounted for, and the family begins planning a long overdue funeral.

Today's researchers benefit from unprecedented access to primary sources. Declassified documents are obtainable with a simple request under the Freedom of Information Act. The National Archives and the

Marine Corps History Division at Quantico are a treasure trove of records; online resources contain many more. Finding clues in primary sources and interviews is a heady experience, and it is tempting to believe that a single overlooked detail is all it takes to prove identity. In some cases, mistakes made by the original record keepers are readily, even glaringly apparent. However, it is no simple feat to argue for the exhumation of remains. An airtight case must be built from multiple sources. Genealogists must trace the family of the deceased and hope to find one willing to submit a sample for DNA testing. Every scrap of information is assembled into a case for submission to the DPAA; the decision to disinter, and the entire identification process, is handled by the government. A successful identification means a funeral with full honors, closure for a family, and another proof of Steere's Thucydidean argument for "fulfilling our nation's promise."

Of course, this is easier said than done. The amount of paperwork attached to each unaccounted for or unknown serviceman can be both dizzying and frustrating. At the individual level, casualty cards, Official Military Personnel Files (OMPFs), Individual Deceased Personnel Files (IDPFs), X-files (pertaining to unidentified remains), Reports of Interment, Weekly Reports of Burial, Disinterment Directives, and cemetery charts are available from the National Archives or the Marine Corps Historical Division. Muster rolls, After Action Reports, war diaries, and unit histories provide additional puzzle pieces; so too do photographs and maps, personal diaries and correspondence, eyewitness reports, and the occasional contemporary publication. These primary sources contain vital details, albeit in various stages of completion and degrees of accuracy. For example, one company's muster roll may include the cause of death, date of burial, and precise map coordinates for every one of its deceased members; another may simply say "buried, details not known" or "killed in action, details later." A Report of Death in an OMPF might read "Buried in Police Barracks Cemetery, Tulagi" while a division-level roster of burials reports "US Naval and Marine Corps Cemetery #3, Grave C." This discrepancy is vexing to the researcher, and may have resulted in the misidentification of the individual in Grave C, as well as the Marine in question. Map coordinates present yet another problem. Period military maps of Guadalcanal were infamously inaccurate or insufficient—one officer even subtitled his memoirs "Remembering Guadalcanal, A Battle Without Maps"—and different units used different reference points at different times. (Most of the 1st Marine Division's trained intelligence men and mapmakers died early in the battle on a poorly planned patrol; none of their remains have been recovered.) With its 1,000-yard grid, the standard "Map #104" could help a company commander direct artillery fire; it lacks the detail required to pinpoint something as small as a grave in the jungle. Even with the naked eye, one can see that some squares are slightly larger or smaller than others, throwing the entire scale into question.

Veteran memoirs and interviews can hold valuable clues—or false memories of incidents and anecdotes. In one example, a Marine battalion commander radioed a report of seven men killed in action in a single skirmish, and that number was picked up by several contemporary and modern histories. Muster rolls for his battalion, however, report ten fatalities in the same incident. One veteran recalled that several men died of wounds overnight; a second remembered burying a buddy where he fell along with four other men; a third insisted that he had personally helped to bury not five, seven, or ten, but thirteen men the following day. By comparing these personal accounts with primary sources, it becomes clear that there were, in fact, ten fatalities—seven killed outright and three who succumbed to wounds—and that they were buried in two distinct groups of five graves each some distance apart. Each veteran told the truth as he remembered it; as with any oral history, one must account for the passage of time and the tricks of memory.

It is not possible for a single researcher to say that every case may be resolved someday, or to say that any individual case is impossible to solve. Nor is it possible for a single book to tell the story of every man who lost his life in the Guadalcanal campaign, or of the families who lived with the lingering uncertainty of "missing in action" or "body not recovered." This one hopes to provide some detail into the last days of a few Marines who have not yet been accounted for, and the ongoing efforts to bring them home.

2

"Current Regulations Prescribe…"

A lieutenant rose to read "Annex E to General Order No. 3," which ended with "Paragraph D: Burial: Graves will be suitably marked. All bodies will bear identification tags."[1]

✸ Richard Tregaskis, *Guadalcanal Diary*

In the grey haze of morning, before the day's first cigarette, Bob Leckie beheld the first dead sailor he had ever seen.

Until that morning, William Francis Buchman was a junior corpsman attached to Leckie's company. A native of the Bronx, Buchman first joined the Army in 1939 and served for eighteen months before his age was questioned. Undeterred by his subsequent "Honorable Discharge (Minority)" in December 1940, Buchman sought out a Navy recruiter, applied for the hospital corps, and passed the basic requirements to become an "HA-Deuce" or hospital apprentice, second class, the following year.[2] While disciplinary infractions kept him at this modest rate, Buchman nevertheless managed a transfer to the Fleet Marine Force and, after a crash course in field medicine, joined the 1st Marine Division in April 1942. As a corpsman, he would go to war unarmed, his only protection a Red Cross brassard and trust in his buddies from Company "H," 2nd Battalion, 1st Marines—a heavy weapons outfit informally called "H/2/1."

Just after dawn on August 7, 1942, the heavy cruiser USS *Quincy* let loose a salvo that crashed into the palm trees of Lunga Point on the island of Guadalcanal. Buchman's battalion, dressed in khakis and laden down with the trappings of war, clambered up the ladders of the transport *George F. Elliott* and watched the bombardment over a breakfast of apples and hardboiled eggs.[3] To Pvt. Robert Leckie, it seemed "there were only a few fires flickering,

✶ A copy of Tregaskis' book in my library. GI

✶✶ A copy of Leckie's book is in my library. GI

like the city dumps, to light our path to history."[4] At the order "Land the landing force," cargo nets spilled over the sides of the transports and Company "H" began the slow, dangerous climb down into their waiting landing craft. Sailors circulated among them, shaking hands, making amends, and asking Marines to "kill one of those (expletive) Japs."[5] Over the rumble of the naval bombardment and the drone carrier-based aircraft, they could hear the crackling of small-arms fire echoing across the water from Tulagi and Gavutu.

Naturally, they thought about death on the way in. In Sidney Phillips' boat, "all the comedians began to wisecrack about enjoying the last few minutes of our life," while Leckie "was praying again.... In the vanity of youth, I was positive I would die.... There were other boatloads of Marines ahead of us. I fancied firing from behind their prostrate bodies, building a protective wall of torn and reddened flesh. I could envision a holocaust among the coconuts."[6]

There would be no fight on the beach. Instead of a bloodbath, Leckie beheld the first wave (the 1st Battalion, 5th Marines) sitting on fallen palms, laughing and sampling coconuts. One hapless man sliced his hand while opening a coconut with a machete; solicitous corpsmen, eager to treat a casualty, surrounded and bandaged him before bundling him off to be treated aboard one of the transports. The rest of the battalion formed into an echelon of companies and struck out for their objective— the "Grassy Knoll"—which lay an indeterminate distance ahead. It was "where the Japs are," asserted the officers, although not one of the estimated five thousand defenders of Guadalcanal had yet appeared.

Before tangling with the enemy, they had to contend with the island itself. Capt. James Howland's Fox Company, 1st Marines, took the lead as the column snaked along. Sandy beaches and the exotic palms of the Lever Brothers plantation gave way to fields of sharp-bladed *kunai* grass that could grow above a man's head. After 2,500 yards, the dense jungle began. Overheated Marines took turns swinging machetes and bayonets at thick vines and creepers, scrambled up and down steep slopes, swatted and swore at insects. Lacking decent maps, they had no choice but to head straight along the azimuth that pointed towards the Grassy Knoll. As the hours went by, they began to suspect that their objective was quite a bit farther away than they had been led to believe. What shaky faith existed in the poorly-prepared map vanished as deep gullies turned out to be shallow ditches, streams turned out to be deep rivers, and steep hills and ridges appeared without warning. Communication and control broke down, units lost contact with each other, and there was "a uniform and lamentable failure to use patrols to the front and flanks."[7]

Cpl James Arthur McCutcheon was holding down one flank of the advance. A stolid NCO from Hasbrouck Heights, New Jersey, McCutcheon was more than halfway through his first four-year hitch in the regular Marine Corps; he had seen jungles before on peacetime deployments to Puerto Rico and fleet exercises in Cuba, but they paled in comparison to what he now encountered. Historian Richard Frank paints a vivid picture of this "education in jungle warfare":

> Great hardwood trees ... soared up to 150 feet and had girths as much as 40 feet across. Their straight trunks sprouted only high branches that formed a "sunproof roof." Their massive flared roots snaked across the surface of the ground and mingled with the creepers and other vines which lay like thick trip wires while other leafy vines festooned the trunks of the trees. The eye could penetrate only a few feet into the foliage of the jungle floor, composed of varicolored plants, bushes, ferns, and at least eleven kinds of thorns. Catcalls from squadrons of exotic birds in the upper canopy mocked Marines as they exhausted themselves and dulled machete blades trying to chop a path through the jungle.... The sour odor of decay permeated the steamy stagnant air, for beneath the lushness omnipresent rot made the yellow clay earth porous. Even the sturdiest-appearing trees sometimes presented only facades for gutted interiors that disposed them to topple randomly on the unwary.[8]

Most Marines were in the prime of their young lives, but spending weeks aboard crowded transports took a toll on their physical condition. "Men whose bodies had softened during weeks of shipboard life scrambled up the faces of muddy hills and slid down the reverse slopes," continued Leckie. "Gasping in the humid heat, bathed in a stream of enervating sweat and burdened with packs and ammunition loads that were far too heavy, the 1st Marines moved through dripping rainforests with all the stealth of a traveling circus." The incredible heat and humidity pressed on the chest like a physical weight, and soon men were shedding their excess gear. Each carried a single canteen, which was quickly empty, and men flung themselves headlong into the streams and rivers they forded, cooling themselves and guzzling the water. Here and there a man collapsed and had to be revived, with teases from his buddies or invective from his squad leader getting him back into the trudging column. Nobody wanted to be left behind.

As they marched, the sky darkened, and suddenly it was almost night. Worn out, nervous, and almost completely lost, the battalion set up a hasty defense. They scraped foxholes into the corner of a grassy field, posted sentries, and wolfed cold C-rations straight from the can. Word began to spread that a man from Company "F" had disappeared during the day's advance. The skies opened with a torrential downpour and men crouched under their ponchos, staring into the darkness, stupefied by exhaustion and the day's events. "The rain fell drearily as we sat hunched in our ponchos, bidden to keep silence, munching the cold rations we took from our packs," wrote Bob Leckie. "We were alone, surrounded by a jungle alive with the noise of moving things which could only seem to us the stealthy tread of the foe moving closer."[9]

Men stood sentry watch in pairs. At 7:05 p.m., Buchman was heard repeatedly calling a challenge. Somebody cursed, and moments later, a pistol shot rang out. The entire line immediately went on alert. A few other men shot nervously into the night, but officers quickly calmed the wild firing. The Japanese were not coming, and Buchman did not call out again.

They gathered around the khaki-clad body at first light. William Francis Buchman lay dead in the field, a bullet wound in his left breast. The word went around that he had gone to relieve himself; startled by the sentry's shout, he flubbed the complicated password. The penalty for confusion was death, "eternity at the mercy of a liquid consonant," as Leckie said. Another narrative unfolded at the battalion aid station as Lt (j.g.) Jacques Saphier—the battalion surgeon and Buchman's boss—interviewed the man who fired the fatal shot. The culprit claimed he had been awakened by a loud voice "and saw a masked figure without a helmet pointing a rifle at him." His natural reaction was to shoot first and ask questions later. Saphier noted that "Buchman was at the time wearing a black mask and no helmet," and that "no one in the party has any idea whom Buchman was challenging or what he suspected."[10] No punitive measures were taken against the shooter.

Facing another day of hard marching—and with a possible fight for the airfield, their new objective, in the offing—Company "H" had little choice but to bury Buchman where he fell. The deed was done by a handful of buddies armed with shovels. "I shall never forget the sad faces of the friends who buried him," said Leckie. "In that dismal dawn, the scraping of their entrenching tools was as plaintive as the scratching of a mouse." The mourners were so engrossed in the unfamiliar task that nobody thought to record the location.[11]

As Company "H" concluded their informal funeral, Company "F" was looking for Cpl McCutcheon. He had disappeared during the previous day's advance—a casualty of heat exhaustion, most thought, although nobody could quite remember the last time they saw him. "He had been wide on the flank ... and had simply disappeared," said Leckie.[12] There was no reason to fear the worst, at least not yet—McCutcheon might have been picked up by another friendly unit or come to his senses and walked back to an aid station to rest. Perhaps even now he was following their trail. Without eyewitnesses, though, nobody was sure: McCutcheon was simply "missing in action," and the company clerks duly updated their records on the morning of August 8. Days of absence turned to weeks, then months. McCutcheon was dropped from company muster rolls; his records were transferred to the Prisoners of War and Missing Persons Department of Marine Corps Headquarters in Washington, D.C. He would be declared dead on August 9, 1943, one year and one day after he disappeared.

Buchman and McCutcheon were the first two Americans to lose their lives on the island of Guadalcanal, and as far as anyone can say, both men are still there.

The combat landings that took place in the Solomon Islands on August 7, 1942, were the culmination of a period of theorizing that dated back to 1906. The first drafts of War Plan ORANGE, intended to ensure American naval supremacy in the Pacific, were built around the precept of subjugating Japan. This plan all but dictated the evolution of the United States Marine Corps in the following decades. After a meteoric rise in military prominence and public perception during the Great War, the Corps faced mounting challenges in the 1920s. With a war-sick public vocally opposed to military spending—especially when it funded expeditionary forces and naval expansion—and with military planners questioning the efficacy of amphibious operations in the wake of Gallipoli, the Corps was nearly made redundant.

The 1919 South Pacific Mandate, which granted former German colonies in the Pacific to Japan, raised American concerns about foreign naval supremacy in the Pacific. If those islands were developed into bases, they could form a barrier between the United States and its interests in the Philippines. The prescient work of Marine Lt. Col. Earl H. Ellis, whose 1921 treatise *Advanced Base Operations in Micronesia* "cast the Corps in roles mandated by War Plan ORANGE," gave Commandant John A. Lejeune the needed direction and rationale to start positioning the Marines as an indispensable force of amphibious warfare specialists.[13] This was a tough sell: Lejeune made his case as the legions of Great War dead were being exhumed in France, and Congress would shortly pass Public Law No. 389, authorizing government funding for the "disposition of remains of officers, soldiers, and civilian employees" who had lost their lives overseas with the American Expeditionary Forces.[14] The Commandant may have passed by to pay his respects at the newly-established Tomb of the Unknown Soldier, and wondered if one of his fellow Marines lay interred beside the marble sarcophagus.

For the next twenty years, Marine training and theory centered on refining this mission, adding in the lessons learned in the "small wars" of Haiti and Nicaragua. Still, even this more modest goal was fraught with difficulty, especially when Depression-era budget limitations restricted the Corps to the bare minimum of personnel and equipment. The most elaborate training, a series of annual rehearsals (Fleet Landing Exercises, or FLEX), were so limited in scale that ship-to-shore movement was emphasized by necessity: there were no resources to practice anything else. "Logistics cost money," commented Lt Col. Merrill Twining, "and we had none. No one had ever seen twenty-five units of fire or sixty days' rations or any other of the weighty allowances needed for combat.... No one had ever seen a completely combat-loaded division until we landed in the Solomons."[15] Even initial publication of the "amphibious bible," *Fleet Training Publication 167*, which contained the accumulated knowledge of these decades of theorizing, was limited due to lack of funds. The Marine Corps accepted the role of the landing force—shock troops who could swiftly seize a beachhead and defend it just long enough for the Army to move in and take over.[16]

The Marine Corps relied heavily on the other services for logistical support, particularly in the cases of technical specialists and quartermaster personnel. Prior to 1939, the Corps staffed only eight specialist training schools; the remainder of training was conducted within combat units, or by farming out candidates to Army, Navy, and civilian schools. "Courses were few and output was low, but they were adequate" for a peacetime Corps that numbered a modest 18,070 men.[17] When authorized pre-war expansion swelled the ranks of riflemen, specialist training struggled to keep up, and only the groundwork for a more robust program was in place by December 7, 1941.[18] Emphasis was naturally placed on roles that would directly support the amphibious mission. Graves Registration was not even a blip on the radar. "Prewar planning for expansion of the Marine Corps devoted no more attention to the graves registration problem than was given by the Army," noted Steere. "Going too far, perhaps, in assuming that the Army actually had a graves registration service, the Navy determined to follow Army standards in this respect and, whenever the two arms participated in joint operations, to work under [the] direction of the Army's Graves Registration Service."[19]

Reliance on the Army for logistical support was one thing in peacetime. It was quite another when a single Marine division was faced with providing the entire ground combat force for an unprecedented and audacious strike against an enemy it had never directly encountered, let alone defeated. This was the situation faced by Maj. Gen. Alexander A. Vandegrift when he was summoned to a meeting in Auckland, New Zealand on June 26, 1942.

The General had arrived in Wellington with the advance elements of his 1st Marine Division just twelve days before. Weary and lethargic after a month-long sea voyage, the Marines were "delighted with the newly constructed camp at Paekakariki, with its complete facilities, pleasant surroundings, and nearness to a liberty town."[20] They would have to earn those precious liberty hours, for "although full advantage was taken of every opportunity and facility for training" before leaving the United States, "it was considered the Division had not yet attained a satisfactory state of combat readiness." The only men exempt from the rigorous schedule were those detailed to work at the docks; a local labor strike compelled the Marines to unload their own cargo ships. It was a less than auspicious welcome to the war, but Vandegrift was not overly concerned: he did not anticipate sending his green division into combat before the new year, after at least six months of additional training and preparation.[21]

Vandegrift and his staff expected to pay a courtesy call on Vice Admiral Robert L. Ghormley, the newly appointed Commander, South Pacific (ComSoPac). Instead, a grim-faced Ghormley handed over a dispatch ordering the 1st Marine Division to "initiate a major naval campaign on 1 August 1942 ... with Tulagi Island as the first objective." Immediately following their assumed success, the Marines would be relieved by Army troops, re-embark, and assault the island of Bougainville—some 400 miles to the north—one week later. Vandegrift was momentarily speechless, and his staff was appalled. "Only five weeks hence!" exclaimed Merrill Twining. "Marines are good, but even so, none of us had an ego that great."[22] Vandegrift managed to secure a slight delay in the proposed timetable—the landing was set for August 7—and planned his operation to include the near simultaneous seizure of not only Tulagi, but the islands of Gavutu-Tanambogo, Nggela Sule (Florida), and Guadalcanal, where Japanese engineers were constructing a valuable airfield.[23] The Bougainville mission was rightly scrapped as too ambitious. Still, the 1st Marine Division faced major deficits in training, reliable intelligence, operational logistics, and supplies for the coming operation. The official codename was Operation Watchtower; Marines later joked that a better name might be "Operation Shoestring."

Problems of logistics and supply weighed heavily on Marine quartermaster units. Available shipping was severely limited, and the Navy was loath to commit its valuable aircraft carriers to such a risky endeavor. The natural priority of the planners was summed up in Vandegrift's approach to supplying his force: "Take only that which is necessary to fight and to live."[24] Prioritizing the preparation of combat men and materiel was unavoidable, but also served to "complicate the mission of most technical services," said Edward Steere. "In any rapid buildup, the just ratio between combat formations and supporting elements is seldom maintained. The problem becomes difficult indeed when a particular service, such as graves registration, is nonexistent." The rapid and improvisational nature of Watchtower preparations "imposed severe restrictions on provisions for care of the dead," continued Steere. "A graves registration doctrine nicely adjusted to conventional methods of land warfare could not be readily adapted to a situation without parallel in the annals of American military history."[25]

The Circular

With no Graves Registration examples to emulate, and without the time or resources to train their own men, the Marines made do with the knowledge they had at hand. *Division Circular 6a-42: Personnel Administration* was released as part of a flurry of paperwork emanating from Vandegrift's headquarters in the weeks before departure. The fifteenth and final topic, "DEATH AND BURIAL," set forth the standards and expectations for handling the inevitable fatalities of the upcoming operation.

> Current regulations prescribe that wherever sea transportation is required for the return to the U.S. of remains of deceased personnel they will be buried locally for duration of war. The conditions under which units of this Division may expect to operate will frequently require burial by organizations. In that connection consideration should be given to the following points:
>
> a.   Proper recording of burial.
> b.   Morale of troops.
> c.   Sanitary protection in the battle area.
> d.   Morale of the home population.

    The second consideration demands that the dead be removed as soon as practicable from the observation of the living; that the removal be conducted with the reverence due the manner of death; and that, when practicable military honors be rendered. Bodies should be covered during movement from the field of battle to the place of interment. Routes should avoid contact with troops whenever practicable and places of interment should be screened from roads [if] the situation permits. The removal should be accomplished with a respectful attitude toward the dead, and any tendency toward improper handling of bodies should be corrected. Whenever possible a Chaplain should officiate at burial and proper decorum should be maintained by all persons who witness the interment.

The third point above demands the expeditious burial of the dead to prevent contamination and the spread of disease.

The fourth point demands that relatives and friends at home, who must be advised of deaths, should also have assurance that the remains were properly interred, and that the graves have been so marked as to insure [*sic.*] the preservation of identities in order that remains may be returned for permanent interment in a National Cemetery or other designated place, and that personal effects of the soldier be returned to the next of kin.

When possible, isolated interment will be avoided. Cemeteries should be designated by the appropriate commander, located in places convenient to where the heaviest casualties are expected or experienced. When possible, they should be located in the open where soil is well drained and easy to dig. They should not be located in swampy ground nor situated near a stream. Graves should be aligned so that headstones will be in alignment, both laterally and longitudinally.

When bodies are brought to the place of interment, the Officer in Charge (Chaplain when available) should search them carefully. All articles of value or interest to the next of kin (unless discreditable) should be inventoried and placed in a separate parcel with the contents of each parcel and the correctness of the inventory being attested by the Officer in Charge. Parcels should be labelled with the name of the decedent and delivered to the Adjutant's Section of the organization concerned for return to next of kin.

Identification will normally be accomplished by means of the identification tags. Where these are missing bodies should not be buried until every effort has been made to establish their identity. A careful examination of personal effects may supply the information or it may be possible to call on men from the same company, if it is known, to establish identity. Failing this, fingerprints will be made by medical personnel when available and the bodies buried in separate graves and accurate records made thereof.

After the bodies have been placed in the graves the Officer in Charge will see that one identification tag of each man remains on the body and that the other is firmly attached to a marker to be placed on the grave. After a record of the location of the grave has been made each body should be covered with a blanket or shelter half and the services of the Faith read. When graves have been filled identification markers should be firmly fixed in place. Locations of cemeteries will be plotted on a map which will be forwarded to higher Headquarters with reports of interment.

BY COMMAND OF MAJOR GENERAL VANDEGRIFT
W. C. JAMES
Colonel, U. S. Marine Corps
Chief of Staff[26]

Col. William Capers James evidently had a copy of the brand-new TM 10-630, "Graves Registration," on hand when writing this directive. The document is a summary of the manual's first twenty pages, and select lines, including the four primary points, are copied almost verbatim. While copies of TM 10-630 must have been available in the Southwest Pacific—there were Army quartermasters in Australia, after all, and graves registration was their responsibility—they were probably somewhat scarce in Marine camps. Certainly, TM 10-630 was less readily available and less readable than a Division circular, so the Chief of Staff's synthesis was likely the extent of most Marine officers' education on the subject. (Technical direction, naturally, was out of Col. James' wheelhouse; the details of body recovery, identification, and burial would be handled in the field.) It was expected that this basic summary, in conjunction with existing Marine methods and a healthy dash of basic common sense, would suffice for a short operation. This did, in fact, prove to be the case on the small islands of Tulagi and Gavutu-Tanambogo where the rapid reduction of resistance led to the quick establishment of cemeteries. The result was proportionally fewer unidentified or unaccounted for casualties, despite heavy losses. Longer campaigns would quickly test the limits of this system.

"Proper Recording of Burial"

The Circular provides no detail on its first consideration; while this may seem like an oversight, Col. James probably thought it would be a given. (The authors of TM 10-630 felt the same: "Consideration A is the primary purpose of this manual and is self-explanatory." One wonders why a self-explanatory process would require a manual at all.)[27] All Marine units were familiar with proper record-keeping procedures. A signification portion of the 1940 Marine Manual was devoted to the minutiae of paperwork. Every company had a detail of clerks and an executive officer to handle their administrative tasks; forms and records went up the chain to the battalion adjutant (who ran the administrative "1-section," as the "Bn-1") and his staff, then to Regiment (R-1) and Division (D-1), eventually landing in the office of the Adjutant and Inspector, Headquarters Marine Corps. Unit strength was recorded by the daily change sheet, "a consolidated report of joinings, transfers, discharges, changes in status of specialists ... and of other events, as they occur, which affect muster and payroll status of personnel" prepared by "all Marine Corps posts, stations, and other separate commands."[28] These reports formed the basis of a unit's monthly muster roll, which was the single most authoritative personnel document.

Strict regulations governed proper formatting, allowable abbreviations, and the type of information to be included in the "Remarks" column next to an individual's name. The Marine Corps Manual of 1940 proclaimed "the importance of correct muster rolls cannot be overemphasized.... Since it is possible that the muster rolls being written today will in a comparatively few years be, at least in part, unsupported, accuracy and completeness are mandatory."[29] (Accurate reporting also helped the Corps control its budget; a surprising number of the regulations involved means of calculating or stopping pay.) In the case of death, the "Remarks" would read:

> Under the heading "Died" show date and hour, place, cause, whether or not Navy Department General Order No. 20 applies, and in the cases of enlisted men, character that would have been awarded if discharged. If death occurs while man is absent on authorized liberty or furlough, show date and hour of actual departure and authorized duration thereof. When interment is near unit to which man is attached, show date and place of burial, with grave location; when remains are forwarded to next of kin or to military or civil authorities, show date, place, and to whom forwarded, and final disposition if known.[30]

Corpsman Buchman's entry in the company muster roll for August 1942 was entered strictly by the book: "7, at Guadalcanal Island in line of duty. GO#20 does not apply. Char. Exc. Buried in the hills with no record of the location of grave."[31] Translated, this means that Buchman was killed on August 7, on Guadalcanal, while on duty. General Order No. 20, which pertains to personal misconduct, did not apply; essentially this means that Buchman's death was not his own fault. His character was considered excellent, the highest possible rating. Since Buchman's exact burial location was not known, the clerk simply typed "in the hills." No mention was made of the friendly fire incident.

Supplementing the muster roll was the Record of Events, a daily journal generated by "companies or similar units, battalions, regiments, or higher units ... on expeditionary duty or maneuvers." While muster rolls were completed on paper printed for the purpose, a Record of Events might take the form of a handwritten journal (blank notebooks were prepared and issued for this purpose), a typewritten form, or simply notes and coordinates scribbled in a log book. The format did not matter so long as it was accurate. "The whole record of events is a permanent record," stated the Manual, "and is therefore to be considered the primary historical record of the organization."[32]

During the campaign, most reports of burial found their way into one or both primary sources. In 1942, Marine ground forces compiled muster rolls at the company level, and the thoroughness of individual clerks varied from unit to unit. The 1st Marine Raider Battalion (Edson's Raiders) and 2nd Battalion, 5th Marines, were assigned the mission of subduing Tulagi on August 7, 1942. Col. Merritt Edson's men landed first and progressed halfway across the island before running into the main Japanese line; clearing the remainder of the island would take three days and cost thirty-nine Raider lives. The dead are uniformly recorded on the muster roll: "Killed in action on TULAGI on [date] and buried on Island; Details later." Unfortunately for the researcher, none of the details were added to the roll. Col. Harold Rosecrans' 2nd Battalion, 5th Marines, lost seven men killed; one was buried at sea, four in the main Tulagi cemetery, and two in the field. Those men—PFCs Henry Huff and A. D. Webster (F/2/5)—were reported "interred one half mile north of beach off road in woods east of ridge road, grave No 1 [Webster; Huff was in grave No 2], Tulagi, B.S.I. [British Solomon Islands]."[33] Fortunately, due in part to Tulagi's small size, almost all American bodies were accounted for shortly after the battle.

The rapid establishment of burial grounds naturally helped improve the accuracy of burial records; the convention was to give the date of burial, cemetery, row, and grave number—for example, "26, died result of gunshot wound, fatal, received in action against the enemy on Guadalcanal, B. S. I. 26, buried 1st MarDiv Cemetery, Row 40, Grave #2." Despite the occasional typo or disagreement over cemetery names—Tulagi's three cemeteries are especially confusing; at least ten variations appear in muster rolls for the few units who fought there—these notations are generally very accurate.

Real difficulties arose when recording field burials, and the primary culprit was a dearth of accurate, consistent maps. The cartographic shortcomings of the Guadalcanal campaign are well known; there never seemed to be enough maps to go around, and those that were issued, especially in the early days, were notoriously poor. First Lieutenant William Hollingsworth Whyte III, an intelligence officer with the 1st Marines, had a map "drawn from the information supplied by a man thoroughly familiar with the terrain shown. It is an approximate pictorial representation drawn from this person's memory. It is not to be construed as being an accurate map."[34] Sgt. Ore J. Marion (L/3/5) complained that "Our maps weren't very reliable. In fact, I never *saw* a map of Guadalcanal until long after I left the island, and I'm not even certain that our platoon leader, Lt. Flaherty, saw one."[35] Terrain features were poorly represented, distances approximated, and rivers misnamed. Plotting a route of march was difficult enough, let alone recording grave coordinates. It is scarcely surprising that several early field burials were simply recorded "in the hills."

Attempts at accuracy were made. Sgt. William J. Steen, an NCO in Marion's company, was returning from an outpost when he was shot by a nervous sentry. The muster roll entry reads "[August] 8, killed in action in vicinity of Teneratu River, Guadalcanal, B.S.I.; GO 20 does not apply; char exc; 8, remains interred in Grave No M598422, Guadalcanal, B.S.I."[36] Map shortcomings are evident here. "Vicinity of the Teneratu"— certainly a mistake for the Tenaru River—was a large area, and the early Marine maps misidentified the Tenaru as the Ilu, and *vice versa*. "Grave No M598422" must be a precise location, but how it was enumerated or coordinated is not known.

Landmarks were sometimes used instead of coordinates. Privates Robert J. Budd and Thomas W. Phillips (both C/1/5) died in an ambush on August 27, 1942; on the following morning their "remains [were] interred in a coconut grove on a narrow strip of low land between the sea and a high coral ridge 1 mile east of Kokumbona and 10 yards north of a trail leading from Kokumbona to Matanikau."[37] Pvt. Frank R. Whittlesey (B/1st Raider Battalion) died protecting a buddy at Edson's Ridge and was "buried 1,000 yards south of Airfield just forward of the front lines on Lunga Ridge."[38] PFC Barney S. Mikus (C/1/7) was shot near the Matanikau River on September 27: "remains interred in Lunga area, only grave in vicinity."[39] Cpl. Robert B. Wallace (E/2/5) was "interred along coast road about 200 yards to front of road junction to CP, 2nd Marines, immediately to rear of O-2 [line]."[40] Of course, the landscape changed as the combatants swept back and forth; many landmarks and graves were obliterated. Only Wallace's marker, located in a relatively high visibility area near a road, survived the battle; Whittlesey's remains were discovered by accident in 1989, and the rest remain unaccounted for.

Maps were updated as rapidly as possible. Surveying was a secondary purpose of the infamous "Goettge Patrol" of August 12–13; the resulting massacre of the Division's most talented mapmakers and draftsmen made the situation worse. The 11th Marines had several skilled draftsmen— maps were essential for plotting accurate artillery fire—and issued "Map No. 101," a single-sheet sketch drawn from aerial photographs on August 18, 1942. This map featured a 1,000-yard grid system and was a marked improvement over the earlier maps drawn from memory. As the Marines tentatively explored further afield, and more photographic flights were made, the maps improved until the twelve-sheet, "Map 104, North Coast Guadalcanal, Lunga Area" was accepted as the standard. The exact date of issue for Map 104 is not clear; some muster rolls begin using its coordinates in late September 1942, though other maps were still plainly in use by other units. The 1st Marines, for example, were using Map 101 through mid-September; Lt. Col. Lewis B. "Chesty" Puller's First Battalion,

7th Marines, had a possibly unique aerial mosaic map for their expedition to Mount Austen later that month.

The introduction of Map 104 marked a significant change in the procedure for reporting field burials. Although degrees of detail varied by individual case and by unit, the amount of information available increases in many cases. The 2nd Battalion, 7th Marines, was particularly good at providing coordinates for field burials. For example, on October 9, 1942, their Company "G" lost four Marines "killed in an engagement with Japanese forces in vicinity of (69.75–200.15) Map #104, Lunga Area, North Coast Guadalcanal." PFC John W. Louder was carried back to the Division cemetery, while the other three were hastily buried in the field. PFCs James M. Lawson and Gerald J. McGettrick were "interred at (69.9–200.2) Map #104" until after the war; both were located and identified by a post-war Army Graves Registration Service (AGRS) expedition. However, even map coordinates were not foolproof. The fourth casualty, Sgt. William J. Cusack, was buried 500 yards east of Lawson and McGettrick (70.4–200.2) but eluded all searches and is still unaccounted for.

Additional information was commonly provided in the form of a map overlay or sketch of the area. These tracings were occasionally submitted in place of map coordinates and were often inserted into an individual's Service Record Book. Even the roughest versions—some were just a set of grid lines and a literal "X" marking the spot—could be a potential help to future searchers. Lt. Col. Dean Ladd, then a junior platoon leader, recalled his friend and executive officer, 1Lt John Murdock, sweating over a map and plotting burial sites. "One of Murdock's responsibilities was to record the location of battle-site graves on an overlay," Ladd wrote. "It troubled him that the locations couldn't always be specifically pinpointed, so there could be no assurance that the bodies would later be found for relocation to permanent cemeteries. He had to write letters to many families, telling them that their loved ones might have to remain in an unmarked, unidentified grave on the battlefield."[42] (This was a valid concern. Six of the nine field burials from Ladd and Murdock's Company "B," 8th Marines, have not been accounted for.) Unfortunately, not all of these overlays have survived the passage of years.

Morale of Troops and Sanitary Protection

These two considerations were closely related. Both dealt with mitigating the effects of the dead on the physical and mental health of the living.

Proactive efforts to care for the deceased were some comfort to the living: if they, too, should die, they could trust that their bodies and belongings would be treated with respect. The ideal outcome, of course, was burial in the island cemetery, and this was done whenever possible. Corpsman John Clayton of the 18th Marines described an effective evacuation following the death of Cpl. Richard B. White in January 1943:

> [The surgeon] turned to me and said, "Take him to Regimental Morgue." Well, I didn't know where the hell Regimental Morgue was. Somebody said it was up near regimental headquarters. So, we loaded his body on a large pickup truck and the driver and his partner rode in the cab. I was going to ride in the cab, too, but the road was so rough, the body threatened to bounce right out of the truck. I had to get back there and sit on him to keep him from bouncing out. I sat on this body going through the jungle. And it was dark and we couldn't turn on the headlights. Well, these guys knew where they were going and we finally got to the regimental morgue and unloaded the body. It was quite an experience.[43]

Location of death and availability of motor transport played a major determining factor in whether or not a fatal casualty could be evacuated. Marines who died on patrols beyond the perimeter, or in major offensives where trucks and jeeps were needed elsewhere, were more likely to be buried in isolated graves; consequently, fewer of these men have been accounted for.

It goes without saying that proximity to the decomposing bodies of one's countrymen has a deleterious effect on one's fighting spirit. There were Great War veterans on Gen. Vandegrift's staff and among the senior NCOs who could personally attest to this grim reality, and it does not take much imagination for modern civilians to conjure up an appropriately gruesome picture. Unfortunately, it was not always possible to effect an immediate removal of the dead.

The 3rd Battalion, 5th Marines, fought a nasty battle on the night of October 8–9, 1942. A sizable group of Japanese troops, with their backs against the Matanikau River, attempted to break through Marine lines and cross a large sandspit at the river's mouth. "It was mayhem first class," recalled Ore Marion of Company "L," "with bayoneting, screaming, shouting, and the constant crackle of small-arms fire in that black night."[44] Dawn broke on a nightmarish scene. "I saw a young Marine lying on his back, his pack under his shoulder and his head resting on a rotten log as if asleep," wrote Sgt. Thurman I. Miller of Company "K":

> A closer look told me he had died in that position. His wound had been sudden and sufficient to drain all the blood from his body, and he was

very white. Nature had already begun the process of returning his body to the dust from which it had come. Little bugs crawled in and out of his nose holes, and a wiggle worm crawled out of one ear. Maggots had begun to eat away his flesh. His gear had already started to mold into a blue-greenish color.[45]

Sgt. Jim McEnery (also of K/3/5) "found the body of Private Emil Student, a Marine I knew fairly well, leaning up against a tree. He almost looked like he was asleep."[46] Marion thought "the after-battle scene looked like an artist's rendition of Dante's *Inferno*"—an oft-repeated comparison in veteran's recollections—and "waited for word—any word—from a superior officer to tell us what to do next."

You knew there were bodies piled up in the brush. Where you could, you dragged them out carefully. They weren't just bodies—they were the guys you lived with. You shared booze with these guys, shared women— and bingo! They were gone. You tried to forget it. Wipe it out. I don't know if you ever can.

One of Marion's buddies lost a particularly close friend in this battle, and Marion recorded how he took the news:

Gerkin didn't say anything. He lowered his head and kicked at the dirt a couple times. He didn't say anything at all, and I didn't say anything either. There was nothing I could tell him. The only decent thing to do was to keep quiet and leave Gerk alone.... In the midst of all the dead and wounded, two men from the 2nd Platoon were rolling Dusty [PFC Luther L. Rhodes] onto a poncho.... Gerkin pulled himself together and went directly to the two men who were getting ready to take the kid's body away. He said to them, "Don't drop that kid while you're moving him in that poncho. Don't bump him on the ground, or I'll kick the shit out of both of you."

"Okay, Gerk," one of them said quietly. "Don't worry. We'll take good care of him."

Larry wandered off somewhere, and it was about thirty minutes before he showed up again. I never heard him mention the kid again or say anything about him. Not ever.... Death was everywhere, but to keep going, we had to push the dead out of our thoughts.[47]

First Sergeant Abraham Felber of the 11th Marines came to view this battlefield and was impressed by the sight of bone-weary survivors tucking into canned rations even as "shiny green blowflies buzzed and swarmed over the adjacent horribly-bloated corpses.... We stayed only a very short while because the men I was with could not stand the awful odor." On the way back to the perimeter, Felber's party was "delayed somewhat by a large truck loaded with dead Marines on the way to the cemetery, which took up most of the road."[48] The 3rd Battalion, 5th Marines, recorded fifteen men killed in action and three missing after this fight; Edson's Raiders, engaged nearby, suffered a similar number of deaths.

In this case, the expeditious removal of the dead enabled the living to carry on with their daily duties, and their own lives. However, it also caused some problems with record keeping. Pvt. Charles D. Taylor of Company "I" was reported on his muster roll as "missing in action since 7:00 PM (last seen in vicinity of the Matanikau River area.)" A 1943 comparison of post-mortem fingerprints revealed that he was actually buried in the First Marine Division Cemetery on October 9, 1942. Similarly, Pvt. Emil Student (K/3/5) and PFC Alfred J. Murther (I/3/5) were noted as "not recovered due to battle conditions"—yet, like Taylor, both were identified in the cemetery by fingerprints. A fourth man, Sgt. Arthur C. Garrett (I/3/5) was found on the battlefield in August 1943; he had also (accurately) been reported as "not recovered due to battle conditions."

Five Marines from this battalion remain unaccounted for after this engagement; given this tangle of records, it is possible that they were in fact buried and are currently interred in a national cemetery as unknowns. In a sad turn of fate, Pvt. Luther "Dusty" Rhodes, whose body Ore Marion saw loaded onto a poncho by his buddies, is one of those Marines who has not been accounted for. He may be one of the unidentified cemetery burials, or he may have been left on the field—although if Marion's memory is correct, this seems unlikely. Rhodes' personnel file refers to an "overlay attached to CRS of STUDENT, Emil S."—further clues may have been recorded in this sketch, but unfortunately, no such overlay can be found in Student's file, and it appears no additional copies survived.

Although the Circular warned that "when possible isolated interment will be avoided," in many cases it was truly unavoidable. Company "A" of the 1st Marines lost three men while patrolling near Papanggu; the bodies could not be carried back to the perimeter and thus were buried "in the hills." Their buddies planned to return and dug only shallow graves, with the dead men's boondocker-clad feet left above ground to aid in their recovery. (The bodies may have been found, but not by Americans. Historian William Bartsch opines that Japanese troops searching for their own dead disinterred the Marines by mistake. What became of the bodies after that is not known.)[49] An isolated burial was infinitely preferable to no burial at all, and the dead were left on the field only in the direst of circumstances. The 1st Marines' Company "B" experienced such a disaster when they were ambushed on September 17, 1942, and were forced to leave half a platoon behind. Eight days later, a burial party managed to return to the site and accounted for all of their dead. After their extended exposure to the elements, the bodies could barely be identified; moving them was out of the question. Still, the act of burying their friends was a solace to the survivors, who in turn could write to the next of kin with a clear conscience. "I asked for and received permission to personally bury Wilbur's remains," wrote PFC Francis J. Ziemba to his deceased friend's family, "and I'm not ashamed to admit that the tears in my eyes at the time of his burial were real and many."[50]

Although such burials were often referred to as "hasty" or "isolated," they were far from careless. Correspondent Ira Wolfert saw the grave of a private standing along the coast road near the Matanikau River. "His friends have trimmed its mound pathetically with coconuts and fashioned a rude wooden cross for a headstone," he reported. "A helmet with three holes in it, the holes as blank as dead eyes, tops the cross and on it is penciled, 'A Real Guy.' Against the cross stands the photograph of a very pretty girl, staring silently.... Her dead man must have loved her truly, for he carried her picture into battle."[51]

Retired Marine Col. Joseph H. Alexander wrote of the Raiders unaccounted for after the battle of Edson's Ridge: "Most of them likely remain in their jungle graves, but at the very least they received a Marine burial. Perhaps only fellow Marines can appreciate the comfort in that fact."[52] The same might be said of every instance where a fighting man was laid to rest along a remote and lonely tree line, beside a nameless trail, or by the banks of a river his buddies would cross and re-cross many times in the months to come.

Battlefield sanitation was an issue throughout the campaign. The subject was part of a Marine's training curriculum but was not always well taught. Cpl. William Rogal's instructor, a heavily-accented old gunnery sergeant, kept the class brief: "I'ma gonna teach you all you need to know about field sanitary. You dig a leetle hole; you sheet in the leetle hole; you cover up the leetle hole. Thatsa field sanitary. OK, class dismissed."[53] On Guadalcanal, this lax performance had serious repercussions. The Division's final report on the operation bemoaned "the absolute lack of field sanitation in combat" and claimed that "empty cans, food particles, and excreta were not properly disposed of at once. This does not concern the advancing party, but is intensely important to the future occupying forces."[54] Standards were eventually established in the rear areas and hospitals, but the front lines were a mixed bag. When the fresh 6th Marines relieved a veteran Marine unit in January 1943, they found a dispiriting sight. "Foxholes marked the outline of the front lines, with occasional machine gun emplacements interspersed. The area was filthy with half-eaten C-ration cans rotting in the sun. A few shallow graves were partially uncovered by the periodic heavy rains."[55]

The lack of attention to proper sanitary procedures drove medical officers and corpsmen to distraction. Flies became a pestilence second only to the malaria-bearing Anopheles mosquito; the spread of dysentery was rapid and far-reaching. Cdr. (Medical Corps) French R. Moore of Company "D," Second Medical Battalion, blamed battlefield conditions. "Line officers and men alike disregarded all rules of sanitation," he complained. "The dead, both our own and the enemy, were not buried as soon as possible, and as a result flies increased very rapidly."[56] Corpsman John Clayton concurred: "The unburied [Japanese] were lying around and eventually a fly problem got to be terrible. The flies would land in the corners of your mouth and eyes and then land in your food.... We had what the Marines referred to as 'the GIs' [dysentery]."[57] A Japanese veteran claimed the voracious pests could reduce bodies to mere bones within two days.[58]

It must be stated that, with very few exceptions, the treatment of Japanese dead was governed by sanitary concerns rather than any pretense of dignified burial. Historian Alvin Stauffer notes that "owing to the uniformly heavy Japanese casualties and the swift deterioration of remains in the hot, insect-laden atmosphere, the disposal of enemy dead came to be regarded throughout the Pacific as a matter of field sanitation rather than of graves registration."[59] A single failed *banzai* charge could result in dozens of dead Japanese troops; a sustained attack, like those aimed at the Tenaru, Edson's Ridge, or Henderson Field, left hundreds of shattered bodies in fairly small areas in and around Marine or Army defensive positions. Although TM 10-630 explicitly mandated that "graves [of enemy dead] will be properly marked and registered and will remain in the custody of and be cared for by the Quartermaster Corps," expedience of disposal was, if not the standing order, at least the order of the day.[60] Stauffer notes that "strict adherence to the Geneva Convention prescribing equal treatment of the dead, whether friend or foe, was impossible.... Only theaters, like the European, which had a large pool of civilian labor as well as a relatively plentiful supply of graves registration units could follow the pattern prescribed at Geneva."[61]

Combat units were thus left to their own devices. John Clayton's company covered enemy bodies with quicklime; their perimeter was marked by "all these white mounds."[62] On Tulagi and Gavutu, many Japanese remains were piled together and cremated. In describing the aftermath of the action that won him the Medal of Honor, Platoon Sergeant Mitchell Paige mentioned an unusual method for cleaning up the battlefield:

There were hundreds of enemy dead in the grass, on the ridge, in the draw, and at the edge of the jungle.... I don't know if there was an order to do it, but almost by instinct we began to drag as many bodies as we could out of the sun and into the jungle. The sun would bloat them quickly and the stink would be unbearable. We buried as many as we could, then we blasted some of the ridge over them with explosives to try to cover them to prevent the smell that only a dead human can expel in heat.[63]

In most cases, however, Japanese bodies were merely tossed into the nearest convenient hole and covered as quickly as possible.

The tendency of Americans and Japanese to regard each other as inferior or subhuman is well documented, and this attitude devolved into a marked callousness that quickly defined the treatment of enemy dead. Jim McEnery described a typical manifestation of this mindset: "I mean, I could sit down and eat my C rations around dead Japs without even thinking about it. But I totally lost my appetite when dead Marines were lying there a few feet away."[64] Japanese troops mutilated American bodies and left them displayed as a warning; Americans affixed Japanese skulls to their jeeps and sent bones home as souvenirs. Keeping remains out of the enemy's hands was a priority, and both sides went to great lengths to do this whenever possible.

There were occasional incidents where human decency outweighed enmity. A patrol sent to find Cpl. Daniel Dermott Sweeney discovered an unusual sight, as Thurman Miller reports:

One patrol [from Miller's K/3/5] was directed to seek out and identify the remains of one member of an earlier patrol. They found his grave and upon digging out the remains found that the jungle had already begun to claim the body. They recognized a tattoo on the forearm of the man, but since there were no dog tags on him, they simply had to list him as missing in action. The strange thing was, the grave had a crude grave marker—a piece of board with the man's name: Sweeney. Apparently, the Japanese had buried him, marked his grave, and kept his dog tags. Why? Our Graves Registration wouldn't have left him there. Was it an apology? A warning? Or was it the natives? We would never know.[65]

A newspaper correspondent visiting the Guadalcanal cemetery in 1943 remarked on "a smaller plot in which a few dozen Japanese officers are buried under green crosses, marked simply 'Officers enemy dead.' Some distance away is a common burial ground known as Bloody Point. There, hundreds of Japanese are interred without markers."⁶⁶ Rather than a potter's field for deceased Japanese soldiers, "Bloody Point" probably refers to the mass graves near the Tenaru River, an area more commonly called "Hell's Point." There was, however, a cemetery plot for Japanese prisoners of war—some of whom were identified by name. This was a rare occurrence, though, and only about fifty of the estimated 19,200 Japanese who lost their lives on Guadalcanal wound up in this cemetery.⁶⁷ Ironically, several of the unknown remains recovered from Guadalcanal and given a military burial in Honolulu showed traits of Japanese or Korean ancestry—clearly not members of the racially segregated American armed forces of 1942.

Morale of the Home Population

When a Marine or corpsman fell in action, a report was to be dispatched to the Secretary of the Navy including the deceased's name, home address, and "disposition that has been made or will be made of the body."⁶⁸ This dispatch, in turn, triggered a long string of correspondence that began with a Western Union telegram ("Deeply regret to inform you...") and lasted for years until final disposition of the remains was made.

Every telegram from Lt. Gen. Thomas Holcomb, Commandant USMC, contained the line "Present situation necessitates interment temporarily in the locality where death occurred." Frequently, the next of kin would write back in search of more information, in which case a second form letter would be dispatched with as much burial information as was known. This second letter also broached the topic of eventually returning the remains as soon as "our dead can be safely removed." In most cases, the subject was not officially raised again until after the war.

In the meantime, the family often received condolence letters written by their Marine's commanding officer. "This communication should be in such language as to show personal consideration for the next of kin," warned the Marine Corps Manual, and as a result, many such missives read like form letters. Every man killed was the most popular buddy and the best fighter in his company, death was instantaneous and suffering minimal, and burials with full rites of faith were invariably performed. Occasionally, the dead man's friends took it upon themselves to write their own letters, and many made personal visits once back in the States. Such communications and connections provided a much-needed element of closure for families and veterans alike.

The personal effects of the dead were carefully collected and cataloged. Anything considered "discreditable" or that might distress the family was removed; government-issued articles, like clothing or equipment, was salvaged for survey or reissue. Paper money and loose change was collected, and a check issued for the exact amount. Everything else went back to the next of kin. PFC Cyrill A. Matelski's effects included a Marine Corps Handbook, a copy of his high school annual, a Bible, two watches, a pipe, and a Japanese undershirt—a souvenir of the Makin Island raid. PFC Gerald Hopkins owned, among other things, a name stamp, a *Reader's Digest*, a rosary, eleven handkerchiefs, and a package of personal letters.[69] Items like these were usually found in the deceased man's seabag or footlocker—which was stored safely with his unit's rear echelon—rather than in his possession. This distinction was not always made clear to families, who rightly wondered why personal effects could be found, but not a body.

Two young Marines from Company "C," 5th Marines, who died together on August 28 had their pockets and packs searched by their buddies, and the effects turned over to the company commander before they were buried. Pvt. Robert D. Budd owned:

26 Jap Bills
1 Rosary Beads [*sic.*]
4 small coins (foreign)
1 Newspaper clipping
8 photos
1 social security card
Several miscellaneous papers

His friend, Pvt. Thomas Phillips, carried:

2 diaries
1 fountain pen
1 cigarette case containing (9 Jap bills, several misc. papers, several trinkets)
1 emergency ration tin containing (85¢ in American money, several small foreign coins)
1 Photo
Several trinkets
2 five-dollar ($5.00) bills, American currency

These small tokens, along with the contents of the young Marines' seabags, were shipped to their families; Blanche Phillips wrote to acknowledge receipt of a check for the $10.85 that was in her son's pocket on the day he died.[70]

Occasionally, removing personal articles bearing a Marine's name led to a misidentification. This was presaged by the Circular, which warned that in the absence of identification tags: "A careful examination of personal effects may supply the information ... to establish identity." Emil Student, who was initially buried as an unknown, had only "a small amount of printed matter and some personal correspondence" on his body when he died. Members of his platoon could not find anything more, "due to the conditions of battle." All "legible" effects, amounting to two personal letters, were sent to his family. Had these letters remained with the body until it reached the cemetery, Student's identity might have been discovered at the time of burial; evidently, he possessed nothing else bearing his name. While Student's case was eventually resolved, many others may have lost their identity because of this practice. On "Dusty" Rhodes body was found "1 purse containing the following articles: 1 driver's license; 9 photographs; 1 piece Chinese money, paper, 50 cents; 1 Subpoena, Royal Domain." The license and King Neptune's subpoena would have given his name; without this information, anyone who had not known "Dusty" in life would have no idea who he was. While his family must have appreciated the return of his belongings, it was little solace when they were informed that his body would not be coming home.[71]

Naturally, the news that a loved one's remains had not been recovered after all came as quite a shock to families who had believed for years that their son, brother, or husband lay under a trim white cross on a South Pacific island. The family of PFC Raymond Schulthies was "exceedingly disturbed, not so much ... by the fact of his death, or even the fact that his remains cannot now be located, as by the exceedingly conflicting statements written to them by various officers in this Corps relative to the location of his remains," explained their attorney, Myron Winegarden, in a letter dated November 12, 1948. "The trouble is, that early letters from the Bureau [of Personnel, USMC] state with considerable certainty that the location of his grave was known. While later letters become more or less indefinite and formal, until finally you will find a letter of July 9th 1946 over the signature of Edwin C. Clark, Captain, USMC, stating definitely that the remains cannot be found." Additional assurances of sympathy were the only reply.[72]

Considering that the 1st Marine Division landed on Guadalcanal with an incomplete understanding of an untested administrative system that they never anticipated having to use in the first place, one might expect the worst—a shambles of record keeping, unreported burials, or an island covered in the isolated graves of men buried where they fell. While this confusion characterized the early days of the battle, the system outlined by Col. James' circular grew into its own over time. Between August 7,

1942 and February 10, 1943, nearly 1,350 members of the United States Marine Corps and their attached Navy medical personnel would die in the jungles and field hospitals of Guadalcanal, on the beaches and ridges of Tulagi, Gavutu, and Tanambogo, and in the seas and skies of the Solomon Islands. Of these, some 667 were identified and buried on Guadalcanal before the Marines departed, with a further 115 in cemeteries on Tulagi and Gavutu. All things considered, this is quite an accomplishment.

Yet James McCutcheon's name never appeared on a cross-shaped marker in the cemetery. Nor did the names of William Buchman, Frank Goettge, Robert Budd, John Langdon, Leon McStine, Charmning Rowe, Gerald Hopkins, Earl Thresher, Ingvard Aasvik, Patrick Milano, John Gnorik, Doyle Asher, Charles Ferguson, Richard Koop, or hundreds of others. At the battle's end, ninety Marines were missing in action, and 198 others lay in isolated graves. For some, nothing could be done, but for others, a simple clerical error, a misjudged good intention, or an improperly marked or situated grave resulted in a decades-long trauma for families and comrades alike.

As Thurman Miller reflected on his role in the battle, he recalled the infamous "Goettge Patrol," which set the tone for so much of the Guadalcanal campaign—and, by extension, the rest of the Pacific War. Miller personally witnessed the aftermath of the massacre and kept abreast of efforts to locate the missing men. "Since 1942, the coast has been heavily developed and excavated, and typhoons have washed away much of the beach," he wrote in 2014. "No sign of Goettge or his men." In his youth, the episode enraged him; men in his company began taking Japanese body parts in retribution. Seventy years later, an article suggesting that Marine remains may have been found and cremated alongside former adversaries in a traditional Shinto ceremony left him without malice.

Perhaps the smoke of our men's bones mingled with theirs, and I wish them all peace, but the island will never be free of ghosts.[73]

3

Blood on the River:
August 1942

The war had been impersonal: shellings, bombings, a few skirmishes, and some straggling prisoners. Now it had come into our tent, to a shortwave radio that no longer had an owner, to an empty desk with a family photograph, to empty cots. We would never be the same.[1]

Karl Thayer Soule, 1st Marine Division

Frank Few lay in his foxhole, wishing the daylight away. Warm seawater swirled into his foxhole, turning pinkish as it mingled with the blood seeping from his chest and arm. Sand was everywhere—stuck to the Japanese blood on his clothes, in his eyes, in the Reising gun he borrowed from Monk and which would only fire single shots. Few counted out his remaining rounds and stuffed them into his mouth to keep the sand and salt water away. Occasionally, a bullet snapped overhead, as if he needed a reminder to keep his head down.

Trapped in a flooding foxhole, wounded, almost out of ammunition, with the sun coming up. It could not get much worse: "The hell with this for a lark," he thought.[2]

Few, a platoon sergeant just twenty-two years old, was what Marines called "really rugged." "This means he is a tough hombre," explained correspondent Richard Tregaskis, "and Few certainly looks the part; he has fierce dark eyes, a wiry, muscular body, and he moves with the swift ease of a cat."[3] His sideburns, beard, and mustache completed the swashbuckling picture, and it was widely known that Few had Cherokee blood in his veins. He was one of the top men in the 5th Marines intelligence (R-2) section, and when word came down that Division intelligence (D-2) was mounting a patrol, Few was tapped to go along. The plan sounded screwy from the start—a night landing in unfamiliar territory, capturing some Japanese, marching overland back to the perimeter—and he was not encouraged at the sight of his companions, a mixture of overaged officers, young kids, non-combat Marines, and a sullen Japanese prisoner. The officer in charge, a burly, fatherly colonel called Goettge, planned to be back the following day.

The plan had not worked. In the first light of August 13, Few could make out the motionless shapes of almost twenty Marines. He could not see the colonel but knew he was dead, along with most of the rest of the patrol. Three men had been sent running for help, but no help had arrived, and the invisible enemy kept sniping away. Few's boss, Capt. Ringer, was still alive and in good shape; so was Caltrider, and a fourth man he thought was Stauffer. The tide was filling in their foxholes, and there was no cover to be had on the open beach. They were running out of time.

On Ringer's signal, they ran hell-for-leather up the beach and to the cover of the tree line. Stauffer managed five steps before five bullets shredded his back; his ammunition belt exploded and he fell, clothing afire. Few whirled around, snapped off a shot at a sniper, saw Ringer and Caltrider go down, and realized he was the last man standing.[4] He spun about, spat out his ammo, and ran for the ocean, stripping down to a pair of white silk Japanese skivvies. Wild yelling erupted behind him as he dove into the waves, then the clatter and rattle of bullets churning the water around him. Few swam underwater until his lungs were bursting, came up for air, and chanced to look behind him. The Japanese had overrun the position. Morning light flashed on their upraised sabers and bayonets.

The "Goettge Patrol" has gone down in history as one of the most brutal episodes of the Guadalcanal campaign. At the time, it was considered propagandistic proof of a treacherous and inhuman enemy who deliberately connived to lure good Americans to butchery. More level-headed critics describe it as a synonym for innocence and ineptitude, a misguided humanitarian effort that cost the lives of twenty-one specially trained Marines and a top Navy surgeon. The loss of the patrol all but crippled the 1st Marine Division's intelligence capabilities at a time when it sorely needed all the information it could gather, and nearly dealt a serious blow to the entire American war effort by exposing a former "Magic" cryptologist to potential capture. At the same time, it served as a wake-up call to Marines who thought fighting the Japanese would be easy. "The Division's mood changed from that of a normal person to a silent, mean person," remarked patrol survivor Charles "Monk" Arndt. "I think each man in the Division changed 180 degrees. The Japanese gave no quarter, and they took no quarter, and that's the way the battle went."[5]

The man for whom the disaster would be named, Col. Frank Bryan Goettge, was a legend in his time. Born in Canton, Ohio, in 1895, Goettge (pronounced Getch-y) was an up-and-coming college football star when the Great War interrupted his education; on May 22, 1917, he exchanged his University of Ohio togs for the uniform of a Marine Corps private. Goettge rose quickly through the ranks, earning a lieutenant's commission in just over a year, and arriving at the Western Front shortly before the Armistice.[6] Stymied at making a name for himself in combat, Goettge quickly attracted attention at inter-service sporting events, including an infamously spirited American Expeditionary Force all-star game. An injury "in the line of duty" sent him back to the United States in 1919.

Rather than return to college, Lt. Goettge decided to stay in uniform, serving in Haiti and aspiring to flight school before being recruited by the Marine Corps football team. His rise to fame was meteoric, first as a fullback, then as an all-around player. "The peerless Goettge," he was called, or "The Human Locomotive."[7] Army footballers adopted a new chant: "Stop Goettge!" Walter Campbell wrote of "Goettge the Great.... He is easily the greatest football player of the present day. He is, indeed, the nearest approach to Jim Thorpe of all time."[8] A four-year service ruling forced Goettge off the gridiron in 1925 with an unprecedented record of thirty-eight wins, two ties, and two losses. The New York Giants offered him the chance to go pro, but Goettge preferred to stay at Quantico and coach Marine footballers.[9] He was more than a talented athlete: in the years that followed, Goettge would serve with the American Legation in Peking, as an aide to two successive Commandants of the Marine Corps and President Herbert Hoover, in command of a battleship's Marine detachment, and as executive officer of the Basic School in Philadelphia.

In the summer of 1941, Lt. Col. Goettge was assigned to the 1st Marine Division as the senior intelligence officer (D-2).[10] He had much to learn; save for a stint as a company-grade scouting officer in Haiti, some twenty years prior, Goettge had little professional experience in this field.[11] Karl Thayer Soule, a recently commissioned second lieutenant with the grandiose title of "Assistant Intelligence Officer for Photography, Division Intelligence Section, D-2," recalled his first meeting with his new boss:

> Colonel Frank Bryan Goettge was as big as an ox. Rising from behind his desk, he looked like a mountain, a huge mass of a man towering above me. He had gray hair, a garden of ribbons on his shirt, and an almost fatherly look in his eyes.
>
> "Welcome aboard, Lieutenant." The voice fitted the man, firm and heavy, but friendly and warm. We shook hands with a tight, firm grip.
>
> "Now," said the colonel, motioning me to a chair, "you can clear something up for me. What the hell is a photographic officer?"[12]

Goettge was willing to learn what he did not know, and his affable nature endeared him to his contemporaries. "Frank had a great personality," wrote one, "and while under the surface he was as hard as the traditional Marine, he had a heart of gold and was a well-polished and refined type of person."[13] Cpl. Joseph Spaulding, a New Yorker assigned to Goettge as a runner, remembered his boss as "an imposing man. His physical stature commanded your attention, and there was a note of authority in his voice…. Goettge gave an order, and people tended to be prompt in carrying it out." His appeal was not universal—Frank Few dismissed Goettge as a "rah-rah football hero"—but most echoed the sentiment of Marine Gunner Edward "Bill" Rust: "You couldn't doubt he was able to do anything … you'd have followed him anywhere."[14]

The expansion of the Corps immediately before the war increased the breadth of its abilities as raw recruits brought civilian expertise to their new roles. Soule "sensed a great deal of know-how and professional pride" among the junior men, some of whom knew Soule's duties better than he did. Soule took immediate notice of Cpl. Herbert Benson, "a good kid with a flair for drawing and telling jokes," and Cpl. Joseph Kashuba, who was "loud, fast, and tough, the old school through and through" and sported a "Death Before Dishonor" tattoo. The section was also blessed with two outstanding senior sergeants—T/Sgt. John Waddick, a military cartographer who thoroughly grasped "the function of intelligence," and a slight, blue-eyed Texan, 1Sgt. Custer, who was the NCO in charge.[15]

Custer was thirty-seven years old when he became Goettge's second in command, the latest post in a colorful career that spanned more than two decades. He came from a military family; three close relatives, including his grandfather, fought for the Confederacy, and George Armstrong Custer of Little Big Horn was a distant cousin. Determined to follow in their footsteps, Alexander Steven Custer lied about his age to enlist in the Army—the ruse went undiscovered for nearly eighteen months before the Signal Corps caught on and kicked him out. Undaunted, the sixteen-year-old Custer simply changed up his name. "Steven Alexander Custer" joined the Marines in 1921 and went off to see the world.[16]

Over the next ten years, Custer ticked all the boxes on an old salt's checklist: sea duty aboard USS *Arizona*, liberty calls in Hawaii and Cavite, duty on Guam, and a litany of stripes earned and lost as he moved from station to station (and, occasionally, from brig to brig). He developed into an exceptional marksman, scoring "Expert" on the rifle range and earning a spot on the 1932 Marine Corps pistol team, for which he was awarded a medal and a letter of commendation. By 1940, Sgt. Custer estimated that he had visited some thirty-eight countries; his service history included everything from clerical duty at Parris Island and fleet exercises with the 5th

Marines to teaching marksmanship to recruits and FBI agents at Quantico. As a recruiting sergeant, he even had the distinction of "enlisting" the country's youngest Marine—his own son, whom he "swore in" at birth.[17] He brought this professionalism to his new assignment. "Goettge was a conscientious and considerate, but remote, commanding officer," wrote a veteran of the D-2 section. "Custer was a father to us. None was more personally fearless, yet more conscious of possible apprehension among his men.... He considered it his mission to mold our character and our competence.... Young and restless in spirit, he at once commanded our respect, for implicitly we recognized his greater knowledge and authority, and [this] inspired our affection."[18]

While the enthusiastic, good-natured Goettge and the charismatic, competent Custer instilled old-Corps values and discipline in the D-2 section, a host of younger officers were inheriting 2-sections whether they wanted them or not. Lt. William H. Whyte III was switched from his rifle platoon to a Bn-2 position "for reasons only [battalion commander Lt. Col. William McKelvy] understood." Professionals like "Wild Bill" McKelvy, whose career began when Whyte was an infant and "the Corps was barely larger than the New York Police Department," took a dim view of young reserve officers, most of whom were college educated and preferred a life of campuses and coeds. This friction sometimes festered into resentment or outright hostility.[19] Occasionally, however, a junior officer fit right in. Wilfred Harvey Ringer, Jr., a reservist from Brookline, Massachusetts, was one of these. As the 1932 Gloucester High School valedictorian, Bill Ringer hoped his academic prowess—plus numerous marksmanship awards and ROTC honors—would translate into an Annapolis appointment.[20] Instead, armed with a degree from Tufts and four years of experience in a reserve platoon leader's unit, he accepted a second lieutenant's commission in January 1939. Called to active duty in February 1941, Ringer led his class at the Basic School in Philadelphia and was assigned to the 5th Marines as an assistant operations officer. He took command of the R-2 section on May 15, 1942; three days later, he was promoted to captain and his regiment left North Carolina for overseas.

Ringer was a talented officer but had no time to work with his men before shipping out. Fortunately, he also inherited some extremely competent NCOs. Plat. Sgt. Denzil Ray Caltrider, an expert rifleman from West Virginia, was the senior man and filled a role similar to Custer's; Plat. Sgt. Frank Few lent a capable hand and was the resident photography expert. Sgt. Charles C. Arndt, a sharp-eyed Mississippian, was one of the best scouts in the regiment. Nicknamed "Monk" for his ability to scramble up trees like a monkey, Arndt was so devoted to his craft that he often practiced stalking around the base and bivouac areas alone, much to the amusement of his buddies.[21] His buddy Sgt. Robert J. Stanfill oversaw the situation map. "We had the same reasons for joining the Marine Corps," said Arndt. "No jobs, no nothing—didn't have two nickels to rub together or buy your girlfriend a Coca-Cola." The two sergeants also shared the experience of parachute school, although only Stanfill completed the rigorous course.[22] Sgt. David Alvin Stauffer, Jr., a former Boy Scout and high school athlete from Berwyn, Pennsylvania, rounded out the group of sergeants; although less experienced than his colleagues, a rapid rise through the ranks bespoke his abilities.

There was talent at the lower levels, too. PFC John L. Delano, a gifted watercolor artist (and former pupil of Capt. Ringer's father at Brookline High School), was applying his talents to mapmaking and was judged "the best draftsman in the division."[23] Cpl. Stephen Serdula was a promising scout, as was Cpl. Aaron Gelzer, shanghaied from Company "L." Theodore Raht, Jr., had only been in uniform since January, yet was already a corporal. A handful of the rest—Blaine Walter, Daniel Gauntt, Jack Kelly, and seventeen-year-old Robert Lovelace—were even greener, and still learning the ropes.

The greenest of all was no stripling private, but forty-four-year-old 1Lt. Merle "Ralph" Cory. Stocky, balding, and reserved, Cory did not fit the picture of a typical Marine officer. Yet he possessed one unique quality: he could read, write, and speak fluent Japanese. Following his journalism studies at the College of Puget Sound and the University of Washington, Cory developed an interest in diplomatic work and was assigned to the American Legation in Peking. While there, he attended Yenching University and was tutored in the Japanese language. As a State Department clerk, Cory worked in Peking and Seoul, and eventually the embassy in Tokyo and the consulate in Nagasaki, where he perfected his language skills and learned much about Japanese culture.

The Navy came calling in 1940. Cory was summoned to Washington to join a secretive program called OP-20-GY—the cryptanalytical section of Navy Headquarters. The United States had cracked Japan's highly secretive diplomatic code ("Purple") and was reading so much traffic that the fifty translators on its staff were overwhelmed. By November 1941, Cory was working late into the night translating the decoded messages ("Magic"); the work was repetitive and prevented him from spending time with his new wife, Carolyn. By chance, a standby order for Japanese diplomats to destroy their codebooks crossed his desk; when translated, it provided the most concrete evidence that the two countries were headed for war. Still, Cory was not satisfied. "I'm going to join the Marines," he confided to a friend. "I'm sick of pencil pushing." He was far too old to enlist, but his language skills outweighed his age and small stature. The Corps offered him a direct commission in May 1942, and after some rudimentary field training, Cory was dispatched to the 1st Marine Division. When he joined their ranks in July 1942, he was one of four men who could speak Japanese; only he and Capt. Sherwood "Pappy" Moran could read and write the language.[24]

The challenge that faced Frank Goettge and his men would have taxed even the most cohesive intelligence units. When Ghormley issued the alert order to Vandegrift, "immediate steps were taken ... to collect all available general information relative to terrain, landing beaches, climate conditions, attitude of natives and relevant topics."[25] "Relevant topics" included everything from enemy strength to how to pronounce the name of the island they were to invade. Marine Corps historian John Zimmerman later categorized it as little more than "a stab in the dark" aimed at "the fog of blank ignorance and some misinformation" that shrouded the mysterious Solomon Islands.[26] "How many Japanese were in the Guadalcanal and Tulagi garrisons? How were they disposed? What weapons did they have? What were the beach and reef conditions at possible landing sites? What kind of terrain would the landing force find inland from the beaches?" wondered Lt. Herbert Merillat, a 1st Marine Division staff officer. "Information on these and other crucial matters was skimpy or nonexistent at Ghormley's headquarters or elsewhere in New Zealand." Merillat, himself a Rhodes scholar, confessed total ignorance of the existence of the Solomon Islands and satisfied his curiosity by locating "Guadalcanar" in an atlas at a public library.[27] "I had never heard of these islands. Nor had anybody else," wrote Lt. Whyte. "What we needed was information. What we needed, especially, were maps."[28] Goettge spent every waking moment collecting information, but the rough sketches, aerial photos, and outdated hydrographic charts that made their way to Thayer Soule's lithographers were woefully inadequate. "It is incredible that the division was committed on such slim intelligence," Soule complained.[29]

Goettge was as surprised as anyone when the Marine landing was unopposed. While the rank and file celebrated with sarcasm and coconut milk, Goettge grew concerned. His preliminary work—interviewing planters, estimating troop strength, studying what was known of Japanese tactics—suggested that the landing on Beach Red would be hotly contested. The entire Watchtower landing plan was based upon that assumption. Now, most of the division had walked ashore standing up. For Goettge, the ease of the assault was no lucky break; it meant the intelligence service had miscalculated or misjudged somewhere along the line. Naturally, he began to wonder what else his section might have gotten wrong.

The progress of August 7 brought no answers. "No knowledge of any enemy front line or forces," he said, as a clerk scribbled in the brand-new D-2 journal. "Deserted enemy positions in Kukum-Lunga Point-Tenaru areas…. Second Battalion, First Marines reported at 2245 Jap patrol of from 150 to 200 stampeding cattle into our battalion lines." Goettge and Custer commandeered a jeep the next morning and followed the 5th Marines' advance across the airfield. They hoped to see some action, but the only unusual sight was the grave of a lone Japanese sailor. While souvenir hunters swarmed over mountains of abandoned supplies, Goettge fretted over possibilities. "No artillery has been located," he complained in his daily report of August 8. "Location, strength, and composition of enemy reserves unknown."[30]

All of this ignorance paled in comparison to the problem of maps, which were wholly insufficient or totally nonexistent. Immediately upon landing, the 1st and 5th Marines struggled to orient themselves to landmarks that were misplaced, mislabeled, or absent from their drawings. "Crude maps can be misleading, and our crude map was very misleading," huffed Holly Whyte after a disagreement over the location of the Ilu River earned him a tongue-lashing from McKelvy.[31] Companies became lost, battalions overexerted, and regiments tangled. Without a map, infantry units could not orient themselves with their surroundings or each other, and artillery batteries could not coordinate fire missions. As days went by, and the grumbling and dissatisfaction grew more pronounced, the cloud over the intelligence section darkened.

Goettge tackled the problem head-on. Ordered to "find, fix, and fight" the Japanese, he attempted to absorb every detail that came to his section: scraps of equipment, reports of abandoned emplacements, and the occasional prisoner. Patrols began to encounter Japanese labor troops, mostly older reservists and conscripts, who had fled from the Marine advance and now wandered aimlessly through the jungle. Those who survived their encounters with the Marines were hauled before interpreters; when plied with sympathy and the occasional nip of brandy, they answered questions and ventured guesses at the size of their own garrison. Marines thought these "termites" low-balled the numbers, but revised their original estimates to "two Navy construction battalions about 1,800 men and under 500 troops," admitting that their earlier estimate of 5,010 Japanese was "a heavy overstatement."[32] The capture of a Japanese camp at Kukum resulted in a wealth of documents and an Imperial paymaster's chest full of occupation currency.[33] Ralph Cory found himself buried, once again, under mountains of paperwork. Lithographers got to work incorporating captured Japanese maps into their own sketches, and penciled revisions to the map were issued starting on August 9.

The disparity in training between members of D-2, R-2, and Bn-2 sections became all too apparent.[34] First Sergeant Custer mentored his men with unceasing patience, "quietly observing all our reactions, helping us along ... it was he who indoctrinated us in intelligence procedure, in scouting, and in warfare in general."[35] Goettge, on the other hand, preferred to do things himself. "Goettge's place was in headquarters," remarked Lt. Soule, "but ever since arriving on the island, he had been at the front or ahead of it. He was that kind of man. In Haiti, he had once been on patrol for eighteen continuous months.... Only the general or chief of staff could order him to change his ways, and neither of them had the heart to do that."[36]

An increasing number of "sanguinary hostile contacts" indicated that, wherever the Japanese had gone, it was somewhere to the west—the sector guarded by the 5th Marines. On August 9, a patrol on its way to the Matanikau River bumped into a heavily-armed Japanese group and suffered several casualties; the Marines returned in strength the following day, only to be pinned down at the riverbank.[37] "There came a sudden spattering of sharp rifle reports," reported Richard Tregaskis. "Deeper-toned rifles took up the chorus, machine guns joined in, and the shower of sound became a rainstorm."[38] Although minor by later standards, this dust-up over a sand spit at the river's mouth—the only natural crossing—was enough to label the area west of the Matanikau a "hornet's nest."

August 12 began auspiciously. The latest map, traced from liberated Lever Company surveyor's holdings and correctly scaled for military use, was ready for the lithographers. Patrols reported seeing a white flag hanging limp and defeated from a pole on the high ground west of the Matanikau. First Sergeant Custer was busily planning a reconnaissance in force of the area, an ambitious plan that would immeasurably enhance his section's knowledge and experience. And, rarity of rarities, a Japanese sailor was caught lurking in the bushes and was brought in for interrogation.

This man, who would prove to be one of the most important figures in the Guadalcanal campaign, is something of an enigma. Historian Stanley Coleman Jersey names him Warrant Officer Tsuneto Sakado, a native of Yamaguchi Prefecture and leader of a machine-gun platoon of the 84th Guard Unit.[39] After several days on the lam, Sakado's blue and white naval uniform was tattered and stained; he was hungry, furious at suffering the shame of capture, "not cooperative in any way."[40] Lt. Col. Merrill Twining recalled "a man in his thirties, powerfully built and of surly demeanor.... He was tied to a tree at the CP for most of the day, with a hawser-size length of manila line around his waist."[41] Sakado must have seemed a tough case, for 1Lt. Cory reportedly conducted the interrogation armed with a generous dose of medicinal brandy. After a few sips, Sakado admitted that he had come from west of the Matanikau and that many of his comrades were starving and dispirited. He thought they might be induced to surrender.

Col. Goettge seized on this new information. He saw a chance to reconnoiter the area west of the Matanikau with minimal risk, to scout the troublesome defensive positions and get a better fix on enemy strength. Americans could prove they were not afraid of the jungle or the Japanese while extending the proverbial olive branch to the non-combatant labor troops caught between the warring parties. The stock of the intelligence section would rise immeasurably. All of this could be accomplished by a single patrol, thought Goettge—a patrol he would lead himself.[42]

This idea met with immediate resistance. Goettge first approached the division operations officer, Lt. Col. Gerald Thomas, with his proposal to take a patrol by boat from Kukum to the uncharted boondocks beyond Point Cruz and return overland. When Thomas expressed reservations about expanding offensive operations, Goettge pulled rank and appealed up the chain of command.[43] Finding Gen. Vandegrift "initially hostile to his request," Goettge turned up the diplomacy, appealing to his boss as an old friend.[44] The general hemmed and hawed before offering a tepid endorsement. "Well, Frank," Lt. Soule heard him say, "I'm not going to *order* you to stay here, but...."[45]

Next, Goettge informed Custer of the change of plans. The senior NCO's reaction was not recorded—Custer, ever the professional, probably kept his opinions to himself. Three of the combat Marines on the roster were replaced by Corporals Herbert Benson, Joseph Kashuba, Joseph Spaulding, and Jack F. Lyons—a scout, a lithographer, a runner, and a draftsman. Not wanting to completely derail D-2 operations, Goettge paid a visit to the 5th Marines. Capt. Ringer was convinced (or ordered) to volunteer almost his entire R-2 section for the mission, including his interpreter, Lt. Cory. Lt. Cdr. Malcolm Pratt, the regiment's senior medical officer, also agreed to go along. The surgeon from Bellefontaine, Ohio, had more than impressive medical credentials: he also wore a Navy Cross awarded for heroism in the Great War. "Doc" Pratt had just turned fifty-one and feared his own poor health would send him home before he got a chance to see some action in his second war. Pratt would be the patrol's only medical specialist.[46]

Time was rapidly becoming a serious factor. Custer had wanted to depart early in the morning; it was now midafternoon. Ringer, already annoyed at ceding control of his section to Goettge, grew increasingly nervous at the prospect of operating after dark—especially after an explicit warning from the regimental exec, Lt. Col. William J. Whaling, to avoid the "hornet's nest" area between Point Cruz and the Matanikau. This foreboding led Ringer to ask Capt. Lyman Spurlock, skipper of Company "L," about the possibility of reinforcements if anything went wrong. Spurlock demurred, saying "it would be difficult at night."[47]

Some of Spurlock's men watched the 5th Marines contingent depart late in the afternoon. Sgt. Ben Selvitelle recognized Cpl. Aaron Gelzer, the former Company "L" BARman. "We talked with him, and he was in high spirits—like the others, he had volunteered to make the patrol," Selvitelle remembered. "There was some discussion about his being rewarded with a medal. As we left Gelzer and returned to our position, we talked about the odd absence of fighting troops with the patrol."[48] Instructed to avoid provoking a fight, Goettge replaced heavily armed combat Marines with intelligence men who could travel light. "We were not a combat patrol, we were more or less a humanitarian patrol," said Monk Arndt. "We had ponchos, a belt, canteen with no cup, one can of C-rations, and one can of fish. No BARs, no grenades at all, nothing like that."[49] The heaviest weapons were a handful of unreliable Reising submachine guns. Even Sakado was brought along, led like a dog with a rope tied around his neck. Col. Goettge intended to change the tide of the battle with a force of twenty-four specialist Marines, one Navy surgeon, and one disgruntled Japanese sailor.

The patrol arrived at the Kukum boat pool on the evening of August 12. Navy lieutenant Jack Clark noted that Goettge's men were "feeling quite confident in their mission.... We were all laughing and talking while they were awaiting the boat which was to take them down," he wrote in his diary.[50] The feeling was not universal. Frank Few had just returned from an overnight patrol; Goettge's mission interrupted his well-deserved night off. Few thought most of his companions were much too green, much too old, or too much of both to patrol enemy territory, and was worried that most of them seemed to regard the expedition as little more than "a lark."[51] Monk Arndt was "more or less disgusted with the higher ups" for his own loss of sleep and the rampant disorganization. "We were just sitting around doing nothing [at Kukum], and that gets old hat," he said. "You don't have anything to eat and nothing to do, so we were just waiting.... Delays just drug on and on, and it was after dark before we actually left Lunga Point."[52] The Higgins boat finally arrived at 6 p.m., a full hour behind schedule. Goettge's men quickly clambered aboard, and the little craft puttered away from Kukum.

From inauspicious beginnings, Col. Goettge's patrol rapidly devolved into "an Intelligence comedy of errors."[53] The men from the 5th Marines were not briefed on their mission until after the boat departed Kukum. As they absorbed the information, someone spotted a signal flare (other accounts mention a fire on shore) shooting up behind them, near Beach Red. Goettge, lacking a radio, did not know what this meant—it might have been a signal intended for him, or not a signal at all—and had the boat turn around so he could relay the information by telephone.[54] When they set out again, it was pitch black. "We really couldn't see where we were going," related Monk Arndt. "The coxswain couldn't tell where the boat was."[55] At 10 p.m., still several miles short of their planned landing site on the far side of Point Cruz, Goettge directed the coxswain to land. This provoked a storm of protest from Sakado, who shouted "*Iie, iie!*"—"No, no!" The colonel and the prisoner started yelling at each other, presumably with Cory translating as rapidly as he could.[56] Goettge prevailed, and the boat headed to shore only to run aground on a sandbar. The exasperated patrol piled out into the shallow water, straining to free the boat while the coxswain gunned the engine in reverse. "The boat made enough noise to raise the dead!" said Arndt. "It took twenty, maybe thirty minutes to get it off the sandbar. That alerted all the enemy in that area. Gave them ample time to set up for us."[57]

Lt. (j. g.) Soichi Shindo was anticipating a quiet evening. The Americans did not like to fight at night; he did not think they would be so foolish as to try to cross the Matanikau in the dark, dominated as it was by strong fortifications. His men, the security force of Capt. Kanae Monzen's 11th Construction Unit, were emplaced around the little village of Horahi, near the western bank of the Matanikau. They had nothing to fear, even from the boat they could hear motoring about offshore. Shindo knew some American sailors liked to pick fights from their little boats under cover of darkness, but these were only a nuisance. After the great victory at Savo Island, the seas were unquestionably Japanese. Whatever its mission, this boat would soon scuttle back to the safety of Kukum.

The sound of the engine grew gradually louder, and the security force realized it was headed in their direction. Suddenly, there was the crunching sound of a boat running aground. The engine roared in protest; splashing and cursing were barely audible over the din. Shindo's men hurried to the shallow trenches guarding the approaches from the beach and from the river, ready to face whatever came ashore.

The Higgins boat grumbled off into the darkness, heading back to Kukum. Goettge's men sloshed onto the beach, set up a quick defensive perimeter, and scanned the dark jungle for any signs of trouble. After a quick conference, Goettge, Ringer, and Custer stepped into the tree line, searching for a place to spend the night. The rest of the men wriggled down into the sand. Plat. Sgt. Caltrider waited near the water's edge, his rifle pressed against Sakado's head as a warning against further outbursts.

There was the sudden report of a rifle; the flat, high crack of a .25-caliber weapon. "That's all we heard, one shot," remembered Arndt. Then came the clatter of Bill Ringer's Reising gun, ending abruptly in a jam. The captain crashed back through the trees, shaken but unhurt. After a few minutes, another few shots rang out, and Custer's familiar drawl rose above the noise: "I'm going to make a break for it!" The first sergeant emerged from the underbrush cursing in pain; blood ran down his face and right arm. Doc Pratt hurried to help. The colonel was nowhere to be seen. "Goettge!" someone called in a stage whisper. "Goettge!" No answer.[58]

Ringer thought the colonel had been hit and wanted to move up to investigate. Frank Few argued with his skipper; if Goettge were incapacitated, Ringer would have to take command, and there was no point in risking another officer. Instead, Few volunteered to go. "Monk" Arndt and a D-2 corporal who introduced himself as Joe Spaulding of New York City would go, too. "This is really Errol Flynn stuff," Spaulding muttered as they low-crawled through the underbrush.[59] They had gone only a few yards when they found Goettge sprawled on the ground. Few reached out to shake the colonel and felt blood all over Goettge's face and shoulders. "My God," he gasped, "he's been shot through the head."[60] There was no pulse, no heartbeat, and no breath. Few dispatched Spaulding back to the beach to get help. He was undoing Goettge's insignia—the enemy must not know they had killed a colonel—when someone moved in front of him. Sgt. Charles Arndt heard shouting and scuffling, the scrape of blade on bone, and some elaborate cursing in English and Japanese. The patrol had wandered into Petty Officer Goro Sakurai's platoon of the 11th CU Security Force.[61]

Shigeru Takamune heard the words "stand up" in English; none of his squad spoke the language, but that was enough to launch them into action. "Petty Officer Sakurai sprung on some enemy and began to scuffle," he later reported. Another platoon leader, Petty Officer Yasou Yamamiya, remembered "the American forces came into the center of our positions.... We desperately assaulted them by bayonet."[62] Frank Few could also fight "like a wild man." A Japanese soldier, possibly Sakurai "let out a war whoop and came at me," Few later told correspondent Richard Tregaskis. "My submachine gun jammed. I was struck in the arm and chest with his bayonet, but I knocked his rifle away. I choked him and stabbed him with his own bayonet." Spotting another Japanese taking aim from a nearby tree, Few grabbed Arndt's pistol and emptied the magazine into the would-be sniper. The Marines turned tail and raced back to the beach. Flares lit the sky and Japanese machine guns opened fire, "so close you could feel the air from the muzzles."[63] The first burst wounded several Marines on the left flank; as they screamed in pain, Capt. Ringer passed the word to dig in. Plat. Sgt. Caltrider executed Sakado with a single shot, then joined his team at the ad hoc perimeter.

Lt. Shindo was playing it safe. His platoons near the beach kept up a steady fire, enough to pin the enemy down while keeping an eye out for other Americans moving in on their flanks. Monk Arndt noted that the fighting was "very slow," and the Marines "all very quiet, except for touching each other once in a while and wondering what was going to happen next." There was no cover on the beach, and Shindo's riflemen took deadly aim. A bullet struck Lt. Cdr. Pratt in the buttocks; gritting his teeth, the surgeon finished Custer's bandages and moved on to the next wounded man. Another round hit Ralph Cory in the stomach, leaving him helpless and groaning in the sand. Capt. Ringer sent a Marine down to the waterline to shoot tracers into the air, a desperate SOS, hoping for the boat to return—or for anyone to send help.[64]

2054. Telephone. Visual observer of 1–5 on beach reports 2 red flares fired across his position. (R-2, 5)

2105. Telephone. Forward observer 11th at Kukum reports 3 red flares along shoreline to NW of Kukum. (R-2, 11)

2118. Telephone. 5 lights, definitely flares, not tracers, seen by 1–5 observer X Visual outpost further reports white light similar to Higgins boat type in same locality as flares X Light shone for about 1 second, has not been repeated. (R-2, 5)

2129. Telephone. 1 more flare observed as above. (R-2, 5)

2305. Telephone. Boat that took Col. Goettge has returned and reports successful landing.

2400. Journal closed.[65]

Pvt. Art Boston of Company "L," 5th Marines, was manning a beach defense position with his buddy, PFC Reno Roy. The night was mostly quiet; a perfect time to grumble about the recently announced reduction in rations or to plan one's next liberty. The sentries knew that an American patrol was operating somewhere out in front of the lines, but did not expect them to return until the next afternoon or later. So it was somewhat surprising when they started seeing tracers arcing into the sky. "Those boys are in deep trouble down there," Boston remarked. "Look at those tracer bullets."[66] Reports of muffled gunfire reached Capt. Spurlock; observers from First Battalion, 5th Marines, saw an unusual number of flares from the direction of Point Cruz. Something was obviously going on, but the word from Headquarters was final—monitor the situation, nothing more.[67] For all anyone knew, Goettge's patrol was safely hidden on the far side of Point Cruz, far from the village sending up all the flares and tracers.

"Someone on our line would get a glimpse of the enemy and fire a shot, and then we would all open fire," recalled Frank Few. "They returned our fire with rifles and machine guns, and apparently every burst wounded at least one of our men."[68] Cries of surprise and pain came from all points of the perimeter; it was impossible to tell who was hit. Despite his own wound, "Doc" Pratt made his painful way from one man to the next. He was tending to a casualty when a bullet smashed through his chest; knowing he was past help, the gallant officer continued to work until he collapsed. With Pratt's death, the wounded were on their own.

Capt. Ringer had no idea how many enemies he faced, or even where on Guadalcanal he was. Without a radio set or an evacuation plan, the only way to save the patrol was for a brave man to deliver the message in person. Monk Arndt was the first volunteer. "If anybody could get through the line, I thought I could," he said. "I was about the only senior scout in the group, and I had taught those men everything they knew.... There was no chance to leave by land, and I was a pretty good swimmer."[69] After trading his weapon for Custer's pistol, Arndt crawled down to the water's edge. He stripped down to his boondockers—the laces snarled, and he could not get them off—tucked the pistol under his helmet, and disappeared into the darkness. His buddies heard scattered rifle shots, followed by the snap of the .45. Fearing the worst, Few suggested sending a second messenger. Cpl. William Bainbridge, a twenty-one-year-old Marine from Hillside, New Jersey, accepted the challenge. He waited for a break in the firing, then took off along the beach, skirting around the area where the shots were heard.[70]

Hours passed. Ringer dispatched a third man, Cpl. Joe Spaulding, who followed Arndt's path down the beach and disappeared into the water. He dared not send any more; his perimeter kept shrinking as more men went down, wounded or killed. As the sky began to lighten in the east, and the tide began to rise, Bill Ringer could count only three other men still able to move. He gave the signal, and they got up and started to run.

A naked, bloody, exhausted man in a dugout canoe came paddling into the boat pool at 5 a.m., screaming "Million! Million!" at the top of his lungs. Monk Arndt had returned to Kukum.

After leaving the patrol and crawling into the surf, Arndt kept close to the shoreline, clambering over razor-sharp coral and swimming as quietly as he could, using a breaststroke to keep his head above water and his pistol dry. He came ashore at the sand spit and was fired upon; two Japanese had followed him along the shore but fled when he fired back. Arndt continued his tortuous progress, wading through the neck-deep water, swimming across the deeper holes. The echoing gunfire from the beach drove him on; a glance back at the tracers arcing above his friends kept exhaustion at bay. He found a dugout canoe with the bow shot off; by sitting at the stern, he could keep the damaged part above water. Arndt paddled along until he spotted an American fire control boat, and fortunately had the presence of mind to remember about passwords.

He beat on the boat's hull with a broken board, obtained the password from the startled crew, and paddled the rest of the way to the beach.[71] Within minutes, he was on the phone to his regimental CP, reporting that the patrol was being cut to pieces.

Joe Spaulding got back at 7.25 a.m. He had followed Monk's route into the water and along the shore, heading inland at the first sign of civilization, thinking he had reached the Marine perimeter. He was within 20 feet when he realized the guard was Japanese. Spaulding turned and ran, evading his pursuers by diving back into the ocean. When he could swim no more, he took a chance and climbed onto a sandbar, strolling as casually as possible and nibbling on a chocolate bar.[72] At the next emplacement, he was relieved to recognize American uniforms. "I walked towards those Marines, and when I was within fifty yards or so, one of them had a submachine gun, and it snapped up, pointed towards me," he said. "It appeared that, ironically, my own men were going to kill me." He confirmed Arndt's story before collapsing at the regimental CP. "This boy Spaulding, I can still see him sitting on the ground right by the CP," recalled Marine Gunner Edward "Bill" Rust. "He was all broken up, he had tears in his eyes telling about his friends that were killed."[73]

Just at daybreak, Art Boston and Reno Roy spotted a figure stumbling down the beach towards their position. The stranger was short, dark-skinned, and wearing a pair of Japanese undergarments; Roy drew a bead, but Boston spoke up. "Wait a minute. Don't shoot now, Reno. He can't hurt us. Look at him. He ain't got nothing on except that pair of shorts. I'm sure he ain't hiding a weapon or anything in there." As the bloody figure came closer, they were shocked to recognize Frank Few. Despite his wounds and a healthy fear of sharks, he swam the better part of 4 miles while Japanese soldiers on the shore took potshots with rifles and a machine gun. Few was delivered to the regimental CP at 8 a.m.; Marines listened agog as he told his story, especially the ending, with the sabers flashing in the morning sun.

Rescue preparations began as soon as Monk Arndt's report reached the 5th Marines' command post at 5.30 a.m. The men there had been anxiously awaiting updates; now their worst fears were confirmed. Gunner Rust volunteered to lead reinforcements out at once, but Col. Leroy P. Hunt urged him to wait; leaving in the dark would only exacerbate the situation. Instead, Hunt alerted Capt. William P. Kaempfer's Company "A" to stand by to move out at first light.[74] The boat pool was alerted, and Kaempfer's men—heavily armed and ready for a fight—departed Kukum at 6.50 a.m.

Unfortunately, nobody knew for sure where Goettge's men were. Arndt estimated covering 4½ miles in his odyssey back to the perimeter but, suffering from shock and exhaustion, could not be more specific. The second man, Bainbridge, had not reported in, and neither Spaulding nor Few could pinpoint the location.[75] So Kaempfer's men headed for the original objective, sailing a full 10 miles down the coast and rounding Point Cruz before coming ashore at 10.10 a.m. Part of Company "L" got into the action, departing at 11.45 a.m. to reinforce Kaempfer and "contact the enemy"—the 5th Marines were looking for some payback. Both companies patrolled through the area but came up empty.

Lt. Col. Whaling, who had warned Goettge to avoid the "hornet's nest" near the Matanikau, realized he was looking in the wrong place and decided to search for the Japanese bivouac reported by Spaulding. A 300-man encampment would be easier to find than the Marines' remains—and might provide some clues and a cathartic opportunity for revenge. While Whaling led Company "L" through the jungle, Kaempfer took Company "A" down the Government Track, a primitive road heading east towards the Matanikau. Both companies made contact. Whaling's men captured a handful of prisoners and sent them back to Lunga under guard, while Kaempfer ran into the fortified village of Horahi. The Marines made a somewhat abortive attack in the fading light, reporting fifteen Japanese K.I.A. The defenders—possibly another platoon of the 11th CU Security Force—took a toll on the Marines in return, wounding two and killing one. PFC Raymond Alphonsus Rosalik, a seventeen-year-old rifleman from Detroit, "was protecting the forward advance of other members of his squad" when, in Kaempfer's words, "a greater order came from Above."[76] As Company "A" withdrew with their wounded, Ray Rosalik's body was left behind on the field.

When the patrols returned to the perimeter, the rumors began. Kaempfer's men claimed to have seen the bodies of Marines near the village; some had been tied to trees, their throats cut from ear to ear.[77] A group from Company "I," 5th Marines, found an American body near the mouth of the Matanikau. Gunner Rust recognized the boy as the missing runner, Cpl. William Bainbridge. They wrapped the body in a poncho and dug a grave in the loose sand near the sea. Bainbridge would be the only member of the patrol buried by American hands.[78]

Officially, the Goettge Patrol was "missing in action."

"As far as the Division's records are concerned," wrote George MacMillan in 1949, "the patrol disappeared into oblivion.... Indeed, the historical monograph on the campaign says that the point where the patrol landed has never been fixed, and that no trace of the dead was ever found."[79] The monograph's author, Maj. John Zimmerman, also writing in 1949, reported that only a few physical effects—Pratt's dispatch case and a scrap of clothing bearing Goettge's name—were located by patrols operating in the area, and "no identifiable remains were found, however, and the members of the ill-fated group continue to be classified as missing in action."[80] For many years, this was the official version of events. Even Gen. Vandegrift, who considered Frank Goettge a close friend, wrote that subsequent patrols "found no trace of Frank's patrol, nor did we ever find a trace."[81]

Reporting the men as missing rather than as killed in action—which terminated in declaring them dead after the customary year-and-a day interval—left a question mark over the story. "First Marine Division headquarters refused to confirm that the slaughter of the Goettge patrol had ever actually happened," wrote former Sgt. James McEnery. "The fact that all three of the survivors ... described the slaughter in detail in interviews, magazine articles, and official reports didn't seem to make any difference."[82] It made a great deal of difference to the families of the missing. A report by Correspondent James W. Hurlbut carefully omitted the names of the dead, but when it hit newspapers a month after the event, it coincided with the release of a casualty list that included Goettge's men. Families began receiving their telegrams at around the same time, which triggered a year of worrisome limbo as they waited for further news.

Ann Lyons learned her son, Cpl. Robert Lyons, was missing on September 3, 1942. In August 1943, she was informed of his presumptive death in action and received a box containing his personal effects. Two years later, still awaiting definitive news of her son's fate, she contacted the Marine Corps. "My son was reported missing September 1942, and then dead August 14, 1943," she wrote, "but so far I do not know just what happened to him. If I could only find out if there is a grave or how he was killed or where. Please let me know." Unsatisfied by the response she received, Mrs. Lyons tried again in 1947. "To this day I have had no further information about my son. I would like to know if anything more has been found out and if by chance he may be buried in the Pacific somewhere. Please give this letter your attention and reply with all information as soon as possible."[83] She received only stock assurances of condolence; nothing more could be done.

Pauline Custer got a package in October 1942. "I received my husband's billfold and personal effects," she wrote. "Does this mean my husband has been found? I haven't received any notice of his being killed in action. I can't understand how his clothes and personal effects could be found and he is reported missing."[84] The missing notice arrived at Steve Serdula's home in Corning, New York, on September 8; his brother, Charles, joined the Marine Corps exactly one week later.[85] Katherine Pratt's and Carolyn Cory's husbands became household names when Richard

Tregaskis published *Guadalcanal Diary*. (The news of Cory's death sent shudders through OP-GY-20; had he been captured and spilled the secrets of "Magic," the Japanese would have immediately changed their codes, ruining the entire project.) Only the Bainbridge family was spared this uncertainty, although they would never receive their son's body.

This was a calculated mystery. In 1942, Gen. Vandegrift was very much aware of what had happened to Goettge and his men—and so were several hundred others, mostly members of the 5th Marines. They were the ones who brought in Spaulding, Arndt, and Few; they were the ones who lost buddies and comrades from their own regimental intelligence unit, and because they were stationed closest to Point Cruz, they were the ones tasked with going out to find the bodies.

When Kaempfer and Whaling returned from their rescue mission, Division HQ believed they had found the main Japanese stronghold on the island. With all intelligence patrols suspended indefinitely—there were no replacements for the skilled Marines lost with Goettge—the 5th Marines sent out a series of combat patrols towards the Matanikau. Second Lieutenant Arthur L. "Scoop" Adams of Company "K," 5th Marines, was charged with such a mission on August 14. They would be searching for any signs of the Japanese, he explained at a meeting of his NCOs, as well as a downed fighter pilot thought to be alive somewhere near the Matanikau. Along the way, they would keep an eye out for the Goettge patrol. Seeing his men were "mad as hell about what happened," Adams cautioned them to "be damn careful out there, don't take any unnecessary chances [and] don't take any prisoners, either."[86]

Sgt. Thurman I. Miller recalled "our approach up the coast through the jungle was made with the utmost caution. We were directed to fire on the enemy only if necessary; we had permission to fire only if we ran into trouble." Sgt. Jim McEnery's squad, acting as flank security, ranged out several hundred yards before gradually circling back to the beach; Miller's squad crept silently in single file along the east side of the sandspit that lay across the Matanikau's mouth, "through long stands of coconut trees and dense brush, across a dry wash."

They found Goettge's men on the east bank of the river.

The smell came first, "a scent that those of us who were there can recall in an instant," said Miller. "What lay beneath the foliage was no longer human.... Sticking out of the sand was a boot, containing the foot of its owner. I scraped in the sand and uncovered another legging with the leg still in it."

"The first thing I saw was the severed head of a Marine," recalled Jim McEnery. "I almost let out a yell because the head was moving back and forth in the water and looked like it was alive. Then I realized it was just bobbing in the small waves lapping at the shore. They would wash it up onto the sand a few inches, then it would float back out again when the waves receded." Their shocked eyes beheld parts strewn in every direction as they slowly worked across the sandspit. The ragged stump of a leg sporting a neatly laced boondocker. A headless, armless torso still clad in a first sergeant's shirt. Less identifiable pieces floated in the water or lay fly-covered and rotting in the sand. Some men began to retch, but most stood stock still in horrified silence. "No one spoke," recalled Miller. "Not a word. Some things are better left unsaid."

Jim McEnery's thoughts centered on a repeated refrain—"I won't ever forget this, not ever!"—and he believed most of his buddies were struggling to understand the spectacle. "It still kind of surprises me that none of the guys in my squad started screaming or cussing or otherwise going hysterical," he said. "Mostly, they just stood frozen in their tracks, like their brains couldn't process what they were seeing." As the platoon congregated along the sandspit, McEnery noticed "pure misery" on Lt. Adams' face. "What should we do with these bodies, Scoop?" he asked. "You want us to try and bury them?"

"Just leave 'em where they are, Mac," came the reply. "There's no time for it right now. Maybe we can send back a burial detail later, but frankly I'd hate to risk it." Utterly unnerved, the platoon continued with its mission.

Adams' directive not to touch the bodies seems unusual, and even callous when considered with the benefit of hindsight. However, he likely had several reasons for this decision. With the Japanese operating in unknown but considerable strength beyond the Matanikau, Adams' top priority was to recon the area with the added goal of locating the downed Wildcat. This meant traveling light, without the impedimenta of stretchers and shovels. Even if the patrol was equipped to handle large numbers of casualties, nothing could prepare them psychologically for what they found along the Matanikau. "Over the next two-plus years, I saw a lot of gruesome sights in the Pacific," said McEnery, "but I can't remember anything worse than what we saw that morning."[87]

In the tropical conditions, the remains were already beginning to deteriorate. Cpl. George W. Kolher, whose mortar squad accompanied the patrol, discovered that "People disintegrate very rapidly because of the heat.... You could be dead today and gone tomorrow. You couldn't even pick 'em up, they were that bad."[88] Adams, known to be a conscientious officer and considerate of his men, may have wanted to spare them the additional trauma of handling the remains. There may have even been some direction from above impacting his decision, as McEnery wrote that "he [Adams] said he was told we were not to touch them."

Finally, Adams had only his platoon, plus a machine gun and mortar squad attached—about sixty men. He had no idea where the Japanese were, and as far as he knew, the remains had been deliberately transported and deposited along the riverbank as a warning. "Why were they here?" wondered Thurman Miller. "Where were the rest? We hadn't made it as far west as the patrol had landed; the remains seemed to be placed for obvious discovery. As we looked over the scattered body parts we could feel the eyes of the Japanese watching us from the jungle.... Had these dismembered bodies been brought to the sandspit as a warning to us? To frighten us?"[89] To collect, attempt to identify, and properly bury the scattered remains might leave the platoon vulnerable to a sudden ambush; Adams might have envisioned his men chopped up and added to the abattoir. He duly reported the discovery, but even though other patrols passed through the area—PFC Donald R. Langer of Company "I," 5th Marines, recalled wading through the Matanikau's chest-high water before encountering "bodies all cut up"—no burial party was sent.[90]

The first official mention of an effort to bring these remains back appears as a secondary objective of an operation west of the Matanikau. Three companies of the 5th Marines would surround Horahi, a Japanese-occupied native village of about twenty-five huts, situated near the mouth of the river. Company "B" would make a diversionary attack across the river mouth to the east (near the spot where Adams' patrol reported finding the remains) and Company "I," after sailing around the objective in Higgins boats, would block any reinforcements or westward escape by occupying the village of Kokumbona. Capt. Spurlock's Company "L" would make the main effort from the south, with "the dual mission of destroying any enemy found there and recovering the bodies of the Goettge Patrol."[91] Gunner Rust, a jungle-wise veteran of Nicaragua, and "Monk" Arndt were attached to Company "L" for the operation.

After hacking through the dense jungle to reach their jump-off positions on August 18, Spurlock's men set up in a bivouac position on Hill 73 above the village—and fired off a message announcing their location "in Morse code ... anyone with a radio could hear it, all over the country." Ore J. Marion, a squad leader in the company's 1st Platoon, believed that this message alerted the Japanese and thwarted the attacks of the other two companies. Nevertheless, Company "L" jumped off at the appointed time and wound their way down a steep jungle trail towards the village. The leading squad found a disquieting sight on their way: "I came across the body of a Marine—one of a group ambushed a week or two ago," recalled PFC Nicholas Sileo. Sileo did not recognize the dead man, but probably had stumbled across the remains of Ray Rosalik from Company "A."[92] A detachment quickly buried the body as the attack continued.[93]

"We could clearly see [2nd] Platoon ahead of us and below us on the embankment, moving downhill in single file, quiet, well-disciplined, everyone alert," said Marion. "Then they disappeared into the foliage ahead of us, and that's when we heard the first small-arms fire.... Next, it was our platoon's turn. As we approached the edge of the village, I saw the 2nd Platoon's sergeant, John Branic, lying face down on the trail. He was dead, but we had to keep moving."[94] Branic, an affable and "extremely sensible" NCO from Madera, Pennsylvania, had taken a bullet in the heart; his death left the platoon temporarily leaderless. Second Lieutenant George Mead, the company executive officer, stepped forward to lead 2nd Platoon through the jungle towards the village. "Enemy forces were well dug in," reported correspondent James W. Hurlbut. "They had trenches and machine gun nests and many snipers in the trees." The fire intensified as the Marines closed on Horahi and Mead, conspicuous at the forefront, was shot down by one of these concealed snipers as he reached the village at about 2 p.m.[95] Gunner Rust took command of 2nd Platoon for the battle that followed.

The two attacking platoons squared off against nearly 150 Japanese naval troops under the command of Capt. Kanae Monzen. After punching through a series of entrenchments, Company "L" broke into the outskirts of Horahi itself, taking cover in and around the leaf-thatched huts. Rifle fire dropped several Marines, and a sniper killed Pharmacist's Mate Third Class William P. Liddle, Jr., as he went to their aid. PFC Sileo killed three running Japanese with a single lucky bullet before he went down with three painful wounds. When the Marines formed a defensive line and held their ground, the Japanese gave "a war chant of some kind" and then came screaming out of the underbrush, "rushing down the path three or four abreast and firing at us." This impromptu *banzai* charge, possibly the first witnessed on Guadalcanal, killed Cpl. Charles Miglin of Company "L" but Marine fire quickly broke up the attack, and the survivors slipped off into the jungle to fight another day. Sixty-five dead Japanese were counted; the Marines took no prisoners.

As Company "L" tended to its casualties, the word was passed to head to the beach. Higgins boats were due to collect the victorious Marines and return them to the perimeter; something big was afoot over in the eastern sector. Their path took them past a shallow trench, defensive fortifications pressed into morbid service. A thin layer of sand covered perhaps a dozen individuals; clothing alone identified them as Americans. Arms and legs protruded from the ground. "The bodies were badly decomposed," said Ore Marion, "and it would have been impossible to recognize ... individual features." Monk Arndt did not need to see faces to know who was buried there. "See the arm sticking up, and the riding boot?" he asked, pointing to the first body in the line. "That's the colonel." Nobody doubted Monk's word. "I believe that every other active member of 'L' Company also saw those bodies," concluded Marion.[96] How many men were buried in this macabre trench is not known for certain. Pvt. Edward Snowden of Company "L" told historian John Innes that he saw "ten to twelve" individuals, with arms and legs all intertwined, while some modern scholars place the number at twenty-one or twenty-two.[97] While these bodies had not been mutilated to the degree of those reported earlier by Company "K," it was still a distressing sight.

Company "L" was no more prepared to handle a mass recovery of the dead than their counterparts in "Scoop" Adams' platoon. Once again, time and uncertainty worked against the situation. The Marines had won one victory but still knew little about their adversaries; the urgency with which they were summoned back to the main perimeter certainly suggested something serious was brewing out in the jungle. Company "B" was beginning the trek from their positions west of the Matanikau, and Company "I" was being summoned back from Kokumbona. Soon the boats were running up on the beach, and a tired Company "L" lined up to embark, staring at or studiously ignoring the shallow burial trench. The wounded were helped or carried aboard. PFC Sileo's stretcher was set down next to "three others who are dead. I hear one of the corpsmen say, pointing at me, 'Is he dead, too?' I surprise him by saying, 'Gimme a cigarette!'"[98]

The "three others" were George Mead, William Liddle, and Charles Miglin. Company "L" brought the bodies of their fallen back to the perimeter for burial in the newly established Division cemetery, where Miglin and Mead occupied the last two graves of the first row. Liddle marked the start of the second; he was followed by PFC James H. Chitwood, who died of wounds suffered at Horahi. Less fortunate was Sgt. John Branic, whose body still lay in a ravine on the slope above the village. Losing a talented NCO was tough for the company—Branic was as friendly as he was capable, and many thought him a sure bet for a commission—but being unable to retrieve his remains left some wounds that would never heal. "We all felt bad about having to leave his body," said Ore Marion, but "there wasn't anything we could have done.... The Marines always make a special effort to evacuate the bodies of their KIAs, but the confusion at the first [battle of the] Matanikau was extraordinary."[99]

A week had now passed since the ambush of Goettge's men. The gathering of Japanese forces along the Tenaru River pulled Marine attention to the eastern part of their perimeter, and as more weeks went by, the mission of recovering the patrol's remains sank farther and farther down the list of priorities. Rather than risk another tragedy, Vandegrift suspended long-range reconnaissance patrols entirely, and the land beyond the Matanikau was left to the Japanese for the time being. Despite multiple reports about the location of the bodies, no further expeditions to recover Frank Goettge's men are known to have occurred during the battle. The trails leading to the riverbank became well-trod paths and eventually grew into roads. As the American ability to wage offensive war grew, the Matanikau itself became an objective line, lending its name to no less than three difficult and bloody battles, each of which resulted in hundreds of dead combatants. The sandspit at the river's mouth became a battlefield and a burial ground for dozens of Marines and countless Japanese. Occasionally, a patrol would report finding a cluster of graves in the vicinity, or an officer would be startled by the sight of a moldering arm still sporting chevrons on a decaying uniform, but by November, even these vague reports ended.[100]

Though it was later overshadowed by bigger and bloodier battles, the Goettge Patrol is still often cited as a landmark event in the campaign for Guadalcanal. For many Marines, the event erased the last vestiges of human empathy towards their adversaries, leading to the sincerely held belief that all Japanese were treacherous, bloodthirsty, and not worth the trouble of taking prisoner. "We were shocked," explained Cpl. T. Grady Gallant. "Shocked and angry and sickened because the Japanese had been able to kill so many.... The loss of this patrol, and the particularly cruel way in which they had met death, hardened our hearts toward the Japanese. The idea of taking prisoners was swept from our minds. It was too dangerous."[101] Lt. Jack Clark scribbled in his diary: "That is the way those devils are. They have on occasion waved a white flag signifying surrender, and as soon as the Marines have come out to get them, the Japs open fire. They respect nothing. The only way to treat them is to kill them all."[102] First Lieutenant Herbert Merillat described the reception for a boatload of POWs—mostly laborers captured on Tulagi—as "unusually hostile.... Glowering Marines gathered around, muttering 'We ought to kill the sonovabitches.'"[103] Correspondent Richard Tregaskis, who arrived on the boat with Merillat and the prisoners, learned of the patrol's destruction when he returned to his billet with the 5th Marines. "Back at my tent tonight, I felt a loneliness that could not be gainsaid," he wrote. "Lieut. Cory and Dr. Pratt, both of whom are missing and believed dead ... bunked in this tent."[104] Aching over the loss of his friends, Tregaskis picked up on the rumor that the massacre had been the result of an elaborate and deliberate ruse; when *Guadalcanal Diary* was syndicated for publication, the story spread across the country, amplified and retold by countless columnists. "This act of treachery on the part of the yellow men sealed the doom of Japs on Guadalcanal," ran the typical line. "From that date on, U.S. Marines were not interested in rounding up captives. They shot Japs out of trees. They dug them out of foxholes and shallow trenches. The Japs paid manifold for the lives of Col. Goettge and his comrades."[105] Local newspapers picked up scoops from returning veterans, like PFC Michael Gullo eulogizing his hometown buddy Steve Serdula while bitterly proclaiming, "You're not fighting men when you're fighting Japs."[106] The false flag story was so popular that the 1st Marine Division's final report included an official account "in considerable detail for the purposes of counteracting sensational versions of the encounter that have appeared in the press."[107] The fate of the patrol had entered and irrevocably altered the public consciousness. "The incident presented a classic tale of Yankee humanitarianism and good will, betrayed by Japanese trickery and brutality," sums up William Bruce Johnson. "By mentioning the 'Goettge Patrol,' anyone could sum up the primary rule of engagement as defined by the Japanese: Show No Mercy."[108]

In 1944, a young PFC named Eugene Sledge was hauling rotten coconuts on a Pacific backwater called Pavuvu. A swarthy sergeant sauntered by, exchanging words with a few old-timers in Sledge's K/3/5. "He's one of the three guys who escaped when the Goettge patrol got wiped out on Guadalcanal," said a Marine in the know. "He was lucky as hell." When asked why the patrol was ambushed, another veteran "looked at [Sledge] with unbelief and said slowly and emphatically, 'Because they [the Japanese] are the meanest sonsabitches that ever lived.'" When Sledge saw combat himself, he understood "the deep personal resentment felt by Marine infantrymen" toward the Japanese.[109]

With the narrative thus cloaked in public myth as much as official obscurity, specific details of the burial site's loss, rediscovery, and possible location threatened to vanish along with the remains of Goettge's men. The post-war search efforts of the 604th Quartermaster Graves Registration Company were an exercise in futility. Armed with map overlays from service record books, eleven men of Search Team No. 3 investigated "Case #7720" from August 18–29, 1947. The beach, river banks, and sandbar were duly searched, locals were questioned and "all foxholes and possible grave sites were thoroughly investigated," but with negative results.[110] In the five years since the fighting, the area had changed so much that a Marine veteran attached to the search party "could recognize very little of the area as it is today."[111] Subsequent searches and attempts to reconcile any patrol members with unidentified remains found on the island were similarly unsuccessful, and all twenty-two men were declared non-recoverable in January 1949.

However, the notoriety of the patrol and the enduring mystery sparked further interest in the decades that followed. In 1978, a Marine reservist named Joseph N. Mueller became interested in the disappearance of Goettge's men and spent the following ten years researching the campaign, traveling to the island, and speaking with American, Japanese, and Melanesian veterans. Among those Mueller interviewed were members of the Matanikau garrison, who recounted the "desperate assault" of the Goettge Patrol that cost them "seven comrades" and told of burying the Americans in old fighting positions.[112] His team conducted a thirty-day search along the old beachfront, now 50 yards inland and covered by a shipping yard and a "squatter's village." Mueller's expedition uncovered three bodies in the search area, one near Kokumbona, and one close to the Matanikau River, complete with American combat equipment. A further six remains, found near Edson's Ridge, were determined to be Japanese and handed over to the appropriate consul for cremation and return to Tokyo.[113] Unfortunately, none of Mueller's finds proved to be Col. Goettge or his men. Twenty years later, a team of students and professors from Radford University joined historians John Innes and Douglas Drumheller for another attempt, but even with the technological advantages of ground-penetrating radar, the site eluded the searchers.[114]

The remains of the Goettge Patrol were reported as buried by sources from both sides and seen by scores of men. Potential search sites are relatively narrow and among the least remote on the island. The number of men buried together—from ten to twenty-one—makes it one of the largest American mass graves on the island. Yet the question of their final disposition remains one of the battle's most tantalizing mysteries. Several theories as to their whereabouts have been put forward over the years. The least optimistic argue that months of fighting, followed by years of construction and operation of a naval base, obliterated any trace of the unmarked graves and destroyed the physical remains. Others maintain that the shallow burials were eroded and washed out to sea, or carried away when the rainy seasons caused the Matanikau to flood. Because of its location—the Matanikau River now runs through Honiara, the capital city of the Solomon Islands—there is the undeniable likelihood of human interference. Graves were frequently, if inadvertently, disturbed by civilians returning to Horahi. The 1988 expedition heard the story of a local gardener who found human remains in her vegetable patch in 1947; after liberating a pair of dog tags, she "just dug another pit and tossed him in without notifying anybody."[115] An untold number of remains must have been shifted, damaged, or destroyed; for an idea of how much a location can change in seventy-five years, one need only look at an aerial photograph of downtown Honiara.

To date, the remains of Frank Goettge and his twenty-one men have not been accounted for. Nor has Pvt. Rosalik, who lost his life while searching for them. Yet those who hold out hope can point to one example straight out of those early, confusing days of the campaign. When construction crews broke ground for the American Memorial on Skyline Ridge above Honiara, they discovered skeletal remains believed to be those of a Marine. Although the Joint POW/MIA Accounting Command (JPAC) collected the remains in March 1992, an immediate identification was not possible, and a plaque honoring the "unknown soldier" was installed at the memorial. In 2004, researcher John Innes learned that a ring inscribed "JHB" had been found with the remains; he also determined that Skyline Ridge was formerly known as Hill 73—the site where Company "L," 5th Marines, commenced their attack against Horahi. Further work by Innes and forensic genealogist Linda Abrams located a matrilineal relative of Sgt. John Harold Branic, and a DNA match confirmed his identity. The announcement went public on August 8, 2006, nearly sixty-two years after Branic was buried on Guadalcanal.

Today, John Branic rests in Arlington National Cemetery Section 69, Site 1532.

As of 2018, the remains of Frank B. Goettge, Malcolm L. Pratt, Wilfred H. Ringer, Jr., Ralph Cory, Denzil R. Caltrider, Robert J. Stanfill, David A. Stauffer, Jr., William Bainbridge, Herbert E. Benson, Aaron L. Gelzer, Joseph F. Kashuba, Jr., Henry L. Kowal, Jack F. Lyons, Robert R. Lyons, Theodore E. Raht, Jr., Stephen Serdula, John L. Delano, Daniel L. Gauntt, Blaine G. Walter, Jr., Jack B. Kelly, Robert W. Lovelace, and Raymond A. Rosalik have not been accounted for.

4

Burying Grounds

There is a cemetery on Guadalcanal where the young, the healthy, the men who were in their first flush of life and vigor, lie row on row, under the strange, tropic palms which they found themselves so unexpectedly defending, under the simple yet deeply felt epitaphs accorded them by their peers in danger and in devotion.[1]

Anonymous, "Guadalcanal Street"

The sentries were shooting at shadows again.

"Shadows or coconuts," thought Abraham Felber, as he scribbled shorthand notes in a green notebook. The stolid former postal clerk from Newark, New Jersey, was keeping a diary of the invasion; although an eleven-year veteran of the Marine Corps Reserve, Guadalcanal was his first time in combat. From his perspective as 1st sergeant of H&S Battery, 11th Marines, war consisted of avoiding sudden rainstorms, eating canned rations, and finding enough idle artillerymen to haul ammunition and supplies on a working party. False alarms abounded, and the young men were edgy. "There is much firing going on all day, and in greatly increased volume at night," wrote Felber. "This firing is done by our men, who imagine they hear or see Japs moving about in the bushes. Lots of the shooting is done by Marines who fire to get the coconuts down from the trees."

Tonight, there was "much promiscuous shooting" going on. Ordinarily, the Top might be out there in the dark, planting a boondocker in the butts of the offenders. Felber was not going to budge, not tonight. "Several Marines have been killed by other Marines through being mistaken for Japs," he noted. "It is not safe to move about after dark."

He knew of one, Sgt. Windisch from Battery "I," who had been shot by his own officer. Another burst of firing broke out, and Felber despaired of ever going outside at night again. Then voices started yelling for a corpsman.

Later that night, Felber returned to his diary. "Sgt. Casey, of Motor Transport, was acting as Sergeant of the Guard tonight," he began. The story took shape from his pen: a dutiful NCO inspecting the sentries, probably telling them to knock off the shooting. A panicked reflex to grab a rifle and fire blindly. A bullet tearing through James Casey's chest. Calling a truck to rush Casey to sickbay.

"This happened at 2245," wrote Felber, with a good 1st sergeant's attention to detail. "At 2310 Casey expired. He is our first casualty." Muster rolls would need to be updated and incident reports drafted. Hell would be raised about the careless firing, and the culprit, one Pvt. Mattice, would be dealt with. There were Casey's buddies to placate, condolence letters to write, and one more concern of paramount importance.

"Casey will be buried tomorrow."[2]

As previously noted, the 1st Marine Division was not fully prepared for many of the challenges they would face on Guadalcanal. A great deal of attention was paid to addressing deficiencies in supply and combat logistics, combined-arms operations with the Navy, intelligence gathering and interpretation, and in the combat patrolling that came to define a large part of the campaign. Fortunately, many of the deficiencies were actively anticipated or rapidly identified, and corrective measures—some quite creative and unorthodox—were put into practice. Using captured supplies, buildings, and equipment was the most obvious adaptation, from finishing Henderson Field with steamrollers made in Japan to field kitchens serving the delicacy of "rice without" (rice without peaches, rice without butter, rice without steak). Special units were established to train scouts on the island. Cooperation with Commonwealth coastwatchers and the local constabulary provided Gen. Vandegrift with intelligence insights he would never have gleaned even if Col. Goettge's patrol had not decapitated his D-2 section.

As the very outcome of the operation, and perhaps the Pacific War, hinged upon solving the myriad issues that would keep the invasion force alive and able to fight, it might seem surprising that much (if any) consideration was given to the question of burying the dead. Yet, as discussed, there were some rudimentary guidelines in place, based on common sense, limited pre-war experience, and the as-yet untested recommendations of TM 10-630. And there were plenty of realists in the Marine ranks. Even the greenest private realized that men would die on Guadalcanal— even if they could not picture such a fate for themselves or their friends.

PFC Mario Sabatelli remembered an address by Maj. Kenneth Bailey, the 1st Raider Battalion executive officer. "'If any Marines are killed, they'll be buried right on Tulagi. Your cemetery will be on Tulagi.' A lot of the guys started to laugh and look at each other and say, 'what do you think of that?'"[3] Men were reminded to wear or carry their identification tags, as prescribed by the General Instructions of the Marine Corps Manual, to "secure the proper interment of those who fall in battle."[4] Shortages of supply and speed of movement, however, resulted in some Marines shipping out without their tags; extra blanks were acquired from New Zealand Army stores.[5] Corpsmen of the 1st Marine Parachute Battalion (the Paramarines) spent part of their voyage to Gavutu punching out new tags with hammers and dies.[6]

Dozens of staff officers were carried on the Division Headquarters muster rolls, but these records do not indicate who (if anyone) was acting as burial officer.[7] It seems unlikely that Vandegrift would have overlooked this important appointment—especially as his staff was taking precautions to account for inevitable fatalities. Col. James' circular called for "the appropriate commander" to designate cemetery sites "convenient to where the heaviest casualties are expected or experienced"—but it is not known whom "the appropriate commander" was, if indeed one was appointed.[8] Fortunately, TM 10-630 provided a solution: take it to the chaplain.

In peacetime, a chaplain's duties revolved around the spiritual needs of spirited young men. Their efforts to enforce morality were traditionally met with resistance by saltier Marines steeped in a culture where to seek succor was to show weakness. General Samuel B. Griffith II famously described the "Old Breed" of 1941 as "inveterate gamblers and accomplished scroungers who ... cursed with wonderful fluency and never went to the chapel (the "God-box") unless forced to."[9] Religious authorities were extraneous appendages, useful only when nobody else was prepared to care. Chronic complainers, for example, might be issued an imaginary "tough shit chit" and instructed to "take it to the chaplain." Many chaplains accepted the ribbing as part of their numerous duties, which included divine services, holding classes in religious and secular subjects, upholding morale, and visiting with the sick and injured.[10] When necessity demanded, and in the absence of civilian clergy, they were also responsible for conducting funerals.[11]

In a section entitled "Chaplains," TM 10-630 explains: "In time of war chaplains will often be charged with duties pertaining to graves registration personnel, particularly in the absence of such personnel within their respective commands." Because the chaplains' function "when charged with burials" was close to that of a Graves Registration officer, they were encouraged to familiarize themselves "with such graves registration regulations as may be in force at the time." (TM 10-630 even included the relevant passages from TM 16-205, *The Chaplain*, to eliminate confusion.)[12] Six of these Naval officers, four Protestant and two Catholic, were attached to the task force for Operation Watchtower and became the "appropriate commanders" for the first American military cemeteries in the Solomon Islands—on Gavutu, Tanambogo, Tulagi, and lastly Guadalcanal.[13] Many chaplains would serve in the long campaign that followed, but the original cadre (Lt. Cdr. Charles A. Dittmar, Lt. Robert M. Olton, and Lieutenants (j.g.) Ansgar E. Sovik, W. Wyeth Willard, James J. Fitzgerald, and Thomas M. Reardon) would preside over hundreds of burials in the field—or in the cemeteries they helped to establish.[14]

The First Cemetery: Gavutu and Tanambogo

There were certainly no civilian clergymen present when Lt. (j.g.) James J. Fitzgerald went ashore on Gavutu. Formerly Father Fitzgerald of the Archdiocese of Chicago, he was on temporary assignment with the 1st Parachute Battalion. Fitzgerald had little time to earn the trust of the Paramarines, many of whom were of the hard-boiled, chapel-dodging stripe—nevertheless, his final pre-battle Mass was unusually well attended. When bullets started flying and men started falling on August 7, 1942, Fitzgerald quickly proved his worth. Eager to help but unsure of his place, he crawled over to Capt. George Stallings and requested permission to perform the last rites for dying men. "Father, that's your department, not mine," snapped Stallings. Fitzgerald hurried over to the prostrate form of PFC Lawton R. Crumpler, Jr., and knelt beside the young Marine. Bullets whizzed and crackled through the air, but "the chaplain didn't appear to be aware of anything but the dying man."[15] Unarmed and undaunted, Fitzgerald kept up his work throughout the day. Stallings would later opine that the chaplain was "a fine man ... and an excellent example for his faith."[16] Fitzgerald was not only providing aid and comfort to the dying; he was compiling a mental list of those to whom he ministered—twenty-seven dead and forty-seven wounded on the beach alone.

The 2nd Marines landed on Gavutu the following day, bringing with them Chaplain Warren Wyeth Willard. The thirty-seven-year-old Willard, a graduate of Princeton Theological Seminary and founder of a Christian summer camp in his native Massachusetts, entered the Naval service in 1941. He was acquainted with Father Fitzgerald; the two had overlapped briefly at the Chaplain's School in Norfolk. Now they were reunited at an aid station established outside the Lever Brothers Plantation store.

According to Willard's memoirs, Fitzgerald's storied composure cracked at the sight of his friend. "Am I glad to see you!" the priest exclaimed. "We've had a terrible time! Thank God, reinforcements have arrived! Some of my best friends have been killed! Several of our officers are dead or wounded! Thank God you've all come!"[17] Willard handed Fitzgerald an orange and began distributing fruit to other hungry men. For the remainder of August 8, the two chaplains worked side by side, tending to the wounded and the dead alike.

Willard got little sleep that night. From the window of the aid station, he could see the flashes of naval gunfire as the Battle of Savo Island unfolded just a few miles away, "as if the sky was cracking to pieces or the heavens were breaking up." It began to rain, softly at first and then in a tropical torrent that poured through the bullet and shell holes in the roof, threatening to ruin the first aid gear. Willard had two personal encounters with death that night. Once, he heard the crack of a rifle and a sudden wailing from "a young Marine six feet to my left.... 'Oh! I'm hit! A sniper got me!' He folded up, clasping his bosom with his hands. A short time later he expired. We took his body to the side of the building and covered it with a blanket." A wounded sergeant was carried in, drenched in blood and rainwater. He had been shot through the abdomen during the failed assault on Tanambogo. By now, Willard could recognize the telltale signs of a fatal injury—the grim looks of the corpsmen, the cold sweat on the sergeant's face—and offered to pray with the wounded man. "I never went much for that stuff back home," grunted the sergeant, "and I don't care for it now." He was "like Gallio of old," thought the chaplain; when the sergeant died, Willard was consumed with remorse at his failure to save the man's soul.

The following morning was Sunday. Exhausted from their ministrations of the past two days, Fitzgerald and Willard decided that no divine services would be held. Instead, they watched as mop-up detachments threw explosive charges into caves and staked out the holes where snipers were hidden. Chaplain Willard explored the ruins of Tanambogo—the "most desolate" battlefield he saw in the Solomon Islands. "Burned buildings and military stores littered the place," he wrote. "Dead bodies and the carcasses of several pigs made the island look like the valley of the shadow of death itself."[18]

Collection of Marine dead began as soon as Gavutu was nominally secured. This sad task was performed by the fighting men themselves, who faced the grim horror of handling the bodies of their recently deceased friends. PFC Robert W. Moore was struggling with an uncooperative Reising gun when summoned by Plat. Sgt. John A. Daskalakis. "It was in my records that I had graduated from embalming college before I went into the Marine Corps," Moore said, "so he elected me to go and take the dog tags off of the dead on the beach." The twenty-two-year-old Paramarine had seen plenty of corpses before and was not particularly bothered by the sight of dead Japanese, but stooping over the body of a friend, rummaging through his shirt, and untying the string that held the tags around his neck was a nightmarish experience. "Many had been shot in the head," Moore related. "Brains were all over.... I remember [Cpl. Harold E.] 'Johnny' Johns; he was a rigger, a real nice fellow. He was in sort of a ditch, shot in the head, brains all over the place." He carefully removed one tag from each body until he had a clinking pile of twenty-eight metal discs.

Meanwhile, Daskalakis collared PFC William Taylor for the unpleasant task of "battlefield sanitation." Nearly 500 Japanese fighters and Korean laborers died on Gavutu and Tanambogo—more than the entire landing strength of the 1st Parachute Battalion. "Wild Bill" Taylor could not argue with "Big John" Daskalakis, and dutifully joined the disgusted band dragging Japanese bodies to an ad-hoc funeral pyre. A column of evil-smelling smoke rose over the island as the clean-up detail shuttled back and forth.[19]

Cpl. Daniel E. Mulcare, Jr. of Company "A" was assigned to a detail of Paramarines who were carrying American bodies from the field to a designated collection point near the aid station at Lever Brothers wharf. Some of the Paramarines had been lying in the tropical sun and rain since Friday morning. Hauling the putrefying bodies was appalling, "the most horrible experience [Mulcare] would ever know.... He tried not to touch them if he could help it and pulled on their webbed cartridge belts." The bodies were gingerly laid in a neat row under the supervision of Father Fitzgerald and Pharmacist's Mate First Class Philip J. McGuire, Jr. "Doc" McGuire inspected the identification tag on each body and entered the name and information into his logbook, taking the utmost care to record everything correctly. "Father Fitz," now a "fighting chaplain" with Reising gun slung over his shoulder, said a final Mass over the collected dead even as occasional sniper fire zinged overhead. He would later be declared an honorary Paramarine.[20]

After bidding farewell to their buddies, the Paramarines boarded landing craft for reassignment to Tulagi, taking Father Fitzgerald with them. The task of establishing the Gavutu cemetery thus fell to Chaplain Willard. Civilian expertise came into play once again: Willard had worked as a mortician in Barnstable, Massachusetts, and had once operated a funeral home. Still, it was "a grim task" as he said. "In tropical countries decomposition takes place much more rapidly than in the semitropical or temperate zones. A strong, foul odor was noticeable in the region round about the rendezvous of the dead." A reasonably flat space just southeast of the aid station was selected, and Willard quickly rounded up volunteers to clear up the remnants of battle, from concrete pillars to iron water containers, and set them to digging the individual graves:

> The sun grew hot in the skies above and scorched the earth beneath. The men's dungarees became wringing wet. As soon as eight or ten graves were dug, we would lay down the bodies of our fallen comrades. There were no caskets, no flowers, none of the niceties which had always been necessities at home. Some of the members of the working party fainted because of the heat or the sight of the bloody and stiffened bodies of their friends. And then I would have to recruit other volunteers, or else from time to time, I would help lower the remains into their final resting place. The working parties seemed to melt away. Sporadic fighting was still taking place on both islands. The sound of the shovels blended with the sound of rifle fire.

Other working parties were carrying in the dead from the 2nd Marines, Willard's own regiment, and he secured three volunteers to assist with the administrative work. These enlisted men drew up a map of the cemetery, retrieved personal effects from the dead, and separated identification tags. It was growing dark when the last grave was filled; a large contingent of Marines and sailors gathered to pay their respects. Willard stood on a platform and began his service: "I am the resurrection and the life." Marines bowed their heads as the chaplain read through the list of names. "It seemed as though all America was represented there in that little city of the dead," thought Willard, as a squad fired three volleys over the graves and a bugler sounded Taps. "Day was done. Farewell, friends, farewell!"[21]

"Gavutu cemetery is small," reported *Leatherneck Magazine*, "but it is believed to be the first cemetery in the South Pacific."[22] Chaplains Fitzgerald and Willard had done an exemplary job in collecting and interring their dead. Furthermore, they had complied with the Division's directive for identifying each set of remains before burial. Photographs of the cemetery are rare; those that exist depict a small plot surrounded by a rough stone wall, with what appear to be three long rows of graves. Later improvements included a cross-topped gated entryway and a sign denoting the "United States Marine & Navy Cemetery." In September 1945, the graves were disinterred, and all remains were moved to the main Army, Navy, and Marine Corps Cemetery on Guadalcanal itself.

Gavutu Cemetery contained fifty-two graves, and aside from conflicting burial dates recorded in battalion records, only three present any persistent questions. Grave No. 1 contained the remains of the only unidentified American body found on the island—a testament to Doc McGuire's thoroughness. Willard himself was responsible for retrieving this man. "On the southwestern end of the island [probably Tanambogo], in the shallow water, I found the bodies of the two corpsmen who had been killed by snipers," he wrote. "Around their swollen and water-soaked left arms were their Geneva crosses.... Not far away was the body of the wounded man they had tried to save.... The bodies, along with two dismembered legs I found in the water, were carried back to the cemetery, where they were buried with a Christian service. We marked the grave where we placed the legs 'Unknown Marine.'"[23] *Leatherneck* ran a photograph of this grave with the caption "This 'Unknown Marine' grave at Gavutu may have been the first one in the South Pacific."[24]

The passage of time did nothing to help the identification of Gavutu's lonely unknown. At the consolidation of cemeteries, he was given the temporary name of "X-257" and interred in Row 182, Grave 3 of the Army, Navy, and Marine Corps Cemetery on Guadalcanal. Three years later, anthropologists in Hawaii examined the leg bones; they described "a short, well-muscled man in his middle twenties," approximately 5 feet 6 inches tall, and weighing perhaps 135 pounds. Without additional physical features, identification was deemed impossible.[25] Only six Marines are unaccounted for from the Gavutu–Tanambogo fighting. Cpl. Raymond L. Bray (B/1st Parachute Battalion) was killed by an American bomb on Hill 148; the following day, Privates William A. James, William H. Pollock, and Merlyn L. Thompson (M/3/2) met the exact same fate in almost the exact same location. Nothing of their bodies could be found. PFC Gerald W. Stetzer (D/1/2) was mortally wounded on Tanambogo and died aboard a hospital ship; he was reportedly buried on Tulagi, location unknown. The sixth man was accounted for at the time and buried in Grave No. 13. It is possible that Willard found the washed-up remains of a sailor killed in the great sea battle off Savo Island, although he was quite confident that he had located a Marine.

A more perplexing mystery of the Gavutu cemetery involves Grave No. 13 and eighteen-year-old Pvt. Robert Lee Liston of Company "I," 2nd Marines. Liston was hit in the spine by shrapnel during the assault on Tanambogo and died of his wounds on August 9, 1942. Chaplain Willard recalled Liston as one of the men he buried on Gavutu. (Willard's memoir includes the names of thirty-nine Gavutu casualties; the first twenty-five, including Liston, are in order of burial.) "Grave #13" was entered in Liston's service record book, casualty report sheet, and certificate of death; company muster rolls and Division burial records were updated, and his family was informed of his temporary resting place.

What should have been an open and shut case took an unexpected turn. All graves in the Gavutu cemetery were exhumed, and the remains brought to Guadalcanal in 1945, yet Pvt. Liston's name could not be found on any reports of interment in the ANMC. Nor was there any information regarding where the remains from Grave No. 13 were reburied. This discrepancy was not noticed until 1947 when the identities of those in the consolidated Guadalcanal cemetery were being checked for final disposition. A Quartermaster Form 371—"Data On Remains Not Yet Recovered Or Identified"—was issued for Pvt. Liston, and forwarded to the 604th Quartermaster Graves Registration Company. This unit returned to Gavutu in 1948 and found the former cemetery site completely overgrown. No traces of the graves remained, and local islanders insisted that all bodies had been exhumed back in 1945. After this somewhat cursory search, Liston's remains were declared non-recoverable. He may still lie on Gavutu, although this seems unlikely. The cemetery was well tended, and graves were in demarcated plots clearly marked with names and numbers. Grave No. 13 would not have been casually missed, even if the wooden cross marker was knocked down or destroyed. A photograph of the cemetery suggests that No. 13 was the first grave in the second row (although, unfortunately, a tree obscures the view). A more likely explanation would be that a clerical error misidentified Liston's remains. Bodies from all over the Solomon Islands were being buried simultaneously; a simple mistake—confusing Tulagi for Gavutu, for example—could throw off a search. Liston may be among the unknowns buried in the Punchbowl.[26]

Finally, there is the case of Grave No. 36. This grave is not mentioned on any muster rolls; Paramarine PFCs Ronald A. Burdo (Company "B") and Emory D. Martin (Company "C") are reported in Graves 35 and 37, respectively on Marine muster rolls or the 1st Marine Division's list of burial locations.[27] However, a photograph of the cemetery clearly shows Grave No. 36 with a marker bearing the name of "J. H. Dudenski."

This may be a case of a multi-level mistaken identity. There was no "Dudenski" on Gavutu, but there was Pvt. John Michael Dudenake, a runner in Company "B." Dudenake, the second man out of his landing craft, was shot in the throat; his entire platoon had to jump over his body on their way to shore. The wound looked awful and, without the quick intervention of two Paramarines who hauled the stricken man onto a boat, may have been fatal. Emergency surgery aboard USS *Neville* saved Dudenake's life. Several months later, while recuperating in New Zealand, he learned he had been officially reported killed on Gavutu. His parents even received a "Killed in Action" telegram.[28]

Dudenake's "resurrection" sparked some newspaper interest, and he told a reporter "as I lay there a captain passed over me and said, 'He's dead.' I was unable to talk and don't blame him for thinking I was dead."[29] Although the company muster roll correctly noted that Dudenake had been wounded and evacuated, it seems that members of his own organization believed him dead, and may have mistakenly identified him as the man being buried in Grave No. 36. The error was then compounded by an inaccurate marker, painted with a similar, but not exact, name.

Like Liston, "Dudenski's" discrepancy was not discovered until 1947. His remains were disinterred from Gavutu and buried in Row 199, Grave 1, of the ANMC. However, during his review for final disposition, it was discovered that no "J. H. Dudenski" existed on the casualty rolls for any service. There were no other clues available as to his identity, and so "Dudenski" became "Unknown X-324." Today, he is buried in the Punchbowl, Section "Q," Grave 946.

Interestingly, the forensic description of X-324 is similar to Pvt. Liston's physical description. Both men were about 5 feet 10 inches tall and weighed about 165 pounds. The dental age of X-324 was estimated at twenty-one to twenty-three years, slightly older than Liston, but not outside the realm of possibility. Photographs of Liston and Dudenake show a distinct physical similarity—slight differences may have been obliterated by wounds or by the initial stages of decomposition. It is possible, however unlikely, that conflicting information confused the men making the identifications, the volunteer gravediggers, and the record keepers to the extent that Liston was mistaken as "Dudenski" and buried in Grave No. 36. A vacant Grave No. 13 might explain the lack of reinterment reports, and why the 604th expedition returned to the Gavutu cemetery site—perhaps no remains were ever found beneath that marker. This is just a theory, however. For now, the stories of Robert Liston and X-324 remain unresolved.

Tulagi: White Beach, Police Barracks, and Chinese Barracks

Once the seat of British colonial power in the Solomon Islands, Tulagi boasted several deluxe amenities. The governor-general's residency was "a rather attractive white clapboard house with lovely porches and breezes going through them."[30] The settled government area supported a sizable radio station and "the physical appurtenances of the white man's rule" including a cricket ground, tennis court, and golf course.[31] There were a barracks and parade ground for the local police and a prison for the local miscreants. Chinese laborers were quartered in the less desirable lowlands near the Government Wharf. It was a pleasantly remote place to serve out one's duty to the Crown—until the Japanese 3rd Kure Special Naval Landing Force arrived in May 1942. The new owners began improving the harbor facilities, constructed headquarters buildings for a seaplane base, and installed a long-range communications center.

Tulagi was a primary target of the American invasion on August 7, 1942; after bombardment by sea and air, the 1st Raider Battalion and 2nd Battalion, 5th Marines, landed on tiny Beach Blue and swept down the length of the island. The Japanese garrison's last transmission was intercepted: "Enemy troop strength is overwhelming. We will fight to the last man."[32] This they did, with a grim determination that surprised Marines expecting quick, easy conquest. When the gunfire started to peter out on August 9, the former landmarks had taken on new meaning. The Chinese Quarters had been a phase line objective. The Japanese staged the first *banzai* of the campaign across the cricket grounds. The radio station was wrecked; the prison was a field hospital. And hundreds of bodies dotted the once beautiful landscape, requiring the immediate attention of the victors.

"In the two days of heavy fighting on Tulagi, about 40 Marines had died and 350 Japanese had been killed," recalled Raider PFC Marlin Groft. "Our job now was to get these bodies under the ground as quickly as we could. In the tropical heat, the bodies bloated up so they resembled sausages. The stench of decay seemed to be everywhere and a lot of guys heaved their guts." Here, as on Gavutu, the disposal of Japanese dead was treated as a sanitary concern rather than a humanitarian one. "Their corpses were rolled or tossed into shell craters and buried *en masse*," continues Groft. "Others were tossed into shacks and the shacks set on fire, the smell of burning hair and flesh now mingling with the stink of death and decay. This had to be a scene straight out of Dante's *Inferno*."[33] Groft's memory stands in stark contrast to the official report, which claimed that "by the end of the first week ... enemy as well as our own troops had been safely and respectfully buried."[34]

As the regional capital, Tulagi had a designated burial ground. Historian Stanley Coleman Jersey mentions "the local cemetery" as a rendezvous point for the Raiders shortly after landing; his work *Hell's Islands* contains veteran references to a spot near the landing site at Beach Blue, alternately called "the native cemetery," "the Chinese cemetery," or "a place where the Japanese had established a small cemetery."[35] An anonymous source from the First Battalion, 2nd Marines, recalled that his battalion CP was established in "a native graveyard, and we made camp there, digging foxholes among the graves."[36] A map of Tulagi indicates "Cemetery (Native)" just inland from Beach Blue; presumably, the three mentions in Jersey refer to the same location. The remoteness of Beach Blue provided a tactical advantage for amphibious landings, but it was less than ideal for the establishment of a military cemetery.

As the victors policed up the battlefield, they carried friendly remains to three distinct sites. Tulagi's landmarks lent their names to the three new cemeteries, the largest of which was located near the old government settlement. Alternately known as "White Beach," "Parade Ground," "Old Radio Station," or the more formal "USN & USMC Cemetery #1," the earliest burials recorded at this location occurred on August 10, 1942.[37] (This may correlate with the arrival of Father Fitzgerald from Gavutu—the Raiders had no chaplain attached to their organization at the time.) Pvt. Louis A. Lovin, a Raider from Burkettstown, Pennsylvania, and one of the first Marines killed on Tulagi, had the distinction of being the first man buried in what would become the longest continually operated cemetery on the island. Some thirty-one Marines were interred in early August; the majority were Raiders killed on the first day of the operation, with a few individuals from the 1st Engineer Battalion and 2nd and 5th Marines. "Our own dead were buried with care," reported Marlin Groft. "Graves were dug using entrenching tools, and the dead were reverently wrapped inside ponchos and their names recorded for notification of next of kin and retrieval for later burial." The first unknown individual buried on Tulagi was also interred around this time. "X-1" was laid to rest in Grave No. 30, between Pvt. Robert S. McKelvy (G/2/5) and Pvt. Robert I. Paine (C/1st Raider Battalion).[38]

Cemetery No. 2, also known as the "Police Barracks Cemetery," was laid out near buildings that once housed the native constabulary; a Raider corporal, Donald Robert Roy Williamson, was buried in Grave No. 1. Despite its designation as the second cemetery, Police Barracks may have been established before White Beach. Muster rolls indicate the burial of Capt. Richard J. Huerth, commanding officer of Company "C," 1st Parachute Battalion, took place on August 9. Several other Paramarines found resting places at the Police Barracks: following Huerth (No. 5) came Cpl. George T. Stosilavage (No. 9), PFC Henry J. Burri (No. 10), and PFC Joseph G. Bresinger (No. 13). Huerth was killed in his landing craft while approaching Gavutu and never made it to shore, while Burri, who died the moment his foot touched dry land, was evidently dragged back aboard his boat.[39] Stosilavage and Bresinger both died of injuries sustained on Gavutu; Stosilavage was mortally wounded in action, while Bresinger was crushed by a falling tree.[40] The remains of both men were sent ashore from USS *Neville* shortly after 11 a.m. on August 9. (The *Neville* also reported receiving hostile fire from the White Beach area on August 9, another indication that Cemetery No. 1 was not being laid out at this time.)[41] The overseer of Cemetery No. 2 is not known, but the arrival of the Paramarines on August 9 strongly suggests that Father Fitzgerald was involved in these burials as well.

Eighteen individuals were initially buried at the Police Barracks; of these, fifteen are known to have been Marines—a combination of Raiders, 'Chutes, and the 2nd Marines. The occupants of Graves 2, 3, and 6 are not known, but may potentially have been casualties of the naval battle of Savo Island. Cemetery No. 2 did not grow much bigger in the weeks that followed. When Sgt. Herbert L. Chivington (C/1/2) was accidentally shot by a sentry on August 13, his remains were interred in Grave No. 19. Capt. Richard Y. Stafford (C/1/2) and Pvt. Joseph Sparks (A/1/2) were killed in a raid on Gourabusu, Guadalcanal, on October 11; their remains were brought back to Tulagi for burial beside their comrades. "Little Joe" Sparks, the first combat fatality in A/1/2, is also the last recorded Marine burial at the Police Barracks cemetery.[42]

Cemetery No. 3 was the smallest of the three cemeteries established after the fighting for Tulagi. The exact location is no longer known; the buildings that bestowed its colloquial name—"Chinese Barracks"—are not specified on maps, though they probably stood somewhere in the neighborhood near Government Wharf, which had a heavy Chinese population before the war. This sector was assigned to the 1st Raiders' Company "B," and was the site of their first exposure to enemy fire. As the 1st Platoon under 1Lt. Eugene Morland "Tex" Key investigated reports of a Japanese machine gun nest near the sea wall, a sniper on the overhanging cliff drew a bead on the Marines. The first shot dropped Pvt. Thomas F. Nickel; when Key instinctively went to his aid, the sniper picked him off as well. The regimental surgeon, Lt. Samuel S. Miles, also attempted a rescue and was shot down in turn. It was a harsh awakening for Raiders who had derided their foes as "yellow monkeys."[43]

Key, Miles, and Nickel were the first three men buried at the "Chinese Barracks," and their graves may have been dug as early as August 7, while the battle raged on. Pvt. Thomas E. Church, killed in action on August 10, was buried in Grave No. 4; he was followed by 2Lt. Russell Nall and PFC George Morris, killed by friendly fire that night and buried on August 11. The occupants of Graves 7 and 8 are not known; Grave No. 9 (Plat. Sgt. Alvin Dismukes, B/1st Raider Battalion) was dug on August 27 and is the last known burial in this area.[44]

Cemetery No. 3 is unique in that it contains the earliest evidence of an effort to consolidate isolated graves and rebury individuals in a more central location. Graves "A," "B," "C," and "D"—the only ones on Tulagi identified by letters rather than numbers—were added to the Chinese Barracks burial ground at an unknown date. The first two contained the remains of PFCs Henry A. Huff and A. D. Webster (both F/2/5). Huff and Webster were killed in action on August 7, 1942, and initially buried "one half mile north of beach off ridge road in woods east of ridge road, Grave #1 and #2."[45] Grave "D" was dug for PFC Elmer L. Speicher (A/1st Raider Battalion), initially buried at King George's Field.[46] All three of these Marines were eventually returned to their families.

Grave "C" was reported to contain the remains of Pvt. George Alfred Johnson. A nineteen-year-old Marine from Coatesville, Pennsylvania, Johnson earned the admiration of his buddies for attacking a sniper's nest with hand grenades on August 9. Although the official story reported by the press and in his posthumous Silver Star citation claimed Johnson was killed in his valiant assault, his OMPF providesthe date of death of August 10, and the clinical cause "WOUND, LACERATED, ABDOMEN, Fatal (Hand Grenade)." This death certificate was completed by a clerk from Company "A," Medical Battalion, Second Marine Brigade, which was temporarily attached to the Raiders.[47] Johnson likely suffered his wounds on August 9 and expired at the field hospital after midnight.

Again, different sources deliver different information. The Raiders, who were rather Spartan in their muster rolls, only recorded that Johnson was buried "on Tulagi." The 1st Marine Division roster of burials recorded the Chinese Barracks grave; this location ("U. S. Naval and Marine Corps Cemetery #3, Grave C") was given to his mother in official correspondence. However, the death certificate states that Johnson was sent to the Police Barracks cemetery and that Company "A," Medical Battalion, was responsible for his burial. Unfortunately, no grave location is given for Johnson at Police Barracks, and no further record of who was buried in Grave "C" is known to exist.

While the Police Barracks and Chinese Barracks cemeteries show little evidence of expansion after August 1942, the White Beach cemetery remained active. The occasional Marine would still be laid to rest here, but beginning in October 1942, the majority of burials were sailors killed in the great naval battles that lasted into December. When the crippled cruiser USS *New Orleans* put in at Tulagi Harbor after the Battle of Tassafaronga, Chaplain Howell Forgy went ashore to plan a service for the dead. His counterpart was none other than Father Fitzgerald, still on duty at the White Beach cemetery. There were so many dead from USS *Orleans* and USS *Pensacola* that an annex had to be added to the burial ground. Thomas J. Larson, a naval officer recently arrived on Tulagi, "saw men carrying buckets of arms and legs and other parts of bodies of our dead men which had been taken out of blasted gun turrets.... What a sad sight—all those poor, dead Navy men which were being taken to a little cemetery and laid out side by side into a long trench." Larson noted the changing demeanor of James Fitzgerald—"this young, handsome Catholic chaplain had so many marines die in his arms that he was really wild and out of his head."[48] Fitzgerald was awarded a Letter of Commendation for his service; after serving briefly with the 11th Marines on Guadalcanal, he was evacuated from the Solomons, his job done.[49]

White Beach Cemetery remained active through the end of the war. Between December 1944 and January 1945, it was consolidated and reorganized into "Cemetery #1, Tulagi." All remains were disinterred and relocated to Guadalcanal in September 1945.

The First Marine Division Cemetery, Guadalcanal

It was early in the morning on August 12, 1942, and Lt. Cdr. Charles Dittmar already had a situation on his hands. Kelley was going to kill Mattice.

News of Sgt. James Casey's death spread quickly through the 11th Marines, reaching the galley and the ears of his best friend, Assistant Cook Joseph A. Kelley. Someone spilled the name of the Marine responsible, and Kelley's shock turned to rage. He went looking for Mattice but ran into "Top" Felber, who relieved Kelley of his pistol and bundled him off to see Chaplain Dittmar.[50]

Dittmar was the senior representative of the Chaplain Corps in the Solomon Islands, serving double duty as both the regimental chaplain of the 11th Marines as well as "padre" for the 1st Marine Division. As a young lieutenant, he ministered to sailors' souls during the Great War; after more than two decades as a blue-water chaplain on ships of the fleet, Dittmar began serving with Marine units in 1939. When Felber deposited the distraught (and disarmed) Kelley at his doorstep, Dittmar calmed the young man down and asked him to make a cross. There would be no field burial for Sgt. Casey: Dittmar was planning a service at the new cemetery.

By dawn on D+5, the 1st Marine Division on Guadalcanal proper had suffered nine fatalities, plus one (Cpl. James McCutcheon) missing in action. Of the dead, five had been buried (two at sea and three in isolated graves) and the remaining four were awaiting burial. Regimental chaplains were already busy with funerals; Lt. Thomas Reardon, attached to the 5th Marines, was reported to have officiated the burial "in a drenching tropical rain ... [of] the first Leatherneck to die on Guadalcanal [probably Sgt. William J. Steen, L/3/5]. It was a temporary resting place, changed the next day, but that burial, as all the ones to follow, was performed with the full rites of the church."[51] The desire to avoid these isolated burials was growing, however; of the four who remained to be interred, two had been waiting for nearly three days—far from an ideal situation.

Defensive positions were now coalescing around the airfield and Lunga Point, which allowed for the establishment of a temporary cemetery. A site near the eastern end of the runway was chosen; the ground was easily dug and easily drained, convenient to fighting positions and rudimentary roads, and, as it soon developed, "located convenient to where the heaviest casualties are expected or experienced."[52] It is not known if there was a specific order establishing the cemetery on this date or at this site, or whether Dittmar as the "appropriate commander" operated on personal initiative. After all, three of the dead were members of his own 11th Marines.

Abraham Felber came to Guadalcanal fully prepared to document his experiences. As the chief administrator of his battery, he could easily justify maintaining a detailed diary when such records were expressly forbidden; a consummate shutterbug, he rarely ventured outside the battery area without his trusty Kodak Monitor. Rightly suspecting that Casey's funeral would be a noteworthy experience, Felber secured permission to tag along. At 3 p.m., the mourners boarded an ambulance and drove nearly a mile to the chosen field.

Felber recorded the experience in his diary:

[The cemetery] was very recently established, and there were only two occupied graves. There were also three open graves. When we reached the field, there was another funeral party there with another body. We all waited for a while, as another body was expected, and all three bodies would be buried with one service. Finally, our chaplain told the one with the other body that he ought to go ahead with his service, as he had far to go to get back before dark, and it was already late.... The other chaplain had the body which was in his care laid in one of the open graves; and while we all uncovered, he pronounced the solemn services. It was a very impressive scene, with the banks of pearly clouds hanging low over the purple mountains and the rumbling thud of artillery drowning out the intoning voice of the chaplain at his melancholy task.

The first party turned to with their shovels, buried seventeen-year-old Pvt. John R. Brotherston (1st Pioneer Battalion) in Grave No. 2, and departed. Dittmar decided to proceed with Casey's funeral; Felber helped carry the poncho-wrapped body to the third grave in the first row. Here the *ad hoc* nature of the cemetery became apparent. "We tried to lower him gently into the grave, but he didn't fit," wrote Felber. "The grave-digging detail had been in a hurry, and as they dug further down, the grave had become shorter and narrower." Dittmar directed the men to rearrange the body, but try as they might, Casey would not lie flat. Finally, one man jumped into the grave and dug out the excess earth, much to Felber's relief. "I would never have been easy again for thinking of poor Casey in his cramped position."[53]

As Dittmar commended Casey to his Maker, another truck arrived with the third body—"a very large man, over six feet, and heavy. He didn't have a poncho covering him, and his feet protruded beneath the blankets.

He had on shoes but was not wearing socks." This was Sgt. Nicholas R. Windisch, also of the 11th Marines, killed in another friendly fire incident on August 9.[54] As soon as he concluded Casey's service, Dittmar simply turned around and repeated his words for Windisch.

The service concluded with a final gesture from the assembled mourners. "On top of each grave we placed a long green coconut palm frond," wrote Felber. "The men with the big body made a cross on the field from a nearby tree and placed it on the grave of their friend. Kelley stuck his cross in at the head of Casey's grave. The grave of the man who had been buried first was without a cross. His friends had gone, so we made one up, fastening the cross-piece with some barbed wire from a nearby fence."[55] Such handmade monuments would become a distinguishing feature of the First Marine Division Cemetery (FMC).

The cemetery expanded rapidly from these humble beginnings. Between August 12, 1942, and January 22, 1943, 940 graves were dug for Marines, soldiers, sailors, and a single Coast Guardsman. Some graves contained more than one body, for on occasion men died so closely together that they could not be separated before burial. Most were known by name, some only by their unit, and some by no designation at all save that they were (or were believed to be) Americans. They were arranged neatly into ninety-four rows of ten graves each; when PFC Walter B. Montgomery (Company "I," 164th Infantry) was laid into Row 94, Grave 10, the burial party moved immediately on to bury Pvt. William H. Matthews (Company "K," 35th Infantry) in the first row of an "annex," which would eventually outgrow the original cemetery by more than two and a half times. The "Army, Navy, and Marine Corps Cemetery, Guadalcanal" (ANMC) would eventually become one of the largest American temporary cemeteries in the Pacific.

Despite their constant growth, and the prominent part they play in veterans' memoirs—nearly all visited a buddy's well-tended grave before leaving Guadalcanal—there is surprisingly little known about how the cemeteries operated on a day-to-day basis. The Gavutu cemetery, along with Cemeteries No. 2 and No. 3 on Tulagi, ceased burial operations just as PFC Oscar J. Grover, Jr., (C/1/1) was being laid to rest in Grave No. 1 of the FMC.[56] These smaller cemeteries (and Tulagi's White Beach cemetery, before it passed to Navy control) were examples of the "burial by organizations" forewarned in Col. James' Circular. Responsibility for postmortem care lay with the deceased's own company, battalion, or regiment.[57] This was a perfect system for battles fought over a small area, just the way Marine doctrine envisioned combat: short, sharp fights centered around beachheads. Casualties might be heavy, but the battlefield would be contained, the dead relatively easy to locate, and the fighting soon over, allowing for a rapid collection and interment. Control of the cemetery, and the responsibility of graves registration tasks, would then be handed over to the garrisoning force.

The same burial by organization system was applied on Guadalcanal, as shown in Felber's vivid account. While the volume of casualties remained small, this was sufficient. For the first few days of its operation, the FMC grew by one or two graves at a time, mostly the unfortunate victims of friendly fire, and there was time for individual units to conduct burials. However, as the two sides gradually came to grips with each other, the number of daily burials increased. Col. Goettge's patrol would have been the first real test, had any of the remains been recovered, and the dead from the First Battle of the Matanikau were few. Two days later, a major battle erupted a few hundred yards from the cemetery itself, testing both the Marines' defensive doctrine and their ability to deal with the inevitable fatalities.

The Battle of the Tenaru—fought over the banks and mouth of a small river called "Alligator Creek" by the Marines and the Ilu River by locals—was the first major encounter between Marines and Japanese on Guadalcanal.[58] Alerted to the presence of a large Japanese force to the east of their perimeter (at the cost of three men whose bodies could not be brought back for burial), Lt. Col. Edwin A. Pollock's 2nd Battalion, 1st Marines, hastily fortified their positions and awaited the onslaught.[59] The Japanese force, an elite group of veterans under the command of Col. Kiyonao Ichiki, charged across the river mouth and slammed into Pollock's line. In the fight that followed, the Ichiki Detachment was all but annihilated at the cost of thirty-eight Marine lives. Three of these men died of their wounds and were buried at sea; a fourth, Pvt. Freeman Blair, was killed in a counterattack the next morning and buried in the field. The remainder wound up at the cemetery, which expanded from thirteen graves to fifty-six in a single day—a remarkable achievement.

Again, the burden of finding, identifying, and transporting the fallen was done by the combat troops. Shocked Marines, deafened by the drumfire of battle, their hands shaking with nerves and exhaustion, picked through Japanese corpses, stacked literally in heaps, to find missing buddies. "The smell of death almost took your breath away," recalled PFC James F. Young of Company "H," 1st Marines. "The chaplains were taking the dog tags off the dead Marines. They said we lost forty men."[60] Lt. (j.g.) Ansgar Sovik, the battalion chaplain, had an intensely personal interest in caring for the dead: he nearly joined their number the night before. As he assisted the surgeon, Lt. Jacques Saphier, with the wounded, a mortar shell struck their aid station. Saphier managed to scream "My God, they got me!" before expiring with a piece of shrapnel lodged in his neck. Sovik continued ministering to the wounded throughout the night, drenched in his friend's blood.[61]

Fortuitously, the cemetery was close to the scene of the battle, and moving the dead from foxholes and field hospitals was only a minor logistical hurdle. Ambulances and stretcher parties made multiple trips as the day went on. The emotional impact of handling the remains of friends was much more pronounced, and it appears that this task fell to the tired warriors as well. PFC Arthur Pendleton (H/2/1) was "volunteered" into a collection detail:

> I remember two riflemen, who were my friends, a big shell landed beside them and killed them both. It didn't just kill them, it blew them to pieces. Their names were Barney Sterling and Arthur Atwood. They would both receive the Navy Cross, posthumously. Our lieutenant gathered me and a couple of guys, and we got ponchos and picked up their body parts. We carried them up through the coconut grove and dug their graves right near the end of the Henderson Field airstrip.[62]

Pollock's men had some additional support in the form of Company "E," 1st Medical Battalion. The Medical Battalion was a relatively new organization in the 1st Marine Division, patterned on an Army medical regiment but built to a smaller scale. Each company was equipped with its own motor transport, supplies, and the ability to set up field hospitals of up to 250 beds.[63] On campaign, these companies—comprised of Navy corpsmen and medical officers, plus a small contingent of Marine Corps administrators—were attached to each of the Division's regiments to treat diseases and facilitate evacuation as needed.[64] When a regiment's organic medical teams were overwhelmed, the medical companies furnished triage support as well. On August 21, the lion's share of the Tenaru casualties passed through the tent hospital established by "Easy Med," and most of them survived. Some, like Lt. Saphier, were too far gone, and the corpsmen wound up assisting with burials as well. Second Lieutenant Edward J. Craig, Jr., (F/2/1) was treated at the field hospital and saw "corpsmen were preparing two who had already expired for a military burial."[65]

PFC Lester C. Clark (H/2/1) was tucking into a can of C-rations after a long night. "The meat and beans were sliding down pretty well when my eyes happened to wander to an area partly screened by a tarpaulin," he said. "There in neat rows lay our dead. These were mostly the same guys we had enlisted with, gone through boot camp with, groused and laughed with, and now they were dead and being prepared for burial. A great lump formed in my throat and I threw the unfinished ration away." He joined a group assembling at the cemetery for a service:

Part of that large, open field on our right flank became Guadalcanal's cemetery. It was inaugurated with our fallen comrades. While over thirty of their buddies were lowered into the soft earth, many of the battle-hardened marines wept unashamedly. Each of the dead was carefully wrapped in captured Japanese blankets, the only burial shrouds we had. With the sad notes of Taps echoing in our ears, we turned away from the gravesites in a gently falling rain.[66]

This courtesy was not extended to the hundreds of Col. Ichiki's men who lost their lives at the Tenaru. For a Japanese unit, a failed assault almost always meant annihilation. This was the case at the battle of the Tenaru: of approximately 1,000 Japanese soldiers who flung themselves at Pollock's battalion, more than 800 lost their lives in the charge or during the Marine counterattack the following morning.[67]

A few hours after turning back the Ichiki charge, Robert Leckie swam the creek to search for souvenirs and beheld the nightmare sight of a coconut grove full of dead men. "The tropics had got at them already and they were beginning to spill open," he wrote. "I was horrified at the swarms of flies; black, circling funnels that seemed to emerge from every orifice: from the mouth, the eyes, the ears. The beating of their myriad tiny wings made a dreadful low hum. The flies were in possession of the field; the tropics had won; her minions were everywhere, smacking their lips over this bounty of rotting flesh."[68] Richard Tregaskis visited the following day and remarked that "the stench of bodies strewn along Hell Point and across the Tenaru was strong. Many of them lay at the water's edge and already were puffed and glossy like shiny sausages.... Everywhere one turned there were piles of bodies, here one with a backbone visible from the front, and the rest of the flesh and bone peeled up over the man's head, like the leaf of an artichoke..."[69] To the victors fell the task of cleaning up the battlefield. Officially, enemy dead were to be properly identified, buried, and reported "in conformity with the rules of land warfare."[70] However, the sheer number of bodies and the rapidity with which they were decomposing prevented any attempts at individual identification.

Curiosity drew sightseers to the battlefield. First Sergeant Felber talked his way into joining a working party headed for the Tenaru on August 23. They smelled the battlefield long before they saw it, and upon arrival found that the burial of Ichiki's men was underway. "A large pit had been dug, and the bodies of some 60 or 70 Japs were thrown therein, one on top of the other, like a bunch of discarded wax figures," Felber wrote in his diary. "About 50 Korean prisoners were collecting the bodies on stretchers and throwing them into the pit. Some of the bodies were so badly decomposed that it was necessary to bury them where they lay.... The sight and the odor was so overpowering that one of the Military Police (who were in charge of the body disposal) took sick as I was talking to him, and the men in our party had their faces all screwed up in horror and disgust…" While Felber allowed that the dead men had once been "brave and confident soldiers," his interest extended little further than "morbid fascination" in watching the burials.[71]

Navy Lt. Jack Clark also visited the Tenaru battlefield. "Prisoners were at work burying the corpses," he wrote:

> They had been working all day. Some of the piles had been buried, but the majority were still in the foxholes they had dug. It was brutal…. The engineers would blast a long trench, then the prisoners would load about 20 bodies on a truck, the truck drove over to the trench, and the Japs would unceremoniously dump or roll the bodies off the truck into the trench. Parts of bodies were just kicked off into the trench. As soon as 40 or 50 bodies were dumped a bulldozer would push sand over them and fill up the hole. No markers of any kind were set up.[72]

Early photographs of the First Marine Division Cemetery show distinct (if somewhat unevenly spaced) rows of graves, "aligned so that headstones will be in alignment, both laterally and longitudinally," as prescribed by the Circular.[73] Markers were fashioned from sticks or scrap lumber. Gravediggers were probably procured from the division's service troops or bandsmen; later, prisoners of war were put to the task. A dental officer, attended by corpsmen, inspected the bodies and confirmed identities when necessary. Chaplain Dittmar, as the ranking officer of the Chaplain Corps, presumably provided additional oversight, and the administrative details were assigned to the record keepers of the Division's D-1 (personnel) and D-4 (quartermaster) sections.

Most chaplains helped to conduct services, and some became familiar figures around the cemetery. Father Reardon was particularly visible, especially when the dead men belonged to his own 5th Marines. Commending them to their Maker was a personal matter: Reardon knew many of the men from happier times when he was the "marrying parson" of New River, North Carolina. "A lot of the boys I married, I buried," he said. "Whenever I buried one of those marines, I felt I was putting in that grave the heart of the girl back home."[74] The popular chaplain spent nearly four months ministering to the sick, the wounded, and the dying in his "parish" around Henderson Field.[75] Richard Tregaskis' *Guadalcanal Diary* made Reardon the face of faith on the island, and he was the basis for "Father Donnelly" played by Preston Foster in the film adaptation. The press nicknamed him "The Padre of Guadalcanal."[76]

The expansion of the cemetery was possible due to the circumstances of battle: for the first month of the campaign, most casualties among the Marine ground forces were sustained within the perimeter. (With very few exceptions, Marines who died on patrol beyond the perimeter were buried where they fell.) Most deaths were caused by shelling or aerial bombing, and these were nasty deaths indeed. On one occasion, the battle-weary Company "H," 1st Marines, lost eleven men from a working party to a single bomb. Even in this extreme example, proximity to the cemetery meant bodies could be moved quickly and with their proper identification. Services were brief. "The burial party for our boys dug the holes," wrote Pvt. James Donahue in his diary. "The men were lowered wrapped in Jap blankets. Chaplain said a few words and they were gone."[77]

This situation changed dramatically in mid-September, with the Battle of Edson's Ridge. Unlike the Tenaru battle, which condensed its terror into a single night, fighting for the Ridge lasted for multiple days. Ground was lost, taken, re-lost, and then retaken as the lines seesawed back and forth in a series of brutal night battles. Massed artillery fire riddled the ground, and many of the corpses "seemed to have been hit repeatedly by the intense gunfire.... Where the shellfire was heaviest, severed limbs and bloody guts littered the ground as if dumped from an airplane," recalled Marlin Groft. "There were headless bodies, body-less heads, and limbless torsos.... Edgar Allan Poe could have set the scene around us."[78] An estimated 800 Japanese were killed in the attempt to take the ridge, and fifty-nine Marines—mostly Raiders, Paramarines, and the 2nd Battalion, 5th Marines—died defending it. Others were killed defending positions elsewhere along the line, or in the daily routine of air strikes, accidents, or disease. All told, some ninety-three men in Marine units lost their lives on Guadalcanal between September 12 and 15.

Retrieving the dead from Edson's Ridge was a particular challenge. Many bodies lay in the field for several days and had been fought over or otherwise abused, deliberately or not, by the combatants. One particularly horrifying episode took place on the night of September 12, when an entire platoon from the Raiders' Company "C" and their supporting machine-gun section was overrun. A single fallen log was the only escape from their lagoon-locked position, and the survivors scattered into the jungle. Several days later, Lt. John P. "Black Jack" Salmon led a patrol back to the scene. "We found three badly decomposed bodies in the near vicinity," he wrote, but "although we were positive that the bodies were those of Marines, positive personal identification was impossible."

Joseph H. Alexander unpacks this statement:

Positive identification of the remains was difficult, grisly work. Slash wounds typically cause much more bleeding than punctures; the features of the dead would have been blackened by dried blood. Also, bodies could readily have been blown up by subsequent high explosives— Charlie Company's battleground the first night became ground zero for countless artillery barrages during the second night's clash. And the Japanese executioners may have looted their victim's belongings, including dog tags. Finally, those conducting the search were hardly forensic scientists or graves registration experts. They were Marines, looking for slain fellow Marines, but in a dense jungle still infested with vengeful snipers and Japanese patrols on the same mission for their own missing and dead.[79]

Of eighteen Marines killed or missing in Salmon's company, only eight were identified when they reached the cemetery.

The first "UNKNOWN" marker went up over Grave 2, Row No. 12, on or around September 15, while the dead from Edson's Ridge were being buried. Seven more quickly followed. Fortunately, the corpsmen working at the cemetery took fingerprint impressions and dental charts of the unidentified men. Unknowns X-1 through X-7 were later identified, during or immediately after the war, thanks to information gathered before their burial. All proved to be casualties of the battle for Edson's Ridge:

X-1	PFC Louis J. LaVallee	G/2/5th Marines
X-2	Private John C. Rock	C/1st Raider Battalion
X-3	Platoon Sergeant John J. Quigley	C/1st Raider Battalion
X-4	Corporal Joseph F. Maye	A/1st Parachute Battalion
X-5	Corporal Ralph W. Barrett, Jr.	HQ/5/11th Marines
X-6	First Sergeant Jerome J. Stark	C/1st Raider Battalion
X-7	PFC Raymond W. Herndon	A/1st Parachute Battalion

The three bodies mentioned by Lt. Salmon—known to be Americans but decomposed past recognition—might have been Rock, Quigley, and Stark.

Unknown X-8 would become the first enduring mystery of the Division cemetery. He was buried in Grave 7, Row 15, probably on September 15 or 16. To his left was Cpl. John W. Heath of the 1st Engineer Battalion; to his right was Cpl. Clyde Farrell of the Paramarines. He probably gave his life on or around September 14, as many who died in the multiple-day battle for the Ridge were so assumed. Several teeth in his maxilla and mandible were knocked out; it is not known whether his fingerprints could be taken, as later laboratory analysis noted that his remains had no hands. He was estimated to be between twenty-four and twenty-six years of age, about 5 feet 9 inches tall, and 145 pounds. The only items found with his body were "one pair Marine Corp [*sic.*] rough leather shoe [*sic.*] size 8EE." To this date, the mystery of his identity has not been solved, and he lies in the National Memorial Cemetery of the Pacific, Section N, Grave 428 as an unknown.[80]

The mass influx of casualties—and the increasing need for oversight in a cemetery now just short of 200 graves—led to the appointment of a division burial officer. That man was Capt. Richard Tonis, skipper of the 1st Service Battalion. A former Massachusetts state trooper, Tonis had a keen eye for spotting malingerers and malcontents—"tagging trash," as he said—regardless of rank. At first, Tonis thought his reassignment was the result of an argument with an influential lieutenant colonel; he later learned that a good friend at Headquarters recommended him for the job precisely because his pugnacious nature could get the difficult job done. Tonis had previously commanded the division's military police company, and these same MPs were now running the work details at the cemetery.

Capt. Tonis accepted his new responsibilities on September 23, 1942. It is not known whom, if anybody, he replaced in this billet, but he quickly got busy "recording the names and locations of those who gave their lives." His memoirs provide a unique sketch of an average day at the cemetery. When casualties were expected, the MPs rounded up a detail of Korean prisoners—likely the same men who toiled over the remains of the Ichiki Detachment—to "dig the number of graves needed." Bodies arrived at the cemetery in various states of decomposition. "If the battle lasted for a number of days, the bodies would become bloated, often with their helmets still on," Tonis wrote. "Due to the swelling and the condition of the body, it smelled bad enough to knock you over." Identity was to be confirmed before burial, but this was sometimes easier said than done as "the Japanese usually took the [identification] tags as souvenirs." When a man arrived with no identification, fingerprint impressions were taken—Tonis had a lifelong fascination, and professional experience, with fingerprinting—and a Navy dentist (probably Lt. Myron G. Turner, Dental Corps) was summoned to inspect the teeth. This was not a job for the faint of heart, and there may have been multiple medical professionals assigned to give each other some relief. Tonis knew one dental officer, a former Quantico classmate now assigned to the Division sick bay. "When a body came in from the front line, unrecognizable and without identification, the two chiefs [pharmacists] assigned to me would call upon him to make a complete examination of his teeth so that the body could possible [*sic.*] be identified at a much later date," he said. "I'm sure it was [in] instances such as these that the dentist wished he had chosen another profession."

Once all avenues for identification were exhausted, each body was wrapped in a shroud. At first, Tonis used captured Japanese blankets—

there must have been an ample supply, as PFC Clark recalled the same practice after the Tenaru battle—but "when one of the commanding officers complained, we began using US Marine Corps blankets." When all was ready, Tonis sent for a chaplain; he found the Catholics, particularly Father Frederic P. Gehring, more amenable to holding services under adverse circumstances, even with "the stench of death hanging in the air" and the "thousand green bottle flies" that swarmed the mourners.[81]

Foul smells and insects were not the only interruptions. The cemetery was quite close to the bull's-eye of Henderson Field; bombs and shells aimed at the Cactus Air Force sometimes fell uncomfortably close to the burial parties. Father Reardon told of making "frequent jumps into newly-dug graves to await the 'all-clear,'" and likely was not exaggerating much.[82] One chaplain volunteered to conduct a burial, "adding with the utmost certainty that we would be bombed," recalled Tonis. "He went on to explain that no matter where he was on the island, that would be where the bombs dropped." Sure enough, when the daily air raid passed overhead, a bomb landed so close to Tonis' shelter that "I felt like I was a rag that had been soaked, then wrung out. I apologized to the priest.... He shrugged it off, saying it was a part of his every day being up front." When the bombers departed, the chaplain calmly finished the burial service.[83] The strain of working in the cemetery took a severe toll. Charles Dittmar came down with malaria and had to be evacuated in October 1942. Thomas Reardon lost 50 pounds in four months; he collapsed while suffering from "malaria and fever contracted from handling bodies," and was flown off the island while unconscious.[84] Months later, Capt. Tonis saw his unnamed "unflinching" chaplain "in a restricted area of a Navy hospital.... The toll of having taken too many bombings was still bothering him."[85]

Capt. Tonis held the billet of Marine burial officer until his division left Guadalcanal. On December 8, 1942, the day before his departure, he signed off on the group burial of three unknowns—X-37, -38, and -39—the last of nearly 550 burials that took place during his tenure as "Marine GRS Officer." Responsibility was handed over to an Army quartermaster officer—potentially Second Lieutenant Edward F. Cogswell and his assistant, S/Sgt. William M. Annetti.[86] Thus ended Marine supervision of graves registration activities in the Guadalcanal area. Edward Steere depicted the situation as unique, "not only for the reason that it was the first of World War II to act in support of offensive action but because of the fact that this service was improvised during the initial phase of the fighting by combat personnel of the Marine Corps."

In *The Graves Registration Service in World War II*, Steere refers to a provisional system involving "a graves registration platoon of combat personnel which was to follow the landing force ashore and make proper disposition of all fatalities." The platoon was to consist of two commissioned officers for oversight, twenty privates for labor, and three pharmacist's mates to identify and prepare remains for burial. (A chaplain was also recommended to perform the proper religious services.)[87] This "organic unit" was very likely the one commanded by Capt. Tonis, and probably provided the model for the first official Marine Graves Registration Unit. Ten men were chosen from the Service Company, I Marine Amphibious Corps (IMAC) at New Caledonia, and placed under the command of Capt. Rex H. Crockett on December 5, 1942. Within a month, this small cadre expanded to the size of a full platoon—forty-six men, including medical personnel. However, most of them had no special qualifications for the work; many were shanghaied from the Second Amphibian Tractor Battalion, and the rest were an assortment of service and supply men from the 2nd Marine Division. Only Capt. Crockett and his successor, Capt. John "Greek" Apergis, both former Raiders, had experienced anything resembling serious combat or witnessed a battlefield burial. Unfortunately, the training methods of this nascent Marine Graves Registration unit are quite obscure, and perhaps with good reason, as almost none of the original platoon lasted more than a few months in this assignment.

Guadalcanal might have proved a training ground for Marine GRS as well as Army, but this was not to be. Aside from a brief visit from Capt. Apergis and a single clerk, no members of this unit are known to have visited the cemeteries once they passed to Army control. Firsthand experience would occur elsewhere in the Solomon Islands.

"He was a Real Guy"

One day before embarking for Australia, a large group from Company "H," 1st Marines, hiked several miles along the coast to view the cemetery one last time. Lester Clark was among them:

> Surprised and saddened at how large it had grown, we filed along the many rows. The first ones contained those of our number who had fallen at the Tenaru back in August. As the campaign had dragged on, the graves showed a chronological history of the many actions and the men who had died in them.[88]

The evolution of the cemetery was also evident in the variety of grave markers that stood in straight rows of ten. In future operations, amphibious forces would carry supplies of ready-made grave markers out of grim necessity. No such provision had been made for Operation Watchtower, and the result was a handmade hodgepodge of styles. The first markers were simply sticks or scrap boards nailed together. Then somebody planted a shaped Gothic cross above Plat. Sgt. Nelson Braitmeyer's grave. Soon, little fences of barbed wire or belted ammunition were appearing around individual plots. Someone hit on the bright idea of making oblique cuts into coconut palms and painting the marker on the angled stumps. PFC Anthony Almeida's cross featured a hand-carved Marine advancing, bayonet fixed. Capt. Rex M. Heap's squadron mates inscribed a salvaged propeller blade—"An Officer's Greatest Achievement Is The Respect And Admiration Of His Men"—and planted it at the foot of his grave. A member of the 11th Marines might have a 105-mm shell for a headstone, while anti-tank men were marked by 37-mm casings welded together in the shape of a cross. The Army got into the spirit, too; one well-respected officer's grave was fenced off with a little garden planted inside. Even when regulation markers started to appear, the individual tributes were often left in place, and some graves featured two or three different styles.

There was a constant flow of visitors—an average of 200 every day, according to one attendant—and men delivered their handmade tributes to their departed buddies. Marines and soldiers alike scratched epitaphs onto mess tins and affixed them to the graves. "Say a prayer for my pal, killed on Guadalcanal" was a common refrain. Bob Leckie noted a few: "He died fighting;" "A real Marine;" "A big guy with a bigger heart;" "Our Buddy;" "The harder the going, the more cheerful he was."[89] Friends of popular PFC Bill Cameron (H/2/1) painted his name and date of death on a broken rifle stock, built a wire fence around his plot, and made a placard with an adaptation of Frank Bernard Camp's poem "Our Hitch in Hell."[90] Some graves were decorated for Christmas, with wreaths made of woven bamboo, greenery, and cardboard stars. Capt. Donald Dickson observed men walking through the cemetery as if in a daze, their minds far away. "When the fighting stopped a little, some would wander among the graves, alone, reading the names on the crosses, aimlessly," he wrote. "Now and then one name would seem to mean a little more than another; there would be a kicking of dirt, a grinding of a heel, never a word, just little actions."[91]

Father Reardon recalled the story of PFC Bernard Fetchko, mortally wounded near Kokumbona on August 27, 1942. Reardon held the young Marine's hand as he died, then walked across the ward to comfort PFC Anthony Fetchko, Bernard's twin brother, who was suffering from malaria. "We carried the ill boy to the cemetery," said Reardon, "and after the services and a mass, I left him there, crying by the grave. He was kneeling in the midst of the crosses."[92] When Anthony recovered, he helped make "a nice white cross inscribed 'gloriously in action'" and put the marker by his brother's grave.[93]

On December 31, 1942, a detachment of the 7th Marines held a full memorial service at the cemetery. The impressive ceremony was attended by all ranks from all services and drew correspondents, photographers, and newsreel crews. Six smartly dressed soldiers, sailors, and Marines stood at attention over a single flag-draped catafalque containing the remains of "an unnamed Navy construction worker who gave his life in the line of duty." The regimental chaplain, Lt. (j.g.) Matthew F. Keough, led a solemn requiem mass from atop a dais of palm logs at the center of the cemetery, followed by Protestant services conducted by Navy and Army chaplains. A squad cracked off the three volleys of a funeral salute, and the assembled men presented arms as Field Music Sgt. Thomas Shepperd played Taps for the fallen. Finally the regimental bandmaster, Master T/Sgt. James T. Tichacek, Jr., led his men in renditions of the Marine Corps Hymn and the National Anthem.[94] When the formalities concluded, the men walked through the graves to say their goodbyes. "It was the last thing we did," recalled Richard Greer. "A lot of tears."[95]

The cemetery remained a popular destination for servicemen throughout the war. Men went searching for the graves of relative or hometown buddies killed during the battle of Guadalcanal; others simply went to view the humbling spectacle of hundreds of graves. Some veterans would pass that way again, on their way to or returning from future battlefields. For many, however, the last goodbye was truly the end. "There would be other battles fought, but not for these gallant men," remarked Lester Clark. "They would live on only in history and in the hearts of those who had known them."[96]

Art Pendleton agreed. "I never cared about going back to Guadalcanal," he said. "A friend told me it's a big cemetery now."[97]

5

An All-Volunteer Patrol: September 17, 1942

The war which seemed like a great adventure before we landed didn't look that way anymore.[1]

Robert Corwin, Company "B," 1st Marines

The coughing stopped, and everything went still.

Private Robert Corwin marveled at the total silence—nothing stirred or made a sound in the heavy, humid air. He lay motionless on the jungle floor, replaying the events of the past few minutes: the red-faced, panicky sergeant yelling that Charlie Debele was down; searching for Charlie and finding him barely alive in a clearing strewn with dead Marines; the sudden blast that laid him out with a bullet in the shoulder; seeing Ralph Ingerson in the foliage beckoning him to run; making a break for it and falling headlong with a second bullet through the leg; hearing Ingerson cough quietly and wetly through the wound in his throat and seeing him slump forward on his knees, head in the mud; and now the absolute stillness that suggested he was the last man alive.

As the shock wore off and the pain set in, Corwin thought about his options. The rest of his company was nowhere to be seen. Ingerson was dead, and he believed Debele was too. Corwin's first instinct was to feign death. Every time he moved, he seemed to get shot. Maybe he could slip back to safety under cover of darkness. A second, stronger instinct quickly took hold: "I'm in Japanese territory … I might be subjected to Japanese bayonet practice."[2] He tried wiggling his fingers and flexing his legs. His right hand was paralyzed, but the wound in his leg was a through-and-through hole in the fleshy part of the thigh. It would be painful, but he thought he could walk.

Corwin lay for a few more minutes, gathering his courage, then scrambled to his feet and bolted out of the clearing.

In the first great American land offensive of the war, the 1st Battalion, 1st Marines, fought largely on the defensive.

After Capt. Charles Brush's Company "A" destroyed the Ichiki Detachment's reconnaissance party at Koli Point on August 19, the battalion went into regimental reserve—"which, under normal circumstances, is about as far from any action as you can get and still be in the same war," they said.[3] Their comrades in the 2nd and 3rd Battalions bore the brunt of the Japanese onslaught across Alligator Creek at the misnamed "Battle of the Tenaru." The 1st Battalion was summoned to help with the mopping up, and between 9.50 a.m. and 2 p.m. completely encircled the Ichiki survivors. They stood firm as a light tank platoon charged back and forth through the coconut grove, spraying canister and machine gun fire and grinding men, living and dead, to pulp beneath their treads. By 5 p.m., the battle was over, "with [the] almost complete annihilation of the enemy."[4]

The slaughter of the Ichiki Detachment represented the first real bloodbath of the Guadalcanal campaign, and after the mop up came the cleanup. Marines from Company "A" were shanghaied onto working parties, removing equipment from dead comrades and "unceremoniously disposing of the enemy in a common grave." The vivid memories would last a lifetime:

> There is no such stench as that of a recent battlefield. Bodies bloat quickly and decomposition starts immediately in the tropical heat. Bulldozers made the job easier and quicker. That was a relief from the standpoint of smell and sanitation.[5]

Seven men from the 1st Battalion, 1st Marines, lost their lives in the counterattack. Six would be buried in the First Marine Division Cemetery, which almost tripled in size after the Tenaru. The lone exception, Pvt. Freeman Bright Blair of Company "D," made a lasting impression on his buddies. Early in the fight, Blair was shot in the side. He refused assistance and fought on until a second bullet that shattered his shoulder. While being carried back to safety, a third bullet struck him in the head. (Blair was awarded a posthumous Silver Star for his gallantry; his body was buried in the field, but the site eluded later searchers.)[6]

After the Tenaru, the battalion settled into a routine which "gave us plenty of time to improve our defensive positions, go on patrols, move the vast quantities of supplies from the dump to the beach area," but felt uncomfortably like being relegated to reserve status.[7] Marines sweated while cutting fire lanes in the tall grass near their bivouac on the Lunga River, and cooled themselves with a quick dip in the sluggish waters. Occasionally, a chosen few were allowed back to the battalion area to hear the latest tunes and propaganda from Tokyo Rose. The dire predictions were shrugged off with a laugh—"them news guys don't know us!"—and the next day, the routine would begin again.

September brought worrisome changes. The food was passable, but no supplies were coming in; meals were limited to two per day, and there was never enough to eat. Necessities became scarce, then coveted, then impossible to find; visions of real toilet paper and new shoelaces danced in the heads of Marines out on yet another working party.[8] And there were the patrols, a constant reminder that the Japanese were out there, somewhere, marshaling for the next attack. Patrols from the 2nd and 3rd Battalions of the 1st Marines skirmished with their Japanese counterparts from September 9–11.[9] Frequency of contact was more notable than the modest casualty count. "Small patrol encounters were of daily occurrence," noted Lt. Col. Merrill Twining, "and it became increasingly difficult to penetrate the area to the east…. The jungle represented a terrific obstacle to be overcome only by weeks of labor at a time when it was all too obvious that only days remained to us."[10] A low ridge just south of the airfield, occupied by the Paramarines and the 1st Raider Battalion, became the focal point of defensive preparations.

The gathering tension hung heavy in the air until September 12, when it finally broke in a furious storm aimed at Henderson Field. Flares lit the night sky, Japanese warships hurled tons of steel into the perimeter, and with a yell the first waves of infantry came swarming out of the jungle. When Maj. Gen. Kiyotake Kawaguchi's bid to recapture the vital airfield finally failed on the morning of September 14, most of the vaunted Kawaguchi Detachment lay dead in the jungle and on the scorched slopes of the formerly nameless rise, which would live in history as Raiders', Edson's, or, to those who survived, Bloody Ridge.

While the 1st Marines played no significant role in defending the Ridge itself, their 3rd Battalion gave a good account of itself on the night of September 13. When their patrols discovered evidence of another strong Japanese force to their front, Capt. Robert Putnam (K/3/1) allowed a listening post of five enlisted Marines led by 2Lt. Joe Terzi to set up shop along the Overland Trail. This proved to be a wise choice. Kawaguchi's right flank, comprised of Maj. Eiji Mizuno's Kuma Battalion, plus attached units (including some survivors of the Ichiki Detachment) anticipated striking a Marine line only one man deep. It would be a devastating blow: a Kuma Battalion breakthrough would leave Henderson Field wide open.

Unfortunately for Mizuno, his lead elements walked into Terzi's listening post, which promptly opened fire. The chaotic effect of six Thompson submachine guns at short range led Mizuno to believe he had hit the main Marine line. Having lost the element of surprise, the Kuma Battalion committed to a headlong attack on "K" Company's lines. The ferocious fight that followed lasted until sunrise, and the Kuma Battalion was halted at the cost of three Company "K" Marines.[11] One of the listening post volunteers, Pvt. Thomas Pilleri, never returned and was listed as missing in action for three days. He would be buried in the field on September 17.[12]

One final drama played out in front of the 3rd Battalion, and it was an object lesson in overconfidence. At first light, a platoon from Company "B," 1st Tank Battalion, sallied forth to harass the Kuma Battalion survivors and returned in triumph. Their second foray, however, ended in disaster. PFC Fred J. Balester of the tank battalion's scout company witnessed the aftermath:

> In looking over the scene, we had to admire the courage and skill of what must have been a very small [Japanese] unit. They had provoked an attack by a much larger force, and with a few light machine guns and one 40mm anti-tank gun wiped out four tanks and got away scot-free. Three of our tanks had been drilled neatly through the turret before they even got close to the gun. One tank had made it to the river, but it was upside down in the water.... The lone survivor was left in shock. He had somehow managed to get out of a burning tank.... We escorted him almost like a prisoner, although he didn't know it ... this fellow was so beat up we honestly couldn't tell whether or not he was a Marine.

Balester excoriated "the trained assault troops of the 1st Marines" for sending tanks to solve an infantryman's problem without support, saying the scouts were "totally disgusted.... The line company did not even offer to support us, so we went out alone."[13] Considering their exertions of the night before, it is perhaps not surprising that the infantrymen preferred to stay in their foxholes.

The activity around the Overland Trail and Edson's Ridge immediately changed the tone of the 1st Marines' campaign. Lt. William H. Whyte III, the intelligence officer of the 3rd Battalion, deemed the effort "a serious effort to improve our knowledge ... through sophisticated patrolling," while the average Marine griped about "a flurry of larger and longer patrols."[14] On the morning of September 14, as the action on the Ridge sputtered out and the survivors of Terzi's listening post straggled back to safety, two companies of 1st Battalion, 1st Marines, moved out of their defensive positions near the airfield and went hunting for Kawaguchi.

Capt. Brush's Company "A" led the trek down the western bank of the Lunga River, hoping to discover the extent of the enemy withdrawal. They ran into one of Kawaguchi's bivouacs a few thousand yards south of the Ridge; the Imperial force, while badly mauled, still managed to get the drop on the Marines.[15] "The Japs opened up on us with machine guns," recalled Pvt. William C. Sparks, Jr. "It was an ambush." Pvt. Claude G. Childers, a seventeen-year-old rifleman from Pleasants County, West Virginia, was shot and killed; Sparks was hit in the hand, and another round struck PFC Francis Z. Humphrey in the foot.[16] The patrol hastily disengaged and withdrew to the perimeter, retrieving their wounded but leaving Childers behind.[17]

A noticeable decrease in Japanese activity on September 15 surprised even Gen. Vandegrift. Occasional stragglers took potshots at patrols or wandered into Marine positions. Numerous machine guns and mortars were found abandoned in the jungle, and after counting bodies and blood trails, Col. Clifton Cates estimated 200 Japanese dead in his regiment's sector alone.[18] When September 16 also passed in relative quiet, some Marines began to speculate that the latest attempt to take Henderson Field was over and that the Japanese were not just bested but soundly beaten. With reinforcements on the way—the 3rd Battalion, 2nd Marines, from Tulagi and the fresh 7th Marines from Samoa—the 1st Marine Division would soon number more than 19,000 men. Vandegrift would be able to complete a cordon defense around the airfield.

As the men dug gun emplacements, sighted artillery, and "virtually swore [the] new line into existence," Vandegrift shifted his gaze outside the perimeter.[19] Worried that holding static positions would encourage a siege mentality reminiscent of the Great War, the general ordered an "active defense" that would dominate the area around the perimeter with regular patrols.[20] The victory at Edson's Ridge, while welcome, illustrated the disturbing fact that the Japanese could advance a large, well-armed force uncomfortably close to the perimeter before being detected. Patrols, sometimes augmented by scouts—either locals or trained Marines—and ranging in size from a squad to several hundred became "Vandegrift's eyes and ears."[21]

The interior of Guadalcanal, with its considerable trails and obstacles, both natural and manmade, was indisputably Japanese terrain. Marines who had quickly learned to defend against Japanese incursions frequently found themselves in difficult situations when operating out in the jungle. Increasing patrol sizes amplified firepower, but taxed the abilities of officers and NCOs to retain control of their men. Trained scouts were occasionally available, but few line officers understood how to coordinate with them, and others were patently unwilling, as illustrated by Balester's experience with the uncooperative 3rd Battalion, 1st Marines.[22] Under such conditions, deficiencies in leadership and basic knowledge of scouting and patrolling became painfully evident. These shortcomings had to be solved the hard way.

Company "B," 1st Marines, would learn a harsh lesson in September, 1942.

When Capt. Rex Williams asked for volunteers to make a combat patrol up the Lunga River, he was not disappointed by the response.

The thirty-year-old South Carolinian was the newest face in Company "B," having taken command from 1Lt. Marshall T. Armstrong on August 24. A peacetime reservist called to active duty in the winter of 1940, Williams was well trained as an artilleryman and transport quartermaster, but had no experience leading an infantry company. The combat patrol might prove an opportunity to get some on-the-job training—and demonstrate that Williams was a worthy replacement for the well-regarded Armstrong.[23]

Volunteers ranged from old salts to green teenagers. Plat. Sgt. Leon Walter McStine was one of the most seasoned men in the company. He was born "Leon Minkstein" in Shamokin, Pennsylvania, on April 10, 1913; at the age of twenty, he moved to Brooklyn, anglicized his last name, and enlisted in the Marines. The Corps had been his home and his career ever since, and he had all the markings of a twenty-year man: service overseas in Cuba, expertise with weapons, high performance as a recruiter, and excellent character marks. Enlisted comrades called him "The Great One" and officer assessments bordered on effusive. "Good leader—stands for no nonsense—gets results without trouble," wrote one commanding officer. "His performance of duty has been outstanding," wrote another. "He is active physically and mentally, sober and industrious, an excellent leader [with] a high degree of initiative and a great sense of responsibility." Two months before landing on Guadalcanal, Lt. Armstrong opined that McStine was "a reliable, efficient, and forceful Non-Commissioned Officer.... He has a thorough knowledge of infantry weapons, and is an excellent instructor on the subject" and recommended promotion to Gunnery Sergeant.[24] McStine was not entirely single-minded, however; he was newly married, and Antoinette McStine was expecting their first baby in the coming weeks.

Sgt. George R. Greenlee was cut from the same khaki as McStine. Between his enlistment in 1938 and the attack on Pearl Harbor, Greenlee served as a recruit instructor at Parris Island, with Special Weapons in the 5th Marines and as a mortarman in the 7th Marines. The twenty-five-year-old Greenlee was also recently married and expecting a child. Other salty NCOs included Corporals Hans C. Jensen and George W. Compton, both "China hands" of five years' service. Volunteering came naturally to Compton, who believed in an emergency "you can be sure the Marines will be in the front and will do their best just as they have always done."[25]

Pvt. Robert Corwin was on the opposite end of the spectrum. He had barely finished his junior year of high school in Northport, New York, before enlisting; at seventeen, he was one of the youngest Marines in Company "B," and still felt that war was a "great adventure." He had a score to settle for a buddy killed at the Tenaru, and for a brother whose cruiser went down off Savo Island.[26] His close buddies, PFCs Charles F. Debele, Jr. and Ralph C. Ingerson, were only slightly older; both were recent high school graduates who put their lives on hold to find out what war was all about. "Freddie" Debele was well-known in Keansburg, New Jersey, where he delivered the *Plainfield Courier-News* to his neighbors and was a familiar face at school track meets and basketball games. Although Debele planned to become a toolmaker, classmates at Middletown Township High School predicted he would become an Army colonel. "Biff" Ingerson, a New Yorker, was an outstanding athlete at Randolph Central School, lettering in soccer, basketball, volleyball, and baseball; he was also a Boy Scout and an aspiring shutterbug. Now he was one of the best automatic riflemen in his platoon. "I'm feeling fine," he wrote a few days after landing on Guadalcanal, "and at the rate things are going I ought to be home soon.... More things have happened to me and I've seen more things than any other kid in town. Tell Bill [his younger brother] that this war is just like the old Indian fighting. It isn't bad at all."[27]

Many of the other junior Marines in Company "B" were just a few months removed from civilian life. PFC Herman R. Shirley was a "gung-ho" Alabama boy with three brothers in the service. PFC Leslie L. Rice was a varsity football star who also played semi-pro baseball, while PFC Morris "Quinn" Curry was an aspiring wrestler. Pvt. Riley D. Shockley, once a truck driver for a Chattanooga grocery, now followed in the footsteps of his grandfather, a Confederate Army veteran. Pvt. Frederick L. Secor of Newark, New Jersey, was a journeyman machinist. Pvt. Mickey A. Boschert wished to be back in Memphis in time to spend Christmas with his family—mostly his new wife. "Pray for me, Mother, that I may get to come home soon," he wrote.[28] These sentiments were echoed by Brooklyn-born PFC Elmer F. Garrettson, Jr. who told his family of a fateful premonition but concluded "I am not afraid. If it is God's will, I will be back with you someday."[29]

Despite these private feelings, morale and expectations were high on the morning of September 17. Corwin estimated that two-thirds of his company were anxious for a fight, and emphasized that every man on the patrol was a volunteer—although some were likely "volunteered" by NCOs or pressured by their buddies.[30]

Rex Williams' volunteers—the bulk of Company "B"—led the way from the perimeter, followed by a similar contingent from Company "A" under Capt. Charlie Brush. A composite platoon of riflemen from Company "D" and a headquarters detachment, including battalion commander Lt. Col. Leonard B. Cresswell, made up the balance of the patrol.[31] Cresswell wanted to advance up the western riverbank, keeping under the cover and concealment of the jungle. This was standard procedure: trails and clearings were obvious sites for ambushes and were to be avoided. However, the thick vegetation was difficult to navigate. "When you start through the jungle, you ain't going nowhere," explained Herman Shirley. Capt. Williams did not want to appear hesitant to close with the enemy, and chafed at the slow pace. "He said 'well, we'll go up the river,'" Shirley continued.[32] Gratefully, the lead platoon of Company "B" stepped down into the dry riverbed and the rest of the column followed suit. The stifling jungle air gave way to a more pleasant climate—"a clear, warm and sunny day like you get on Long Island in July or August," recalled Corwin, who glanced up to watch shark-nosed Army Airacobras buzzing overhead to strafe Japanese positions. The show of air superiority was a real confidence boost.[33]

PFC Francis J. Ziemba and his buddy, Pvt. Wilbur "Mack" McElvaine, were near the front of the column when the point squad captured a Japanese soldier. From the man's excited shouts and gestures, "it was easy to assume that ... he was trying to tell us there were more Japs further up the Lunga," wrote Ziemba. Pleased with this unexpected success, the Marines set off to investigate. They walked and sweated along the riverbank for another thirty minutes, lulled by the gentle rippling of the water and the warm day, draining their canteens as they went. Ziemba and Mack walked companionably along. "It never dawned on any of us that perhaps this Jap was leading us into a cleverly concealed trap."[34]

The Japanese sprang the ambush just after 3.30 p.m.

As they splashed across the Lunga, Robert Corwin and Charlie Debele ducked out of line to fill their canteens. A few Marines ahead of them on the eastern bank had the same idea. As Corwin watched, "the stillness was broken by a burst of fire. One of the two Marines just collapsed like a sack of wheat. The other hesitated for a moment, the machine gun spat again, and then he went down too. Neither of them made a sound."[35]

Six Japanese machine guns emplaced on the riverbanks opened fire on the startled Marines, dropping five men in just a few seconds. The shock of the sudden attack was bewildering. "There was firing all around us," said Pvt. Jack W. Morrison. "I looked around and felt something hit me in the side."

A bullet smashed through his arm and into his chest; Morrison yelped and fell into the bushes.[36] As the Americans scrambled to get out of the riverbed, more Japanese troops raced through the jungle to cut them off.[37]

"Everything happened out of a clear sky," recalled PFC Ziemba. "We soon discovered that we were in the middle of a circle of Japs and that our position was hopeless."[38] The 1st Platoon of Company "B" had walked into a perfect killing zone. "Come here, please," called the Japanese gunners, their accented English rising over the din of battle and the cries of the trapped men. "Come here, please."[39]

As the ambushed men fought to free themselves from the trap, Corwin's platoon rushed to the banks of a small island situated in the middle of the river. Pushing through the shoulder-high grass, they came across a strange sight: two unarmed Japanese, one lying under a blanket, the other kneeling beside him. "I shouted 'stand up, you're under arrest' or something equally as silly," admitted Corwin. The Japanese ignored him. Lacking time or inclination to deal with prisoners, Corwin hustled over to the eastern side of the island. He heard the "swoosh" of an American mortar and watched the proceedings with interest. "It was the first time I'd seen a mortar team in action," he recalled. "I could see smoke and dirt being thrown up where the mortars landed. After a while, the machine gun didn't fire anymore."[40]

The rest of the battalion stopped dead in its tracks. Brush's Company "A" was fording the Lunga when they "came under fire from a machine gun on a bend in the river." Caught in a vulnerable position, and mindful of being ambushed themselves, they hit the deck "strung out between logs, rocks, and other cover." Lt. Col. Cresswell's commanding presence intervened. Lighting a cigarette with a steady hand, he coolly issued a perfectly Marine Corps order: "Let's move out and eliminate those people." Duly impressed, Company "A" got into action. A mortar squad under Cpl. William L. Billingsley, Jr., sent three rounds arcing upriver, which "either sent [the Japanese] to meet their ancestors or helped them make up their minds to move."[41] The Marines managed to silence three enemy guns with mortar and automatic weapons fire, but the remaining three kept any would-be rescuers at bay.

As the mortars went to work, Capt. Brush summoned 2Lt. John Jachym, an energetic and capable officer with an outstanding patrol record, to find out what was happening at the point. Jachym led his platoon over to the Company "B" command post, where a discouraging scene was playing out: "four of the company officers wringing their hands over the possible fate of a rifle platoon that had been ambushed and was pinned in the dense undergrowth." Machine-gun fire and a near miss by a dud mortar round added to the dismay. In Jachym's opinion, "the demoralized B

Company officers were not about to commit themselves to bailing out the lost platoon."[42] He dispatched a runner back to Capt. Brush and waited with the indecisive officers, listening to the trapped platoon attempting to break free.

The stalemate continued until almost 6 p.m. Word of the patrol's predicament reached the 1st Marines' command post, and was forwarded to Division HQ for advice. The decision rendered was not a welcome one: disengage and withdraw. Dusk would be falling soon, and neither Regiment nor Division was willing to risk the balance of two companies to save a single platoon.[43] Pvt. Corwin recalled Capt. Brush shouting vainly that "some of his men had been trapped in the jungle by the Japs," but there was little the frustrated officer could do.[44] Unless something was done quickly, the ambushed men would be forfeit.

One Company "B" officer, 2Lt. Lawrence W. Smith, Jr., was not prepared to leave anyone behind. Pvt. Shirley recalled Smith's decision to "go up on the left-hand side and see if we can find out where that machine gun nest is, see if we can get them people out of the river down there."[45] Shirley, Charlie Debele, Fred Secor, and a handful of others followed Smith along a little path to the top of the riverbank, searching for a route around the machine guns. The remainder of the patrol prepared to return to the perimeter.

Pvt. Shirley was up front with Lt. Smith when, as he said, "all hell broke loose." They were in a room-sized clearing; bullets whipped overhead, but the enemy machine gun was well hidden. Some of Smith's men went down. "I want three volunteers," the lieutenant barked. "Go up that trail and find out where the fire's coming from." Pvt. Fred Secor, the nineteen-year-old machinist from Newark, stepped forward at once; so too did Charlie Debele.[46] Smith locked eyes with Shirley and made an emphatic hand motion. Shirley knew what that meant—"Go! Hit 'em, boy!" Obediently, he followed Debele and Secor up the trail. The staccato chatter of a Nambu cut through the air, and the two New Jersey Marines went down hard. Shirley, unscathed by pure chance ("why I didn't get it, I'll never know") spun around and hightailed it back to his platoon. Smith pounced on the retreating private—what had happened to Debele and Secor? "They got hit," was all Shirley could gasp.

"Well," said Smith, "let's get out of here."[47]

The men did not need to be told twice. Robert Corwin was shocked to see "the rescue squad came running back, led by a sergeant, his face hot and flushed with fear." The panicked NCO told of the second ambush and broke the news that several more Marines, including Charlie Debele, were down. Corwin immediately volunteered to go back up the river, and Ralph Ingerson grabbed his BAR. They joined a group of eight other Marines, heading out to rescue the would-be rescuers.[48] "There was no sound as we made our way cautiously through the thick green foliage," Corwin said. The lack of gunfire was disconcerting: evidently, the Japanese had finished off the group in the riverbed, too. If any Marines were still alive out there, they must not be in any condition to fight back.

After fifteen minutes, Corwin spied a small clearing about 20 feet in diameter. It was a horrific spectacle. Seven Marines lay motionless, spread around the fringes of the little clearing. And there, on the ground, was his friend.[49]

"That you, Charlie?" he called.

Debele lifted his head a little. He was shockingly pale. "Yeah…"

"Don't you worry, we'll get you out of here."

One moment Corwin was kneeling over Debele; the next he was down on the ground, wondering what hit him. "My helmet fell off, and I dropped my rifle," he later recalled. "The bullet had gone through my shoulder near the neck and out below the shoulder blade." He could hear nothing, but saw Ralph Ingerson hiding in the bushes, waving frantically, "get up and run out of there." Corwin managed a few steps before the enemy rifleman fired again. The .25-caliber bullet drilled through the fleshy part of his leg and hit Ingerson in the throat. Corwin lay still, afraid to move. All was quiet except for Ingerson's dying coughs; when those finally ceased, Corwin realized he was truly alone.

After a few moments, Corwin decided that bullets were preferable to bayonets. He lurched to his feet and, despite his leg wound, "took off the trail so quick a jackrabbit would not have passed me," he said. "I shouted 'B Company! B Company!' and after a few minutes I caught up with the last of our group." His company was already withdrawing down the river. Numb from pain, shock, and morphine, Corwin lay back on a stretcher. "I made the rest of the trip on my back, watching the stars come out as night fell."[50]

Meanwhile, Pvt. Jack Morrison was fading in and out of consciousness. He had had the good fortune to fall wounded into some bushes that lined the narrow trail, and as bullets whined overhead and struck down his buddies, managed to wedge himself under cover until only his feet stuck out in the open. Like Corwin, Morrison noted the sudden, ominous silence that permeated the area as soon as the firing stopped. The survivors of his group, if indeed there were any, melted into the undergrowth. Morrison could see the motionless form of Pvt. Harry Dunn and hear the muffled groans of a Marine behind a log a few yards up the trail.

The Japanese soldier appeared as if from nowhere, his camouflage blending perfectly with the surrounding jungle. He ran swiftly down the track, leaped over the log, and with a swift motion ran his bayonet through the wounded Marine before disappearing once more. Morrison wiggled farther into the bushes, clenching his teeth to keep from crying out. To his horror, more Japanese appeared, laughing and calling to each other while rifling Marine bodies for supplies and souvenirs. Even after they departed, Morrison lay still as death, too scared and hurt to move, waiting for someone to come to his rescue.[51]

Cresswell's battalion stumbled into their bivouac at 8.30 p.m., so utterly exhausted and upset that they were placed in regimental reserve.[52] The optimists among them believed they had killed some fifty Japanese during the patrol; the realists pointed to the fact that twenty-seven of their own men were missing in action. PFC Robert H. Cline of Company "B" nursed a slight wound while Pvts. George Lundgren (Company "A") and Bob Corwin were rushed off to the Division field hospital. Neither would fight again. Corwin's leg wound was relatively minor, but the bullet through his shoulder caused partial paralysis in his arm. He was sent back to the States and spent some time on the War Bond circuit, a genuine hero of Guadalcanal.

Survivors from Company "B" began to trickle in the next morning. Corporal James Serroka, Pvt. John J. Ell, and Pvt. Robert J. Mitchell reported in at 8 a.m. on September 18; Cpl. Eugene Robertson, Jr., and Pvt. George Hill appeared at 3 p.m. Plat. Sgt. Edward L. Clark turned up on September 19 and was hospitalized.[53] Each of these men doubtless had an exciting escape story to tell, but none proved so harrowing as that of Jack Morrison and Harry Dunn.

Morrison passed out after evading the Japanese at the ambush site. He was awakened after dark by a heavy hand across his mouth and a voice whispering "Don't move. It's me, Harry Dunn." The wiry gunner from Springfield, Ohio, had escaped injury earlier in the day, concealing himself in an abandoned Japanese foxhole. Alternately playing dead— even, allegedly, as the Japanese stripped his equipment—and fighting off intruders, he was preparing to slip back to Marine lines when he discovered Morrison, unconscious but alive. Dunn bandaged Morrison's chest with a shirt, then crawled around the bodies of their dead friends looking for canteens. Finding none, he crawled to the Lunga but fled after spotting Japanese soldiers lounging on the bank. The two Marines spent the next day hiding at the ambush site battling thirst, pain, and swarms of flies and ants attracted by the moldering flesh of the dead. Only after dark on September 18 did they make it to the Lunga. Dunn half-carried, half-dragged Morrison all the way to the river's mouth, where they were discovered by a friendly outpost just after dawn on September 19. Both men were hospitalized, but ultimately survived; Dunn later received the Navy Cross for rescuing Jack Morrison.[54]

These successful escapes kindled some hope in the company's record keepers. Seventeen Marines and one Navy corpsman were optimistically entered on the rolls as "missing in action" rather than killed. As the days passed, though, it became clear that nobody else was coming back. Rumors began to spread through the regiment. Pvt. James Donahue of Company "H" heard that one officer lost his job over the debacle. "He is being sent back to the States and has been relieved of his command," Donahue wrote in his diary. "He holds the record for leading men into ambush. He lost 18 men the first time. If you can't produce in this outfit, out you go."[55]

At 6.45 a.m. on September 25, one week after the Lunga ambush, Maj. Marion Fawcett led Company "B," reinforced by two platoons from Companies "A" and "C," north towards Edson's Ridge and passed through the front line. "Mission: burial party," noted the battalion's war diary. At 10.30 a.m., they arrived at the scene of "our recent engagement" and began searching for their missing friends. Seventeen of them were found where they fell, and individually identified by members of Company "B." Only Pvt. Mickey Boschert was missing, but Fawcett received a report from a Raider patrol that mentioned burying a lone body in the vicinity and concluded that must have been Boschert. Remains were searched for personal effects and the area scoured for weapons: surprisingly, the Japanese had left behind a Browning machine gun, a pistol, four BARs, and seven rifles—a veritable arsenal.[56] This done, the grave digging commenced.

This was an intensely personal moment. Francis Ziemba knew where to find Wilbur McElvaine; "Mack" had died after volunteering to get help for the stranded men. "I asked for and received permission to personally bury Wilbur's remains," he wrote to the McElvaine family, "and I'm not ashamed to admit that the tears in my eyes at the time of his burial were real and many.... Mack died a hero's death.... In my own mind and heart, Wilbur will be forever remembered as the one to whom I owe my life."[57] Charlie Debele's buddies stuck a cross in the ground; other groups likely did the same. After a week, the heat, humidity, and indigenous life of Guadalcanal rendered the physical remains of dead friends a gruesome sight. Maj. Fawcett noted that "due to the advanced decomposition of all bodies, it was impossible to ascertain whether or not wounded men had been mistreated or bayoneted." Pickets spotted three Japanese loitering on the left bank of the Lunga while the burial went on, but the American mission was "not primarily combat," and the Japanese had no desire to tangle with a reinforced company. Both sides watched each other warily and eventually withdrew.[58] The patrol returned to bivouac at 4 p.m. after a physically and emotionally draining day. Chaplain Robert M. Olton held a memorial service on the morning of September 27, "in memory of our departed comrades ... buried on the 'field of battle.'"[59]

While the ambush on the Lunga was the single bloodiest patrol action since the Goettge massacre, it was also "only the latest in a series of patrolling failures." It would never attain any degree of notoriety or publicity, coming as it did on heels of the tactically significant and hero-heavy battle of Edson's Ridge. However, it did have an immediate impact on the conduct of the battle. Historian Richard Frank notes that "To Vandegrift, this episode … highlighted the need to cultivate men with a special aptitude in jungle craft and navigation." Three men meeting these requirements were selected from each rifle battalion and combined into a special Scout Sniper Detachment under the tutelage of Col. William J. Whaling, a "highly capable woodsman and one of the finest marksmen in the Corps." Training with the "Whaling Group" was a highly desirable temporary assignment; "men returning to their units spread the warrior gospel" and "combat morale and effectiveness rose continually despite losses." As scouts grew more adept, line company officers grew more willing to let "the weirdest characters you've ever seen" accompany patrols.[60] Risks were never entirely eliminated, but never again would an ambush claim so many lives.

The misfortune of Company "B" may have advanced Marine tactics, but unfortunately did little to progress the Americans' ability to recover bodies lost beyond the perimeter. The eighteen ambush victims were officially reported as killed in action by "gunshot wounds" at 10.30 a.m. on September 25—this is the time when they were found, and their fates verified, rather than the precise moment of death—and "buried [the] same date in the field." Their personal effects were collected and processed. Leon McStine's belongings—a keyring, campaign medals, and a collar clasp—were found folded in a handkerchief. Charlie Debele's mother received his Benrus wristwatch, cigarette lighter, and a package of letters and photos.[61] Notifications were sent to families, although in at least two cases these were misleading; the families of Morris Curry and Leslie Rice were informed their boys were missing in action, only to be corrected a few days later. The telegram to PhM3c James F. Pierce's family was delayed: they received returned mail stamped "DECEASED" before the official notification of his death.[62] McStine's widow, cousin, and creditors wrote letters of inquiry to Headquarters, Marine Corps; each received the stock answer that he was dead and more details would be divulged in time.

The Lunga ambush was the worst day of the war so far for 1st Battalion, 1st Marines. In a single afternoon, they suffered more than half of the total number of KIAs they would lose in the entire campaign. Company "B" alone had nineteen men killed during their tour on Guadalcanal; eighteen of those were lost on September 17, 1942.[63] When they departed the island in December 1942, the battalion had more men buried in the field than in the cemetery. It was also one of the most extreme instances of the standing policy to "inter locally temporarily all bodies recovered, if practicable."

Only the 1st Battalion, 5th Marines, after being mauled at the Third Battle of the Matanikau in early November, would conduct a more extensive field burial.

It appears that no deliberate search for the site was undertaken, and the graves remained undisturbed for more than two years until someone stumbled across the graves in October 1944, and a Graves Registration team was dispatched.[64] Morris Curry and Elmer Garrettson were identified and reinterred in the ANMC on October 5, followed by Ralph Ingerson, Charlie Debele, and PFC Carl J. Gorczysky on October 6. Wilbur "Mack" McElvaine and George Compton were laid to rest the next day, along with a set of remains labeled as X-117—eventually identified as corpsman James Pierce. Hans C. Jensen was reinterred in January 1945; evidently, he was found separately from the rest.[65] Thus nine of the missing men were identified, leaving the others unaccounted for.

Why these nine and not the others? This question may never be satisfactorily answered. One of the more frustrating aspects of researching unaccounted for personnel are the gaps in the historical record. As has been mentioned, a lack of original documentation might be the result of oversight, ignorance, or incompetence on the part of the original record keepers. When the sources closest to the event are inaccurate, even by a few feet, a miss is as good as a mile. It happened countless times in the 1940s when the scars of war were just starting to fade. With each passing year, the job of responsibly reconstructing that event becomes immense, and the margin for mistakes grows exponentially

In many more cases, however, individuals were inclined toward exactness. Maj. Marion Fawcett may stand as an example. Record keeping was a primary responsibility of a battalion executive officer, and Fawcett—a professional officer and Annapolis graduate—was thoroughly steeped in proper protocols. Professional duties aside, it would be unlikely, even unthinkable, that Fawcett would have led Company "B" back to an area of such terrible trauma unprepared to record every detail of what he saw and where he saw it. This he did, in a full page typed report augmented with a pair of enclosed overlays. One showed the exact route to and from the ambush site; the other not only diagrammed the graves but "shows the exact location of the bodies in relation to one another." As an added measure of caution, he plotted the coordinates more precisely than most: (59.65–112.35) on his battalion's map. Maj. Fawcett performed his duty to the letter.[66]

Somehow, this document survived the culling process that determined which of the countless reports generated during the war would be preserved in the National Archives at College Park. It is tucked away in the back of a folder containing the battalion's war diary. Unfortunately, the overlays are no longer present. Drawn as they were on thin tracing paper, map overlays were fragile at the best of times, and they may have long since been destroyed. Or—equally tantalizing and frustrating—they may be elsewhere in the labyrinthine holdings of the archive system, misfiled, misplaced, or reassigned over the years. Divorced from the context of their accompanying report, they may appear as worthless diagrams rather than the answer to the mystery. They may yet be found someday, but until then, researchers will need to examine other sources.

Reconstructing the narrative using eyewitness accounts and a sample of other period files may shed some light on the issue. The memories of Robert Corwin and Herman Shirley suggest that there were two significant castastrophies on September 17: the initial ambush site, which both observed at a distance, and the small clearing where the rescue attempts were stopped. If there were two distinct places where heavy casualties occurred, there may have been two corresponding burial sites. Call them the "Ambush Group" (including Dunn and Morrison) and the "Clearing Group" (including Corwin, Shirley, Debele, Secor, Ingerson, and Smith).

Finding the ambush site is the first hurdle. Thanks to Maj. Fawcett, map coordinates are available, but we must recall that the Major could only work with the materials he had at hand. His battalion was using Map No. 101, one of the earliest maps issued in the field on Guadalcanal. A surviving example held by the Archives Branch of the Marine Corps History Division is dated August 18, 1942. Unfortunately for researchers, the map's detail (which is questionable at best) extends only about two hundred yards south of what we now known as "Edson's Ridge." Maj. Fawcett's coordinates, (59.65–112.35), are about 2,000 yards south and west—smack in the middle of a blank square. Corpsman Pierce's Official Military Personnel File contains a map overlay (proof that some, indeed, survive) but it shows only his grave, bracketed by coordinates, on an otherwise featureless sheet. Still, this is another important clue. When placed on Map 101, the overlay roughly maps to the location in Fawcett's report. Double confirmation is a good place to start; although the researcher is still confronted by the blank space.

When Company "B" walked into the ambush, Map 101 was in the process of being replaced by Map 104, a more detailed (though still questionably accurate) map spanning a much larger area. The Lunga River is extended, snaking down the page with a multitude of turns before the drawing tapers off into a muddle of blobs indicating jungle and foliage. Roughly superimposing Map 101 over Map 104 results in an approximate location just off the eastern bank of the Lunga, coordinates (80.30–196.30) on the newer map. Here we must mention a seemingly minor but potentially crucial omission in Maj. Fawcett's report: perhaps ignorant of the coming cartographic change, he neglected to specify which map he was using.

Additional details about the location—and, importantly, the terrain features around it—can be extracted from statements of those who were there. "I don't know how far we went," recalled Herman Shirley, "but the river made a little left-hand turn, and when we got around there a machine gun opened up."[67] In 1992, Robert Corwin reported hearing the ambush at a point "perhaps half a mile south of our lines;" in his 2002 interview, he stated "we made contact about five miles south of our perimeter on the east side of the Lunga." Accounts of Dunn and Morrison's escape describe distances up to two and a half miles.[68] The "small island" which appears in Corwin's narrative was evidently noteworthy: a 1943 newspaper article about the event mentioned "strong Jap positions on the shores of a nearby island."[69] Although the distances vary, the natural landmarks together are another piece of the puzzle. Search up (which is to say south) the Lunga River until it turns left, creating a mid-river island.

While period maps show many turns in the river, neither Map 101 nor Map 104 depicts an island. With a rough idea of the area and notable landmarks, the researcher can turn to modern satellite imagery of Guadalcanal. Maj. Fawcett's coordinates place the location a few hundred yards from the village of Mbelaha. There, the Lunga makes a turn—to the left, if facing along the Marine line of advance—and forking around a substantial island, the only one in the vicinity. The eastern riverbank describes a significant upward slope, making it an ideal place for an ambush. While the naturally changing shape of the river and reliance on notoriously inaccurate 1940s maps prevents pinpoint accuracy, this is almost certainly the approximate location of the massacre.[70]

Now one can attempt to orient the two groups to each other. In the opening moments of the ambush, Corwin saw two Marines "on the opposite bank come down towards the water's edge" only to be killed one after the other. (Corwin was crossing from west to east; "opposite" likely refers to his destination.) Herbert Merillat's *The Island* suggests that the Marines were actually down in the riverbed when the attack occurred: "The patrol was making its way up the right [eastern] bank of the Lunga River.... Suddenly six machine guns, in position on both sides of the river, opened up on the leading elements of the patrol."[71] Herman Shirley recalled "a bunch of the First Platoon got in ... a little place in the riverbed" and said the Lunga "at that time of year didn't have no water running down it, just a little stream."[72]

More sensational references to the Ambush Group's location come from secondary sources describing Dunn and Morrison's escape; all focus around the pair's desperate search for water. *Leatherneck Magazine* set the scene "on the bank of the Lunga River. Water was only a few feet away," while the 1992 veteran's history depicted Dunn crawling "several hundred yards" to reach water.[73] The most exciting account, penned by Ted Shane, has Dunn hot-footing up hill and down dale and through the very middle of a Japanese bivouac before diving headlong into the Lunga and swimming underwater to safety—all with Morrison in tow. (Shane, a former Hollywood screenwriter, peppered his account with imaginative movie-ready banter: "Jesus, Harry, how'd I get here?" "You flew, you boot. Didn't you know we'd joined the Air Corps?")[74] If the ambush did not actually take place in the riverbed, it certainly seems to have been close by.

It is known that Capt. Williams had his men moving along the riverbed instead of through the jungle; for trained Japanese gunners, the lead platoon would have been like fish in a barrel. Lt. Lawrence Smith would have known better than to rush his men straight into the crossfire. Smith's sensible decision to attempt a flanking maneuver was reported by Herman Shirley, who said his platoon went up a trail on the left-hand (which is to say eastern) side of the river.[75] Smith probably wished to gain a height advantage on the suspected ambush site; unfortunately, he chose a trail that led into a Japanese fire lane. It is likely, therefore, that the Clearing Group is some distance to the east of the Ambush Group, somewhere up the riverbank.

Once again, without precise coordinates, one can only make an educated guess as to the location of the two groups. However, the sources seem to suggest that the Ambush Group, consisting of part of the 1st Platoon and a machine-gun section, were down at a low elevation near the river, possibly the riverbed itself. And there is a corresponding likelihood that, if they were buried where they fell, the markers or the bodies themselves were washed away once the rainy season returned to Guadalcanal.

The third challenge is to determine who died where. The clearing claimed the lives of Debele, Secor, Ingerson, and an unknown number of others; a 1943 newspaper account of Corwin's adventure mentioned "seven of [his] buddies dead and spread around the fringes of the small clearing," while Corwin in 1992 recalled only that "several Marines lay apparently dead."[76] Pierce may well have been among them; a corpsman's skills would have been badly needed by the rescue party, and his map overlay suggests that he was farther up the riverbank.

The Clearing Group accounted for at least some of the remains recovered by Graves Registration in October 1944. Ingerson, Debele, and Gorczycki were the first and, possibly, the most readily identified. Debele at the very least appears to have had a well-defined field burial; the GRS Form No. 1 (Report of Interment) in his OMPF states "Body disinterred from isolated burial. Identity established through name on cross marking the grave." Ingerson was similarly identified; Gorczycki's difficult surname was rendered as "Gorszyzski" and no first name was given.[77] Pierce, McElvaine, and Compton were found around the same time and buried the following day. Because Pierce had no legible marker or means of identification, he was the only one of the six not immediately identified. Remnants of medical equipment were found with his remains; this clue, combined with "comparison of physical and dental characteristics, and by facts and circumstances of death and recovery" led to his eventual identification in May 1950.[78]

An additional clue in the files of Debele and Pierce may also indicate a distinction between the two groups. In 1942, Debele's body was found with "1 package of letters; 1 billfold containing 51¢, personal papers & photographs; 1 watch, wrist (Benrus); 1 lighter, cigarette." Besides his medical equipment, Pierce's remains in 1944 included "1 wrist watch, 1 ring, 1 Jap coin." Evidently their bodies were not stripped for souvenirs, as Morrison claimed to witness in the Ambush Group. By contrast, Plat. Sgt. McStine's few effects may suggest that anything of greater value— from jewelry to identification tags—wound up as a Japanese trophy. Fawcett's men also located a surprising number of Marine weapons, including a light machine gun. It was highly unusual for the Japanese to ignore abandoned American weapons. (These may have been deliberately disabled by Marines; of four BARs found, only one had its trigger group present, suggesting that the rest had been deliberately sabotaged.)

A final word on the Clearing Group. Fred Secor from New Jersey was, according to Herman Shirley, killed in the same burst of fire as Charlie Debele. Like the others in the clearing he was reported "body found and buried in the field," and a "package of letters and photos" was retrieved. However, Secor was never reported buried in the ANMC, and to this day remains on the list of non-recovered. His marker, if he had one, may have been lost or destroyed, or he may have been buried apart from the rest and simply missed by the Graves Registration team. As in many cases, the news that his remains could not be found was a doubly hard blow to a family still trying to process their son's death. "I certainly hope you will do all that is possible to find my boy's body," wrote Mrs. Florence Secor in 1945, "after all he gave his life for this country and I feel he should rest here.... It would help me a lot to know just what did happen.... My husband died Nov. 3 1945 indirectly [related] to the loss of the boy, so I would appreciate any news you could get for me."[78] None was forthcoming.

Determining the identities of the Ambush Group is more difficult by dint of the fact that there were fewer survivors from the trapped point of the patrol. Aside from Jack Morrison and Harry Dunn, no account mentions a Marine from the Ambush Group by name. Their numbers are likewise unknown, though the anniversary history of the battle (to which Morrison contributed) references a "ten-man patrol." Presumably, this refers to trapped men only; a platoon with attached machine gunners would have numbered closer to forty. Francis Ziemba's account indicates that others may have escaped:

> We soon discovered we were in the middle of a circle of Japs and that our position was hopeless unless we could get word of our predicament to the main body of marines on the beach. The commanding officer had no alternative but to call for a volunteer whose job it would be to slip through the Jap circle and reach our lines on the beach to get help. Wilbur was the very first man to volunteer.[79]

If Ziemba is correct (and truthful—the account, written a year after the fact, was expressly intended to console Wilbur McElvaine's family, and Ziemba admitted "past events are kind of mixed up in my mind") then some unknown number of Marines must have managed to escape from the trap to fight another day. The remainder were left to their fate.

A final coincidence arises: of the nine unaccounted for, only Secor can be convincingly placed with the Clearing Group. When one adds the two survivors, Dunn and Morrison, to the remaining eight—McStine, Greenlee, Rice, Boschert, Kuhl, Lilly, Luecking, and Shockley—the "ten-man patrol" figure looks much more convincing.

In September 1947, the 604th Quartermaster Graves Registration Company went out in search of the men from Company "B." They were provided with a map overlay, but it did them no good. Whoever prepared the sketches used Maj. Marion Fawcett's original coordinates but captioned them "Map 104" instead of "Map 101." The resulting discrepancy set the site miles outside the zone of Marine operations on Guadalcanal. A radiogram for additional details returned only the vague information that the men "were believed killed in the area between the Tenaru and Nalibmbu [sic.] Rivers." This was not only wildly inaccurate, but a huge area to cover. Nevertheless, three teams spent four fruitless days trudging from the Tenaru to the Malimbiu at Koli Point, investigating old foxholes and possible graves. They returned empty-handed, reporting "negative results." After "careful consideration," the nine cases were declared non-recoverable and were closed.[81] Despite Maj. Fawcett's careful attention to detail, erroneous information led the 604th astray, and they never came close to the river bend where nine Marines may still lie in temporary graves.

The remains of George W. Compton, Hans C. Jensen, Morris Q. Curry, Charles F. Debele, Jr., Elmer F. Garrettson, Jr., Carl J. Gorczycki, Ralph C. Ingerson, Wilbur McElvaine, and James F. Pierce were recovered from the field and identified between 1944 and 1950. They have since been returned to their families.

As of 2018, the remains of Leon W. McStine, George R. Greenlee, Leslie L. Rice, Mickey A. Boschert, Philip S. Kuhl, John R. Lilly, Bernard J. Luecking, Frederick L. Secor, and Riley D. Shockley have not been accounted for.

Ghosts on the Trail:
September 24–25, 1942

We're marching along merrily on our way when baby! everything lets loose around us as dusk comes. The Japs had ambushed us. They were all around us, in the trees, dug into foxholes, firing machine guns, snipers picking away at us, and mortars in the rear tossing shells into our midst. It was hell.[1]

Walter Bodt, Company "C," 7th Marines

Willie Rowe, or someone who sounded a lot like Willie, was crying in the darkness.

PFC Gerald White could not blame Willie. He felt a bit like crying himself. His battalion of the 7th Marines left the Lunga perimeter full of fight, ready to prove they were no Johnny-come-lately laggards but the warriors who would turn the tide on Guadalcanal. Now they were a "weary and dejected band" dug in on a nameless hill overlooking an unfamiliar stream, an anonymous location with no known landmarks save those they named themselves.[2] The field where Fuller found the cooking fire; where Chesty placed their guns; the tree where Goble hid; the trail where Randolph died. Unremarkable places, except that men bled for them. They could not even be placed on a map; they lay somewhere below a blank white expanse unhelpfully labeled "CLOUD."[3]

White could not care less about maps at the moment. His head was throbbing. When the bullets were flying and Col. Puller yelled for a machine gun squad, White responded on the double, as one did when "Chesty" raised his voice. His crew put down a base of fire as the riflemen advanced, milled about, retreated. For his troubles, he had been shot in the helmet, the bullet punching through the steel shell and fiber liner to run a gouge through his scalp. He would live, the corpsmen said, but it still hurt like hell and though he was exhausted it kept him from sleeping.[4]

On another nameless hill, some 300 yards away, were White's Japanese counterparts, machine gunners whose fire stopped a whole battalion. A few yards closer were the bodies of "Eddie" Edwinson and Manuel Pimentel. Closer still were the wounded who made it partway back, anxiously awaiting their buddies who even now were searching for them in the dark. Just a few yards away was Willie Rowe. Rescuers zeroed in on his cries. "Leave me alone," the wounded man gasped. "I'm going to die where I am."[5] His buddies disagreed, rolled him onto a stretcher, and carried him up the hill where Doc Schuster was working his way through half a platoon's worth of casualties.

Willie Rowe would die by daylight and join nine of his comrades in field graves in the foothills of Mount Austen.

Samoa seemed like an age ago, Stateside like another life.

The men of the 1st Battalion, 7th Marines, were ready for action—or thought they were. When word of an imminent deployment reached their camp at New River, North Carolina, sick Marines were "miraculously" healed, and two would-be deserters experienced a sudden change of heart.[6] They received the best equipment, the best personnel, and the best motivation from their commander, a formidable hard-charger named Lewis Burwell Puller. A month of sailing brought them to the unfamiliar shores of Upolu, the island they would garrison and fortify into a bulwark of the Pacific. They dug trenches, moved supplies, traded cigarettes for coconuts, and waited for an attack that never came.

Samoan duty suited some Marines just fine. Gerald Pendergast White, a somewhat reluctant warrior from Hutchinson, Minnesota, much preferred reading *Harper's* and *The New Yorker* to long marches and endless inspections. While he prided himself on taking everything the Corps could dish out, he was "thoroughly, even proudly reconciled to never becoming a first-rate soldier" and frequently went AWOL in search of local delicacies and the grave of Robert Louis Stevenson.[7] Pvt. Leland DeRocher enjoyed camping on landscaped polo grounds where there were "pineapple and coconuts ... also fresh water to bathe in. We played baseball and were allowed two cans of beer a day."[8] Even the "Old Man" Puller enjoyed a game or two, PFC Robert Cornely remembered, and "got in there and played like a kid himself."[9]

Lt. Col. Puller had not come to Samoa to play ball. The famously aggressive "Chesty," whose nickname bespoke his physical stature and pugnacious nature, found Samoa more purgatory than paradise. Commissioned in 1918—before many of the officers and men in his battalion were born—Puller was a storied "coconut warrior" who fought Haitian Cacos and Nicaraguan Sandinistas. He earned two Navy Crosses in the Banana Wars, did two tours in Shanghai, and once commanded the 2nd Battalion, 4th Marine Regiment. Puller fully expected to be knocking down the doors of the Imperial Palace in August 1942; instead, he garrisoned a backwater post while the rest of the 1st Marine Division fought on Guadalcanal.

Garrison duty notwithstanding, Chesty enforced a punishing training routine of forced marches and field exercises. As months passed and the 7th Marines came no closer to combat, the rough training created some enmity. Puller was "occasionally ruthless" to his junior officers; his communications chief, Capt. Joseph Griffith, complained that "this lousy outfit has failed completely in giving the men anything to look forward to … [they] just don't give a particular damn about anything."[10] Some tried to impress Puller, but failed; one captain who berated his men for poor performance on a march incurred the "Old Man's" wrath and found himself transferred out of the battalion.[11] Others, however, showed genuine promise as well as enthusiasm for serving under a *bona fide* war hero. First Lieutenant Alvin Chester Cockrell, Jr., was one of Puller's protégés. At twenty-three years old, Cockrell was making the first real strides of a Marine Corps career that began in a platoon leader's class in 1937, his sophomore year at Ole Miss. After earning his degree and his commission in 1940, Cockrell began the long, slow climb of a junior officer in the peacetime Marine Corps, earning positive if somewhat unenthusiastic praise from his company and battalion commanders of the 1st Marine Division. This changed when he met Chesty Puller. The gruff Virginian took an immediate shine to the young lieutenant, noting that despite a "violent temper" he would still be glad to have Chester Cockrell under his command. "I believe he will make a fine combat officer."

Cockrell's temper bested him on one memorable occasion. A group of enlisted Marines enjoying liberty at the White Owl Tavern near Kinston, North Carolina met an outgoing man dressed in civilian clothes who proceeded to "associate with them in conversation and drinking." The conversation became heated, somebody threw a punch, and the Military Police were summoned to the scene. The "civilian"—Cockrell, out of uniform—was ejected from the tavern, where he picked a second fight with 2Lt. Monson McCarty, another officer in his battalion. Both men were hauled before their regimental commander, roundly scolded, and suspended from duty. Such a brawl might have ended two promising careers, but Puller's recommendation kept both officers at their posts.[12] Cockrell would soon have a chance to prove that Puller's trust had not been misplaced.

The battalion's Samoan sojourn ended in September 1942, with the receipt of movement orders for Guadalcanal. Excitement rapidly changed to the abject boredom of shipboard life, as USS *President Adams* sat at anchor for several days before sailing for the Solomon Islands. Even Gerry White was anxious to be ashore and in action. Like many of his comrades, he ruminated on the causes of war, the prospect of death, and how he would fare under fire. "Noble thoughts ought, I suppose, to be filling my mind," mused White, "but I find instead rather grim opinions on the folly and stupidity of warfare."[13]

The *Adams,* along with the rest of Transport Division Two, arrived off Kukum at 5.50 a.m. on September 18. Many of the sailors were making their second trip to Guadalcanal; their lurid stories of dive bombers, sunken cruisers, and stranded Gyrenes were "not a pretty tale to hear." (Marines countered with pointed comments about the Navy turning tail and abandoning the "First Maroon Division.") Rivalries aside, the transport sailors were intent on making good for the debacle of the August landings. The first squads of the 7th Marines stepped onto the Kukum beach at 7 a.m.: when the transports hauled anchor at 6 p.m., they had not only put the entire regiment and its equipment ashore, but also the 5th Defense Battalion, thousands of barrels of aviation gas, hundreds of tons of rations and ammunition, tools and construction equipment, and medical supplies.[14] "This was undreamed-of wealth," said Merrill Twining. "We made the most of it. All hands turned to…. Half rations ended that night."[15] The heavy overcast, nature's own deterrent to marauding Japanese aircraft, was more than welcome.

This impressive logistical feat was overshadowed by some of the "folly and stupidity" that bothered Pvt. White. Sailors and Marines worked at a frantic pace, knowing full well that the Japanese controlled the seas. Sgt. Joe Goble, an NCO with Company "B", 7th Marines, was toiling with his squad when "at about 10:30 a.m. word passed down the beach that at exactly 11:00 a.m. each day the Japs would hit us with an air raid. We got jumpy!" As the clock ticked down to "Tojo Time," Navy gunners began scanning the cloudy skies. Reports of exploding bombs and friendly destroyers shelling targets inland added to the tension. Suddenly, the gong-like General Quarters alarm echoed across the water. A single low-flying aircraft appeared out of the overcast; the gunners on the *President Hayes* opened fire, followed by those on the *Adams* and the *President Jackson.*

Sgt. Goble watched as "the plane banked to the right to try to escape the fire, but it was too late. The engine began smoking, and the pilot made a 5- or 6-mile circle up past the Matanikau River and back—to crash just offshore in front of us."[16] Pvt. White, whose Company "A" was then disembarking from the *Adams,* had a ringside seat. "It was an American, not a Jap plane," he noted in his diary. "The pilot of the plane that was shot down was rescued.... Shot in the leg but rumor has him expected to recover."[17] Not everyone recognized the mistake: Lt. Herbert Merillat wrote that "the stars on the plane's wings were plainly visible, but the newcomers refused to believe the plane was ours. When the poor devil crashed into the water, a great cheer went up from the apes on the beach, who seconds before had stampeded into the palms."[18] The aircraft was a Douglas Dauntless dive-bomber belonging to VMSB-232. Second Lieutenant Leland Evan Thomas, a promising young pilot recently recommended for the Distinguished Flying Cross, was returning from an anti-sub patrol when the friendly ships shot him down. His radioman, PFC Edward Eades, was plucked from the water, but Thomas went down with his plane.[19] (Later, it was learned that the Japanese planned to send twenty-seven bombers and thirty-seven Zeros against the convoy, but were foiled by the same bad weather that doomed Lt. Thomas.)[20]

As the new arrivals marched up to the airfield, they passed dozens of Marines heading the other way. The remnants of the 1st Parachute Battalion were being evacuated, along with those wounded, exhausted, and "too lean" after a more than a month on the 'Canal.[21] PFC Charles M. Jacobs remembered a brief exchange with a veteran unit. "The group coming out hollered 'where you guys from, what are ya?' We said, 'We're A/1/7, what are you?'" On an impulse, Jacobs asked after a sergeant named Mihalek, the grandson of one of his father's employees. "Some guy hollers 'he got killed last night.' That was the first real meaning of what a war is."[22]

The Imperial Japanese Navy reinforced the lesson that night. Frustrated at missing the transports, a cruiser and several destroyers threw shells at the airfield. "They gave us a real circus that night," said Cpl. Walter Bodt (C/1/7). The infamous aerial nuisance "Washing Machine Charlie" dropped blinding flares, "making the whole goddamn grove bright as day." PFC Jacobs was "so scared my knees were knocking... that was the first time in my life that I was ever petrified." Gerald White was also "thoroughly frightened," yet managed to convince himself that friendly artillery was responsible for the chaos. Marines who had earlier been too tired for digging developed an intense interest in foxhole construction. A 5-inch shell landed 15 feet from Joe Goble but failed to explode. "I got the most rude awakening you ever saw," said PFC Richard Greer (A/1/7). "A fourteen-inch shell came in and burst in that coconut grove—I was laying on my side digging, then! That was the only night for the next four months they ever caught me without a foxhole."[23]

"People don't realize that when you get shelled, you have no place to go," explained PFC Ed Poppendick (D/1/7). "You're trying to dig a hole, and you can't.... That shrapnel, it's razor sharp. When it hits you, you're going to feel it." Poppendick's buddy, PFC William Hartry, was hit in the legs and chewed through his poncho to keep from screaming in pain.[24] Another shell hit the communications center of the 3rd Battalion, 7th Marines, killing PFC Dorr I. Sprague and Pvt. Eugene V. Friedrichsen. "An old truck removed the bodies for burial after dawn," records historian Burke Davis. "The faces of the men in the grove were already much older."[25]

It was almost a relief to leave the perimeter and strike out into the unknown. "Chesty Puller got us going first thing," recalled Poppendick. "Patrols and everything."[26] On Vandegrift's orders, Puller led his battalion on a probing mission along the upper banks of the Lunga. As they crossed the low-running river at "Bayonne Bridge," there was the sudden crack of a Japanese Arisaka rifle. "Whew! but that was a tough stretch!" exclaimed Cpl. Bodt. "When you hit the deck so hard you just about knock yourself out, and you feel that one of those bullets just about parted your hair in the middle—well, then you know you're in the war."[27] Inexperienced and overexerted Marines scattered left and right until Puller intervened. Oblivious to the danger, Chesty stalked along the trail, browbeating his men into action. Company "A" killed three Japanese in the fracas, but lost one of their own. "Corporal Don Beamer ... unlike most Marines [was] personally a thoroughly likable fellow," wrote Gerald White. "After he was shot, no one could find him, indicating he might have been slightly wounded."[28] Three days later, Beamer would be found dead in the field, shot through the throat. Fortunately, his body was returned to the Division cemetery.[29]

Puller's men bivouacked on a ridge that night, nervously shot up the shadows, and continued their operation the following day. "We contacted an enemy patrol and had a little clambake with them," quipped Bodt. The oppressive heat and rugged terrain were more memorable than the handful of brushes with the Japanese. White "very nearly passed out from heat prostration and thirst," while Bodt discovered "what a drink of water could mean if you didn't have it."[30] Thirst overcame discipline and men threw themselves headlong into the Lunga River without stopping to purify the water.

That evening, the battalion returned to the perimeter, flushed with success as well as the heat: they had completed their mission and killed twenty-four Japanese at the cost of three casualties.[31] One of the wounded Marines was Maj. John Stafford, the skipper of Company "B." It was a freak accident: as one of his Marines struggled with a rifle grenade, Stafford bent over to help just as the missile exploded in its launcher, mangling the major's ear, face, and throat. Puller had him placed on a stretcher, which slowed the patrol's pace to a crawl. Command of the company passed to the executive officer, Lt. Alvin C. Cockrell.[32]

This minor operation imparted many useful lessons to the battalion. Some birds sounded like wounded men crying for help; thirst could drive a man to drink doglike from a muddy river; snipers hid in trees; American weapons were dangerous to friend and foe alike; dead bodies were a foul fact of life.[33] They had unexpected reactions to being under fire—"I kept humming, for a stupid and unknown reason, an old silly ditty 'Listen To The German Band,'" said White. And not all of them would survive. "Some guys got hurt, a few got killed. You don't get used to it," said Charles Jacobs. "War was beginning to come home to me now."[34]

As previously noted, the arrival of the 7th Marines allowed for a cohesive cordon defense around the airfield. Patrols were sent out into the hinterlands to ensure the Japanese would not interfere with preparations for a renewed offensive. Smaller groups on reconnaissance tended to perform better than the larger unit sweeps: the disaster that befell the 1st Battalion, 1st Marines, on September 17 illustrated the difficulties of larger combat patrols. Fortunately, an expert in the subject had just arrived on the battlefield and was more than ready to put on a demonstration.

Few men on Guadalcanal understood patrolling as well as Puller. As a young officer, he cut his teeth in countless small-unit actions during the "Banana Wars" in Haiti and Nicaragua. Guadalcanal was developing into a similar operation, a "small war" of maneuvering and limited engagements (quite different from the hit-hard-and-get-out operation envisioned by Marine planners of the late 1930s). Puller—along with his peers Herman Hanneken, Sam Griffith, Evans Carlson, and others— helped write the Marine Corps manual for propagating such a battle.[35] Ten years might have passed since the occupation of Nicaragua, but its veterans were running the fight for Guadalcanal.

To the south and west of Henderson Field lay "the broken terrain and heavy jungle of the upper Lunga," an area "so bewildering as to beggar description."[36] Its confounding effects on troop movement were demonstrated by the uncoordinated attack on Henderson Field; however, it was plain that the Japanese could and did move about in the area at will. "Lacking the force to hold it permanently, it was decided to dominate the area ... by a series of small operations designed to clear the area of small forces and to prevent larger forces from consolidating" noted Merrill Twining.[37] The first such expedition called for an overland march through the rugged terrain to the very slopes of Mount Mombula (which most Americans called Mount Austen) to the headwaters of the Matanikau River. A Japanese trail was thought to exist out in the boondocks; such a trail might provide a route around the formidable defenses along the

Matanikau's northern banks. A strong, well-led unit could conceivably make this march and be on hand for a flanking maneuver to coincide with a Raider operation to establish a patrol base at Kokumbona. Such a unit required a commander who had the experience to operate autonomously, but whose men were not used up by weeks of fighting. Puller's battalion was an obvious choice, and Puller was already hounding headquarters to let him loose on the enemy.[38] "We thought if any person could get a battalion up the river, get it across and above the Japanese, it would be Lewie Puller," said Col. Gerry Thomas.[39]

They set out from Lunga early on the morning of September 24.[40] Puller adapted a patrol configuration that served the Marines well in Nicaragua, scaling it up to accommodate an entire battalion.[41] Two leading companies—"Able" under Capt. Thomas Cross and "Baker" under Lt. Cockrell—formed the main body. Chesty himself walked close behind the point squad. In the event of a surprise, the two lead companies would immediately deploy from column into line and advance aggressively to envelop the enemy's flank, while supported by a detachment of mortarmen from "Dog" Company. "Charlie" Company, led by Capt. Charles Kelly, formed the rear guard. "This is a time tested and proven formation which works," Puller proclaimed. "It is okay to say that an outfit cannot be surprised, but it is bound to happen in this type of warfare; so, therefore, your outfits must know what to do when ambushed."[42]

The trail that snaked off into the jungle was a Japanese thoroughfare, cleared by hand, mile after miserable mile with machetes and picks. Although only a few yards wide, it had borne many battalions on their way to attack Edson's Ridge, and the occasional imprint of a hobnailed boot, discarded piece of equipment, or rotting bloodstained bandage showed that it had been used in their retreat as well.[43] Where it led was not entirely known. Puller was equipped with "one of our atrocious maps of Guadalcanal, based on photographs taken … during a single flight on a cloudy day."[44] Copies of Map 104 were evidently unavailable; Puller would rely on a 1:20,000-scale, five-sheet aerial mosaic covering nearly 20 miles west to east, roughly centered on Lunga Point. Gunner Edward "Bill" Rust of the 5th Marines and a local islander accompanied the patrol as guides.

The morning was miserably hot, and the route led through dense jungle ravines and up bare, sunbaked ridges that looked "like a large desert" to Sgt. Joe Goble. "We were so hot and dry that we had no energy to climb."[45] Water discipline broke down under such conditions. Despite Puller's dire warning "if you don't save water, you'll regret it," many men were bone dry by midday. Moldering Japanese bodies were dragged off the trail and relieved of their canteens.[46] A passing cloudburst sent

Company "B" scrambling for their ponchos, not to stay dry but to catch rainwater. Marines poured what little they collected into homemade bamboo containers. It rained just enough to saturate the ground and turn the trail to slippery mud. "For every two feet up, you went back five," said Ed Poppendick.

The going was particularly rough for Marines lugging crew-serviced weapons and ammunition. Poppendick saw one of his newer buddies, Pvt. Randolph Ray Edwards, struggling along with his mortar team. The lanky Southerner volunteered to join the 7th Marines in hopes of getting into combat, and he was now getting his wish. Although Edwards was comparatively old (twenty-two) and well educated (two years of junior college), his status as the new man doomed him to carrying the heavy mortar baseplate. Edwards was "a nice kid," thought the nineteen-year-old Poppendick, but it remained to be seen how he would hold up once the shooting started.[47]

Early in the afternoon, an American bomber buzzed the patrol, circling and gyrating as the pilot tried to communicate with the Marines on the ground. When they failed to respond, one of the crew scribbled a message, tied it to a spare tool, and dropped the makeshift missile to the ground. His aim was poor; the object fell into the tall grass beside the trail and was lost forever. The plane departed, and the Marines got back in motion. This struck some as an odd choice, given the scarcity of information at their disposal. "I thought Colonel Puller should have had the whole patrol search until the message was located," remarked Sgt. Goble.[48]

Everyone was exhausted by 5 p.m. The approach of dusk signaled the end of the day's marching—"who wanted to go down into the next valley in the dark?" reasoned Poppendick—and when the head of the column reported running water just ahead, Puller decided to make camp for the night.[49] Gunner Rust led his scouts across the stream, lacing them with well-chosen invective when a few broke ranks to fill canteens. The Company "A" platoon under Capt. Robert Haggerty followed some distance behind, the squads spreading out to provide security.[50] Capt. Regan Fuller, also of Company "A," was told to find a bivouac site and led Cpl. Harold Turner's squad into the tall grass. Company "B" filed down to the water's edge, filling canteens and splashing their reddened, sweat-streaked faces. Joe Goble found two dead Japanese in the stream, and a third body on the bank, rifle still aimed menacingly at the ford.[51] The mortar train and rear guard (Kelly's Company "C") remained on a hill a few hundred yards down the trail, awaiting their turn at the stream.

It was a perfect spot for a bivouac, and it was already occupied.

Marine commanders estimated that the Japanese below Mount Austen were a disorganized and demoralized group of about 400 men. They had good reason to believe this: after defeat at Edson's Ridge, Gen. Kiyotake Kawaguchi's survivors faced a torturous retreat through 6 miles of Guadalcanal's worst terrain. Only scattered stragglers remained in the jungle in front of the Ridge itself. However, American knowledge of Japanese dispositions was sketchy at best. Historian Stanley Coleman Jersey notes that "the Marines had little intelligence beyond what their patrols had discovered in the past few weeks, and thus they continued to act without the benefit of adequate information."[52] Despite the proven Japanese acumen for effective rear-guard ambushes, a well-led battalion would be able to gather intelligence and handle the demoralized and disorganized remnants of Kawaguchi's force. Or so Vandegrift's headquarters believed.

Col. Akinoske Oka thought differently. His 124th Infantry Regiment, bloodied but not decimated on the Ridge, was entrenched in strong defensive positions, forming a secure wall to protect their reorganizing comrades. Anticipating a new American incursion across the Matanikau River, Kawaguchi organized some 4,000 troops to hold them off. Most of this force was concentrated near the river's mouth, but one battalion was to occupy the foothills of Mount Austen to collect any stragglers still making their way along the trail. Oka chose his Maizuru Battalion for the job. They knew the area well; after all, they had cut the path leading to the American lines.

These men from Kyoto were seasoned veterans, blooded in the Borneo campaign, well-schooled in fieldcraft. They camped near the point where their trail crossed a stream—an ideal place to collect starving stragglers, treat the wounded, and intercept any pursuers. They set guards to keep watch and equipped their outposts with heavy machine guns. If the Americans dared show themselves, these outposts would fight valiantly, delaying the intruders until the main encampment was ready to withdraw. Oka did not intend a full-scale engagement: he needed his men alive for the next offensive.

The fifty-odd men on outpost duty were not expecting trouble on the evening of September 24.[53] They had collected a handful of emaciated, exhausted stragglers; those who did not return would be waiting at *Yasukuni Jinja*. In another day or two, they expected to be called back to their regiment. Guards kept a relaxed eye on the trail, a cooking detail meandered down to the stream to collect water for the evening rice, and the remainder of the detachment went about their daily rituals of cleaning weapons, writing in diaries, and thinking of home.

The rapid popping of a pistol shattered the quiet and sent them rushing to their posts. Clips were fitted into Nambus. Snipers scaled into trees. They waited, breath baited, for what was coming down the trail.

As Cpl. Turner and Lt. Fuller explored up the grassy hill in search of a bivouac site, they stumbled—literally—onto the Maizuru Battalion's field kitchen. "We almost stepped on two Japs," Fuller recalled. "They were as astonished as we were, and we all scrambled. I fired three clips from my .45 and killed one of them." The other made a break for freedom, but ran straight into Turner's squad and was shot down in his tracks.[54] Fuller was just getting over his surprise when "the Old Man bobbed up behind us"—Chesty, as usual, was not far behind his point squad. Grinning, the battalion commander made a big show of dipping a bowl into the Japanese rice pot to sample the enemy's cuisine.

The encounter alerted the entire area. Ed Poppendick heard a few shots and someone—Puller, he believed—crowing "I got a couple of the bastards!"[55] Down below, Sgt. Goble's squad tumbled into the stream bed, taking up defensive positions behind the 4-foot-high bank. Goble could see Marines ahead of him, perhaps alerted by the gunshots, heading for a tree line. Others were easing over a felled mahogany tree, eyes peeled for trouble, but the Maizuru gunners were already taking aim.

Much later, Goble would think to himself, "Our patrol ran into the trap that the pilot had been trying to warn us about."[56]

Five Marines in Capt. Bob Haggerty's platoon went down with the first burst of fire. Gunner Rust hit the dirt and "pulled his head into his shoulders" as a storm of bullets whipped through the trees and bushes.[57] The Maizuru Battalion had at least five, and perhaps as many as nine, heavy machine guns arranged in a horseshoe that effectively swept every inch of ground. The effect of the sudden, concentrated fire was so intense that the platoon broke apart, leaving Haggerty temporarily without a command. Another Nambu zeroed in on Chesty Puller's group; one bullet knocked the rice bowl from his hand while another tore the throat out of his runner, PFC Richard J. Wehr.[58] Marines flattened themselves in the grass. Only Puller remained upright, bellowing orders at the top of his considerable lungs. "The Old Man didn't find too many leaders right there," admitted First Sergeant William Pennington. "He was the only Marine you could see standing on that hillside." Fuller watched his battalion commander duck and weave down the slope, popping up to shout orders and rolling away, keeping the Japanese gunners "buffaloed" while his men hustled to form a skirmish line.[59]

Chesty established himself in the deep stream bed and summoned his scouts. Gunner Rust made his report: he had not seen much, but his point men were returning fire as well as they could. Three wounded men were dragged back to the safety of the bank; Corporals John "Eddie" Edwinson and Manuel Pimentel were dead and not retrievable.[60] The rest of Company "A" gamely tried to deploy, but with Haggerty's platoon scattered and Fuller's pinned down, this was easier said than done. Japanese forces on Guadalcanal rarely enjoyed fire superiority, and the Maizuru detachment made the most of it. "Trying to set up our light machine gun we, [PFC Rolland D.] Robey and I, were sprayed with fire," recorded Gerald White.[61] Forward movement was no longer an option for Company "A."

Meanwhile, 1Lt. Alvin Cockrell had successfully maneuvered Company "B" into position along the stream. The mercurial Mississippian had earned Chesty's confidence since taking command from the wounded Maj. Stafford. Now, Puller would rely on Cockrell's natural aggression to counterattack the hidden enemy positions. They planned a classic envelopment: 2Lt. Walter B. Olliff would take 2nd Platoon around to the left, while 2Lt. James W. McIllwain brought 3rd Platoon up the middle. Cockrell himself would lead 1st Platoon on the right, where the fire was heaviest. At Puller's shouted command—"Bring 'em up, Cockrell!"—the three platoons lunged forward. The Japanese immediately shifted their attention to the charging Marines. "The bushes and leaves waved and bent over as if there was a gale," said Lt. Olliff.[62] He saw a BARman, Pvt. Anthony Jarzynski, go down with a nasty bullet wound to the thigh; moments later, Jarzynski's assistant was shot in the face and Pvt. Robert Eddington took a slug through the shoulder. Olliff went to throw a grenade, but a bullet hit his left hip, exiting through the right leg. Helping hands dragged him behind a tree.[63]

McIllwain's platoon struggled to get moving. "Just as we cleared the stream bed, two machine guns opened up on us," said Sgt. Goble. "Some of us rolled back into the water, others lay flat and got behind anything they could find. Bullets were spraying everywhere." Goble rolled behind the mahogany log as bullets stripped the bark and showered him with splinters. Behind him in the stream bed, he could hear an increasingly incensed Puller yelling for Cockrell to advance on the right.[64]

As minutes passed and Cockrell failed to materialize, Puller considered his other options. Artillery support was out of the question; although an observer team from the 11th Marines was along for just this purpose, the "atrocious" maps made calling an accurate strike impossible.[65] Closer at hand were the 60-mm mortar squads of Company "A." PFC Mathew C. Constantino recalled Puller's order: "Old man, I want you to set a barrage out there." When the squad leader hesitated—the range was dangerously close—Puller lost his temper. "Son," he barked, "set a barrage out there!" Constantino knew that when Chesty called you "son," he meant business, "and you'd better rectify [your] mistake to get back to 'old man' again."[66] The mortars opened fire, ducking their own shrapnel as well as the combined fury of enemy machine guns that zeroed on their position.

Next, Puller ordered Company "D" to deploy their mortars. Under normal circumstances, a battalion commander could call upon his "hip pocket artillery"—the 81-mm mortars of his weapons company fired lethal shells weighing 7 pounds—but they were wickedly heavy and difficult to carry through the jungle. The 60-mm version was less powerful, but far more portable, and Puller seems to have substituted "the small mortars" in the interest of mobility. On his command, Company "D" began the complicated dance required to get their weapons into action. Squad leaders staked out sites for their guns. Heavy baseplates were thrown down, bipods extended, and tubes fitted into place. The sights, carried carefully by gunners in special leather pouches, were set in place. Ammunition carriers wriggled out of their heavy vests, passing rounds to the front as the squad leader and gunner calculated range and direction. A good squad could be assembled and ready to fire in well under a minute. The need for haste was essential—and may have led one Marine to make a fatal mistake. Ed Poppendick was watching the proceedings when a tall Marine carrying a baseplate stepped out onto the trail itself. "Geez, they just riddled him right down the side with a machine gun," he recalled. "He really got it." Pvt. Ray Edwards, the "nice kid from Louisiana," was likely dead before he hit the ground. Nobody else tried to go down the trail.[67]

Darkness was falling fast. In the stream bed, Sgt. Goble could barely distinguish friend from foe. He could hear, however, when a Marine splashed up to Chesty Puller and reported that Lt. Cockrell was dead, his platoon scattered. Puller placed Capt. Zach Cox (Company "A") in charge of Cockrell's company, and began planning a withdrawal. Pressing the issue in the dark would serve no purpose and his men, while well-trained, were more than a little shocked by their first pitched battle. "We were having a little trouble putting into practice our tactics," admitted one chastised NCO.[68] Ed Poppendick explained the impossibility of anticipating "what's going to happen in a battle. Even if you had all the time in the world to explain it, there's always a new situation.... You had to learn a lot of things real fast, and your previous training was never enough."[69] (Unbeknownst to the Marines, the Maizuru detachment was also beginning a withdrawal, leaving behind a rear guard to operate the machine guns and discourage any pursuit.)[70]

The battalion was about to improvise a withdrawal under fire. Capt. Kelly's rearguard set up defensive positions on a hill a few hundred yards from the ambush site. Squad by squad, Company "A" broke contact and began to withdraw, prompting a final fusillade from the Maizuru Battalion. As his gun crew broke down their weapon, "Pow! A shot went through my helmet," wrote Gerald White. "I was conscious of the fearful ringing in my ears ... and a few moments later realized that my skull had been grazed." Bullets whipped overhead, wounding more Marines, and White "gave an involuntary groan as I heard bullets land in Jim Tanzi and Willie Rowe."[71] In the precipitous "advance to the rear," several of the wounded were left behind. Company "B" provided covering fire, putting out a last few rounds in the general direction of the Japanese before withdrawing back up the hill. "Coming back through the jungle was really scary!" said Joe Goble. "There was no moon or light of any kind—just blackness." They reached an open area on the hillside and dug in, bayonets fixed.[72]

If hauling ass was frightening for the able-bodied, the wounded faced a far more harrowing ordeal. Lt. Walter Olliff lay behind his tree, pistol in hand, bleeding from three different wounds. He was numb from the waist down. Not far away, Eddington was howling in pain and fear—"I'm dying! I've been hit!"—and Olliff struggled to keep his own nerves under control. A corpsman appeared, did what he could without morphine, and disappeared into the darkness. Six Marines materialized in his place, hoisted Olliff fore and aft, and carried him back up the hill where another corpsman was organizing the evacuation of casualties. Olliff was placed on a poncho, dropped, loaded onto another poncho, and then bodily hauled up the steepest part of the hill before passing out. He awoke in a makeshift field hospital.[73]

From start to finish, the fight for the stream bed had lasted about thirty minutes.[74]

Lt. Lawrence E. Schuster, the battalion medical officer, was up to his elbows in casualties. An accomplished surgeon in civilian life, Schuster could splint, bandage, and operate as well as any MO on the 'Canal, but twenty-eight wounded men would have strained the capacity of a hospital back at the perimeter. Schuster was operating in the field, with limited supplies and only a dim flashlight for guidance. Some men needed only a bandage or a kind word: Pvt. Connell, dislocation right shoulder; PFC Hinnant, lacerated knee; PFC Miller, shock—but there were a distressing number of stretcher cases. Puller got on the radio to request reinforcements, an airdrop of water and additional stretchers, and to report his casualties: seven dead, twenty-five wounded.[75] (In fact, the aid station treated twenty-eight Marines.) Privately, the old "coconut warrior" sorrowed over his casualties, particularly Lt. Cockrell. Puller vowed to find the Mississippian's body at first light; he also intended to recommend Cockrell for the Navy Cross.[76]

PFC Charles Jacobs hurried over to the aid station. He was unwounded, but had seen a buddy, Pvt. Monjet Higginbotham, shot through the chest during the ambush. "I went around to see who got hurt," he said. "They had a sort of little field hospital; a lot of the guys were hurt or dead." He spotted PFC Charmning "Willie" Rowe, a good friend from rural Florida, lying on his stomach. Rowe was wearing a "funny, quizzical" look, the combination of morphine and shock. Jacobs bent down. "Hey, where'd you get hit?"

Willie grunted, "Got hit in the butt."

"Oh that's good, you'll get to go home."

"Yeah...."

Jacobs moved on, searching for Higginbotham, troubled by the look on Willie's face.[77]

"Rowe? He died during the night."

It was early morning on September 25, 1942. Marines were enjoying the first smoke of the day, swapping stories of the fight and the night just passed. Puller was vindicated: the Japanese had kept quiet. "We sure had the Japs stymied," bragged Cpl. Bodt. PFC White thought about the enemy tracer round that passed between his legs and was grateful to escape with only a head wound. "27 years old today," he scribbled in his diary. "I trust St. Pete doesn't begin to lower that Jacob's Ladder for me again soon."[78] The rumor mill turned and men swore up and down they'd seen Puller lighting his pipe to draw enemy fire and Cockrell charging into the teeth of a machine gun with blazing pistols in each hand. Reinforcements arrived at dawn, the battle-tested 2nd Battalion, 5th Marines, breathless and sweating after a four-hour march.[79] Company "B" was moving out to investigate the battlefield, and Charles Jacobs was staring in disbelief at a battalion corpsman, the bearer of bad news.

"He was shot in the butt. What'd Willie die from?"

"He wasn't just shot in the butt. He had three bullet holes in his stomach. That's what he died from."

"Friends of mine are starting to have problems," Jacobs thought. Three poncho-covered bodies lay near the aid station; Marines from Charlie and Dog Companies carried over two more.[80]

Sgt. Joe Goble and Company "B" were stalking through the jungle. "We circled around the battle area about a mile out, to come in from the north," he recalled. "We wanted to surprise the Japs by hitting them from that direction."[81] They were too late: the Maizuru Battalion was long gone, leaving only spent brass, abandoned emplacements, and a handful of fresh graves.[82] The Japanese buried only their own; the bodies of five Marines were found lying where they fell. Among them was Alvin Chester Cockrell, "shot through the head ... the bullet had gone on through the mouth," according to Goble. "He must have been looking up for snipers in the trees."[83] A Marine removed Cockrell's sterling silver identification bracelet, which was later returned to his parents in Hazlehurst, Mississippi. Burial parties set to work on shallow graves, hoping to complete their unpleasant work before the day grew too hot.

Meanwhile, Puller was making dispositions to continue his mission. In their radio conversation the night before, Vandegrift gave Puller the autonomy to "continue the attack or return as you decide" as commander of a two-battalion force. Chesty chose a third option, attaching himself and Company "C" to the 2nd Battalion, 5th Marines. He would lead this combined force onwards to the Matanikau crossing, while the balance of his battalion headed back to the perimeter under command of Maj. Otho Larkin Rogers. "This was a strange decision," comments Jon T. Hoffman, "since it placed [Chesty] in charge of a force he did not know. Possibly he thought this veteran but depleted unit was in better shape for action than his recently bloodied companies. He also might have considered it important that his own men take care of their own wounded."[84] Of the twenty-five wounded men in 1st Battalion, 7th Marines, eighteen were stretcher cases.

The march back, on "the hottest day of all," was torture. "The Marines could not go for more than a few hundred yards without stopping to rest," said Joe Goble. On the way, they stopped to take some potshots at a Japanese patrol clustered around a fallen Marine aircraft. Goble had the added burden of helping carry Lt. Olliff's stretcher. "He was swollen like a balloon and his tongue was black," Goble continued. "I thought sadly that I would never see him again."[85] Incredibly, all twenty-five wounded Marines survived their trip back to the perimeter.

Puller's skirmish with the Maizuru Battalion was only the overture to what would become known as the Second Battle of the Matanikau, but played a significant role in its outcome. By electing to continue, Puller committed to his original objective of a coordinated attack with the Raiders. The unexpected encounter with Oka's troops ruined the delicate timetable, however, and resulted in the "unfortunate decision" to proceed down the eastern bank of the Matanikau rather than rolling up the Japanese flank on the western bank.[86] Exposed to harassing mortar fire and unwilling to listen to the input of unfamiliar junior officers, Puller eventually tried to cross the Matanikau at its mouth on September 26. In the ensuing slaughter, thirteen Marines lost their lives. Second Lieutenant Paul Moore (F/2/5) watched as "one platoon went over and got annihilated:"

Another platoon went over and got annihilated. Then another. We were lined up just behind the shore, ready to go. Ours was the fifth to go over, and you know we all realized it was insane.... When I got back I asked if I could see Colonel Puller, just to report to him what had happened.... I saluted and told him that I'd just started the platoon across and what had happened.... He not only didn't answer me, he didn't even turn his head to speak to me. It's as if I hadn't been there. After a while I just left.[87]

Attempts to cross the Matanikau continued on September 27, but the fully-alerted Japanese put up a fierce defense. An amphibious attack carried out by Maj. Otho Rogers' command attempted to get behind Japanese lines at Point Cruz. Rogers, a reservist better known as a government philatelic agent than a combat leader, neglected to tell his own subordinates about the attack plan; he was killed by a mortar shell in the opening moments, and Japanese troops surrounded his men. Individual heroism, naval gunnery support, and the timely return of the landing craft prevented their annihilation; still, twenty-two of Puller's Marines were lost in this "Little Dunkirk." The episode was deemed "the only thoroughly unsuccessful operation of the entire Guadalcanal campaign."[88] In the two-day offensive, thirty Marines were buried in the field or left behind. Only two were later accounted for.

The Maizuru ambush burial site (or, rather, "sites" as two separate locations were used) was situated in Guadalcanal's backcountry, in an area devoid of ready landmarks. Identifying the exact site today requires reconciling military maps whose accuracy ranges from questionable to "atrocious," without the benefit of anchoring points like Point Cruz or the Lunga River. Fortunately, enough eyewitness accounts with geographical data, and an unknown Marine's attention to detail, provide some excellent clues.

Muster rolls and individual personnel files indicate that two separate burial sites were selected on two different ridges; lacking proper names, these were designated "Hill 'X'" and "Hill 'Y.'" These locations were almost certainly chosen for convenience and, perched on ridgelines away from tree cover, for visibility to aid future search parties. Five men were buried at each location; given the known circumstances of several of their deaths, it can be argued that one hill was at or near the night's bivouac site, while the other was closer to the ambush site.

Hill "X" is likely the ridge where Puller's battalion established their night defense. In this cemetery, Graves 1 through 5 were reported to contain the remains of Pvt. Randolph "Ray" Edwards (Company "D"), PFC Morris E. Canady ("C"), PFC Erwin S. King ("B"), PFC James R. Walters ("B"), and Pvt. Charmning "Willie" Rowe ("A"). According to Ed Poppendick, Edwards was killed while moving along the trail to set up his mortar. Puller's configuration for a battalion-sized patrol kept the mortars—Edwards' section—towards the rear of the formation; this makes perfect sense as mortars are a support weapon with no business at the forefront of the attack.

The exact fate of PFC Canady, a twenty-two-year-old Marine from Goode, Virginia, is not known. Modern historians make no mention of his company's participation in the day's action; as the rearguard, they were probably lightly engaged, if indeed they deployed at all. Cpl. Walter Bodt provides a rare and dramatic eyewitness account—"machine guns, snipers picking away at us, and mortars in the rear tossing shells into our midst"—but considering that Canady was the only Company "C" Marine killed or wounded, it seems that they avoided the main part of the action and were not near the main ambush site.[89]

We also know from casualty reports that three Marines died of wounds sustained in action. One of these is Rowe from Company "A"; he died at the aid station, according to Charles Jacobs. While no eyewitness accounts detailing the deaths of PFC King or PFC Walters are known to exist, their burial in proximity to Rowe and two other individuals who were arguably towards the rear of the column, suggests that they also succumbed to their wounds overnight.

Ed Poppendick witnessed the burial on Hill "X." "I had to identify Randolph's body.... A group of us buried [him]." This was Poppendick's first field funeral, and he took note of the process. Each of the five Marines was buried "right on the spot ... in his poncho, [we would] take his canteen and put all the information in the canteen and bury him with it." Furthermore, "someone [made] a map of the graves so they could go back and dig our guys up." The overlay sketch attached to Ray Edwards' personnel file shows the contours of Hill "X" and five graves in a crescent shape, with Edwards at the center. A dotted line extends into an area marked "WOODS," possibly designating the trail. The placement of the graves in a clearing on top of a hill, plus the ad-hoc "bottle burial" of information in a canteen, were to ensure the eventual retrieval of the dead men. "We always went back for the fallen when we had the chance," claimed Poppendick.[90]

Five more graves, designated "A" through "E," were dug on Hill "Y." These reportedly contain the remains of PFC Richard Wehr (HQ Company), Pvt. Joseph P. Karnaghon ("B"), Corporals Manuel J. Pimentel and John E. Edwinson (both "A"), and Lt. Alvin C. Cockrell ("B"). This location was probably close to the ambush site; given the difficulty in evacuating the wounded under fire, the dead were necessarily left where they fell. Wehr and Cockrell are known to have died at or near the fighting front, Wehr near the cook fire and Cockrell leading his charge. Two Company "A" Marines were killed in the first moments of the ambush; with Rowe accounted for, this leaves Pimentel and Edwinson as the two candidates. Karnaghon's fate is not known for sure, but using proximity as a guide, we can argue that he, too, died at the fighting front.

Sgt. Joe Goble was with the patrol that found Cockrell's body and witnessed the interments on Hill "Y." Like Poppendick, Goble states that all men were buried "on the ridge" with "a canteen and a dog tag [in] each grave." (He was also convinced that thirteen bodies were found: "Marine Corps history records only seven dead ... I helped to bury thirteen men.")[91] The graves were arranged in a single row, running along a ridgeline from WSW–ENE.

Because the grave sites were plotted on an unusual map—only the 1st Battalion, 7th Marines, is known to have used this map to mark burial locations—Army graves registration units transposed the location to their own documents. In 1947, the 604th QMGRC referred to "Map 104, 25th Division Map," probably an Army reprint of the Marine map of the same name. Hill "Y" was determined at coordinates 74.8–197.3. When plotted to the Marine Map 104, this coordinate falls on the very edge of a grassy ridge, just 300 yards from a giant blank area labeled "CLOUD." Comparable coordinates for Hill "X" were not recorded. (It should be noted that the Army fought over a pair of hills designated "X" and "Y" as part of the "Galloping Horse" offensive in January 1943. These locations, however, are much too far to the west to be the same hills noted by the 7th Marines.)

Of interest, however, are the overlays themselves. The OMPFs of Ray Edwards and Alvin Cockrell contain detailed sketches, not only of each man's grave, but of all burial sites, topographic information, and proximity to tree lines—the only landmarks available. These were made in the field, as witnessed by Ed Poppendick, and although there is no key save for a compass reading, they must have been aligned to the aerial mosaic map. The two overlays have no overlapping features, but if one trusts the cartographers of the 604th QMGRC, an interesting picture emerges. Rough similarities appear between the ridge described at coordinates (74.8–197.3) and the topographic lines indicated on Cockrell's overlay— and Cockrell, the reader will remember, was buried on Hill "Y." About 1,000 yards due north is a little hill. Bowl-like depressions on either side, as well as the proximity of tree lines, are roughly analogous with the Hill "X" overlay included with Randolph's file; the lines of the sketch indicate very steep sides, which feature prominently in descriptions of the night bivouac. Neither sketch aligns with north on Map 104 (although 104 does not have a compass orientation, "up" is simply assumed to be due north), but when aligned with terrain features, the overlays orient with each other, and the dotted line, believed to represent a trail, points directly to Hill "Y."

It is not known if any Graves Registration personnel ventured in search of these ten Marines during the war; the location was quite remote and if any attempts were made, they were not successful. The first recorded effort was made by the 604th QMGRC in 1947. They sweltered in the sun on August 26 and 27, digging up "foxholes and all possible grave sites" they could find on what they believed to be Hill "Y." No graves or remains were found. A subsequent expedition in February 1949 repeated the search, noting "many evident signs of heavy fighting in the area," but again could find no human remains. Interviewing the population of nearby Matanikau Village No. 3 was likewise fruitless; Chief Kotusi "stated that his natives had made many searches since the war, but they had been unable to find any remains." He offered to bring the Americans to Hill "X," but although this too was dotted with old foxholes and possible graves, the 604th returned to their camp empty handed.[92]

The individual files were closed and the men declared non-recoverable in 1949.

In 2016 and 2017, research teams from the Defense POW/MIA Accounting Agency traveled to Guadalcanal to conduct search operations in the jungle. In one location, they reported discovering the remains of five individuals, all believed to be American servicemen. The graves of Hill X or Hill Y may have been discovered at last, but no official identification has been made.

As of 2019, the remains of Alvin C. Cockrell, Jr., John E. Edwinson, Jr. Manuel J. Pimentel, Morris E. Canady, Ervin S. King, James R. Walters, Richard J. Wehr, Randolph R. Edwards, Joseph P. Karnaghon, and Charmning Willie Rowe have not been accounted for.

Beach Road, Beach Ridge: November 18–20, 1942

I knew the men who had been killed. They were my friends and had served under me. They were B Company's first KIAs, and their deaths hit us all very hard. A real shock: the first friends to die in combat. There would be more, many more. But these were the hardest to take.[1]

Dean Ladd, Company "B," 8th Marines

The nameless kid strolled past the bivouac on an errand of his own. Although he walked casually, he attracted an audience.

He had been on the 'Canal for more than two months. His green cotton twill utilities were torn and stained, a uniform in name only. Beneath the tattered fabric was an emaciated form, the result of two meals a day, constant exertion, and probable bouts of malaria, dysentery, or both. Still, he radiated an unmistakable aura of cheerfulness, and his step was confident. He had been through the wringer and lived to tell the tale. He held a rope in one hand; a white object bounced in his wake, trailing through the dust like a puppy on a leash.

The kid's audience was cleaner, better fed, healthier by far. They were Baker Company, 8th Marines, and they had been on Guadalcanal for only a few days. Even the old-timers among them were new to combat. The aftermath of a fight between two Army battalions, grass trampled, flattened, soaked and reeking of blood, the cries of the wounded and the awful stillness of the dead, made the stop and fall silent. "I had been a Marine since 1939, and had been at war for the better part of a year, but I had not yet experienced war, not really," remarked 2Lt. Dean Ladd. "In all that time I had been practicing for war, preparing for it—or so I thought. But I wasn't prepared for this. It was an ugly, ugly sight—just sickening." That night, their first on the line, the Marines bloodied themselves with friendly fire, evacuated two men, and never saw a Japanese. Ladd, nursing a thumb gashed by a C-ration can, felt anything but confident.

The kid felt the eyes upon him, grinned, and whipped his rope like a lasso above his head. The bleached skull of a Japanese soldier whistled through the air. Merrily swinging his trophy, the kid continued on his way. "He was doing just fine," Ladd realized. "He had found a way to keep his spirits up. He had 'acclimated' to conditions on Guadalcanal."[2]

This anonymous young man embodied the 1st Marine Division of November 1942. Individually, he may have been "fine" but as a fighting man, he was approaching the end of his rope—exhausted, hungry, sick, a shadow of his former self. The tables were gradually turning; American air and naval power in the Solomon Islands were in the ascendant, attacking Japanese "rat runs" and landing reinforcements a few battalions at a time.[3] However, "gradually" was not soon enough for Marines who had fought without pause since August. When the early November offensive failed to hold its conquered ground, Vandegrift's headquarters declared "the infantry regiments were no longer capable of offensive operations."[4] Securing air and sea meant the once-isolated 1st Marine Division could be resupplied, reinforced, and finally relieved by fresh troops of 2nd Marine Division and the Army's Americal Division.

The 8th Marines had waged a defensive war thus far, occupying the southern California coast after Pearl Harbor and deploying to Tutuila, American Samoa, in January 1942. Ladd described Samoa as "a place of surpassing beauty, at once spectacular and restful in aspect"—an incongruous place to watch the war run steadily against the United States.[5] Guam and Wake were already lost; when Bataan and Corregidor fell, the 8th Marines faced the realization that they could do little more than delay the seemingly inexorable Japanese march across the Pacific. Nevertheless, they built fortifications, laid telephone wire, sighted guns, and manned their beach defenses until Midway stalled, then scrapped any Japanese plans to invade Samoa. Instead of a potential battlefield, the islands became a training and staging area for troops headed west across the Pacific.

The original cadre of Company "B," 8th Marines that left the States together was a tightly bonded group. Many of the older NCOs, like Ladd's platoon sergeant Rhynette Spell, were "plank owners" present when the company was formed in 1940, and whose personnel files told a story of years, even decades, in uniform. These venerable old salts formed the backbone of the company. Most of the younger NCOs were Depression kids who joined the Corps in peacetime, willing to undertake the "twenty-year man's" long climb through the enlisted ranks.

William Albert Smith was typical of the younger set. Born on May 15, 1919, Smith spent his childhood on the road as his single mother, Mazie, searched for cooking jobs across several states. By 1932, young Bill and his sister, Christella, were wards of the State of Indiana, living with foster families several miles apart. Bill's early teens were spent tending chickens on Mrs. Artemecia Howard's farm in North Vernon; "Stella" moved in with the Rochat family in Rising Sun. Mazie married one Scott Ague in 1935; while the children occasionally came to visit her in Knightstown, they were not fully reconciled, and Bill would refuse to adopt the Ague surname.

After completing a year at North Vernon High School, Bill set out to make his own way. Six years on the chicken farm prepared him for hard work, and he spent several months as a carpenter at CCC Camp 596 in Versailles before leaving Indiana behind. When a stint as a farm driver in Oklahoma failed to pan out, Bill headed for Colorado and wound up in the Denver recruiting office. When he enlisted in Denver on July 28, 1938, he named Mrs. Howard as his next of kin. He had no other witnesses to his character—a nameless official from the Department of Public Welfare granted permission for Bill Smith to enlist.[6]

In three years of service in California and Hawaii, Bill developed into a good Marine with a reputation for reliability. He was promoted to corporal shortly before joining the 8th Marines in September 1941; with the outbreak of war, he was bumped up to sergeant and placed in command of a machine-gun section. The rapid rise from junior NCO to section leader tested Smith's abilities; his officers initially thought him somewhat shaky in command, and one subordinate got in trouble by calling Smith a "jawbone sergeant" to his face. Experience inspired confidence, however, and by the time of the "Samoan sojourn," Smith was being considered for promotion to platoon sergeant. He was so busy that he fell behind on letters to his family; Mazie resorted to writing to her son's officers, who promised encourage Bill's correspondence.[7]

Doyle Hugh Asher was one of Smith's squad leaders. The red-headed corporal was a few months younger than his sergeant, and enlisted just a few days later, but came from a markedly different background. Hugh and Hattie Asher raised their boys, Doyle and Irvin, on a farm just outside of Chanute, Kansas. Doyle, a high-school athlete, entertainer, and Future Farmer of America, enlisted a few days after graduation, bringing with him a sheaf of required paperwork: parental permission, signed statements from the Chanute chief of police, and references who praised him as "a good hard worker—very energetic" and "above average morally." He spent his first Marine years in California and Hawaii (crossing paths with Smith at Pearl Harbor) and showed a great deal of talent with automatic weapons. His proficiency with the heavy Browning Automatic Rifle earned him a specialist's rating, a promotion to corporal and, eventually, a role in the weapons platoon of Company "B."[8]

New faces were added to the company as the months went on. Some wanted to fight with family: PFC Marshall P. Smith was with a unit bound for Guadalcanal until he ran into an influential figure—his big brother, Sgt. John W. Smith, a bodyguard for Samoa's military governor. The elder Smith pulled some strings to have Marshall reassigned as a staff driver; when both tired of the assignment, they transferred to Company "B," 8th Marines.[9] The Smith brothers became "Big Smitty" and "Little Smitty," just like "Big Outlaw" and "Little Outlaw," Claude and William, brothers from Waco, Texas. Others arrived with a degree of civilian celebrity: boxing fans clamored to befriend professional middleweight Pvt. Tony "Punchy" Almeida, and cheered when Pvt. Barney Ross defended his Golden Gloves title against a massive Samoan fighter.

A few joined by compulsion, arriving with disciplinary black marks that only service with a combat unit could dispel. Pvt. Raymond Joseph Schulthies had few qualms about this course of military justice: he was right at home in Company "B." Before enlisting, Schulthies was a part-time business student who held jobs as a hotel clerk and a Ford foundry worker. Finding that "opportunities for betterment are few at best" in his hometown of West Branch, Michigan, he joined the service in 1939. His Marine career took off fast: selection for Sea School, assignment to the famed 6th Marines, and promotion to private first class within a year. In April 1940, he was posted to Company "B" for the first time; within a few months, he rose to the rank of corporal.[10]

When the war in Europe heated up in 1941, Schulthies volunteered to rejoin the 6th Marines and go overseas. Instead of action, he endured months of cold-weather boredom on garrison duty in Iceland, with only the occasional German reconnaissance plane to break the monotony. He would not return to the United States until the spring of 1942. After a two-week furlough with his family, Cpl. Schulthies was assigned to the newly formed 22nd Marines to provide some professional leavening for the influx of new recruits.

In July 1942, the 22nd was put on standby to head overseas. A handful of men overstayed their liberties by a few hours; a few went AWOL for a last fling in San Diego, accepting the punishment of a fine or a few days in the brig as a low price to pay. This leniency may have convinced Cpl. Schulthies to gamble on his perfect disciplinary record, or perhaps he wanted to say a proper goodbye to his girlfriend, Miss Belen Mendivil. Where he went is unknown, but the results were disastrous: while he was absent, his regiment sailed for Samoa.

When a handful of hangdog 22nd Marines reported back to Camp Elliott on July 20, they were immediately arrested. Instead of a simple slap on the wrist, they faced a much stiffer penalty for missing their ship. Their voluntary surrender spared them imprisonment, but each man was busted down to private and held at Camp Elliott for the next two months. Fortunately, the mark of desertion was removed from Ray's record; in return, he was immediately assigned to a combat unit, which happened to be his old home in Company "B," 8th Marines. "Peepsight" Schulthies, as he was called, was assigned to a rifle squad and earned back one of his stripes.[11]

Reorganizing and training continued through mid-October 1942. The new men were folded into the 8th Marines, which was finally able to conduct exercises on the platoon and company scale after being spread across Tutuila for several months. "Recruits straight out of boot camp and recently activated reservists, officially Marines but hardly more than civilians, arrived to fill the ranks," said Dean Ladd. "Integrating the new men into their units was a difficult task."[12] Acclimating to the jungle environment was particularly difficult on the newer men. "It was long, hot, gasping work," said Barney Ross. "We hiked, we marched. We tested ourselves on short rations, we crawled, waded, and sneaked through swamps and brush that was as formidable as barbed wire.... It turned us into a tough team of jungle warriors.... The time we spent on Samoa was a godsend."[13] Schools were held for those who hoped to advance in rank. Ladd, who arrived on Samoa as a corporal, entered a machine-gun leadership program hoping to become a sergeant; he left with a second lieutenant's commission, outranking Bill Smith and Doyle Asher, his former NCOs. Morale was high despite the hardships. PFC Howard J. Schlesinger eulogized the experience in a poem, patriotically titled "It's Worth It!" which concluded a laundry list of complaints with the couplet "Now we didn't mind these hardships and all the many more/For we had a cause, a cause worth fighting for."[14] They left Samoa in late October, bound for Guadalcanal. "Ready or not," commented Lt. Ladd, "we were going to war."[15]

They made a strange sight on November 4, 1942, tumbling over the sides of their Higgins boats and traipsing the same Beach Red where the invasion forces waded ashore nearly three months before. With their flat-brimmed 1917-model helmets, khaki uniforms, and Springfield rifles, they might have been headed to Belleau Wood or Château-Thierry. The Marines and GIs they encountered were "a hard-bitten lot ... gaunt, sallow-skinned and grimy, their clothes in tatters—scarecrows in green." These veterans were spare with words: their appearance spoke volumes. "Brown as berries, tough as a barbed-wire fence," thought Pvt. Frank P. "Nick" Nicolli, as he bantered with a Marine guarding the beach.[16]

PFC Marshall Smith, "smart enough to bring socks and cigarettes," gave a pack of Lucky Strikes to a bearded Marine whose dungarees were held together with safety pins. "He lights up, and that's when I knew that I was in hell," said Smith. "His hands were shaking. His buddy said, 'What's the matter, Red? You nervous?' The guy was suffering from combat fatigue.

When I saw that young corporal's hands shaking ... I volunteered to give up my job driving a colonel for this?" Big Smitty needled his brother with a well-timed "Well, you happy?" As if on cue, the air raid alarm sounded and interrupted the brotherly quarrel.[17]

The 8th Marines scattered. Pvt. Nicolli's "tough guy" act evaporated as he searched for one of "those famous foxholes. I see one about twenty yards away, towards the woods, and I make for it like a rabbit and flop in head first ... I think Christ, if Mary saw me now ... so this is war."[18] The scramble provided some comic relief for the veterans. "You don't have to dig in," one said, voice heavy with sarcasm. "They're bombing the airfield, they're not after you."[19] Completely unfazed, the veterans went about their business, ignoring the Japanese bombers with the confidence born of experience. The newcomers were chagrined and amazed. Lt. Ladd summed up the impression: "They were something else, something different. They were warriors."[20]

Campaigning began on November 6, with a 7-mile trek east of the Ilu River to support an advance of the 164th Infantry. For inexperienced troops, the learning curve of Guadalcanal was no less steep three months after the invasion. No amount of conditioning could prepare one for marching through *kunai* grass and rainforest "in the heat of a relentless sun that scorched our helmets and baked our brains." Humidity pressed against a Marine's chest like a physical force, thick vegetation limited his visibility to the man beside him, the unfamiliar sounds of birds and lizards worked on his nerves, and malaria-bearing mosquitoes flew thick and fast. Although supplied with the standard Map 104, Company "B" was in unfamiliar terrain and eventually became so lost that it simply halted in place for the night, making camp quite literally on the trail beside the Malimbiu River.

The following morning, they discovered the site of a "friendly fire incident"—a pitched battle between two battalions of the 164th. "We were horrified," said Ladd. "You're not supposed to get killed by your own people. And there was so much blood. Twenty guys shot and blown apart can pump a lot of blood." The company executive officer, Lt. John Murdock, concurred: "That's the first time I smelled blood.... I'd never smelled it in my life before. That made you stop and quiet down. Everybody's thinking, 'Oh, shit.' Not a man said a word." On the night of November 7, their battalion engaged in a friendly fire fracas of its own that wounded two men in Company "B." When their operation concluded at Koli Point, they had yet to fight a Japanese outfit—"but why should the Japanese bother as long as we were doing such a good job of attacking ourselves?" Ladd asked.[21]

Disheartening as this patrol was, the 1st Battalion, 8th Marines, was comparatively fortunate. On November 10, the 3rd Battalion drew a similar assignment, following the veteran 2nd Marines into some extremely rugged terrain west of the Matanikau and suffering the same physical discomforts. They had the misfortune to run into determined Japanese defenses in a ravine. Company "K" was hardest hit, losing four men killed and one missing in the span of an hour before breaking contact. Rumors of a Japanese convoy resulted in a general withdrawal to the Matanikau defenses; 3rd Battalion was unable to recover or even bury its dead.[22]

"There is such blinding, life-and-death reality about everything when you're waiting for your last minute to come," thought Barney Ross, "that all your lifetime before seems pale."[23] Ross had plenty of time to contemplate his mortality as Company "B" manned the Matanikau defenses against the forecasted Japanese attack. Squad-sized patrols on "security routine" ranged across the river and along the beach for up to ten hours at a time.[24] Two fleets crashed together in a night battle on November 13, transforming the company into "a vocal audience, awestruck and profane" during the action and open-mouthed gawkers at the naval carnage the next morning.

They began to acclimatize, though at different rates. To some, it seemed almost easy. Cpl. Herschel J. Wilsky developed an almost pathological obsession with patrolling, sneaking off alone to "hunt Japanese like quail." "'Skee' was a one-man army," said Ross. "He was always disappearing on us; he even ducked away at chow time. Shooting Japanese was more his favorite pastime than eating. He didn't have any other recreation."[25] Mindful of the regimental edict "Do not try to win the war singlehanded, use teamwork and live," Wilsky was assigned a hunting partner. Marine Gunner Otto Lund, a seasoned old salt, was respected by officers for his "courage, competence, and common sense" and idolized by the "kids" of his platoon.[26] "Gunner" and "Skee" became inseparable. "It was a prize to see the two of them melt off together, the little blond and the big blond with the busted nose," said Barney Ross. Lund made a point of shepherding young Marines through the jungle, delivering his wisdom with an ever-present cigar clamped between his lips. Ross, who made his first patrol with the venerable Gunner on November 17, commented that "new Marines coming in learned their profession and saved their lives by going out with him on their first patrols and seeing what he did."[27]

The Americans were preparing to launch another westward offensive across the Matanikau. The Army's Brig. Gen. Edmund Sebree planned to capture a ridgeline running 2,500 yards from the base of Point Cruz over a series of unremarkable rises with the unromantic names of Hills 66, 81, and 80.[28] These objectives would become a starting point; from here, Sebree would oversee further operations towards the Kokumbona and Poha Rivers. Two infantry regiments from Sebree's Americal Division—the veteran 164th and the newly arrived 182nd—were slated to make the main effort, with the 8th Marines in support.[29] Engineers stood ready to throw a footbridge across the Matanikau. The attack would begin early on November 18.

Capt. Osborne "OK" LeBlanc put his company on alert the evening before the attack. As night clamped down, the men prepared themselves for what they would face in the morning. Barney Ross could hear Japanese voices in the darkness—"I often wondered when they slept"—and noted the common phenomenon of being able to smell his adversaries. "It makes the back of your neck creep, a night like that." Thin wires ran between the foxholes; "Peepsight" Schulthies looped one end around his wrist and waited for the tug that signaled a buddy going off watch, or an infiltrator getting tangled in the wire. Sgt. Smith's machine-gun section crouched behind their heavy weapons; Cpl. Asher took turns on watch with his crew. A few men managed to sleep. No Japanese appeared but, as Ross said, "don't get the idea that it isn't spooky."[30]

The offensive began with a simple command: "Let's move out."

"No pep talks. No looking at the captain's wrist and saying, 'in 30 seconds it'll be time for the push, men,'" reported Ross.[31] With simple efficiency, Capt. LeBlanc had his company on the road to the Matanikau crossing by 6.30 a.m. The engineers were putting the finishing touches on the footbridge when Company "B" arrived, and the entire company was across by 7.15 a.m.—the talkative Japanese having decamped before dawn.[32] The green 2nd Battalion, 182nd Infantry, crossed under Marine protection and began the tiring struggle up Hill 75; overloaded with water and ammunition, the "doggies" soon began to drop from heat prostration.

As the Army disappeared up the slopes of Hill 75, LeBlanc's Company "B" split into two combat patrols, each about the size of a reinforced platoon. The captain led one group up the western slope of "Beach Ridge" to cover the Army's flank against any surprises. The second—Gunner Lund's platoon, with Sgt. William Smith's machine guns attached— swung out towards the coast to provide security along "Beach Road," the regiment's name for the Government Track that was the main thoroughfare leading to the enemy stronghold at Point Cruz.[33] The surf hissed and lapped not fifty yards from their right flank; to the left, thick jungle muffled the occasional boom of mortar and artillery rounds. Lund ordered his platoon into line and advanced up the road.

Private First Class Marshall Smith felt like he was being watched, not by the Japanese, but by his buddies. "One of the things you're told in the Marines is not to volunteer," he explained. "So I didn't. But on platoon patrols, every [other] squad leader had volunteered to take his squad out. I couldn't live with myself; I was the last one that hadn't been on a patrol, and some of the other corporals had been on a couple."[34] He wanted to prove himself to Gunner Lund and the dozen-odd men of the squad he led. Little Smitty donned his "modern" steel helmet, borrowed Big Smitty's pistol, and put on a brave face.[35] So far, patrolling was not too terrible. He just had to explore down the road until told to stop, wait for the Army to move in and set up shop, and then he could head back across the Matanikau, his job done and honor satisfied.

They reached the eastern base of Point Cruz before the shooting started.[36] A few quick pops rang out to the right of the road. Little Smitty signaled his squad to hit the deck and rolled behind a tree. A Marine burst through the brush. "We've made contact!" he blurted. "Sergeant Smith got shot by a sniper!" Little Smitty's blood froze for a split second until he realized the man meant the "other" Sgt. Smith—Bill Smith, from the weapons platoon— and not his brother, John. At the same moment, he knew Bill Smith was dead because the messenger now carried his pistol. "You couldn't wait for his body to get cold?" he snapped as the other man scampered off.

Lund materialized out of the brush, issuing commands. "That's our flank. Stay there, don't let anybody come around." Little Smitty lay prone, a weapon in each shaking hand. He regretted bringing the pistol: a sniper might mistake him for a valuable target, like a corpsman or an officer, and so he had no intention of moving from behind his tree.

"What the hell is going on?"

A Marine appeared before him, cradling a Tommy gun in the crook of his arm. Smitty recognized Cpl. Doyle Asher from the weapons platoon and was astonished to see him there, anxious that Asher was standing upright without a care in the world. "They shot Sergeant Smith," he blurted. "Not my brother, the other one." The words didn't seem to register on Asher. "There are Japs here somewhere," Smitty insisted. "See where they must have been cooking rice? There's a fire over on the right—"

A bullet struck Asher full in the head, killing him instantly. The corporal hit the ground hard, his flat helmet bouncing along the ground to land at Smitty's side. Smitty ducked down, cursing, sure now that the sniper had his number. "He knows where I am. That noise I was making with the corporal ... he might be lining me up...." There was no way he was going after Asher, not even for a coveted Tommy gun.[37]

A few yards behind Smitty, Gunner Lund was weighing his odds. It was about 10.45a.m.; according to the plan, the Army should have been arriving soon, but there was no sign of any support coming down Beach Road. He could not know that exhaustion and overexertion were slowing the Army's advance to a snail's pace, but he did know that a single platoon was no match for any sizeable Japanese force. Lund knew the difference between a hero and a fool—"the first one has common sense as well as courage"—and decided to head back to the safety of supporting units.[38]

First, however, he had to do something about his casualties. The Gunner worked his way up to Little Smitty. "Look, we've got to pick up Sgt. Smith and Cpl. Asher. We're gonna pick up the bodies. We've been here long enough; the Army should be dug in by now, and we're gonna withdraw back to the Matanikau."

Smitty swallowed hard. It was do-or-die time, quite literally, and both his life and his pride were on the line. "Your reputation as a Marine depends on doing what you're supposed to do, and not running the other way," he later said. "So I passed the word along to my guys to get ready to move." On Lund's signal, Smitty's squad jumped up and ran forward in a frantic dash to reach the prostrate forms of the fallen Marines.[39]

The Japanese sniper was well trained. If he was a seasoned veteran of Guadalcanal, he knew Americans fixated on retrieving their dead; probably he was staking out Little Smitty just as the young Marine feared. His third shot caught Little Smitty in the chest, tore through his lung and out his right side, and sent him crashing to the ground practically on top of Asher's body. The squad faltered and Lund called them back, yelling "get Smith outta here, he's not dead yet." A makeshift stretcher was thrown together, and Smitty was transported by hand, rubber boat, and jeep back to an aid station.[40] The wound was too large for a standard battle dressing, so a corpsman stuffed him full of gauze, bound him with tape, injected him with morphine, and sent him off to the Division hospital. Fortunately, Smitty survived his ordeal.[41]

Meanwhile, Gunner Lund wisely called off the retrieval effort, planning to "leave the bodies here … we'll come back for them in the morning."[42] He pulled his platoon back about 50 yards—no Matanikau retreat after all—and linked up with Capt. LeBlanc's group on the northern slope of Beach Ridge, creating a single line. The company was stunned by the setback. "I had served in Weapons Platoon in Samoa, and I knew the men who had been killed," said Dean Ladd. "They were B Company's first KIAs, and their deaths hit us all very hard. A real shock: the first friends to die in combat. There would be more, many more, but these were the hardest to take."[43] Platoon Sgt. Rhynette Spell shook off the shock with pragmatism. "We don't leave our dead unburied," he declared. "Maybe the Army does, but we don't. We go up and get our wounded and bring 'em back. If they're dead, we bury 'em." Ladd recounts that Spell organized a group of volunteers, and that the patrol only withdrew once Smith and Asher were buried.[44] A casualty report sent to regimental headquarters made no mention of any burial, however.[45]

Capt. LeBlanc's contingent, which included Dean Ladd and Barney Ross, was more fortunate; no casualties were suffered on Beach Ridge itself. Ross recalled a busy day of constant sniping back at the Japanese.

"There were so many of them, you couldn't miss," he told a reporter. "We held those 300 or 400 yards, and spent another night in foxholes. But this time we felt like we were going someplace."[46] Before the smoking lamp went out, Company "B" was alerted for movement the next morning.

The remainder of the company, augmented by a platoon of machine gunners from the battalion weapons company, crossed the Matanikau bridge at 8 a.m. on November 19. Thus reinforced, LeBlanc's men would act as a spearhead for the 1st Battalion, 182nd Infantry, retracing their steps along Beach Road towards Point Cruz. Led by Lt. Ladd, 2nd Platoon would traverse the length of Beach Ridge along its crest and hold up at Hill 78. Gunner Lund's 3rd Platoon stretched down the slope of the ridge and across the coastal flats to meet 1st Platoon, which took the left flank along the beach. The Marines began moving at 9.15 a.m., preceded by a rolling barrage reminiscent of the Great War. American artillery fire saturated the base of Point Cruz before dropping the range to a few yards ahead of the platoons advancing along Beach Road. Company "B" was taking no chances today: all potential strong points were targeted by mortars, artillery, and machine guns. Fire superiority seemed to be working. From the summit of Hill 78, Ladd observed that "the enemy was conspicuous by his absence."[47]

Unknown to Ladd, the Japanese were executing an offensive as well. Fresh reinforcements landed days before at Tassafaronga Point were bearing down on Point Cruz from the west, just as the untested Americans were advancing from the east. Warned of trouble by the start of the barrage, Japanese units hurried toward the battle zone, hoping to force the decisive battle that would return Henderson Field to their control. Their advance troops soon spotted Company "B." Lone riflemen began taking potshots at the Marines—one talented individual pinned Ladd's platoon until Ladd personally brought him down—and their mortars and artillery came into play as well, ranging along the open ground near Beach Road.

The 3rd Platoon ducked a round or two before one mushroomed in their midst, sending three men sprawling to the ground. Pvt. Lionel Lejeune was riddled with shrapnel, but would survive. PFCs Tony "Punchy" Almeida and "Big" Claude Outlaw took the full brunt of the blast and were instantly killed. At some point, the company traversed the area where Bill Smith and Doyle Asher died, although no mention was made of seeing their bodies in the field.

Japanese resistance, surprisingly, seemed to peter out as the Marines "inched up" on Point Cruz. Pvt. Nicolli recalled that the attackers even paused for a lunch of "can rations, cold coffee, and three pieces of green mint candy."[48] About 400 yards west of the Point, their NCOs yelled to hold up: they had advanced far enough.[49] "We'd gotten so far that we were separated from our objective only by a road about fifteen feet wide," said Nicolli. "We began establishing our firing line there."[50] A company from the 182nd Infantry deployed on their left, further reducing the risk.

A holiday atmosphere took hold. "Not a Jap could be seen," said Barney Ross. "The sky was blue; the sun was warm. Our fellows in broken formation were sitting around, talking to one another, and smoking."[51] Closer to the coastline, PFC Harold "Porky" Park stood idly swatting bugs, occasionally glancing down the road, his BAR held loosely at his waist. Pvt. John "Whitey" Onnen, Park's teenage assistant, wandered to and fro, edging away from Park, testing his boundaries. Porky harped on Whitey, Whitey was sorry, and then they heard the footsteps, soft as sandals on a beach.

"I turned around, and there were these two Japanese point men for a bigger unit," Park recalled. "All of a sudden they were right in front of me." They were so close that Park could see every detail of their uniforms and the confusion on their faces. American and Japanese stared at each other for an eternity that lasted two or three seconds. Park's finger was a fraction away from the trigger.

A *"Banzai!"* and a rifle shot broke the trance. Whitey Onnen was no more than 6 feet from his adversary when the first bullet ripped through his lung; a second bullet caught him in the back as he fell. Park shot down both assailants and saw "a whole damn column of Japs" piling off the road and into the brush. "Porky! What in hell are you firing at?" yelled one of his buddies. Park did not have time for stupid questions; he simply called "The Japs!" and reloaded. Every Marine within the sound of his voice opened fire, and the Japanese responded in kind.[52]

"They were so close they could have thrown a cup at us," recalled Nick Nicolli. "They laid down a regular wall of fire. The bullets whizzed by, flipping past your ears...."[53] Barney Ross and PFC Richard "Heavy" Atkins crawled over to give Park some fire support. They spotted Whitey writhing on the ground and dragged him into cover while others called for a corpsman. The shooting died away as the Japanese column melted into the jungle. A small crowd gathered around Whitey, who kept mumbling "I'm alright, fellows, don't worry about me."[54] A corpsman administered first aid, but Whitey would need more than that to survive. As if on cue, runners appeared with the word to withdraw. Company "A" of the 182nd had arrived and established a defensive line; the Marines were to get back to safety as quickly as possible. Heavy Atkins, Pvt. Leo Freeman, and Pvt. Francis Monick stripped off their dungaree jackets for an *ad hoc* stretcher and lifted the groaning Whitey aboard. Barney Ross, Pvt. Leo Washvillo, Pvt. Myron Guarnett, and a few others—perhaps including Ray Schulthies—formed a rearguard. The little group set off down Beach Road, hoping to catch up with their buddies.

Capt. LeBlanc's company moved quickly, but in good order, back to their assembly area. At times, John Murdock could see the Japanese battle line not more than 100 yards away, and one Marine was shot and killed as the main column passed Point Cruz. He had to be left behind for now; the corpsmen had their hands full with the wounded. Nick Nicolli was one of them, spun and concussed by a mortar shell that "felt as though two sledgehammers hit me simultaneously on either side of my head.... I was picked up in the air about four feet, whirled around like a matchstick.... I felt as if I was gathering myself together, as though I'd been separated and had to pull myself together..."[55]

The Japanese counterattack was gaining steam. From his hilltop position, Ladd could see "the green 1/182 was receiving its baptism of fire in a big way." Some of the inexperienced and overexerted young soldiers began to flee back towards the river. Ladd saw "the wild-eyed expression and the sickly pale, green-at-the-gills pallor that signaled the onset of panic and heat exhaustion" on some of the doggie's faces. As the hard-pressed Army battalion struggled to maintain its defensive line, Company "B" recrossed the Matanikau.

They did not yet realize that six of their men were left behind, stuck 50 yards west of Point Cruz.

"We walked exactly two yards down the road with our litter," said Barney Ross. "Then hell happened."

A Japanese machine gunner opened fire on the little group carrying Whitey Onnen to safety. Either the range was very close, or the gunner was very talented, because a single burst destroyed the evacuation party. Atkins, Monick, and Freeman were wounded and dropped the stretcher. Another Marine tried to pull Onnen to safety and was killed in the attempt; his sacrifice was in vain, as Onnen had been hit again and was dead before he hit the ground. Washvillo and Guarnett melted into the grass, and Ross tumbled tail-over-teakettle to get out of the line of fire.

He wound up in a hole, protected by a fallen tree. More machine guns opened up ("going kak-kak-kak-kak a mile a minute") so hot and steady his wounded buddies could barely move. Monick managed to roll into the hole, bleeding from a leg wound. Two soldiers from the 182nd ("it was their first time under fire ... they were scared") jumped in with him. Ross waged a one-man war through the night, fired eighty rounds of his own ammo and 200 from the soldiers' Garands, threw twenty grenades ("and saved the last one for a pinch"). Bullets nicked his helmet, explosions showered him with dirt, shrapnel sliced into his arms and feet ("my shoe got full of blood"), and rain filled the crater. They fixed bayonets, prayed, and survived. In the morning, as he got ready to drag the wounded men back himself, who should arrive but "a vision of the Lord" in the form of Capt. LeBlanc, Lt. Murdock, and a corpsman. The wounded men were saved, and when LeBlanc heard how

Above left: "Farewell, friends, farewell!" Father James J. Fitzgerald holds a service at the Gavutu Cemetery. Building in the background is probably Lever Plantation store, used as an aid station during the battle. (*United States Naval Academy, Edward J. Steichen Photography Collection W-FU-25-40487*)

Above right: A late war view of Gavutu cemetery. Markers appear similar to those placed in 1942, but individual plots have been marked off and flowers planted along a walkway. Graves No. 1 (Unknown) and No. 13 (reported as Liston) are just out of frame on the left. Note Grave No. 36 with name "Dudenski"—there was no such Marine, and this individual is currently unknown. (*Official USMC Photo*)

Below left: Colonel Frank Bryan Goettge, the Division intelligence officer, poses with a trunk of Japanese currency captured on Guadalcanal. Not long after this picture was taken, Goettge led a patrol behind Japanese lines. Twenty men, including the Colonel, were killed. (*Official USMC photo by Karl Thayer Soule, collection of Clifton B. Cates (COLL/3157), United States Marine Corps Archives & Special Collections*)

Below right: Tough, intelligent, and experienced, First Sergeant Steven A. Custer was the senior NCO of the 1st Marine Division's intelligence section. "Custer was a father to us," said one of his men. "He considered it his mission to mold our character and our competence." Custer was killed on the Goettge Patrol, August 13, 1942. (*Official USMC Photo*)

Above left: Luther Leru "Dusty" Rhodes of L/3/5 was also known as "The Kid" for his youthful appearance. He was killed in action on October 9, 1942, and may have been buried in the 1st Marine Division Cemetery as an unknown. (*Rhodes OMPF*)

Above right: This is the earliest known photograph of the 1st Marine Division cemetery on Guadalcanal, dated August 1942 and probably taken a day or two after the Tenaru battle. The photographer stood at Row 5, Grave 1 (PFC Richard Holcombe, G/2/1). First graves described by Felber are at upper left—note crude stick crosses. Palm fronds cover the graves. (*NARA*)

Prisoner of war detail assigned to clean up Japanese dead after the Tenaru River battle, August 21, 1942. The photographer, 1st Sergeant Abraham Felber, reported "The sight and the odor was so overpowering that one of the Military Police took sick as I was talking to him; and the men in our party had their faces all screwed up in horror and disgust." (*NARA*)

Marines visiting the cemetery bow their heads in a moment of silence. They have gathered around the graves of the fallen from the Tenaru battle; the visitors may be members of 2nd Battalion, 1st Marines, soon to be leaving the island. Note that this older section of the cemetery looks rather overgrown. (*NARA*)

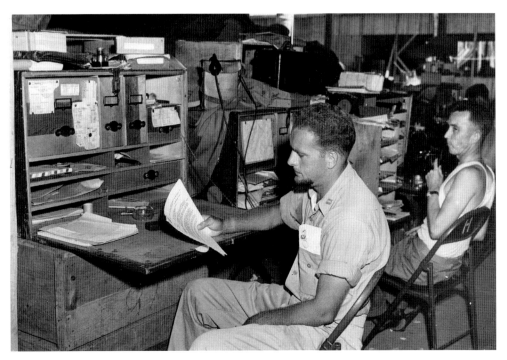

Captain Richard Tonis at the Division field office, sometime in 1942. Tonis arrived on Guadalcanal as a supply and service officer; he was appointed Division Burial Officer in September 1942. (*Official USMC photograph from the Thayer Soule Collection (COLL/2266), Archives Branch, Marine Corps History Division*)

Above left: William Cameron was one of ten Marines from H/2/1 killed when a Japanese bomb hit their working party. "Bill Cameron's face keeps coming before me at night," wrote one of his friends. "He had everything in the world to go home to. Why should he have to go, of all people?" His squad decorated his grave, including the poetic placard. Photo by MG John F. Leopold, February 18, 1943. (*NARA*)

Above right: A Marine unit heads for the Matanikau River during the November offensive. The Matanikau area was the scene of heavy fighting for most of the campaign; many isolated burials were made in the vicinity. (*NARA*)

Gathering the dead for temporary interment in the field. Although this photograph was likely taken during a later campaign (note apparent P42 camouflage utilities on three men, not issued until mid-1943), this would have been a familiar scene to veterans of the Guadalcanal campaign. (*NARA*)

Above left: "A crude cross, his shrapnel-torn helmet, his bandoleer and a marker made by his comrades from a mess kit" mark the grave of Cpl. Robert B. Wallace (E/2/5). Wallace was killed on November 2, 1942 during the Matanikau offensive and buried beside the "coast road" (visible in background). He was reburied in the ANMC in June 1943. Photograph by MG John F. Leopold, February 2, 1943. (*NARA*)

Above right: "HERE LIES A DEVIL DOG." MG John F. Leopold found this isolated burial close to the water somewhere in the Lunga area on February 15, 1943. Note remnants of M1 Garand stuck in the rocks. A marker this small, in an out of the way place could easily be damaged or destroyed by the elements—or overlooked by a search party. It is not known whether this individual was eventually recovered. (*NARA*)

Another "hasty" burial located somewhere on Guadalcanal. Tag reads "Here lies a Marine or Soldier unknown but to God." Stick marker is braced by Japanese machine-gun clips; the M1917A1 "Kelly" helmet was frequently worn by troops coming from duty on Samoa, notably the 8th Marines. (The photographer, Sgt. Ernest J. Diet, was attached to the 8th Marines; the man buried here might have belonged to that regiment.) Note how small this marker is, and the presence of a fragile paper tag. (*NARA*)

Above left: The grave of Pte. Anthony "Punchy" Almeida (B/1/8) in the Division cemetery, September 1943. Note the differences in spelling and initials between marker, dog tag, and plaque. To the left rear is the raised altar that stood at the center of the cemetery, also a flag pole and what appears to be a bulletin board or directory. (*NARA*)

Above right: The first three rows of the "annex"—or Plot "A" of the Army, Navy, and Marine Cemetery, Guadalcanal—shows the variety of individual grave markers. Note the propeller blade (Sgt. William D. Myers, VMF-122), dual markers and helmet (Pte. Rudolph J. Lukas, 10th Marines), coconut tree stump (Cpl. George R. Calloway, 6th Marines), and welded 37-mm artillery shells (Cpl. Robert F. Wilson and PhM3c Elmer L. Hopkin, Weapons Company, 6th Marines). (*NARA*)

The ANMC as seen on Easter Sunday, 1943. Note the distinctive graves of Wilson and Hopkin (previous photo) behind the two men at far left. The visitors are looking at the graves of PFC John R. Weigel and Pte. Emory F. Gess (A/164th Infantry). Weigel and Gess were killed in November 1942; their burials in January 1943 were among the first field recoveries effected on Guadalcanal. (*NARA*)

This photo from September 27, 1944 shows Row 44, Plot "B,' of the ANMC. Building in the background is the Memorial Chapel. Four individuals recovered by the 45th QMGRC are shown. The two Stars of David are Pte. Morris S. Kaplan and PFC Barnett Klass (C/182nd Infantry), killed November 20, 1942 and buried May 17, 1943. PFC Jerrold Miller (E/2nd Raider Battalion) died at Asamana on November 11, 1942, and was buried May 2, 1943. "Unidentified #57" consisted of a skull, scattered leg bones, and a pair of GI shoes. He has not yet been identified. (*NARA*)

Above: The FMC plot as seen from Row 86 in February 1943. Note the uniformity of many grave markers. This photo was taken around the time that Warrant Officer Chester Goodwin was appointed Graves Registration Officer. (*NARA*)

Below: The same view, taken near the end of the war in 1945. The ground has been landscaped, and all markers replaced with uniform crosses or Stars of David. (*NARA*)

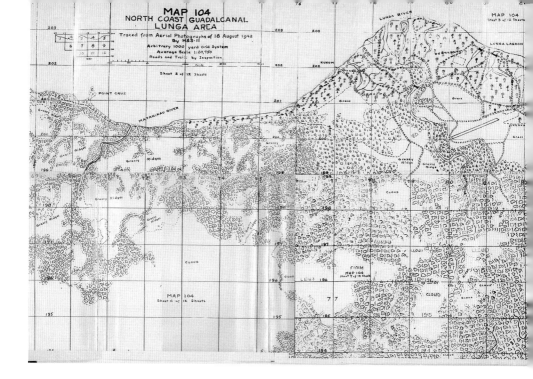

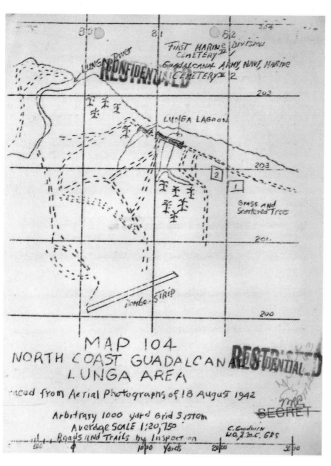

Warrant Officer Chester Goodwin created this map overlay showing the location of the 1st Marine Division Cemetery and the Army, Navy, and Marine Corps Cemetery early in his tenure as a Graves Registration officer. (*Washington National Records Center*)

Above: This was the standard map of Guadalcanal, in use through most of the campaign. Coordinates were plotted in 100-yard increments on the 1,000-yard grid; e.g. the tip of Point Cruz is at 70.5–201.3. (*NARA*)

Below: A detail of Map 104 with coordinates of the five B/1/8th Marines buried in the field. Note that an apparent clerical error places Smith and Asher's graves out to sea. (*Map courtesy of NARA; official USMC photos*)

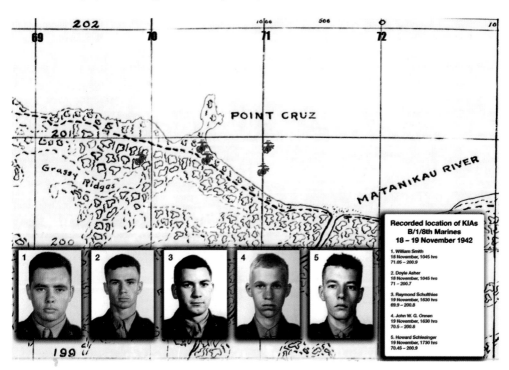

Recorded location of KIAs
B/1/8th Marines
18 – 19 November 1942

1. William Smith
18 November, 1045 hrs
71.05 – 200.9

2. Doyle Asher
18 November, 1045 hrs
71 – 200.7

3. Raymond Schulthies
19 November, 1630 hrs
69.9 – 200.8

4. John W. G. Onnen
19 November, 1630 hrs
70.5 – 200.8

5. Howard Schlesinger
19 November, 1730 hrs
70.45 – 200.9

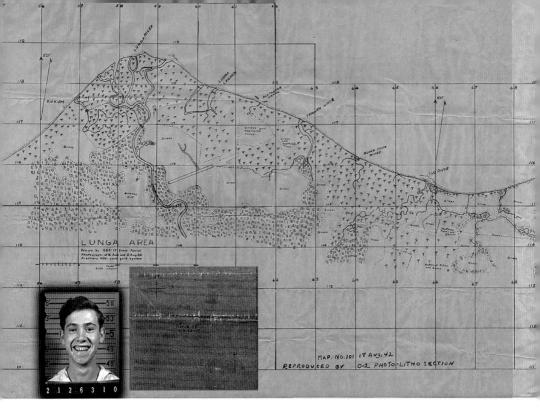

Above: The older standard diagram, Map 101, was in use by 1/1st Marines at the time of their ambush on September 17, 1942. Pharmacist's Mate Third Class James F. Pierce (insert) was buried at the location marked on the map—note the lack of detail. (*Map courtesy USMC Historical Branch; official US Navy photo*)

Below left: A list of personal effects recovered from the body of Private Frederick L. Secor, B/1/1, before his burial in the field. (*Secor OMPF*)

Below right: Report of Interment for Charles F. Debele, Jr., of B/1/1, after his remains were recovered by the 49th QMGRC in October 1944. A copy of this form was forwarded to Washington; another was buried in Debele's new grave to aid with his final identification. (*Debele OMPF*)

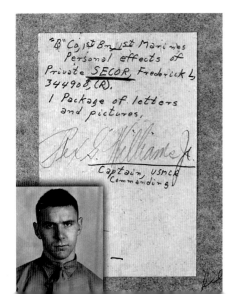

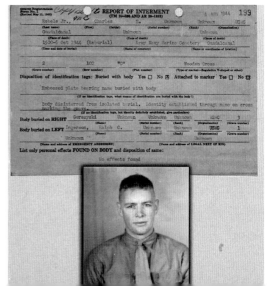

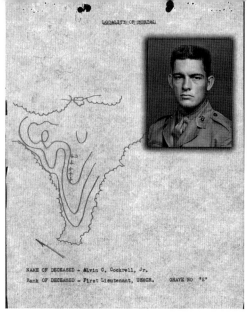

NAME OF DECEASED - Randolph R. Edwards   SERIAL NO - 364854
RANK OF DECEASED - Private, USMC.   GRAVE NO - 1

NAME OF DECEASED - Alvin C. Cockrell, Jr.
Rank OF DECEASED - First Lieutenant, USMCR.   GRAVE NO "E"

Above left: Sketch overlay of five graves on Hill "X" where members of 1/7th Marines were buried on September 25, 1942. Note the lack of coordinates; without the corresponding map, this overlay was all but useless. Private Randolph Ray Edwards (insert) was buried in Grave No. 1. (*Edwards OMPF. Photo of Edwards courtesy of Anne Anderson*)

Above right: Map overlay showing five graves on Hill "Y." This is one of two locations that might have been located by a DPAA research team. Lieutenant Alvin C. Cockrell, Jr., (insert) lies in Grave "E." (*Cockrell OMPF*)

Below: A detail of Map 104, showing some of the sites targeted by the first AGRS expedition in August 1947. The expedition recovered Lawson and McGettrick (No. 6) and accidentally discovered "Isolated Burial #2" who was later determined to be of non-Caucasian origin. (*Map courtesy of NARA*)

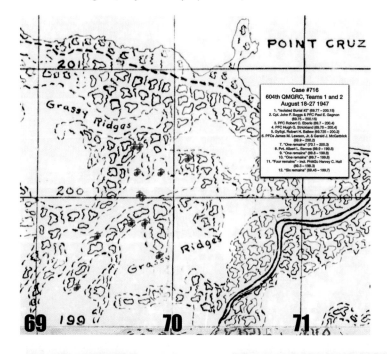

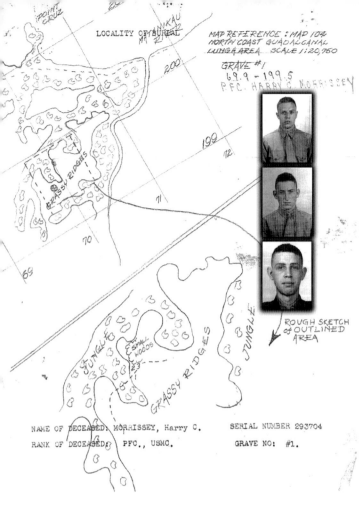

MAP REFERENCE : MAP 104
NORTH COAST GUADALCANAL
LUNGA AREA SCALE 1:20,750

GRAVE #1
69.9 - 199.5
PFC. HARRY C. MORRISSEY

ROUGH SKETCH
of OUTLINED
AREA

NAME OF DECEASED: MORRISSEY, Harry C.   SERIAL NUMBER 293704

RANK OF DECEASED: PFC., USMC.   GRAVE NO: #1.

Left: Overlay of Map 104 showing the burial location of three members of 1/7th Marines—Harry C. Morrissey, Francis E. Drake, Jr., and Albert L. Bernes. (*Map and first photograph from Morrissey OMPF; photographs of Drake and Bernes from their respective OMPFs*)

Below: Members of the 604th QMGRC conducting an "area sweep" for isolated gravesites during their Pacific expedition. The exact location is not known, but conditions on Guadalcanal were similar—and frequently worse. (*NARA*)

Above: A soldier of the 604th QMGRC excavates a suspected grave on a Pacific island. (*NARA*)

Right: Corporal Albert L. Hermiston (insert) was killed in action while serving with Company "B," 2nd Raider Battalion, on December 4, 1942. This form (minus the photo) provided most of the information available to the 604th QMGRC during their search in 1948. "Case 7703" was declared non-recoverable. (*Hermiston IDPF*)

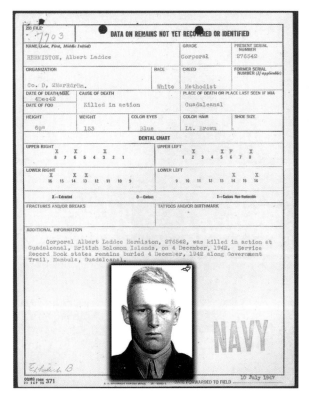

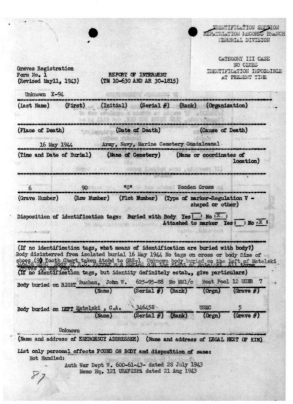

Graves Registration
Form No. 1   REPORT OF INTERMENT
(Revised Mayll, 1943)   (TM 10-630 AND AR 30-1815)

Unknown X-94

(Last Name) (First) (Initial) (Serial #) (Rank) (Organization)

(Place of Death)   (Date of Death)   (Cause of Death)

16 May 1944   Army, Navy, Marine Cemetery Guadalcanal
(Time and Date of Burial) (Name of Cemetery) (Name or coordinates of location)

6   90   "C"   Wooden Cross
(Grave Number) (Row Number) (Plot Number) (Type of marker-Regulation V - shaped or other)

Disposition of identification tags: Buried with Body Yes ☐ No ☒
                                    Attached to marker Yes ☐ No ☒

(If no identification tags, what means of identification are buried with body?)
Body disinterred from isolated burial 16 May 1944 No tags on cross or body Size of shoe (2) Tooth Chart taken Attchd to GRS-1 Unknown body buried on the left of Matelski
(If no identification tags, but identity definitely estab., give particulars)

Body buried on RIGHT Buchan, John W. 625-95-88 No MM1/c Boat Pool 12 USNR 7
                    (Name)   (Serial #) (Rank) (Orgn)   (Grave #)

Body buried on LEFT Matelski , C.A. 346458   USMC   5
                    (Name)   (Serial #) (Rank) (Orgn)   (Grave #)

Unknown
(Name and address of EMERGENCY ADDRESSEE) (Name and address of LEGAL NEXT OF KIN)
List only personal effects FOUND ON BODY and disposition of same:
Not Handled:
        Auth War Dept W. 600-61-43- dated 28 July 1943
        Memo Hq. 121 USAFISPA dated 21 Aug 1943

87

Report of Interment for an unknown individual, designated as "X-94, Guadalcanal." Note the details under "Particulars," which give the names of two other individuals found in the same location. Richard C. Farrar and Cyrill A. Matelski were members of Company "B," 2nd Raider Battalion, killed in action on December 4, 1942. (*Albert L. Hermiston IDPF, Washington National Records Center*)

IDENTIFICATION DATA

| 1. REMAINS OF UNKNOWN | | | | | 2. DATE OF REPORT |
| Unknown X-94 Guadalcanal | | | | | 23 March 1948 |

3. NAME OF CEMETERY	4. PLOT	5. ROW	6. GRAVE	7. DATE OF
U. S. Army Mausoleum #1		C	5	DISINTERMENT / REINTERMENT
Formerly of Guadalcanal Cemetery.		90	6	23 Mar '48 / 23 Mar '48

PHYSICAL DESCRIPTION Age 22 to 24 years.

| 8. ESTIMATED WEIGHT | 9. ESTIMATED HEIGHT | 10. COLOR OF HAIR | 11. RACE |
| 155 lbs. | 5' 10" | U. T. D. | White |

12. GIVE DESCRIPTION OF ANY OFFICIAL IDENTIFICATION FOUND WITH REMAINS
One (1) embossed metal grave marker reading: Unknown X-94, Plot,C, Row-90, Grave-6, (attached to end of box).
One (1) embossed metal grave marker, with remains reading: Unknown X-94, found buried with: Farrar, R. C., 336677 USMC.
        Matelskt, C. A., 346458, USMC.

13. GIVE DESCRIPTION OF TATTOOS OR SCARS ON BODY AND/OR SUCH INFORMATION OBTAINED FROM OTHER SOURCES
None   UNIDENTIFIABLE
            BY REASON OF LACK OF SUFFICIENT IDENTIFYING DATA
            CYRIL U. DISNEY
            1st. Lt., FA 0-1167396 Cyril C. Disney 30 Jan 1949

14. WAS BODY BURNED?	TO WHAT EXTENT?
☐ YES ☒ NO	
15. WAS BODY MANGLED?	TO WHAT EXTENT?
☐ YES ☒ NO	

16. DESCRIBE EVIDENCE OF HEALED FRACTURES AND BONE MALFORMATIONS
None

17. LIST EVERY ITEM OF CLOTHING, EQUIPMENT AND PERSONAL EFFECTS FOUND, SHOWING THE TYPE, COLOR, SIZE, MARKINGS, SERVICE, ETC. (IF laundry marks are indistinct such notation should be made and specimen forwarded through channels for examination when facilities are not available in the area)
One (1) left shoe size, 9½ E- }
One (1) right shoe size, 9½ E- } G. I. Field type, dark brown.

Incl 20

Form 1044 was filled out at the Central Identification Laboratory in Honolulu. Guadalcanal X-94 was investigated in March 1948. (*Hermiston IDPF*)

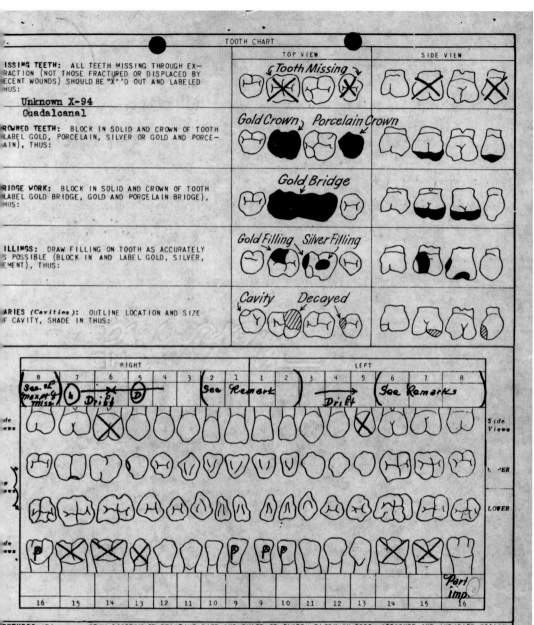

TOOTH CHART

	TOP VIEW	SIDE VIEW

ISSING TEETH: ALL TEETH MISSING THROUGH EX-
RACTION (NOT THOSE FRACTURED OR DISPLACED BY
ECENT WOUNDS) SHOULD BE "X"'D OUT AND LABELED
HUS:

Tooth Missing

Unknown X-94
Guadalcanal

ROWNED TEETH: BLOCK IN SOLID AND CROWN OF TOOTH
LABEL GOLD, PORCELAIN, SILVER OR GOLD AND PORCE-
AIN), THUS:

Gold Crown   Porcelain Crown

RIDGE WORK: BLOCK IN SOLID AND CROWN OF TOOTH
LABEL GOLD BRIDGE, GOLD AND PORCELAIN BRIDGE),
HUS:

Gold Bridge

ILLINGS: DRAW FILLING ON TOOTH AS ACCURATELY
S POSSIBLE (BLOCK IN AND LABEL GOLD, SILVER,
EMENT), THUS:

Gold Filling   Silver Filling

ARIES (Cavities): OUTLINE LOCATION AND SIZE
F CAVITY, SHADE IN THUS:

Cavity   Decayed

RIGHT / LEFT

8	7	6	5	4	3	2	1	1	2	3	4	5	6	7	8

See Remark ... Drift ... See Remarks

| 16 | 15 | 14 | 13 | 12 | 11 | 10 | 9 | 9 | 10 | 11 | 12 | 13 | 14 | 15 | 16 |

ENTURES (Plates): DRAW DIAGRAM OF RELATIVE SIZE AND SHAPE OF PLATE, BLOCK IN TEETH ATTACHED AND INDICATE RETAIN-
NG CLASPS ON NATURAL TEETH WITH THE WORD, "CLASP."

REMARKS:
- L-16 might have been forced farther in to jaw, mandible fractured in that area.
- Either R-1 or R-2 is extracted and the same for L-1 and L-2. The tooth present s missing posthumously.
- L-4 is in torsi distal version.
- There is one upper left molar present with an A - O filling.
  I feel that at least one upper left molar is extracted.

MC FORM
8 MAR 47   1044a

Technicians at the CIL charted the teeth of X-94 and recorded their findings, including any missing teeth or postmortem changes. (*Hermiston IDPF*)

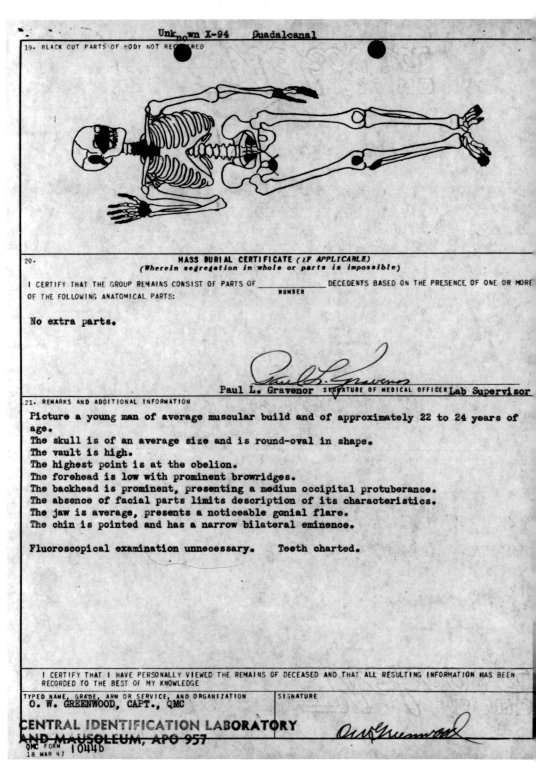

Unknown X-94   Guadalcanal

19. BLACK OUT PARTS OF BODY NOT RECOVERED

20.
MASS BURIAL CERTIFICATE (IF APPLICABLE)
(Wherein segregation in whole or parts is impossible)

I CERTIFY THAT THE GROUP REMAINS CONSIST OF PARTS OF _____ DECEDENTS BASED ON THE PRESENCE OF ONE OR MORE
OF THE FOLLOWING ANATOMICAL PARTS: **NUMBER**

No extra parts.

Paul L. Gravenor   SIGNATURE OF MEDICAL OFFICER Lab Supervisor

21. REMARKS AND ADDITIONAL INFORMATION

Picture a young man of average muscular build and of approximately 22 to 24 years of
age.
The skull is of an average size and is round-oval in shape.
The vault is high.
The highest point is at the obelion.
The forehead is low with prominent browridges.
The backhead is prominent, presenting a medium occipital protuberance.
The absence of facial parts limits description of its characteristics.
The jaw is average, presents a noticeable gonial flare.
The chin is pointed and has a narrow bilateral eminence.

Fluoroscopical examination unnecessary.   Teeth charted.

I CERTIFY THAT I HAVE PERSONALLY VIEWED THE REMAINS OF DECEASED AND THAT ALL RESULTING INFORMATION HAS BEEN
RECORDED TO THE BEST OF MY KNOWLEDGE

TYPED NAME, GRADE, ARM OR SERVICE, AND ORGANIZATION | SIGNATURE
O. W. GREENWOOD, CAPT., QMC

CENTRAL IDENTIFICATION LABORATORY
AND MAUSOLEUM, APO 957
QMC FORM 1044b
18 MAR 47

As the dental exam was going on, anthropologists inspected all the bones present. Note
that X-94 is missing some of his facial bones—the possible result of a wound—which
limited the lab's ability to describe his physicality. (*Hermiston IDPF*)

Ross had killed twenty of the enemy all on his own, he made Ross a corporal on the spot. Instead of celebrating, "the fightingest Marine" collapsed with malaria and woke up in the hospital ten days later.

That, at least, was the story that the newspapers picked up and ran in a thrilling ten-part syndicated feature title "Barney Ross at Guadalcanal."[56] After recovering from the double punch of sickness and wounds, Ross was plucked out of his company, awarded the Silver Star, and sent back to the States to work the war bond circuit. It began to sound like he had blunted the advance of the Imperial 38th Division singlehanded. There was truth to his tale—"Ross was certainly brave," recalled Dean Ladd—but details were lost as the story was told, retold, and reprinted across the country. "Ross' version of events is about three parts baloney and one part truth," said Ladd. "Guarnett and Washvillo were the real heroes."[57] The three Marines and two unnamed soldiers survived a terrifying night and a pre-dawn attack that shoved the 182nd back 400 yards. Washvillo slipped away to find help at first light; he ran into Capt. LeBlanc's rescue party around 7 a.m. and led them to the wounded Marines. Atkins and Freeman were placed on makeshift stretchers and toted back to Marine lines; Monick was treated by Army medics. No mention was made regarding the disposition of the dead Marines.[58]

In the two-day action west of the Matanikau, seven Company "B" Marines lost their lives. Tony Almeida and Claude Outlaw were brought to the Division cemetery, where a handful of their buddies attended a brief service on November 20. "Big Outlaw" was laid to rest in Row 63, Grave No. 9; among the mourners were his older brother, PFC William "Little" Outlaw, and childhood friend PFC James Harris. A hand-carved depiction of "Punchy" in action was affixed to the marker at Row 64, Grave No. 1.[59] "I wept all over my chest as we buried poor Tony," said Barney Ross.

The remaining five—Bill Smith, Doyle Asher, Raymond Schulthies, John Onnen, and Howard Schlesinger—were all recorded as "buried in the field." As the company executive officer, John Murdock had the responsibility of verifying each death and plotting burial locations on a map overlay. His guide was the ubiquitous Map 104, and it caused him no end of headache and heartache. "It troubled [Murdock] that the locations couldn't always be specifically pinpointed, so there could be no assurance that the bodies would later be found for relocation to permanent cemeteries," remembered Dean Ladd. "He had to write letters to many families, telling them that their loved ones might have to remain in an unmarked, unidentified grave on the battlefield."[60]

Smith and Asher were the first recipients of Murdock's attention. The exec confirmed that the Marines were "instantly killed by enemy gunfire while on patrol" at "71.05–200.9" and "71–200.7" respectively—about 200 yards apart. They were "buried in the vicinity of" those coordinates on the standard Map 104—whether separately or together is not known; no detailed overlay survives in their records.[61]

The immediate and most striking problem with this information is that these coordinates, when plotted on Map 104, are some 500 yards east of Point Cruz – and 100-300 yards into the ocean. Their position relative to each other seems accurate, especially in light of Marshall "Little Smitty" Smith's recollection, but neither coordinate falls on land. How Murdock, a college-educated officer with pre-war service in the reserves, made such an error is not known. He may have received misinformation about the coordinates, or he may have simply misaligned the overlay by a few centimeters, throwing off the plot. Whatever the cause, these coordinates were entered in each man's personnel file, repeated in official correspondence, and finally relayed to the 604th Quartermaster Graves Registration Company.

Such a basic error regarding the burial sites of Smith and Asher leads to the follow-up question of whether they were buried at all. For several hours after they died, the area was too dangerous to attempt even picking up remains, let alone dig and mark a pair of graves. The Japanese were still present and active, as Company "B" reported several infiltration attempts overnight. Any attempt to retrieve Smith and Asher would have been conducted in enemy controlled territory, far from supporting units, and with night approaching—hardly ideal conditions for a thorough search.

If we assume that Sgt. Spell's group was successful in locating their dead friends, then they elected to bury the bodies in the field, together or singly, instead of transporting them back to the safety of the rear. They would have been working quickly and presumably buried their friends at quite a shallow depth. Grave markers, if any, were likely large sticks or rocks; weapons and helmets could not be left in enemy territory, and the Japanese might have scrounged them up already, especially Asher's Tommy gun. No personal effects or identification belonging to the two men were found; either Japanese souvenir hunters took these items or Spell's men simply buried everything they could find. Furthermore, working in the near darkness would have made reckoning a precise location difficult: Spell's men would not have had maps with them, and this might be the source of Murdock's incorrect coordinates. Any one of these factors could result in the loss of the gravesites. While they could not have left their friends unburied, any well-meaning but amateurish burial efforts may have made the situation worse.

Finally, it must be remembered that the battlefield did not stay quiet. The morning after Smith and Asher died, American artillery dropped a barrage on the area surrounding Point Cruz, and the ground changed hands multiple times before becoming reasonably secure on November 21. If Spell's men did succeed in burying their friends and setting up grave markers, there is a decent probability that the markers and possibly the graves themselves were destroyed in the fighting that followed.

On August 18, 1947, a Graves Registration Search and Recovery team under 1Lt. Howard D. Wolenberg went looking for the remains of William Smith and Doyle Asher. Because the coordinates provided were "about 200 yards out in the ocean," Wolenberg instructed his men to search along the beach instead. "Just off the beach inland were former bivouac and living areas of several port companies," he later reported. "Area was at one time either built up, or leveled off and filled in. No graves could be located." Eighteen months later, another team searched the area accompanied by Chief Kousti of Matanikau Village. By now, the former bivouac was covered in tall *kunai* grasses "which made the search very slow." Although Chief Kousti pointed out the locations where remains had been found, and the team sunk test holes and excavated old foxholes, the searches were negative. Smith and Asher were declared permanently non-recoverable on May 27, 1949.[62]

Of those lost on November 19, Schlesinger, Onnen, and Schulthies had the misfortune to die in the afternoon. Outlaw and Almeida could be evacuated; a unit on the advance had time for such luxuries. In the retreat, however, the ability to properly handle the dead was greatly reduced. Battalion muster rolls report that all three men were buried in the field on November 19; however, given the hasty withdrawal of American units, this is unlikely. In fact, personnel files for all three men report that "due to battle conditions it has been impossible to recover his body or to obtain proper identification prints or tags"—and this on November 30, 1942.[63] The 8th Marines withdrew from the area, which passed to Army control. The 182nd Infantry, reinforced by the veteran 164th Infantry, blunted and then turned back the Japanese advance on November 20. It appears that one of these units located and buried at least two of the fallen 8th Marines alongside the soldiers who lost their lives in the attack.

John Onnen was buried in the field near Point Cruz, at coordinates (70.5–200.8). The likelihood that he was buried alongside Army dead is reinforced by the fact that the GRS team initially mistook him for a soldier, PFC Albany Doucette, of the 182nd Infantry. "Whitey's" remains were transported to the Army, Navy, and Marine Cemetery on February 20, 1943, and he was interred as Doucette in Row 26, Grave 2, alongside other members of the 182nd. This error would not be noticed until long after the war, when laboratory technicians discovered Onnen's corroded ID tag name among "Doucette's" remains. Confirmation of identity was received with joy by the Onnen family—and, presumably, renewed sadness by the Doucettes.[64]

PFC Howard Schlesinger, the budding poet from Weapons platoon, was killed at 5:30 p.m. on November 19, making him a likely candidate for

the last Marine killed in the withdrawal. A detailed overlay created by
Lt. Murdock places his last known location at coordinates (70.45–200.9)
near the eastern base of Point Cruz.[65] This overlay may have played a part
in the speedy identification of his remains. On May 17, 1943—possibly
alerted by surveyors scouting for the aforementioned port company
bivouac—a team from the 45th Quartermaster Graves Registration
Company exhumed several graves near Point Cruz. One was marked
with "an identification tag and a rough cross" identifying Cpl. James
L. Farley, late of the 182nd Infantry. The others had no ready means of
identification. Working on the assumption that the four were buried at
the same time, the GRS men checked a list of burial coordinates supplied
by the 182nd Infantry to tentatively identify the remaining three.[66]
Schlesinger's grave was exhumed on May 18; his name was either on a
marker, on his identification tag, or deduced using records available to the
Graves Registration team. Pvt. Schlesinger was buried in Row 45, Grave 1,
of the ANMC on May 18; four years later, Joseph and Eleanor Schlesinger
had their son permanently interred in the Punchbowl.

Ray Schulthies was not so fortunate. Only one eyewitness account of his
death has been located; Barney Ross said "'Peepsight' Schulthies crumpled
beside me," but provided no further details.[67] John Murdock recorded that
Schulthies died at 4:30 p.m. and was "buried in vicinity of (69.9–200.8)."
The hour is consistent with the approximate time of the withdrawal, and
the location is consistent with the approximate location of the ambush
site "50 yards forward of the western base of Point Cruz," if not a little
beyond.[68] This reported time and location suggest that Schulthies was
the Marine killed in the attempt to rescue Whitey Onnen. How close he
was to the ambush site when he died cannot be determined; if Ross is
to be believed, it must have been fairly close, but far enough that he was
not located by the rescue party. This area was shelled and fought over for
hours after Schulthies' death, and did not return to American control until
later on November 20 or 21. As in the cases of Smith and Asher, it cannot
be said for certain who buried Schulthies, if indeed he was buried at all.

The Schulthies family initially accepted Ray's death, although it was
naturally "a great shock and one that will not be easy to get over for
quite some time," wrote his sister, Dorothy Schulthies. "Please let us know
how we are to go about it.... Or how long it will take before we can get
his body shipped home to us as that is one thing we do want." Matilda
Schulthies followed with another request. "I would appreciate anything
that you could do in order that we could get at least a little of his personal
belongings to keep," she wrote. "I realize that this is a great task, but it is
also hard to give up your son." Barney Ross visited the family during one
of his tour stops, relating how "he was with Raymond while going across

and also at the time he was killed, and told us about his nice burial." Then doubt began to creep in. An anonymous Marine on liberty in San Diego told Miss Belen Mendivil that Ray was not dead, but in a hospital in Pago Pago. Miss Mendivil—Ray's former girlfriend—wrote to Matilda, who grabbed on to the hopeful thread. "He wrote and told us that he was at a very quiet place and getting lots of sleep and not to worry about him," she explained. "Raymond was rather careless in wearing his identification tags, he told us he sometimes carried them in his pocket, don't you suppose that he could have lost them and perhaps the captain in charge could have thought he had been killed and filed papers to that effect?... I do realize that I am not the only mother in this country to lose a son in this war, but I'm sure you will agree with me that it is worthwhile trying to find out if he is alive."

Dorothy and Matilda accepted the reality of Ray's death by 1945, but grew increasingly frustrated over the unsatisfactory information received from the Marine Corps. "Now that the war is over it is my mother's, as well as myself, one desire and wish that my brother's body be returned," Dorothy wrote on September 13, 1945. "I would like to know the name of the cemetery where he is buried & the exact location of his grave," she continued in September 1948. "It seems strange to me that it should take this long.... My mother is getting rather worked up over not hearing from the Marine Corp [*sic*]." A family friend interceded: "His family is exceedingly disturbed, not so much as of this date by the fact of his death, or even the fact that his remains cannot now be located, as by the exceedingly conflicting statements written to them by various officers of the Corps." Each letter was met with renewed assurances of sympathy, but with the same stock answer: Raymond had not yet been found. Finally, on December 8, 1948, a more detailed form letter arrived, admitting the impossibility of locating isolated graves on Guadalcanal. This final letter seems to have killed the last remaining hopes of the Schulthies family. Raymond was declared non-recoverable on January 14, 1949—another casualty lost in the hills beyond the Matanikau.[69]

As of 2018, the remains of William A. Smith, Doyle H. Asher, and Raymond J. Schulthies have not been accounted for.

Nor have the following members of the 182nd Infantry killed in the November offensive: Allan Russell, Albany A. Doucette, John J. Falardeau, Stanley M. Kondziolka, Leonard F. Meuse, Edward J. O'Leary, Lincoln H. Ackerman, Benjamin Azarva, Andrew F. Lepine, Chester J. Menzenski, and Lloyd C. Williams.

"An Indigenous Growth": Graves Registration, Cemeteries, and Field Recoveries, 1943–1946

We made every effort to bring the men back for burial in our own Marine cemetery, but there were many graves out in the jungle. Graves marked with the man's helmet perhaps, his name penciled on it, and probably now other parties have gone out and brought those men in and interred them in the cemetery.[1]

James W. Hurlbut, combat correspondent

On February 9, 1943, as the 132nd and 161st infantry met at the village of Tenaro, Maj. Gen. Alexander "Sandy" Patch sent a radio message to Admiral William "Bull" Halsey. "Total and complete defeat of the Japanese forces on Guadalcanal effected 1625…. Tokyo Express no longer has terminus on Guadalcanal."[2]

"There it was," ruminated naval historian Samuel Eliot Morison, "2,500 square miles of miasmic plain, thick jungle and savage mountains in American hands, after exactly six months of toil, suffering, and terror. What had it cost? What was the return?"[3] The transformation of the Lunga area from a defensive perimeter to forward base was well underway. "Tent cities replaced the early primitive bivouac areas," wrote Herbert Merillat. "Machine shops, repair facilities for vehicles and aircraft, supply depots sprang up. Tulagi Harbor teemed with combat ships, transports, freighters, and landing craft…. In Robert Sherrod's phrase, Guadalcanal was growing up." The operation once called "Watchtower" and derided as "Shoestring" was replaced by "Drygoods" as the Navy began stockpiling supplies and equipment. Tellingly, Guadalcanal's codename changed from "Cactus" to "Mainyard."[4] An Island Quartermaster's Office was established to handle the ballooning administrative needs of a growing base, and to balance the ledger with the cost in lives that had secured such a beneficial return.[5]

Morison maintained that in the "brutal scale of lives lost against lives risked," the price "had not been excessive" with 1,592 Army and Marine Corps lives lost on the island, plus additional Navy dead "never to this day compiled."[6] Marine historians calculated that their units alone suffered 954 killed in action, 103 died of wounds, and 145 "missing, presumed dead."[7] Several hundred of these men had been buried in the formal cemetery, but a worrisome number had not. Their recovery, identification, and reburial became a persistent issue in the administration of Guadalcanal—never a preeminent concern, but a constant reminder of the cost of military progress.

"Guadalcanal Street"

The 1st Marine Division burial ground reached its capacity of approximately 940 graves on January 21, 1943. In the four weeks that followed, nearly 270 more were added to a nearby plot. The Marines called it an "annex," the Army called it "the island cemetery," and the press dubbed it "Guadalcanal Street." On January 24, the official name was announced as "Guadalcanal Army, Navy, and Marine Cemetery."[8] The ANMC would be active through the end of the war and beyond; more than 3,000 servicemen of all branches would eventually be interred or reinterred within its eight plots.

The end of combat operations naturally coincided with a sharp decrease in the number of deaths reported on Guadalcanal, and one might expect the frequency of burials to drop as well. Col. Joseph H. Burgheim, of the Quartermaster Service Command on New Caledonia, certainly thought so. On February 24, he issued a report that read, in part:

> No attempt has been made to date to move battlefield casualties to the cemetery owing to the battered condition under which these bodies were interred and the rapidity with which decomposition takes place in the tropical climates, and these bodies must wait for a considerable time before they can be exhumed and reburied in proper cemeterial plots.[9]

However, burial reports issued by the Island Command suggest otherwise, and in fact show a rapid increase in the size of the ANMC between the period of February 16 and March 8, 1943. These reports are limited to basic information: dates of burial, at the very least, with names, serial numbers, and units if known. While death dates are not included in these reports, it is a relatively simple matter to find this information using names and serial numbers—and this reveals an interesting pattern. The overwhelming majority of men buried in the ANMC during these three weeks were Army personnel recovered from the battlefield.

On paper, the Army had a well-established procedure for the proper burial of the dead. The standard manual at the time, TM 10-630, cautioned against battlefield interments unless absolutely unavoidable: "every isolated burial renders liable the loss of a soldier's body, as well as making registration and maintenance of the grave difficult." A group of fewer than twelve individuals was considered an "isolated" burial. Whenever possible, burials were to be consolidated into a "cemetery" (twelve graves or more) and were not to be moved until the declaration of an "armistice."[10] Because the Graves Registration Service itself was only organized in time of war, the initial burden for burials would fall on officers and NCOs serving with units on the line, supported by the administrative expertise of their division quartermaster. Responsibility traveled up the chain of command from there: the XIV Corps Field Order No. 1, issued January 16, 1943, included the edict that henceforth "Burial will be by the Quartermaster in Island Cemetery."[11]

"American dead are always brought back from the places where they fall—wherever that may be—to be interred in the cemetery which has been established on Guadalcanal," said Capt. Francis C. Rockey of the 164th Infantry. "It isn't an impressive cemetery, as compared to the ones we know.... But it is a true cemetery, and mothers and families of men who have died there may take comfort in this fact."[12] This was a nice sentiment for the folks back home, but the reality of the situation was quite different. Army combat units faced the same difficulties as their Marine counterparts: rough terrain, extreme heat, and a lack of trained personnel and motor transport. Under such conditions, Edward Steere notes: "... any persistent effort at evacuation of bodies to a centrally located burial place only tended to defeat the purpose sought in first removing the dead as a sanitary precaution and as a means of preserving combat morale." When Maj. Gen. J. Lawton Collins, commander of the 25th Infantry Division, saw dead soldiers carried to the rear while wounded men lay suffering on the ground, he enforced a policy that made field burials a rule, not an exception. In Steere's opinion, Collins' attitude that "undue concern for the dead at [the] expense of succor to the wounded was an expression of false sentiment that had no place in war" showed a willingness to accept "realistic measures ... in making the best of an admittedly difficult situation, rather than attempting to realize an unattainable ideal."[13] Questions of military efficiency, sanitation, and morale had to supersede emotional farewells. Soldiers spent a moment of silence and pressed on, while well-marked burial sites sprang up in the hills and jungles.

Of course, Gen. Collins did not intend to leave his men in the field permanently, and took a personal interest in the proper administration of the established cemetery. When the assigned officer struggled with his new responsibility, Collins tapped a personal favorite, 2Lt. Ernest J. Panosian, to assist. Panosian, a UCLA graduate who rocketed through every enlisted rank within a year of enlisting and earned his commission in 1942, was a 25th Division quartermaster. Graves Registration was an additional duty (Panosian was also leading his quartermaster unit following the accidental death of the original commander) and he had no specialized training in the subject. However, he was intelligent and hardworking, and Collins—who may have been grooming Panosian for a spot on his staff—considered this sufficient. The exact dates of Panosian's tenure as Graves Registration Officer *pro tempore* are not known, but he was present when the first field burials were reinterred in the ANMC.[14]

Once the island was officially secured, Army combat units had the time, resources, and manpower to revisit their old battlefields, salvage the debris, and collect the dead. The first interment of "recovered" individuals (indicated by a lapse of more than a week between date of death and report of interment) occurred on January 22, 1943, when five soldiers from Company "I," 164th Infantry killed in action on November 21, 1942, were buried in the First Marine Division Cemetery.[15] Coincidentally, they were the final five men buried in the Marine plot; the ANMC extension was begun that same day. Between January 22 and February 3, eighteen more men from the 164th were reported as interred in the ANMC—they, too, were killed on various dates in November 1942. A pattern quickly emerges. Men who served in the same company and were killed on the same day were frequently buried sequentially: eight from A/1/164 on January 24–25; one from L/3/164 on January 30; eight from B/1/164, plus one medic, on February 3. Each of these groupings in the ANMC almost certainly represents the exhumation of a corresponding group burial in the field. (The 164th Infantry was particularly adept at retrieving its men; only five soldiers are still listed as non-recoverable.)[16]

The task of recovering the dead fell to the recently relieved combat troops. Survivors of the Gifu and the Galloping Horse had a few blessed days in the rear before returning to the battlefields to retrieve their buried buddies. On the surface, this made sense: the friends of the dead were already familiar with the terrain, the location of the graves, and had a personal stake in finding and correctly identifying the remains. In one instance, an Illinois soldier named PFC Arthur A. Drach was buried in a grave near the Gifu strongpoint. One of his hometown buddies, Clarence Ellinger, helped to dig Drach's grave, and was later able to locate the remains. Ellinger attended Drach's second burial in the ANMC, and then his third in Cullom, Illinois, after the war.[17]

This personal attention, plus the relatively short time between burial and reburial—three months at the outside—resulted in remarkably few soldiers being misidentified or unidentified. The process, however, was horrific. Robert Kennington of the 25th Infantry Division was tasked with such a mission in February 1943:

> After about five days [in the rear], my company commander called me in to talk to him. He asked me to handle the worst thing I had to do in the war. He told me that five men from our company were buried in marked shallow graves in the jungle. He requested a group of volunteers to go up there, dig them up, and bring them to the rear. Because they were men that we all knew, I got five other volunteers. We went up in a two-and-a-half-ton truck. We had buried them in ponchos and marked the graves. We started digging.
>
> When we got down to the bodies it was something you can't really visualize unless you were there to see and smell it. It was very hot and the soil dank. When we got down to the bodies there was nothing left: it was like soup. They had dissolved. All of us took turns about three minutes each. That was as long as we could stand it. We had a cloth across our face. We were puking. It was terrible. After a while, we got everyone out. The flesh did not adhere to the bones. We could really only get the bones out. Having in your mind what the guys looked like alive, and then seeing this was horrid. But we finished our job and turned them over to graves registration so they could be returned to the States and buried properly. I know the families appreciated that. I know I would have wanted it. But I would never do it again.[18]

Hidden in the horror of Kennington's memory is a crucial detail. The Island Quartermaster's Administrative Division now had a Graves Registration section—the sort of organization Edward Steere described as "an indigenous growth, improvised for the express purpose of meeting a series of local emergencies."[19] Improvised it certainly was, conceived by necessity and born from a radiogram message from Lt. Gen. Millard Fillmore Harmon, Jr., commanding US Army Forces in South Pacific Area (USAFISPA). Harmon's directive, distilled into General Orders No. 38 and issued by Maj. Gen. Alexander Patch at XIV Corps Headquarters, authorized the organization of the First Platoon, 45th Quartermaster Graves Registration Company, on February 18, 1943. The new unit—eight men strong—was drawn from the 101st Quartermaster Regiment stationed on Guadalcanal, and a junior warrant officer named Chester Elmer Goodwin was placed in charge. A former chauffeur from Milton, Massachusetts, Goodwin had been in the Army for just over two years and arrived on Guadalcanal as a field artillery NCO. However, when his previous training as a mortician was discovered, the twenty-eight-year-old corporal was snatched out of his battery, promoted, and transferred to the Quartermaster Corps, with seven enlisted men and a team of local laborers under his command.[20]

It is doubtful whether any of the quartermaster men had any real preparation for the work they were about to undertake. Although the technical aspects of Graves Registration service were laid out in Army field manuals, the actual implementation of such efforts at this point in the war was still being tested. Insofar as casualty collection and handling was concerned, the Army arrived on Guadalcanal as ill-prepared as the Marines they were to relieve. "The peacetime US Army had no organizations of this sort, for commercial morticians were always available to care for its dead," notes Alvin Stauffer's history of the Quartermaster Corps.[21] Administrative tasks such as keeping burial records and taking inventory of personal effects could be done by any intelligent man, but handling remains and certifying identifications could not be learned as quickly. Soldiers might become familiar with the sight of dead bodies, but the fortitude required to inspect the remains of a man several weeks dead—to go through his pockets looking for letters, to reach into a chest cavity to extract identification tags, or pry open a mouth to make a dental chart—was not taught in Army clerical schools.

"Over It Presides Lieutenant Goodwin"

At last, there was a Graves Registration presence on Guadalcanal, but the provisional First Platoon was only eight men strong. The buildup of training areas, supply dumps, and naval facilities required tremendous amounts of labor and resources, putting manpower and motor transport at a premium. Guadalcanal was still a dangerous place: men were killed in traffic accidents and airplane crashes, drowned while swimming on liberty or when their harbor boats capsized, died in hospitals from tropical disease and battle wounds. There were also a small number of Japanese POWs; these men occasionally died and were buried, if not reverently, at least in marked graves. These casualties all required the attention of the GRS platoon.

Goodwin had his work cut out for him. His first priority seems to have been organizing records for the existing cemetery plots, which meant going case by case through more than 1,000 individual burials. Each grave was supposed to have a GRS Form No. 1—Report of Interment (ROI)—filled out in triplicate: one copy buried with the body, one for Goodwin's office, and the other to be forwarded to the Quartermaster General. Goodwin's signature appears on ROIs for men interred long before he arrived on the island, which indicates that the 45th needed to re-file a considerable amount of paperwork. Meanwhile, Lt. Panosian was signing ROIs for new burials through at least the end of February, possibly to give Goodwin a chance to learn the ropes of the Quartermaster Corps. When Panosian returned to his regular duties, Goodwin assumed command of all Graves Registration activities on the island.

In the first four months of 1943, there appears to have been no deliberate effort made to search for isolated Marine graves. At least, it is certain that Marines were not being reburied at the rate of Army personnel. This does not mean that they were being deliberately neglected or ignored. Instead, a lack of information and staff is probably to blame. Exactly which records were provided to Goodwin's office by the Marine Corps is not known, but they were likely quite sparse. Two representatives of the new Marine Graves Registration unit, Capt. John Apergis and Pvt. Walter Karus, Jr., visited Tulagi and Guadalcanal between February 24 and March 8, 1943. The details of this mission are not known, but probably included the delivery of documents like casualty lists or service records to Goodwin's team. Even following this visit, most Reports of Interment for unknowns in the FMC plot contain a common complaint: "… no further information left at this office by Marine GRS unit." If Goodwin was struggling to account for the Marines buried right in the cemetery, he probably had no idea where to start searching for Marines buried out in the field.

Even supposing that Goodwin was provided with detailed map overlays and eyewitness accounts, he did not have enough men or resources at his disposal to mount extended search and recovery efforts. Running the cemetery occupied the full attention of his little staff, and "volunteering" combat troops for extra duty was not an option. If Robert Kennington "would never do it again" for men from his own company, one can imagine how enthused a soldier would have been to search for strangers. This was not only the case on Guadalcanal, as Edward Steere notes: "Search and recovery activities in the Pacific Theater were carried out on an individual case basis. Graves Registration units, assigned to garrison forces, investigated their areas of responsibility as time and opportunity permitted, but much remained undone, and no region could be regarded as thoroughly combed."[22] The dead "leathernecks" and "dogfaces" would have to wait.

Two Marine graves were discovered during the first significant influx of recoveries, although these were probably found by accident rather than design. Pvt. Francis L. Roberts (C/1st Raider Battalion) lost his life on September 14, 1942, during the Battle of Edson's Ridge; his battalion noted his burial "in field approximately 300 yards from Pioneer Bridge on eastern branch of Lunga River."[23] This bridge was now a well-traveled span across the Lunga; Roberts' grave may have been visible to passers-by or discovered by troops out sightseeing near the famous Ridge. He was disinterred and brought to the ANMC on February 25, 1943. Eighteen-year-old PFC George Payne Clark (Company "A," 6th Marines) disappeared from his company on January 10, 1943, the morning of a major Army offensive. Since the 6th Marines had no enemy contacts, Clark was declared AWOL; when he failed to return, his unit labeled him a deserter. On March 3, 1943, his body was found in the jungle among the dead from an Army unit. It was decided that Clark had indeed gone AWOL, but rather than running from a fight, he had been searching for one. Still, the mark of desertion carried on his file for nearly a year; it was only expunged when reports of his death were confirmed in January 1944.[24]

The provisional Graves Registration platoon did a magnificent job handling their first challenge, due in no small part to the efficiency of Ernest Panosian and the excellent leadership of Chester Goodwin. The Army could have scarcely picked a better man. Conscientious and hardworking, Goodwin not only filled out the retroactive Reports of Interment; he restructured the alignment of the old Marine plot to align with the Quartermaster General's specifications and took it upon himself to write personal letters to the families of the fallen.[25] His seven enlisted men worked as record keepers and administrators; the grave digging was done by a small battalion of local laborers.[26] When the concerted recovery effort ended on March 8, 1943, the ANMC had grown from twelve rows to thirty-nine, or nearly 270 graves. Of these, perhaps a dozen were interred within a day or two of their death; the remainder, almost all of whom were Army personnel, spent an average of six to eight weeks in the field before burial in the ANMC. Incredibly, only ten of these men were buried as unknowns—five were later identified—and two others, buried under the wrong names, were resolved after the war. By the numbers alone, this was by far the largest and most succesful effort undertaken to recover battlefield burials on Guadalcanal, and Goodwin received a well-deserved promotion to lieutenant on March 29, 1943.[27]

Goodwin's efficient implementation of proper Graves Registration protocol played a major role in this success. Receiving bodies from details of combat soldiers was an important first step in confirming identity; reports from a dead man's comrades could solidify a location, a unit, or a name. Confirmation was obtained through a careful search for personal effects, or other "identifying media." There was little else they could do; often they handled skeletal remains. After a few experiences like Kennington's, where soldiers were compelled to sift through the putrefying remains of their former friends, it was decided to let the bodies rest in place until most of the flesh was gone. Visual identification or fingerprinting was already out of the question, and moving dry bones was easier on the stomachs and morale of the exhumers. Clerks grew accustomed to typing "Flesh decomposed. No identifying marks on body. Impossible to take fingerprints or tooth chart." This information was entered on a Report of Interment, along with any possible clues that would aid future identification—date of death, a unit designation, and the bodies buried on either side. (Unfortunately for modern researchers, one key piece of information—a field for describing the location where a body was found—was often left blank.) A copy of this report was inserted into a bottle and buried at the head of the grave; another was forwarded to the Quartermaster General. Goodwin and his senior NCO, S/Sgt. Chester Grant, personally signed off on every Report of Interment.

After the reinterment of five soldiers from Company "E," 132nd Infantry, on March 8, the rate of field recoveries dropped dramatically. Only six are known to have occurred between March 16 and April 27, 1943. The reassignment of Army combat units, who appear to have shouldered most of the burden for locating, excavating, and transporting remains from field to cemetery, played a role in this sudden slowdown. The Americal Division shipped out for Fiji on March 5; the 25th Division remained to garrison Guadalcanal but, having retrieved most of their fallen, focused on training for operations elsewhere in the Solomon Islands. Occasionally, an isolated grave or unburied bones would be found as if by accident. Of four bodies reburied in April, only one—Capt. Samuel N. Moore of USS *Quincy*—was found under a legible marker. The other three were buried as unknowns.

Instead of combing through the boondocks, Goodwin appears to have made initial efforts to identify some of the forty-six unknowns already buried in his cemetery. The service record for Pvt. Emil Student includes a memorandum to the Bureau of Medicine and Surgery inviting comparison between the "finger impression ... of Unidentified #13, U.S. Marine Corps, probable date killed in action, October 7, 1942, buried in Row #25, Grave #8, First Marine Division Cemetery, Guadalcanal ... [and] Emil Stanislaus Student #352326." The Bureau agreed that the fingerprints were identical; Student's identity was confirmed, his mother was notified, and his grave on Guadalcanal appropriately marked.[28] At least ten Marines are known to have been identified in this manner, and there may well have been more:

Pvt. Louis J. LaVallee (G/2/5th Marines): killed in action 14 September 1942, buried in Row 18, Grave 2 as X-1.

Pvt. John C. Rock (C/1st Raider Battalion): killed in action 14 September 1942, buried in Row 12, Grave 2 as X-2.

Platoon Sgt. John J. Quigley (C/1st Raider Battalion): killed in action 14 September 1942, buried in Row 12, Grave 3 as X-3.

Cpl. Ralph W. Barrett, Jr. (HQ/5/11th Marines): missing in action 13 September 1942, buried in Row 19, Grave 2 as X-5.

PFC Raymon W. Herndon (A/1st Parachute Battalion): missing in action 14 September 1942, buried in Row 18, Grave 1 as X-7.

Pvt. Emil S. Student (K/3/5th Marines): killed in action 8 October 1942, buried in Row 25, Grave 8 as X-13.

Pvt. Bill N. Pope (C/1st Raider Battalion): killed in action 9 October 1942, buried in Row 27, Grave 2 as X-15.

Pvt. Frank J. Panarisi (A/1/7th Marines): killed in action 25 October 1942, buried in Row 42, Grave 5 as X-17.

Cpl. Patrick L. Marotta (D/1/7th Marines): missing in action 25 October 1942, buried in Row 45, Grave 9 as X-21.

PFC Theodore Guesman (E/2/7th Marines): killed in action 9 November 1942, buried in Row 57, Grave 2 as X-28.

The simple expedient of taking fingerprints before burial played a crucial part in returning identities to these men and bringing closure to their friends and relatives. It is unlikely that the provisional platoon attempted any exhumations of unknowns in the cemetery itself. Goodwin would not have strained the already taxed resources of his men—many of whom were still learning their craft—and risk destroying physical clues into the bargain.

War correspondent Mack Morriss paid a visit to the cemetery on April 14, 1943. It was his first chance since January, and he was struck by how large it had become. "A new plot, almost as large as the first, is full," he wrote. "Apparently, some of the men were exhumed in the hills and brought back. I wish every person back home could walk between these crosses, see the names and read the inscriptions. All the outfits I was with were represented there.... Nobody walks in there and speaks except in a lowered voice. I suppose that is convention, but I think it is also sheer respect born of understanding." Morriss paused and uncovered at the grave of Cpl. Edwin Bickwermert. "There is nothing particularly morbid about [the cemetery], with the faded palm fronds still over some of the mounds, and almost all of them decorated in some way by the men who fought here, but I couldn't help but remember Rickenbacker's statement in *LIFE* [Magazine] that he 'wouldn't give the life of one American boy for the whole damned island.'" As he wandered through the rows, Morriss noted: "There were more than 50 graves marked 'Unidentified.'"[29]

As Guadalcanal transformed into a permanent base, construction crews ventured further out into the boondocks, sometimes unknowingly traversing old battlefields, and occasionally encountering field burials. The 14th Naval Construction Battalion (Seabees) began building new airfields at Koli as early as December 1942, not long after fighting in the area ceased. They quickly established a fighter crash strip and laid the groundwork for a larger installation called "Bomber 2" (later Carney Field, in memory of their commanding officer). As air strikes against the northern Solomons increased, surveying teams went scouting for another site, which would become "Bomber 3" or Koli Field. This brought them to the banks of the Metapona River and the tiny village of Asamana. On November 11, 1942, the 2nd (Carlson's) Raider Battalion fought a pitched battle over a river crossing near Asamana; ten Raiders were killed in and around the village, including one who was captured, tortured, and castrated by his foes. All were buried in the field the following day. Three well-marked graves—PFC Jerrold B. Miller, PFC Lorenzo D. Anderson, and Pvt. Joseph M. Auman—were discovered on May 2, 1943, just days before the construction of Koli Field began. These men had fallen while fighting in the village on the western bank of the river, close to the site of the proposed airfield. Unfortunately, the other Raiders were likely buried on the eastern bank; development did not extend far across the Metapona, and parts of the area were prone to flooding, which may have destroyed their markers. The remaining seven are still unaccounted for.

Four more Marine remains arrived at the ANMC on May 18. Cpl. Edwin A. Howard (Headquarters & Service Company, 2nd Marines), killed on a ridge halfway between the Matanikau and Point Cruz on November 3, and Pvt. Howard J. Schlesinger (B/1/8), buried at the base of Point Cruz itself on November 19, were probably discovered by construction crews working on the new Navy base. Pvt. Daniel R. Cashman (H/2/7) was killed by an exploding shell on October 28 and buried in the field three days later; his remains were found near the ridge where his platoon-mate Mitchell Paige won the Medal of Honor. The fourth was found under a cross marked "Pop, 7th Marines," and believed killed in action on October 19, 1942. Unfortunately, no further identification was found, and the 7th Marines had no information to help with identification. "Pop"—described as a "rather short, slender man in his middle twenties with very narrow shoulders"—was found wearing only a pair of size 7 GI shoes. Most of his facial bones and ribcage were missing, which prevented any chance of identification. He was buried as X-98.[30]

Operations in June uncovered a further five bodies in the jungle. Cpl. Robert B. Wallace (E/2/5) lost his life on November 2, 1942, and was buried near a road junction two days later. His buddies scratched his name into a mess tin and topped the marker with Wallace's helmet. The grave was in a highly visible location and was even photographed by Marine Gunner John F. Leopold in February 1943. Wallace's remains were brought to the ANMC on June 8 for burial in Plot B, Row 47, Grave 10. A greater mystery surrounded scattered remains found in the Point Cruz area on June 1; no identifying information could be found, and the individual was designated as X-61. Laboratory analysis conducted several years later identified him as PFC Ralph Harless (A/1/7), killed in action at "Little Dunkirk" on September 27, 1942. Another individual found on the same day, "a rather short man of 30 (plus) years of age … exceptionally well-muscled" and missing most of his lower body was buried beside Harless. He was tentatively identified as "W. L. Fleming, USMC" but no individual by that name appears on Marine casualty reports from Guadalcanal.[31] How this misidentification was made is not clear, as the Report of Interment signed by Goodwin and Grant states that X-86 (as he was known) was unidentifiable at time of burial in Row 47, Grave No. 2. The report for X-61 (Harless) appears to be the culprit, stating that the body to the left of Harless was "Fleming." (The discrepancy was discovered in May 1944 and referred to the 2nd Platoon, 49th Quartermaster Graves Registration Company, who confirmed that "Grave 2 Row 47 is occupied by the remains of unknown X-86. No record can be found pertaining to W. L. Fleming, USMC, deceased.") Later in the month, the mostly intact skeleton of a teenaged soldier was found out in the jungle, still clad in his steel helmet and a single GI service shoe. The only identifying physical traits recorded were traces of wavy auburn hair. Lt. Goodwin speculated that the deceased might have been part of the 161st Infantry, but could not be certain, and reported the burial of X-63 on June 28.

Details are unfortunately scarce about the precise locations where these men were found and the circumstances that led to their discovery. The story of PFC Seraphine "Buddy" Smith, a nineteen-year-old Marine from Canton, Ohio, is different. On September 8, 1942, the 1st Raider Battalion staged a daring raid on a Japanese marshaling point near the village of Tasimboko. They surprised and routed the few guards protecting the Kawaguchi Brigade's supply base, ransacked or ruined piles of foodstuffs and medical supplies, burned field packs and other supplies, and dragged captured armaments and artillery into the ocean. While successful, the raid was not without cost. Six Raiders were wounded; Cpl. William D. Carney was killed by a Japanese shell and Buddy Smith went missing. The Raiders withdrew with their casualties, leaving Smith behind; he was reported as missing in action.[32]

Nine months later, the Raiders were back on Guadalcanal, preparing for the next offensive in New Georgia. Between exercises, there was free time—"in quite sharp contrast to the last time we were here," commented PFC Marlin Groft. The new guys were wildly curious about the island, taking hikes up to Edson's Ridge and peppering veterans with questions. Groft had no desire to revisit the Ridge, but when his cohort expressed interest in Tasimboko, he wrangled a trip with a group of Raiders testing weapons on abandoned Japanese barges near the village. Seeing the burnt remains of a village still littered with debris from the raid had "a surreal quality," but "I gave the new fellows the ten-cent tour." The green Raiders were suitably impressed by the ruined base, until one called out "Oh my God. Over here! Quick!"

"I ran over to his side and stared down in the direction of his pointing finger," said Groft. "There, amid the underbrush, were the skeletal remains of a Marine, killed nine months ago and somehow missed when we withdrew. Something glittered in the sunlight beneath the man's rotting shirt. It was his dog tag. I did not touch the body, but we left him where he had lain since September 8, the day his life ended." Groft reported the discovery to his commanding officer, and a quartermaster recovery team was dispatched to collect the remains. Identification tags and circumstances of loss confirmed the identity of "Buddy" Smith on June 24, 1943. "The poor soul was buried in the Marine cemetery with our other fallen," concluded Groft. "I felt satisfaction that at last his family, who most certainly had gotten a 'missing in action' telegram, would have closure, although the sight of the decomposed corpse did unnerve the new guys."[33]

June also saw a few changes in the makeup of the First Platoon, 45th QMGRC. Sixteen enlisted men were assigned in the middle of the month, tripling the platoon's strength. On June 24, Lt. Goodwin and four enlisted men were placed on detached service with the 43rd Infantry Division for the invasion of the Russell Islands. (This turned out to be unnecessary; the landings were unopposed.) Chief Warrant Officer H. M. Garland, Jr., oversaw the section in Goodwin's absence. Routine operations kept the temporary supervisor busy—even in "quiet" periods, there could be as many as eight burials on a single day—and there were no "unsettling discoveries" in the boondocks for several weeks.[34]

Help was on the way. On July 31, 1943, SS *J. H. Kincaid* arrived at Guadalcanal and debarked the 2nd Platoon, 49th Quartermaster Graves Registration Company, led by Lt. Alfred D. Torrence.[35] The 49th was the first Stateside Graves Registration unit to reach to South Pacific; since being organized at Camp Rucker, Alabama the previous year, its men had studied GRS duties exclusively.[36] Guadalcanal was not their permanent station, but a chance to practice their craft before further assignments elsewhere in the Solomon Islands. On-the-job experience was quick to come. The field grave of Pvt. LuVerne H. Trimborn (I/3/2, killed in action October 25, 1942) was discovered in early August, and the 49th handled his reburial in Row 58, Grave 3, on August 6.

The following day, a mass grave was found in an old bivouac belonging to the 1st Battalion, 11th Marines. Japanese battleships bombarded this area on October 16, 1942 and scored a direct hit on a dugout where a geoup of Marines were huddled. "The command post had been located about a half mile from the guns, on the reverse side of a hill. It was just about as safe a spot as you could get," said Warner Pyne of the 11th. "It must have been caught by a fourteen-incher because there was nothing left. I mean, that's all she wrote, nothing! The men at the post were all blown out of town."[37] The bodies of PFCs Hobert T. Price and Lytle E. Whitley, Jr., were pulled from the rubble after the shelling and buried in the Division cemetery. Five others—Sgt. Horace M. Wise, Cpl. John L. Kimmel, and PFCs John J. Hynes, Kenneth C. Schneider, and Bernard Seiden—were reported buried in the field, quite possibly in the dugout where they died.[38] The confused tangle of bones presented a real challenge to the 49th. Seiden, Kimmel, and Hynes were identified before reburial, but the shattered remains of perhaps five other individuals were not so easily separated. Two were interred in the same grave (X-65 and -66, later identified as Wise and Schneider), while the other three received individual burials as X-67, -68, and -69.

The 49th QMGRC recovered Sgt. Arthur C. Garrett (I/3/5) from the banks of the Matanikau, and a headless skeleton designated X-70, on August 11, 1943. Plans for any additional expeditions were shelved when a Japanese air raid sank the attack transport USS *John Penn* two days later. The 49th, suddenly presented with immediate combat casualties, put their training into practice. It took twelve days to find, process, and bury the remains of thirty sailors, fifteen of whom could not be identified. Interestingly, a much older set of remains (designated X-80) was also discovered around this time. They were later identified as Maj. Michael M. Mahoney, a popular officer in the 7th Marines, who died in an aircraft ditching on October 23, 1942. Mahoney became trapped in the plane as it sank; all things considered, it is remarkable that his remains were found at all.

Guadalcanal was gradually being "civilized" by the American military, but the boondocks still held their mysterious appeal to newcomers. The 77th Naval Construction Battalion (Seabees) arrived on September 3, 1943, and stayed for three weeks. During that time, "guards were posted within sight of one another along [the beach] road to keep any stray Japs from infiltrating our camp, and to keep souvenir hunters and curiosity-consumed 'bees of the 77th from infiltrating the jungle." Among the debris of war and much-sought Japanese mess gear were "shallow graves where wild boars had rooted up the bones, Jap skulls bleached white.... We were told to keep out of there. A few days before a Marine patrol had found two American bodies back in the hills. Who? We couldn't tell. They'd been decapitated. We stayed out."[39] Two bodies were, in fact, recovered during the 77th's brief stay on the island: PFC Dale Utecht of the 164th Infantry and a partial skeleton that was not immediately identifiable, yet was listed on the Weekly Report of Burial as "D. Tewell, USMC." (No such Marine existed, and the redoubtable team of Goodwin and Grant did not propagate the error; this individual was designated Unknown X-92. Later laboratory analysis suggested that X-92 may have been Japanese.)

United Press correspondent Francis L. McCarthy visited the island in September 1943 and was impressed by Goodwin's handiwork. "Sixteen hundred American dead lie buried in Guadalcanal," he wrote. "A volunteer honor guard pays them constant tribute.... Flower beds surround the rows of neat, white crosses. An almost never-ending line of fighting men of the United Nations wends its way, night and day, between the rows, paying last respects to dead soldiers, sailors, and marines.... The cemetery's chapel is the first of its kind build in a war zone. Over it presides Lt. Goodwin, the first Graves Registration officer, so far as it is known, to go into actual combat." McCarthy was particularly moved by the personal touches evident on graves like that of twenty-five-year-old Cpl. John W. Ross:

Johnny boy—sweetest fellow,
Lovable and very mellow,
Easy going—full of fun,
God accept this worthy one.[40]

Another distinguished guest visited the cemetery on September 16, 1943, the day Utecht and "Tewell" were buried. Eleanor Roosevelt was in the middle of a goodwill tour to Australia and New Zealand, and after countless visits to hospital wards full of Guadalcanal veterans, she had a strong desire to see the island where her son, Jimmie, had fought and "where these men had left their health or received their injuries."[41] Her sincerity impressed the usually intractable Admiral Halsey, who went against the President's wishes and flew the First Lady to Henderson Field. Eleanor arrived on the night of September 15 and spent the following day visiting hospitals and mess halls, chatting with wounded soldiers and sentries, and inspecting downed Japanese aircraft. Naturally, the cemetery was on her itinerary. "One of the things which I shall never forget on Guadalcanal is my visit to the cemetery," she wrote in her diary:

The little church there was built by the natives and given to the soldiers; they even made an altar and the altar vessels, carving them beautifully and decorating the church with symbols which have special meanings for them—fishes of various kind which mean long life, eternity, etc. It was very moving to walk among the graves and realize how united these boys had been in spite of differences in religion and background. The boy's mess-kit or sometimes his helmet hung on the cross which some friend would have carved with the appropriate symbol of the Jewish or Catholic or Protestant faith. Words that came from the heart were carved on the base, such as "He was a grand guy"—"Best buddy ever." The cemetery is carefully tended and flags wave over the graves. The chaplain told me he took photographs and sent them home to sorrowing families in the United States.... On Guadalcanal, as in many other places, I said a prayer in my heart for the growth of the human spirit, so that we may do away with force in settling disputes in the future.[42]

In the grainy color of an Army newsreel, one can see the First Lady walking through the cemetery, her Red Cross uniform standing out in a gaggle of khaki-clad officers and half-dressed soldiers. She stops before the grave of Pvt. Joseph Werry Burt, Jr., of Company "K," 6th Marines, and says a few words which the silent film does not record. She reads the mess tin inscription left for Cpl. Stanley Friedrich of Company "L," 8th Marines. At a pilot's grave, decorated with propeller blades and belted ammunition, she stops to dry her eyes. The camera cuts away.

The 1st Platoon, 49th QMGRC, arrived on Guadalcanal in the last days of September 1943; shortly thereafter, both platoons of the 49th sailed off to support the New Georgia campaign. Goodwin and the 45th continued their operations on Guadalcanal, recovering PFC Kenneth G. Quist (A/1/7) on September 28 and a headless, armless, unidentifiable man, X-85, on October 2. An expedition to the northwestern tip of the island on October 6 turned into one of their greatest achievements as they recovered, identified, and buried all eleven crew members of a B-24D (*Alley Cat*) which crashed near Cape Esperance the previous July. Next, a pair of Marines were found in isolated graves on a grassy ridge. Cpl. James W. Roach (1st Engineer Battalion) and Cpl. William H. McArdell (F/2/7) gave their lives to defend Henderson Field on October 26, 1942; almost a year after their deaths, they were buried in Plot B, Row 72, of the ANMC.[43]

Roach and McArdell were the last two identified Marines recovered in 1943. The 45th also handled the recovery of an airman—Sgt. Bruce W. Osborne of the 42nd Bombardment Squadron, whose B-17 (*Bessie the Jap Basher*) ditched just 50 yards offshore of Doma Cove in September 1942—and a medic, PFC Joseph Moloney of the 147th Infantry. The year's end brought a slowdown in the number of burials and the number of field recoveries, despite the return of 1st Platoon, 49th QMGRC, from New Georgia. In the next four months, only one Guadalcanal campaign casualty (PFC Chester Staszak, 132nd Infantry) was brought in from the field. During the winter of 1943–1944, an "Allied" plot was established for the remains of non-American casualties: New Zealanders, Fijians, even Raymond L. Cartier of the Free French Navy would be buried in this small section.

The next recovery occurred on March 18, 1944 when six sets of remains were found on an old battlefield near the Matanikau River. Four were swiftly identified: Sergeants Louis P. Kovacs and Harland P. Swart, Jr., Cpl.

Terrence J. Reynolds, Jr., and Pvt. Albert E. Ausili were all members of the 1st Battalion, 5th Marines, killed in action on November 1, 1942. These four were buried individually in Plot C, Row 85; the other two, designated as X-90 and X-91, could not be separated and were buried together.

An interesting story may relate to this discovery. On October 7, 1944, a *Marine Corps Chevron* article, entitled "Promise to The Dead Kept By Marine," told how Sgt. Merton F. Taylor, 29th Marines, returned to Guadalcanal to visit the graves of four buddies. Finding they had not been recovered, Taylor spent two days searching in the hills before locating the graves, marked by crude crosses made from sticks and bayonets. He is pictured making his discovery with Lt. John L. Stewart and PFC Anthony Pincairo of the 49th QMGRC. Taylor fought on Guadalcanal with Company "C," 5th Marines—the same company as Kovacs, Swart, and Ausili—and may have known Reynolds, a squad leader from Company "D."

However, there is a discrepancy in the dates. On March 18, 1944—the date of the recovery as given by Graves Registration Weekly Report of Burials—Lt. Stewart was still en route to Guadalcanal. Sergeant Taylor was not visiting his old battlefield; he was attending Combat Intelligence School in North Carolina. Neither man would actually be present on the island until much later in the year. If Sgt. Taylor did visit his old battlefield, he must have come up empty handed. The *Chevron* story and photograph might have been a dramatic recreation for the benefit of correspondents.[44]

There must have been other remains in the vicinity—the 5th Marines recorded the burial of thirty men in an area "about 400 yards west of Point Cruz, about 600 yards inland from the sea"—but their graves were not discovered. No other members of the 5th Marines are known to have been recovered in 1944.

The 49th Takes Over

The March 18 recovery was the last for Chester Goodwin. The 1st Platoon, 45th Quartermaster Graves Registration Company, departed for New Caledonia on April 5, 1944, having spent fourteen months on Guadalcanal.[45] Their replacements were Lt. George M. McVeigh's 2nd Platoon, 49th QMGRC, who had just returned from New Georgia and would remain on Guadalcanal for the rest of the war. McVeigh's men got off to a strong start; in mid-April, they accounted for Clarence Evans, Gilbert Gray, William Florence, William Richey, and McCoy Reynolds—all members of the 1st Battalion, 8th Marines, who had lain in isolated graves since November 1942.[46] One month later, a trio of graves were found along a trail leading up Mount Austen. Identification tags for Richard C.

Farrar and Cyrill A. Matelski, formerly of the 2nd Raider Battalion and killed in action on December 4, 1942, were found on two of the bodies. The third man had no means of identification and no personal effects, save for a pair of GI field shoes, size 9.5E. He was buried as X-94.[47]

Base construction continued to turn up bodies—a bulldozer working near Fighter Strip No. 2 dug up some shattered bones with bits of American equipment and clothing, classified as X-95—but now the Graves Registration team could take to the field on more complex missions. Shattered aircraft dotted the islands; on May 31, 1944, a wrecked Dauntless dive-bomber was found along with what remained of its crew, Cpl. Alfred Hozempa and X-96, later identified as 1Lt. Herbert Bass. Under the leadership of McVeigh's successor, 1Lt. John L. Stewart, the 2nd Platoon even undertook two multiple-day "marches" to aircraft crash sites on Florida and San Cristobal islands in August 1944. In both expeditions, detachments retrieved every man they set out to find.[48]

While the second of these "marches" was happening, another team was combing the Point Cruz area. Skeletal remains found in a gas dump triggered the search, which began in the ridges south of the point on August 22, 1944. The marked graves of Marines Rollen Mullens, Edwin Langley, and Alba Jenkins (E/2/7), victims of the Third Battle of the Matanikau, were discovered. A grim collection of scattered bones and equipment fragments were found near the ridges 500 yards inland from the Point; a shallow grave contained two incomplete skeletons, both wearing Marine boondockers. Lt. Stewart and his senior NCO, S/Sgt. Richard Moyer, processed these remains but could not establish identity.

The last group recovered by the 49th was also its most noteworthy. On October 5, 1944, a burial site was located several miles up the Lunga River. Investigating teams found the remains of Corporals Morris Curry and Elmer Garrettson, late of Company "B," First Marines. Over the next two days, six more graves were found in the area; five were identified as Ralph Ingerson, Charles Debele, Carl Gorczysky, Wilbur McElvaine, and George Compton, all from Company "B." The sixth had no identification, but from the remnants of medical equipment he carried, the GRS rightly assumed that he had been a corpsman; he would later be identified as Pharmacist's Mate James F. Pierce. In January, Cpl. Hans C. Jensen's remains were found in the same vicinity, bringing the total number of recoveries at the site to nine. These men had fallen in an ambush back in September 1942; the 49th could not have known that another nine Marines were left behind.

On January 29, 1945, a massive explosion shook the Quonset huts at Lunga Point. The cargo ship USS *Serpens* had been loading depth charges not far off the beach when something went catastrophically wrong. The sight was "an awe-inspiring death drama" according to an eyewitness. "As the report of screeching shells filled the air and the flash of tracers continued, the water splashed throughout the harbor as the shells hit. We headed our boat in the direction of the smoke and as we came into closer view of what had once been a ship, the water was filled only with floating debris, dead fish, torn life jackets, lumber and other unidentifiable objects.... This was sudden death, and horror, unwanted and unasked for, but complete." The disaster claimed the lives of 197 Coast Guardsmen, fifty-one Army stevedores of the 231st Port Company, and a civilian physician aboard; one soldier on shore was struck and killed by flying shrapnel.[49] Of the fifty-six bodies that could be found and brought to the cemetery, Graves Registration was able to identify only three. It was the last major military calamity to occur on Guadalcanal. Following the *Serpens* disaster, Lt. Stewart's unit—redesignated as the 109th Quartermaster Graves Registration Platoon on February 1, 1945—maintained a nearly static cemetery, with only the occasional single grave requiring their attention.[50]

There was one incident, however, which was unique among all their experiences in the war. On March 20, 1945, Army Pvt. Robert A. Pearson met his death on Guadalcanal. He was not the victim of combat, accident, or disease, but of military justice. Pearson was charged with killing a fellow soldier, Pvt. Frederick D. Johnson of the 368th Infantry, on April 4, 1944. His conviction carried the death sentence: Pearson's hanging was the only execution of an American soldier carried out in the Solomon Islands. In accordance with military tradition, the disgraced soldier's body was buried in a separate plot.[51]

A handful of recovery operations were undertaken in the closing months of the war. On April 3, four unidentified remains were found with an aircraft wrecked on South Malaita, and two more were found with a Navy dive bomber downed off Rennell Island.[52] In July, another wreck was discovered about a mile inland from Guadalcanal's Doma Cove. The plane was readily identified as a Navy SBD-type bomber, a type that saw heavy service during the campaign. Key pieces of the aircraft—the landing gear, cylinder head, engine housing, and fuselage—still had legible serial numbers; the squadron number "21" was painted in 18-inch letters on either side of the fuselage. A nearby grave marker bore a maximum speed plate from the plane and the inscription "2 Men." "Bones of two different bodies were found in this isolated grave," read S/Sgt. Moyer's report. "Impossible to separate.... At time of disinterment almost all bones which were found were broken." The two aviators were buried in Plot D, Row 117, Grave 4, as X-182 and -183 on July 10, 1945.[53] They would be among the last wartime recoveries on Guadalcanal.

Consolidation of Cemeteries

News of the Japanese surrender on September 2, 1945 sent a wave of jubilation through military camps across the Pacific. Combat troops rejoiced that the planned invasion of the Home Islands was canceled, and service troops in rear echelons began counting the months, weeks, and days until they could go home. The end of hostilities, though, did not mean the end of the Graves Registration mission. The Naval policy forbidding the shipment of human remains had been strictly observed since the beginning of the war, but now the war was over. The bodies of 61,656 fighting men in 133 Pacific cemeteries would need to be disinterred, identified, and assigned a final disposition per the wishes of their next of kin.[54]

The Army-Navy Joint Policy Memorandum of February 19, 1945, called for the consolidation of smaller cemeteries into "such larger cemeteries as may be located nearest such places where there will be an Army installation and as may be readily accessible to promote expeditious repatriation of all our service dead."[55] The Solomon Islands were under the auspices of the Army Forces, Mid-Pacific (AFMIDPAC), whose zone encompassed the Hawaiian, Gilbert, Marshall, Mariana, and Bonin Islands. "The AFMIDPAC area included two distinct types of cemeteries," wrote Edward Steere and Thayer Boardman, "which presented differing disinterment problems when bodies were exhumed preparatory to concentration of remains in a few centralized points. One group of cemeteries included battlefield burials. The second type comprised base command cemeteries ... where no fighting had taken place.... In general, concentration operations proved more difficult in battlefield cemeteries, where many scattered interments were made in haste and where records were either incomplete or missing." Thousands of men were buried in the Solomon Islands, on battlefields and bases alike. Due to the distances involved and the number of remains to move, the Solomon Islands were assigned two concentration points. The dead from the northern Solomons campaigns—New Georgia, Rendova, and Bougainville—were brought to the Finschhafen cemeteries of New Guinea.[56] Those who had died on Tulagi, the Russell Islands, or Espiritu Santo and Efate in the New Hebrides, became the responsibility of the 109th QMGRC on Guadalcanal.[57]

The monumental task of disinterring these remains and shipping them, along with their reams of attendant paperwork, to Guadalcanal's Army, Navy, and Marine Cemetery commenced even before the surrender was announced. Between July 10 and August 28, 1945, at least 127 individuals from other islands were reburied in the ANMC, and this was barely a tenth of the estimated 1,200 that would eventually arrive. A look at a grave chart reveals neither rhyme nor reason to the organization; dates, services, and locations of death are all intermingled, making it impossible to tell exactly how and when the shipments of remains arrived.

While most of the remains came from "base command cemeteries" and were properly identified, there were several dozen unknowns as well. The majority of these came from Cemetery No. 1 at Tulagi Naval Base. Tulagi, of course, had once been an active combat zone, and many of the unidentified men had been buried there following the great naval battles of 1942. To further compound the confusion, Tulagi cemeteries had undergone a reorganization in December 1944; in some cases, remains were exhumed, moved, and reburied three or four times before arriving at Guadalcanal. This was a textbook case of "interments made in haste where records were incomplete or missing" leading to mistakes. Graves Registration clerks had to work backward, tracing each set of remains from grave plot to grave plot, often finding that the information they needed most—a complete report filed at the time of death—was missing. Remains were reburied with the information on hand, reliable or not; the only change made in many cases was to update the X-number to match the ANMC sequence (for example, X-7 from Tulagi became X-225 in the ANMC). The usually meticulous 109th completed few, if any, tooth charts for the reinterred unknowns—likely due to the sheer number of remains they were handling every day—but the price of expedience was to add yet another twist to complicated burial histories and kick the question of resolving identity even further down the field.

Even well-kept records sometimes failed to produce results. An unknown (X-13) arrived from Espiritu Santo Military Cemetery with a completed Report of Interment that included his date and cause of death (October 23, 1942, intracranial injury), the date, time, and location of burial, a map of the cemetery, and a full set of fingerprints. Of course, these no longer helped with skeletal remains, and the individual was buried again as X-190.

The Graves Registration troops were still occasionally called into the field. In September 10, 1945, the 109th interred ten separate sets of remains. One was identified as Cpl. William F. Wheeler (C/1/5). Six were found on a hill approximately a mile inland from Point Cruz. They were in poor condition after long exposure to the elements. "No identification," typed S/Sgt. Moyer. "Probably body of man who was killed in that area in 1942. No tooth chart could be made. Only the skeleton remained." Two more were found buried together in a common grave; Moyer's team lacked the experience to separate them, and they were buried together as X-217 and X-218. Oddly, these ten graves were arranged in a column, occupying the fourth graves of Rows 141 to 149.

The number of field recoveries dwindled in the weeks that followed; those found were often in a pitiful condition as recorded by T/5 William H. Tussey, the hard-working clerk for the 109th:

X-308:   Body found in isolated grave approximately 3 miles inland from Kukum. No identification found. Only skeleton remained. No tooth chart could be taken. Burial 29 September 1945.

X-311:   Probably the body of a man killed in action in 1942. Initials R. B. T. found on helmet liner, also a Catholic Crucifix. No tooth chart could be taken. Burial 12 October 1945.

X-312:   Body found on Hill #27 located on Guadalcanal Map 104 coordinates 71.7–195.7. No means of identification found. Probably the body of a man killed in action in that area in 1942. No tooth chart could be taken. Burial 12 October 1945.

X-313:   Field burial, probably the body of a man killed in action in 1942. Initials L. W. L were found on cross marking the grave. Tooth chart could not be taken. Burial 12 October 1945.

X-314:   The initials R. R. were found in helmet liner with body. Also serial number 3602924? Couldn't make out the last number. This skeleton was located on Guadalcanal Map 104 at coordinates 71.7–195.7. Probably was a casualty during the invasion. Only skeleton remains. No tooth chart could be taken. Burial 12 October 1945.

X-320:   This skelton [sic.] was found approximately 100 yards from the beach directly in front of Lever Brothers Manager's Home on Gavutu. An American helmet and shoes were found with the body. Burial 29 October 1945.[58]

Six Marines were among those brought to the ANMC during the consolidation period. Four were identified at the time of burial; two were interred as unknowns and identified after the war.

Private Glenn L. Mitchell (A/2nd Raider Battalion): killed in action 1 December 1942 and buried in the field; reinterred in Plot D, Row 140, Grave 1.

Corporal William F. Wheeler (C/1/5th Marines): killed in action 1 November 1942 and buried in the field; reinterred in Plot E, Row 143, Grave 4.

Private Edward J. Cunningham (G/2/8th Marines): killed in action 25 November 1942 and not recovered; reinterred in Plot E, Row 144, Grave 2.

Unknown X-213 (PFC Louis J. Huettman, G/2/8th Marines): missing in action 23 November 1942; reinterred in Plot E, Row 145, Grave 4.

Platoon Sergeant Harold F. Drain (C/1/8th Marines): killed in action 13 January 1943 and buried in the field; reinterred in Plot C Annex, Row 174, Grave 8.

Unknown X-321 (PFC James L. Blair, C/1/8th Marines): killed in action 29 December 1942 and buried in the field; reinterred in Plot C Annex, Row 174, Grave 9.

"Blackie" Mitchell was killed by a sniper while searching for airdropped supplies near Mount Austen. His buddies made a marker clad in salvaged biscuit tins; this metal covering might have helped it to survive in legible condition.[59] Wheeler was buried at the site of a major battle "about 400 yards west of Point Cruz [and] about 600 yards inland from the sea"—an area previously explored by the 45th QMGRC in March 1944, and recorded in muster rolls as the burial place for thirty men from the 1st Battalion, 5th Marines. Huettman's company attacked a heavily fortified ridge in the same area on the day he was reported missing in action; both his battalion and the Third Battalion, 164th Infantry, suffered terribly and were unable to hold their ground against "practically impregnable" Japanese positions "on the reverse slope of a bare ridge with interlocking grazing fire of numerous machine guns." Cunningham's death came as his battalion held their meager gains; there was "aggressive combat patrolling" during this time, and Cunningham may have been lost on one of these sorties. (Unknowns X-210, 211, 212, 214, and 216 might be Marines or soldiers lost in the failed assault, but to date only X-213—Huettman—has been identified.)

The 1st Battalion, 8th Marines, later occupied this ridge; there were the usual combat patrols, one of which cost the life of PFC James Blair. Two weeks later, Plat. Sgt. Harold Drain was killed when his company ran into a heavily defended draw near Hills 78 and 80. All told, five Marines from the battalion were killed in the day's action, and four were buried in the field. Drain was comparatively lucky: the remains of PFC Eugene W. Wade, Pvt. Joseph J. Diamond, and Pvt. Hobart M. Fiscus, Jr., went undiscovered.[60]

Drain and Blair were the final field recoveries made during the consolidation period. In November 1945, labor troops dug the last grave, and ARM1c William J. Stribling joined his countrymen in the Army, Navy, and Marine Cemetery. Not long thereafter, the 109th Quartermaster Graves Registration Platoon was relieved of duty, and for many months, the chief activity in the cemetery was groundskeeping. Back home, however, the American Graves Registration Service was coming to realize that the 3,350 graves on Guadalcanal were not nearly enough to contain all those reported dead—and the families of those not recovered were demanding an accounting.

9

Tell Me About My Boy

World War II brought death to more than 300,000 Americans who were serving their country overseas.
While the war was on, most of these honored dead were buried in temporary United States military cemeteries. Some were buried in isolated graves. These latter are being located as fast as possible and are buried in these temporary military cemeteries. Some were lost at sea. Other remains shall never be recovered.

Quartermaster Corps pamphlet, *Tell Me About My Boy*, 1946

Mr. Charles Kendrick flatly rejected the decision of Headquarters USMC. He was determined to find his son.

Second Lieutenant Charles Kendrick, Jr., was one of the heroes of the Cactus Air Force. The young man's star had risen quickly with the fighting squadron VMF-223; he was an ace pilot, and Admiral Chester Nimitz had personally decorated him with the Distinguished Flying Cross. The day after the ceremony, "Red" Kendrick failed to return from an intercept mission. His wrecked Wildcat was found on its back a few miles from Henderson Field; two pilot friends buried him by a distinctive rock near the crash site, and they wrote as much to the Kendrick family. A family friend, Col. George Stimmel, visited the grave two months later and brought photographs back to California. It was impossible, argued Mr. Kendrick, that his son could not be recovered.

Mr. Kendrick was not just a bereaved father. He was also Maj. Kendrick, a decorated veteran of the Great War, a prominent figure in the American Legion and leading citizen of San Francisco, where he helped spearhead the War Memorial Opera House. As president of Schlage

Lock Company, Mr. Kendrick earned the government's thanks for his professional and personal contributions to the war effort. He was, to say the least, extremely well connected. After acquiring map annotations from his son's former comrades, the seventy-year-old businessman used those connections to secure a seat on a military flight bound for the Solomon Islands. On February 12, 1947, he stepped onto the tarmac at Henderson Field, Guadalcanal.

Accompanied by an Australian mine manager, a Marist priest, and representatives of the Solomon Islands Constabulary, Mr. Kendrick headed into the hills. It took ten days to find the Wildcat, and yet one more to locate "Red" Kendrick's grave. The military funeral that followed was well attended, with an honor guard of American soldiers and Solomon Islander scouts. "Kendrick's search also led to the location of several other graves on remote hillsides," related a reporter, "and the graves registration unit will be told of these."[1]

Of thousands of grieving parents, Charles Kendrick the only one with the means and influence to make a personal search for his son. The rest were left dependent on the Army Graves Registration Service.

Renewed Assurances of Sympathy

16 July 1946
My dear Mr. and Mrs. Rhodes:

It is with regret I inform you that the remains of your son, the late Private First Class Luther L. Rhodes, U. S. Marine Corps, which were temporarily interred on the field of battle, have not been recovered.

During the course of the invasion and ultimate conquest of the islands of the Pacific, the combat forces made every effort, as far as battle conditions permitted, to mark the temporary graves of deceased personnel in order that the remains might be recovered at a later date. However, shortly thereafter, when the Graves Registration Units began operating in the occupied areas with a view toward recovering the remains for reinterment in a military cemetery, they found that despite their utmost endeavors, many of the graves could not be located. Inability to find the graves was due to changes in the appearance of the terrain caused by the rapid growth of thick underbrush and tropical vegetation, and by extensive destruction wrought by artillery barrages and aerial bombing attacks.

This information was not furnished you at an earlier date pending receipt of the reports of the final searches made of the Pacific Theater of

Operations for missing personnel and isolated graves. These searches are now considered completed.

A number of our dead have not yet been identified but the American Graves Registration Service is attempting by every scientific means to establish identity. This procedure, however, entails long and careful investigation and will require many months to complete.

Although it appears improbable that the remains of your son will be recovered, you may be certain that should his remains be positively identified you will be promptly informed and furnished the necessary application blanks to be completed in connection with the return of his remains.

Sincerely yours,
EDWIN C. CLARKE
Captain, U. S. Marine Corps.

The form letters went out in the thousands, to homes where the joy of victorious peace was tempered by the loss of a loved one. Frequently, they came as a shock to families who wondered how official sources could know so little about something so important. It was confirmation without information, certainty without finality, and cast doubt on all the correspondence that came before. Had they been told the truth about their loved one's death? Had his sacrifice made a difference, or was it all inconsequential? Or, if no body was found, was he really dead at all?

July 25, 1946
Commandant of the Marine Corps, Washington D.C.

In reply to your letter of July 16 it is with deep sorrow we read the news that the body of our dead Son PFC Luther L. Rhodes serial no 327928 has not been located as we hope to have his body returned to his beloved Land the U.S.A. for his final resting place. Thank you and if any further information is obtained concerning his remains please do not hesitate to notify us we remain yours truly

Mr. & Mrs. Harley B. Rhodes

Personal letters began flooding into Headquarters, Marine Corps. Expressions of anger and confusion, sorrow and understanding, heartfelt requests for more information, for personal effects, for what to do next. More than anything, families wanted to know what had happened. "'Tell me about my boy' is the request most frequently sent to the Quartermaster

General of the Army by next of kin who want additional information on the progress of the War Department's program for the return and final burial of those who died overseas in World War II," began a Quartermaster Corps pamphlet produced in 1946. "Seeking information from unauthorized persons is inadvisable. Official sources alone should be sought to avoid the dissemination of erroneous information and the disappointment which a wrong answer might bring."[2]

The official response to a plaintive request was often disappointment enough:

11 August 1946
My dear Mr. and Mrs. Rhodes:

I have your letter of July 25 regarding your son, the late Private First Class Luther L. Rhodes, U. S. Marine Corps.

This office received a report that your son was buried in the First Marine Division Cemetery on Guadalcanal, British Solomon Islands. However, a recheck was recently made of that cemetery and I regret to inform you that no record was found of his grave.

It may be that your son's remains could not be identified at the time of interment and were of necessity buried among the unidentified in one of the military cemeteries. You may be certain that no effort will be spared in attempting to identify our dead and every scientific means will be utilized to this end. The identification of remains is an extremely slow process but is progressing and will continue as long as there is any possibility for further identifications. You can doubtless realize that the terrific explosive power of modern weapons of war makes it extremely difficult, and in some cases impossible, to establish identifications after death.

I can understand your desire to have your son's remains recovered and any further information obtained will be forwarded to you.

With renewed assurances of sympathy, I am
Sincerely yours,
D. Routh
Lieut. Colonel, U. S. Marine Corps.[3]

Disbelief or mistrust also crept in as families received (or perceived) conflicting messages. Many could not understand why they had received personal effects when a body was supposed to be missing. Others provided condolence letters or grave photographs sent by comrades of the deceased or friends of the family. Mrs. Opal Alward of Linton, Indiana, went straight to the Secretary of Defense. "My son was killed in Oct. 1942 in the Guadalcanal," she wrote, "and I have saw in newspapers here they have brought back boys from there for burial and I haven't had any papers or any kind of word concerning my boy.… My boy was a Marine and his name is Albert Leroy Bernes, so if you can tell me what to do or could send me the necessary papers." Unsatisfied by the reply she received, Mrs. Alward tried the Commandant of the Marine Corps. "I received the letter in regards my Son Albert Leroy Bernes and that his remains have not been recovered and identified and can't understand how that can be for I had a letter soon after from The Marines telling me he was buried in grave number 2," she wrote on March 23, 1948, "and giving his tag no. and also wish to say he was wounded on the 7th of Oct. 1942 and died on the 9th of Oct. 1942 and I don't see why he wasn't buried along with the others who died along the same time. One boy from this little city of ours told at one time he had saw Leroy's grave. So I am hoping that you may locate him and soon for I am in very poor health and this worries me very much."

While Commandant Clifton Cates was no doubt sympathetic to Mrs. Alward's plight—he was himself a Guadalcanal veteran—he could do little to help. Her hopes were crushed in August of 1949 by another letter from the Casualty Division: "It is regretted that the American Graves Registration Service was not successful in locating the remains of your son. You may be certain, however, that everything possible was done to effect the recovery and identification of his remains."[4]

The words, while well-intentioned, must have been small comfort indeed.

Back to the Islands

Despite Capt. Clarke's assurance that "final searches … are now considered completed," the reality was that organized searching "began very late," as Edward Steere relates. "Such activity prior to 1947 was at best haphazard and somewhat piecemeal, since various local island commanders of separate branches of the service carried out search operations for isolated burials." The scarcity of reliable information was astounding. In December 1946, Army Graves Registration Service, Pacific Zone (AGRS-PAZ) acknowledged only seventy-nine active cases "when, as a matter of fact, several thousand unrecovered dead lay scattered throughout the PAZ. Hundreds of Navy servicemen were missing from the Pearl Harbor disaster alone."[5] In January 1947, as Mr. Kendrick pursued his personal crusade, the AGRS began a similar effort on a much larger scale. Their survey of records included individual service files, After Action Repots, muster rolls, correspondence between quartermaster outfits, and base closeout reports. The Adjutant General's Records Division handed over some files, and "AGRS 'arm-chair' detectives" who pored over other sources "discovered names of missing persons, boats, and aircraft in books or magazine articles, which were not listed in Graves Registration files." Newspaper reports prompted individuals to volunteer information. Veterans provided clues about their buddies; relatives of the missing contributed letters and photographs. By September 1947, AGRS-PAZ had 4,303 missing person cases, and the number was still climbing.[6]

The AGRS was racing to meet a timetable. Congress ordered that the program of recovery in all theaters of the war be completed in five years; Quartermaster General of the Army Thomas B. Larkin thought his men could accomplish the task in less time.[7] An initial phase—planned as much "to uphold the faith of the next of kin in the program" as to gauge the effort and resources required to meet an aggressive schedule—kicked off in the spring of 1947. Hawaii was chosen as the proving ground; 3,200 remains were to be disinterred, identified, and processed within nine weeks. A new organization, the 9105th Technical Services Unit (TSU), was created to handle this job.[8] On paper, each of the eight Field Operating Sections of the 9105th would be fully manned, equipped, and provided with ample transport between military cemeteries on the islands.

In practice, however, the results were not encouraging. Transport problems abounded; even in the Hawaiian Islands, the 9105th TSU required logistical support by land, sea, and air. Only some of the Field Operating Sections were able to deploy all of their men and equipment, while the rest worked piecemeal. The most persistent problem was one of manpower: the 9105th was far from a desirable assignment for men of any rank. There was a shortage of experienced Graves Registration officers, and finding new ones to train was a challenge. Most officers arrived in Hawaii expecting pleasant duty like the pre-war years; some even arranged to have their families join them. Those who found themselves assigned to the 9105th expressed "keen disappointment," and some went so far as to request a transfer or a discharge from the service.

Qualified civilians were sought to make up the difference, but few warmed to the prospect of sailing between remote islands and tramping through swamps in search of dead bodies. Even less-than-ideal candidates proved difficult to convince, and only a third of the planned number of embalmers and clerks were hired before training commenced in July. When the exhumations began in earnest, many of the civilian workers took off—daily turnover rates approached 10 percent, and replacements could not be sufficiently trained. Chief among the many lessons learned was that "the hasty inauguration of exhumations" was not always worth the litany of problems.[9]

As the 9105th TSU cut its teeth in the cemeteries of Hawaii, other units were working in more challenging conditions across the Pacific Theater. The 604th Quartermaster Graves Registration Company (QMGRC) had been overseas since 1943, performing every task that might be asked of a GRS unit, up to and including support of combat operations in New Guinea and on Iwo Jima. After the surrender, the company's four platoons conducted cemetery consolidation work at various stations and battlefields—most notably in the Tarawa atoll, scene of an infamously bloody battle in 1943. More than 1,000 Marines and sailors died storming the beaches of tiny Betio Island, and many more were killed in accidents and mishaps in the two years that it functioned as an airfield and naval base. The fifty-man detachment of the 604th under Lt. Ira Eisensmith anticipated that consolidating so many bodies into the new Lone Palm cemetery would be a challenge. They did not expect the nearly impossible task that awaited them. Betio alone had forty-three separate burial sites, from single bodies to hundreds of remains in long trenches. To make matters worse, the island garrison constructed memorial cemeteries on the island, which meant placing crosses and memorials in areas convenient for the growing base while removing the original markers erected over actual graves. When remains were found beneath markers, there was no guarantee of a matching identity. Corroded identification tags, decomposed bones, incomplete records, and live ammunition added to the challenge of recovery. In three months, the 604th located only about half of the remains they sought, and only a few of those could be identified before reburial in Lone Palm.[10] Eisensmith's team departed in July 1946; a second detachment of the 604th disinterred Lone Palm between December 1946 to January 1947 and prepared those remains for shipment back to Hawaii.

Meanwhile, the ongoing AGRS survey "uncovered sufficient data to warrant the formation of an extensive search and recovery operation."[11] Planning commenced in March 1947, and the mission got the green light in May. Solving cases that had bested every wartime search effort was a daunting task, and the passage of time would only make circumstances that much harder. "The Pacific area was particularly inhospitable and reluctant to give up its dead," writes Michael Sledge, "nor did it hold particular appeal to U.S. units charged with the responsibility of working little-known islands, lagoons, and jungles."[12] The mission was also clearly beyond the abilities of the recalcitrant civilians of the 9105th TSU, so the 604th QMGRC—the most experienced organization in the theater—was chosen for this job. Their 1st Platoon, scarcely returned from its lengthy assignment on Betio, was told to prepare for yet another voyage out into the Pacific. Difficulties in procuring equipment delayed the departure;

in the interval, the remaining platoons of the 604th were disbanded and sent home. The remaining soldiers—eight officers and fifty-six enlisted men, under the command of Capt. Clarence Hawkins—plus a civilian mortician, "Mr. Dunman," boarded *LST-711* and set sail for Kwajalein on July 15, 1947.[13]

The first leg of the voyage was devoted to planning and preparation. Guadalcanal was the priority objective, and Capt. Hawkins assigned the bulk of his platoon to the task. "1st Lieutenant Eugene I. Agnew was to be in command of the detail," noted expedition scribe Lt. Robert I. Trapp, "with 1st Lt. Howard D. Wolenberg, 2nd Lt. John H. Mooney to assist, and 1st Lt. Chun Kwok Bung [and] CWO John R. McBee, as observer. These officers and a detail of thirty-three men are to remain in Guadalcanal to search for the missing personnel on that island." The balance would work cases on smaller islands and proceed to Australia for provisions, then rejoin the Guadalcanal party. Following stops at Kwajalein and Nauru Island (where the recovery of several bodies was followed by a festive lawn party for all hands), the 604th proceeded on to the Solomon Islands.

LST-711 arrived at Guadalcanal on August 7, 1947, the fifth anniversary of the invasion. As the ship unloaded supplies, vehicles, and machinery, representatives from the 604th connected with the Army detachment stationed on the island, including one Capt. Johnson, who was the current cemetery superintendent. Lt. Agnew's shore detachment moved into huts at the Lunga Point base, where a friendly Army engineer unit helped set up generators, lights, and water tanks. Three days later, *LST-711* sailed off for other targets in the Solomons—along with Lt. Trapp and the official expedition diary.[14]

The story of Agnew's team may be glimpsed in the reports they filed, which ended up in the personnel files of the men they sought. They were supplied with copies of Quartermaster Form 371—"Data On Remains Not Yet Recovered Or Identified"—which provided pertinent data to match against identification tags, a physical description (including a rudimentary dental chart) of each individual, and as much additional information as was available. In most cases, this amounted to details from muster rolls or wartime reports of death. Search teams carried prints of Map 104, augmented by reports from Army engineers who remembered seeing graves while surveying the hills.

Agnew's Search and Recovery (S&R) teams hit the field on August 15 and began working areas close to camp. One of the first men they found was in the Lunga area. He still wore his service shoes and a pair of canteens, his ammunition belt still held five clips of .30-caliber ammunition, and two quarters were found where his pockets had been. Most of his left arm was missing, and his skull—except for a single tooth—was gone. No means of identification were found, but the S&R team noted a name scratched onto a canteen cup. "C. Wiglehart" became the first unknown isolated burial found by the 604th, and one of its first enduring mysteries: there was no "Wiglehart" on Guadalcanal. (Later analysis of the cup clarified the inscription as "C. W. Iglehart" but this name also came up empty.) The remains were carefully collected, boxed, and brought back to camp.[15]

On August 18, two teams headed for the Matanikau to work Case Number 716, which involved twenty-one Marine Corps personnel. Lt. Wolenberg's investigation report provides a rare glimpse into the difficult working conditions—and intense frustration—that would dog the 604th for their entire stay on Guadalcanal:

From the coordinates given, seven bodies were concentrated on a narrow grassy ridge or two small finger ridges projecting from it. The area is difficult to reach and shows few signs of occupancy after the battle. There are numerous foxholes on the ridges and in the ravine between the two finger ridges. All foxholes and possible grave sites were thoroughly investigated, but no American remains were found at the coordinates indicated. However, the remains of Guadalcanal Isolated Burial Number 2 was found at coordinates (69.77–200), Map 104.... If the remains laboratory can definitely establish the race of Guadalcanal Isolated Burial Number 2 as American, remains might possibly be those of one of the seven men listed below.

PFC Gagnon	69.75–200.15
Cpl. Suggs	69.75–200.15
PFC Eberle	69.7–200.4
PFC Strickland	69.75–200.4
Sgt. Ballew	69.725–200.2
PFC Lawson	69.9–200.2
PFC McGettrick	69.9–200.2

[The men in question were all members of the 2nd Battalion, 7th Marines, killed in action on October 8 and 9, 1942, during the Second Battle of the Matanikau.]

One remains was [*sic.*] supposed to be at coordinates (70.1–200.3) which is further east on the long grassy ridge. This area was thoroughly searched, but no remains could be found.

[The identity of this individual is not known.]

Three reported remains at coordinates (69.9–199.55), (69.8–199.8), and (69.7–199.8) respectively. This area was on the slopes of a grassy ridge and in a ravine ... directly south of the ridge indicated in paragraph two.... All foxholes and possible grave sites were thoroughly searched, but no American remains could be found.

[The first set of coordinates was Pvt. Albert L. Bernes, killed in action on October 9, 1942. Bernes was buried with two others from the 1st Battalion, 7th Marines: PFC Harry Morrissey and PFC Francis Drake, Jr. The two remains in the ravine are not known; this was the site of an engagement involving Company "E," 8th Marines, in November 1942.]

Coordinates (69.3–199.3), where four remains were reported buried, are located approximately at the junction of a high grassy ridge and a smaller finger ridge. All foxholes and possible burial sites in the area were thoroughly searched, but no American remains could be found.

[Pharmacist's Mate Harvey C. Hall of 2nd Battalion, 8th Marines, was reported buried at these coordinates following his death on November 22, 1942. The identity of the other individuals is not known, but they were likely members of the same battalion, which lost fourteen men in action on this date. Only two had been recovered by the time of the expedition.]

Coordinates (69.45–199.7), where six men are reported buried, is located on the wooded east slope of a low, very narrow ridge, which connects with two high grassy ridges. Signs of heavy fighting can still be traced through the area. All foxholes and possible burial sites were thoroughly searched, but no American remains were found.

Recommend that this case be closed.

[The identities of these six individuals are not known.][16]

Two officers and twenty men spent a total of nine days searching for the remains of Case 716. They returned all but empty handed, with only Isolated Burial No. 2 to show for their efforts. It is possible, even likely, that the searchers found the remains of Japanese fighters on the old battlefields—note that Wolenberg specifies "no American remains were found"—and presumably left those remains to lie where they were. (Ironically, laboratory analysis indicated that Isolated Burial No. 2 was almost certainly a Japanese soldier.) A second search was apparently made and returned with Isolated Burials No. 3 and No. 4—later identified as PFCs Gerald J. McGettrick and James M. Lawson, Jr. (both G/2/7). Still, it was a disappointing start to the recovery mission.

Other teams fanned out across the island. Personnel from the 604th headed for the Point Cruz area to search for Marines and soldiers lost in the numerous attempts to push through to the west. Here, too, the S&R teams found they could not always rely on the information provided. Form 371 for AGRS-PAZ Case No. 7176 (PFC Raymond Schulthies) included map coordinates, and a team dedicated August 19, 1947, to searching the reported location but could not locate any clues.[17] Any men assigned to search for Sgt. Bill Smith and Cpl. Doyle Asher must have thrown up their hands in disgust: the same incorrect coordinates that placed their graves out into the bay were the only ones supplied on their data sheets. Further frustration, but no further remains, was all they found at Hill "Y," where "Chesty" Puller's battalion was ambushed in September 1942. The soldiers dug up foxholes and potential graves for two days without finding a trace of the ten men buried nearby.[18] The infamous Matanikau sandspit was given a "thorough search" on September 5, but not one of the Marines buried in the vicinity was located.[19]

Some reports had additional details, but even these could do more harm than good. The team detailed to find PFC Jack H. Gardner, Pvt. George H. Grazier, and Pvt. John C. Buckhalt must have been dismayed at the forms they received. Gardner and Grazier were simply "buried in the Hills" in August 1942. Buckhalt's form, however, had additional information gleaned from a letter written by his sister. His grave, she said, was located "at the first bend in river approximately 200 to 250 yards inland, grave was about 10 yards from river bank on right side going upstream. Grave was marked by white cross made out of coral and placed flat across center of it. There was also an identification tag tied to a bayonet." As proof, she included a picture. Her source for this information is not known, and was unfortunately incomplete. The letter did not specify which of Guadalcanal's many rivers to use as a starting point, so Lt. Agnew's men investigated "all river banks through the battle area for a distance of five hundred yards inland."[20] On September 27, the 604th decided the case was hopeless and called off the search.

Not every effort met with failure. Isolated Burial No. 10, for example, consisted of fragmented and charred bits of bone, a broken denture, and an ID tag for "L. H. Pratz, 281869." Isolated Burial No. 12 produced a trove of personal effects, the remains of multiple men, and another ID tag for "T. J. Christie, 331305." The 604th collected all potential American bones, crated them, and stored them at the Lunga camp. Not many names were crossed off the search list.

LST-711 returned on October 18 to find Lt. Agnew's frustrated detachment engaged in an area search of the island "in addition [to] the cases that were being covered." This activity continued for the next six days.

"Unless one has been to these Islands it would be difficult to understand just what difficulties an area search team is up against," reported Trapp. "The island is very large ... covered with numerous rivers, low land, thick jungle and mountains reaching up to 8500 feet, making it most difficult in covering any area." The search was confined to "an area starting at Henderson Field and extending west for approximately six miles, and to an average of three miles inland" because "most of all the cases referred to this area of the island." Capt. Hawkins called off the Lunga area search on October 25, and the 604th returned to quarters aboard their LST for the next few weeks, checking out individual crash sites and cases at the southeastern end of Guadalcanal and on the surrounding islands with varied results. Hawkins, Trapp, and Chief Warrant Officer John McBee made a final trip to the west bank of the Matanikau between November 7 and 8. "This river changes from time to time in its course to the ocean," reported Trapp, "and although CWO McBee, our Marine observer, had fought in this area during the fall of 1942, he could recognize very little of the area as it is today."[21]

One area the 604th did not search was the cemetery itself. The old burial grounds would be the responsibility of the 9105th Technical Services Unit, due to arrive in November 1947. Exhumation operations were only just concluding in Hawaii, and the powers in charge were rightly worried that the problems experienced in those civilized islands would only grow worse in the remote reaches of the Pacific. Preparations for the unit's arrival began on October 20, with a pair of liaison officers who secured housing, equipment, shipments of fresh meat and vegetables, and the assistance of local labor. Administrative, supply, and storage buildings were refurbished; old barracks buildings were cleaned and equipped. Everything was made as ready as possible, and the officers set back to await the arrival of USAT *Goucher Victory*.[22]

"Approximately 400 men leave Honolulu to write the final chapter of the war in the South Pacific," announced the *Honolulu Star-Bulletin* on October 29, 1947. "These field operating sections are made up of about 360 civilians, the remainder army officers and enlisted men.... Nearly 200 of the civilians are from Honolulu."[23] This rosy summation belied the troubles that still plagued the 9105th TSU. Seventeen of the thirty-three officers—including the commander—joined just a few days before sailing, replacing officers who resigned in disgust at the prospect of leaving Oahu. There should have been 500 civilians, not 360, and thirty-nine of those who signed on for the voyage skipped out on sailing day. "Many of those who did report were in an intoxicated condition, slovenly-clothed, dirty and unshaven," commented Edward Steere. "Some of them even carried dangerous weapons." When confronted by the ineffective authority of inexperienced officers, the "wretched group of workers" instigated "ill feeling and disputes of all sorts."

After what must have been a touchy voyage, the *Goucher Victory* arrived at Guadalcanal on November 9, 1947, and deposited four Field Operating Sections, most of an Army port company, and their baggage and equipment. "A formidable task lay ahead of them," reported Steere. "Over 3,000 remains were to be disinterred, processed, and casketed within 62 days, during the worst of the rainy season."[24] The 9105th settled into their accommodations, acclimatized to the weather, and waited for supplies of caskets to arrive. They were bolstered by 136 Filipino laborers and two lieutenants, O'Neil and Radner, transferred from the 604th to provide some professional oversight. The remainder of the 604th departed for the Russell Islands on November 18. They would return briefly to pick up some spare parts, but the work of the first S&R expedition to Guadalcanal was considered complete—with fewer than forty remains to show for their efforts.[25]

Exhumations in the cemetery began on November 27, 1947. The first remains were carried to the "Processing Center"—two large huts separated by a long passageway. The 9105th used a relatively new "processing line" system developed during the Hawaiian phase of the program. Previously, technicians moved between each exhumed individual, carrying out the difficult and time-consuming task of documenting and "casketing" the remains at the graveside. This process was deemed inefficient, and the diggers tended to outpace the few trained technicians available. Processing lines involved two embalmers, one or two clerks, and five to eight laborers who received, cataloged, charted, and casketed remains as a team. On Guadalcanal, each hut at the Center contained three processing lines, with two embalmers and a Graves Registration officer assigned to each line. The huts themselves were likely overseen by the most experienced officers, Lieutenants O'Neil and Radner.

A typical shift in the Processing Center began at 11 p.m.—the buildings were too hot during daylight hours—and ran through 7 a.m. Remains exhumed during the day were delivered to the Center with the burial bottles left by the original Graves Registration teams. The Report of Interment was extracted from each bottle and checked against the master Disinterment Directive; the individual's name was embossed on a metal plate which would stay with the remains. Once the officer in charge of the line was satisfied, the remains were placed in a "final-type casket" and readied for shipment. A second officer double checked the remains and confirmed that the tags were correct before the casket was sealed, crated, and stacked outside the Center. Every morning, the port company transported the caskets to separate storage areas based on their intended destination—distribution centers in Hawaii or the continental United

States, according to the wishes of the next of kin. The Center worked quickly and efficiently. Between November 27 and December 20, a total of 3,346 exhumations were performed in a total of twenty-seven working days, and Steere reports that "the number of remains handled daily [at the Processing Center] about equaled the exhumation rate."[26] Assuming every single exhumation passed through the Processing Center, an average of 124 bodies were casketed during every eight-hour shift—meaning each of the six lines averaged one body every fifteen minutes.

The 9105th was charged with confirming identities, but exactly how much time the Processing Center devoted to unknowns is a mystery.[27] Edward Steere notes that individuals "destined for the Identification Laboratory at Schofield Barracks"—where all unknowns were sent— "were delivered directly from the cemetery to the port unit and stored in Quonset huts." This seems to suggest that unknown individuals skipped the Processing Center entirely. If true, the decision was probably made in the interest of time; identification was a laborious process, and it was simpler to put "X-8" in a box and let the professionals in Hawaii solve the mystery. It is certain that unknowns were handled differently than identified individuals. They were wrapped up and placed into "temporary containers" rather than "final-type caskets," making it easier to examine the remains later, and "great care was exercised to make certain that all clothing, equipment, personal effects and other items of possible identification" were packed in with the wrapped remains. (Later, lab techs in Hawaii spotted a few ID tags packaged in with unknown remains, which further suggests that accurate processing was not always done.) Reports of Interment and embossed plates bearing their X-number and location of burial—e.g., "Unknown X-16, Plot FMC Row 27 Grave 3" or "Unknown X-52, USA, 27th Inf. P-A R-29 G-2"—were included with the remains or attached to the casket itself.

Morale was never high in the 9105th TSU, and working conditions on Guadalcanal did nothing to help. Laborers worked six days a week under a blazing sun or in heavy rain. Most of the remains they handled were uncasketed, and live ordnance was occasionally found among the bones. Recreational facilities amounted to "the provision of some movies and library materials" and were roundly deemed "inadequate." Pay was delayed, and supplies occasionally ran out. The enmity between civilians and officers grew so pronounced that Steere mentions "an incident on Guadalcanal approaching the proportions of a riot of civilians against military jurisdiction." (Unfortunately, he does not go into greater detail.) Whatever its shortcomings, however, the 9105th accomplished its task. When the last casket was ready for shipping and a final check was made against the disinterment directive, there was not a single discrepancy to be found. The Army, Navy, and Marine Cemetery at Guadalcanal was finally closed.[28]

"Expidition No. 2"

The 604th Quartermaster Graves Registration Company returned to Honolulu on February 17, 1948. Seven months of effort garnered a disappointing result: thirteen "known" and fifty-six "unknown" remains, for a grand total of sixty-nine. The Solomon Islands had been the most successful search, with thirty-nine remains retrieved, but this was barely 1 percent of the estimated number of non-recovered the region.[29] Planning for a second expedition began as soon as the shortcomings of the first could be analyzed. New equipment, from folding shovels and machetes to surf boats and diving gear, was requisitioned. *LST-711* got a thorough scrubbing from stem to stern. She departed on June 10, 1948, again carrying the 604th QMGRC, a team from the 561st Engineer Diving Detachment, and the redoubtable mortician "Mr. Dunman."[30]

A log book for "Expedition No. 2" reports that the searchers arrived on Guadalcanal early in the morning of February 7, 1949. Connections were made with the British administrators and American Army personnel, and the following day four teams went ashore. As before, the LST departed on other errands while search teams worked ashore; as before, the keeper of the diary stayed with the ship. *LST-711* stayed mostly in local waters for the two-week stop in the Solomons. Most American remains had been recovered from the smaller islands of Malaita, Nugu, and Tulagi, and little recovery work was accomplished. With the guidance of Mr. A. P. Peebles, assistant district officer on Tulagi, a group went to visit what remained of Chaplain Willard's cemetery on Gavutu. "The Cemetery was overgrown with heavy underbrush 6 to 10 ft. tall," reads the report. "The natives said they assisted the Americans in removing the bodies several years ago about the time the Americans moved from the Florida Islands. [We] asked them about Graves #1 [an unknown Marine] and 13 [Pvt. Robert L. Liston, I/3/2] to which they replied that all were removed at the time. We looked for any possible signs of remaining graves but found none."[31]

Meanwhile, the search teams on Guadalcanal were methodically working through their checklist. While the 1947 expedition was characterized by sweeping area searches, Capt. James E. D'Entremont's men focused on specific, targeted areas that were felt to merit closer attention. The Matanikau area was first on the list. Cpl. Nesmith led a team to "Chinese Village" on February 8, in search of members of the 7th Marines reported buried along the western bank of the Matanikau. Mindful that maps had not helped the earlier expedition, Nesmith questioned two merchants, Leong Him and Chow Leoo. Both men denied knowledge of any remains and explained that due to heavy rains and flooding "the mouth of the Matanikau River had extended in the past five years to cover an area almost twice the size that it was originally." Mr. Him and Mr. Leoo led Nesmith's team to the Matanikau and helped search "from the mouth of the river far back into the jungle.... The entire east bank of the river was searched for remains that might have washed to that side but to no avail." Only a single grave was found, but the remains it contained could not be associated with any of the men they sought.[32] Three separate searches were made for the Goettge Patrol on February 11, 12, and 22—two AGRS teams guided by the local constabulary and assisted by Chiefs Barnaba, Kaus, and Kousti of the Matanikau villages—but again, the changes in terrain and the rapid jungle growth obscured all traces of the fighting. A few weathered foxholes and gun emplacements were excavated, but not even a scrap of American equipment could be found.[33]

They had no more luck in the more remote areas. The team assigned to AGRS-PAZ Case No. 729—1Lt. Alvin C. Cockrell of the 7th Marines—dug up foxholes and "possible grave sites" on what they thought was the correct hill, but had no success. A team returned to Hill "Y" on February 13, 1949, to find "many evident signs of heavy fighting in the area, several foxholes and what appeared to be grave sites" still plainly visible. Human remains were elusive, but this time the team turned to local help. Headman Chief Kousti showed the Americans where the population of his Matanikau Village No. 3 had searched since the war, and even guided them to another local landmark—Hill "X," where five more Marines were reportedly buried. Again, the scars of battle were evident, but remains could not be found.[34] The mission reports of the second expedition began to sound much like those of the first:

HQ AGRS (PAZ) S&R Expedition #2, APO 958, 21 March 1949

1. On 10 February 1949 a search team led by Cpl. Nesmith and including PFCs Marshall and Pfaffle left the 30th Engineer Base Camp on Guadalcanal Island for Cactus area at Grids 69.9-199.8 on Section 2 of Aerial Map 104, North Coast Guadalcanal in search of conclusive information concerning case 7676 involving Pvt. Joseph Francis Setzer.

2. The team stopped at Honiara Village, BSIP, and contacted Mr. Arthur Whitten, Labor Control Officer, and questioned him concerning the case. Mr. Whitten had no knowledge of this case but provided the team with two guides who were very familiar with the area.

3. The team then proceeded accompanied by Native Police Boy Gaia of Honiara and Native Boss Boy Ceole Stivens of Honiara as guides.

Upon arrival, the Cactus Area and surrounding ridges and gullies were thoroughly searched. The search continued through 15 Feb 49.

4. During the search the team with the aid of the two guides and natives from Tupakau Village dug in all foxholes, gun emplacements, and suspicious indentations that may have been graves or filled in foxholes, but could not locate any American remains.

5. After negative results on the ridges, the team searched along the stream beds running along the ridges with negative results. The undergrowth in both areas was very thick and hampered the search somewhat, however it is believed that the five day search was conclusive and no further information can be obtained concerning this case.

6. In view of the foregoing, it is recommended that Case 7676 be closed.[35]

Unfortunately, there is also some evidence that not every team was as scrupulous, or as honest, as they should have been. AGRS-PAZ Case No. 727 was investigated on February 11. The graves of Privates Robert Budd and Thomas Phillips, a BAR team from Company "C," 5th Marines, were supposedly located a mile east of Kokumbona village, 10 yards north of the only road in the area, at a natural choke point where the coastline noticeably narrowed. Although the site had eluded the 604th in 1947, the 1949 team had precise instructions—which they duly recorded in their report, noting that test holes were dug and local missionaries interviewed without success.[36] In 1985, Ken Budd came to Guadalcanal in search of his brother's remains, and by chance met a local man named Mingara who had worked as a laborer for the 604th. Mingara told Budd that no digging had been done at all: "Army guys just ride jeep into next town. We drink, then go back to camp."[37] Maintaining morale was a problem in the 604th—one man attempted to desert on the voyage—and while the Army never officially confirmed Mingara's story, it is certainly possible that some disgruntled soldiers decided to take a night off. The price for their dalliance is the ongoing hurt to the Budd and Phillips families, whose Marines have not been accounted for.

The 604th wrapped up their search activities on February 19 and sailed from Guadalcanal four days later.[38] They had recovered thirty-eight remains during their brief time in the Solomon Islands, a healthy percentage of the expedition's eventual total of 109. Capt. D'Entremont's expedition was deemed an improvement over Capt. Hawkins' effort, and while "officials felt confident that the journey's varied experiences would aid any future search and recovery operation," the AGRS-PAZ zone was closed to further searches effective May 13, 1949. "After careful consideration of all the facts involved," the Board of Review declared 9,049 servicemen in AGRS-PAZ permanently unrecoverable.

A grand total of 178 recoveries were made by the two official expeditions. Of these, approximately fifteen were Marines from the Guadalcanal campaign.[39]

"Picture a young man..."

The penultimate stop for remains returning from the Pacific was the Army Central Identification Laboratory (CIL), located at Schofield Barracks in Hawaii. This facility was established in 1947 for the express purpose of identifying Pacific war dead, and grew quickly from its humble beginnings in outdated facilities. The lab supervisor, an experienced (and aptly named) mortician-turned-AGRS officer named Paul Gravenor, and Dr. Mildred Trotter, Professor of Anatomy at Washington University in St. Louis, implemented a training program that taught physical anthropology and skeletal reconstruction to every new lab employee. To ensure impartial analysis, technicians were not allowed to access deceased personnel files: relying on their own research efforts would prevent false positives, improving accuracy and inspiring the confidence of the next of kin.[40] Queries requiring records were handled by the Identification Branch of the Repatriation Records Division, and a third entity, the Board of Review, confirmed or rejected the findings. Under the leadership of Gravenor, Dr. Trotter, and Dr. Charles Snow, Professor of Anthropology at the University of Kentucky, the CIL handled thousands of cases during its brief existence. (While working at the CIL, Dr. Trotter devised a new method of estimating the stature of the deceased by measuring long bones; she earned special recognition for her work from the Office of the Quartermaster General and from her peers. Her 1952 publication with Dr. Goldine Gleser, *Estimation of Stature from Long Bones of American Whites and Negroes,* was heavily influenced by her examination of Pacific War dead.)[41]

The USAT *Cardinal Victory* delivered the remains exhumed from Guadalcanal by the 9105th TSU to the Schofield Barracks mausoleum in January 1948.[42] The CIL was tasked with "an orderly examination of all remains from a particular cemetery"—in other words, confirming the identities of every individual.[43] "Authenticity was mandatory," writes Robert C. Williams, "and no remains were ever delivered to a family without positive identification and absolute certainty."[44] It was well that they took this extra step. While wartime Graves Registration efforts had been executed to the best of abilities—and, in most cases, with accuracy—they were not infallible, and the CIL began uncovering mistakes. In one instance, what should have been a routine check turned into a complete reevaluation of identity. Remains buried in Plot "A," Row 26, Grave No. 2, arrived at CIL with paperwork bearing the name of PFC Albany A. Doucette, ASN 31033450, 182nd Infantry. As the bones were being cataloged, however, someone noticed a little piece of metal in the distinctive shape of a Navy-issue identification tag. A thorough cleaning revealed the inscription:

ONNEN, J W G
310329 TYPE O
T 8/41
USMC

An inquiry to the Identification Branch returned information that Marine Corps Service Number 310329 belonged to Pvt. John William George Onnen of Company "B," 8th Marines. Onnen was killed in action on November 19, 1942, and buried in the field; in 1946, his family was informed that his remains had not been recovered. Here, however, was evidence of an error; Onnen had been buried as Doucette since 1943. The remains were compared to dental charts and physical characteristics recorded in each man's personnel file, and Onnen's returned a "very favorable" match. The AGRS dispatched letters to the Onnen family in Cut Bank, Montana, and the Doucettes in Beverly, Massachusetts. When Mr. George Onnen accepted the findings, the identification was made official, and Pvt. Onnen was buried in the National Memorial Cemetery of the Pacific.[45] This success came at the heartbreaking expense of a family who learned that their boy was not coming home after all: Albany Doucette is still unaccounted for.

In other instances, remains were attributed to individuals who were either alive and well or never existed (recall "W. L. Fleming" and "D. Tewell"). Some skeletal remains, especially the fragmentary ones recovered in 1945, were determined to be of Asian or Melanesian origin; in the most unusual case, remains of Unknown X-87 proved not to be human at all. (Any remains of undeniable Japanese or Korean origin were cremated and buried at sea, while all unidentifiable human remains, regardless of presumed national origin, were buried with honor in the National Memorial Cemetery of the Pacific, where they rest to this day.)

Under laboratory analysis, individuals long buried as unknowns began to regain their identities. However, some cases defied even the experts. Cases X-12, X-13, and X-14 were all buried side by side and on the same day on Guadalcanal. X-13, it may be recalled, was identified as Pvt. Emil Student by fingerprint comparison in 1943. This method did not work for his compatriots, who were examined at the CIL in February and March 1948. Both arrived with a collection of personal effects packaged by the 9105th TSU. The CIL recorded their findings:

X-14 (examined 13 February 1948)
2 gas masks—marked on facepiece "U. S. N.-U."
4 canteens—one reads: P J R Heller—Jimmy Elnore—U.S.M.C.—Rocky, one sent to Lab for further examination of indistinguishable name scratched on bottom of canteen
2 rounds .45 caliber
1 empty soluble coffee can, small, probably from C type ration
1 "fog pruf" kit
1 pair of shoes—sent to Lab for examination for size
1 poncho
1 first aid kit
1 spare parts kit for B. A. R.

X-12 (examined 22 March 1948)
1 gas mask with marking "U.S.N.-U."
1 first aid packet
1 packet of lens fog-proofing
1 can of soluble coffee
1 Webb belt (pistol)
1 pocket comb with case
1 pair of shoes, size 8E
1 mess fork
1 "top part of saber (a type of knife)"
Fragments of mattress cover (no markings found)
Fragments of 1 rain coat (service) (no markings)
Fragments of shelter one-half (no markings)
2 water canteen[s] (no markings)

Neither set of effects helped with establishing identity. The canteens buried with X-14 likely seemed a promising lead, especially when the lab discovered the name "H. Patterson" on the bottom of the corroded specimen. However, there was no good match with any "Patterson," and the canteen inscribed to "Heller" certainly belonged to Pvt. Paul Heller of Company "K," 5th Marines, who was buried three graves to the left of X-14.[46] The shoes also proved to be of different sizes; the left was a 5, the right a 6½. The presence of the BAR kit suggested that X-14 had been an automatic rifleman, assistant automatic rifleman, or squad leader, but this was not enough to make a reliable assessment of identity. The mismatched shoes, plus the surplus of canteens—Marines typically carried only one or two—and the definite association of one canteen with another burial is enough to cast doubt on every other piece of equipment that arrived with X-14. He may have been buried with them in 1942, or careless handling by the 9105th might have mixed up personal belongings.

While some technicians sorted through the personal effects, others worked to catalog the remains themselves. Using skeletal reconstruction techniques taught by Drs. Trotter and Snow, the bones were laid out in their proper places on an examining table. Dental data was regarded as the most definitive means of establishing identity, so tooth charts were made with the utmost care. Fillings, cavities, bridgework, and extractions were sent to the Identification Branch for comparison with records filed in service books. Unfortunately, several remains arrived at CIL with damage to their skulls (or no skulls at all), lost teeth, or, in a surprising number of cases, a perfect set of teeth, indistinguishable from every other perfect set. Trained eyes looked for clues in the condition of the bones, such as physical anomalies—X-14 had a distinctive and unusual fusion of his fourth and fifth right ribs—or healed fractures. Charred or burned bones were noted, as was evidence of "mangling." X-12 had a broken left tibia and right femur, X-14 had several broken ribs, and both had multiple fractures of the skull and pelvis. Missing parts were common; after years in the ground and multiple reburials, nearly every set of remains was incomplete to some degree. Delicate phalanges and vertebrae were often missing, having decayed or been overlooked and left behind by the exhumers, while larger bones were sought among the remains buried on either side.

"Parts not recovered" were blacked out on an illustrated diagram. While X-12 was relatively intact, his compatriot was not so fortunate: the right forearm and entire left arm were missing from X-14, and the skull diagram shows a disturbing pair of holes that obscure half of the facial bones. It is tempting to view this diagram as evidence of killing wounds—entry and exit wounds in the head, for example, might have destroyed X-14's face; he might not have been fingerprinted because his hands were blown away. However, it should be remembered that damage to remains or the "acquired absence" of parts might have been the result of postmortem handling at any point in the six years between death and examination at the CIL. The technicians, in any case, were careful to avoid jumping to any conclusions about the cause of death—a benefit, perhaps, of keeping personnel files in a separate location.

After estimating the height, weight, and age of the individual, the technicians crafted a description of what the deceased might have looked like in life. These descriptions, while clinical, are also often somewhat poetical. Dr. Snow approved the following assessment of X-14:

Picture a short well developed young man 20–21 years of age, with a relatively large head. The skull is of average size, forms a rather broad oval in outline. The occipital and parietal bones are outstanding. It is likely that the back projected. The vault is fairly wide across the parietals. The face is rather long and narrow with flat sides. In profile, the face is fairly straight. The chin appears to have average prominence. The chin presents a rather rounded eminence of average width.[47]

Paul Gravenor signed off on X-12:

Picture a young man of 18 to 20 years of age, with small, slender build. The skull is small and oval. The backhead projects. There is a left cranial asymmetry. The vault is somewhat ill filled. The forehead is narrow, and there is a very marked right facial asymmetry. The face is average in size. The nose is straight with a wide bridge and an average nasal opening. The palate is wide and presents some alveolar prognathism. The mandible is rather deep and has a median eminence. The angle of the lower jaw is very smooth with negative gonial flare.[48]

The completed laboratory report was forwarded to the Identification Branch for comparison against Reports of Interment, personnel records, unit reports, and burial charts. X-12 and X-14 were buried alongside Marines and corpsmen who lost their lives along the Matanikau River between October 5 and 10. The Identification Branch might have investigated the small, lightly-built X-12 as Luther "Dusty" Rhodes, "The Kid" whom Ore Marion and Larry Gerkin saw taken away for burial. X-14 might have been checked against the records of twenty-year-old PFC Joseph Normand Roger Dionne of Company "I," 5th Marines, who was reportedly shot in the head and chest. Or possibly Salvatore "Sammy" Speciale, who went missing the night of the battle, or Pvt. John H. Brown, Jr., who disappeared along with Sammy, or any one of several possibilities. None of the information provided was deemed sufficient for positive identification.

Isolated burials recovered by the 604th were also processed by the CIL and numbered separately from the established roster of X-cases of the ANMC. Many of these men were found with field gear and personal effects exactly as they had been buried in 1942 or 1943. A single case may serve as an example. "Isolated Burial 12"—distinct from the ANMC X-12 described above—involved the remains of three individuals ("A," "B," and "C") who had been buried together in a single grave, along with a large haul of personal effects and equipment:

Isolated Burials 12A, 12B, 12C (examined 2 March 1948)

1 dog tag bearing the inscription "Christie, T. J., 331305, Type O, T 1/42, USMC"
1 pair shoes size 10.5 EE
1 pair shoes size 8.5 EE
1 shoe, size unknown
1 mess kit spoon
1 oil and thong case
1 .30 caliber shell
2 .32 caliber shells (automatic)
1 firing pin and safety lock of an "03" rifle
1 No. 19 hypodermic needle
2 fragments of leather
1 Bakelite cap off a bottle marked "Bakers" on top
2 pieces of a first aid pack
Multiple buckles from field pack
1 key off Master Lock
3 helmets
1 canteen with "N. L. Hamilton" engraved onto the cup and "Pepe" engraved onto the canteen
1 canteen and cup
1 Masonic ring (10K gold)
1 celluloid toothbrush holder
1 Navy type gas mask eyepiece cleaner
1 USMC insignia
2 used morphine oprettes [*sic*.] & a few medical tubes[49]

The first task was to segregate the remains into individuals. An anthropologist's trained eye could match bones of different ages and comparable sizes, and as they worked, technicians placed separate remains on separate working tables. A close watch was kept for "extra parts" that could not be associated with the remains. It was not unusual to find anything from a scapula or some ribs to entire articulating limbs—particularly when processing uncasketed burials where remains might have been in physical contact, or when the disinterring party was rushed or careless when packing remains for transit to the laboratory. When "extra parts" were found, they were checked against the remains of those who had been buried near the individual being processed. If that failed, the parts were assigned their own CIL X-number and treated as a new case. Despite a few overlaps—12C had "two upper 3rd molars present; they may or may not belong to this maxilla"—the three remains from Isolated Burial No. 12 were successfully segregated with no extra parts reported.

Once the segregation was complete, a detailed examination began. An anthropologist theorized that 12B might have been between twenty-two and twenty-four years old, 68.5 inches tall, and "a fairly young heavily muscled man weighing approximately 160–170 lbs":

> Skull is oval in outline and small average in size. It has a pronounced right symmetry. Backhead is projecting and probably had a palpable external occipital protuberance. Forehead is rather narrow and upright with prominent brow ridges. The face was probably straight. Jaw was fairly prominent with flat sides. Chin was of narrow bi-lateral type, protruding more on left side than on right.[50]

A skull in good condition was an important clue. Despite some damage to the nose, eyes, and upper right jaw—indicated by blacked out areas on the skeletal diagram—the description above paints a clear picture, even in medical terms. By contrast, 12C was "a rather short young man in his early twenties weighing approximately 120–155 lbs." but his skull had been shattered and "due to the absence of majority of face parts, description is impossible."[51] Armed with these descriptions and tooth charts, the technicians could begin to search for potential matches in *antemortem* service records.

Equipment and personal effects were also analyzed for clues. The identification tag was an obvious starting point: Thomas John Christie, service number 331305, was killed in action at Guadalcanal on November 3, 1942. His body was not recovered by his buddies in Company "B," 1st Battalion, 2nd Marines, and was last seen "300 yards west of Position 03." The location where the remains were found—plotted at (67.9–201.35) on Map 104—was in the correct vicinity. The field of potential identifications could thus be narrowed to a specific date and location. Ten Americans—nine Marines and one corpsman, all from the 1st Battalion, 2nd Marines—fit these criteria. Although he was three years younger and 6 inches taller than estimated, "dental records of the remains recovered from Isolated Burial #12B were found to compare very favorably with those of Pvt. Thomas J. Christie," and the presence of the dog tag quickly solidified the case. The Board of Review recommended the change in identification on April 22, 1948.[52]

Among the debris were a No. 19 hypodermic needle and "a few medical tubes" of unknown origin. The presence of these supplies suggested that a corpsman might have been nearby; the used morphine "oprettes" (the typist probably meant "syrettes") indicated that he had been busy. Pharmacist's Mate Third Class Bruce Bertram Bender lost his life on

November 3, 1942; although he was on the muster rolls of the Second Medical Battalion, documents in his personnel file confirmed that he had been attached to Company "B," 2nd Marines, when he died. According to eyewitness reports included with his certificate of death, Bender "proceeded forward of the main firing line to render aid to injured patient" and was shot while on his mission of mercy. No help could reach him, and the Marines ultimately withdrew, leaving the area to the Japanese. Bender was an older man (all of twenty-seven) and his age, physical stature, and all-important dental chart matched those of Isolated Burial No. 12A.[53]

With two identifications rapidly resolved, investigators probably felt confident of securing the third. However, No. 12C eluded them. The markings on the canteen and cup would have been investigated; however, there was no "N. L. Hamilton" on casualty lists—or, indeed, attached to any Marine unit on Guadalcanal. Nor was there a "Pepe" that matched the time or location.[54] Furthermore, Bender and Christie were the only two fatalities in Company "B," 2nd Marines, that matched the date and location. Individual 12C might have been another member of the battalion—potential candidates include Raymond H. Hesslink, Doyle K. Miller, Raymond E. Sanders, Dalton W. Whittington (of A/1/2) or Donald H. Beale, Lee H. Duren, Bernard A. Fling, William B. Schultz, Jr. (of C/1/2)—but evidently none of these was a conclusive match. The damage to 12C's skull smashed the facial bones and damaged his maxilla, destroying all the teeth on the upper left side of his mouth; the scant few physical details gleaned from examining the bones were not enough to establish identity. As Bender's and Christie's next of kin gladly accepted the findings of the Board and prepared to have the remains permanently interred, 12C was declared unidentifiable. He was buried in the National Memorial Cemetery of the Pacific as an unknown on June 22, 1949. Visitors can pay their respects at Grave 784 in Section "Q."

Many of the isolated burials were found to contain parts of more than one body. IB-10, located by the first 604th expedition, was little more than a group of burned, fragmented bones accompanied by two pairs of American field shoes, a partial denture, and an ID tag belonging to "L. H. Pratz." Under close inspection, IB-10 was segregated into three individuals. The Records Branch revealed that 2Lt. Leroy H. Pratz died on Guadalcanal while serving with Company "E," 2nd Marines; his body was not recovered from the field by members of his unit. The tag and dentures were assigned to IB-10C, and Pratz's identity was confirmed.[55] Two other members of Company "E"—PFCs James C. Wiseman and Jewell D. Wood—died under similar circumstances; unfortunately, the remains of IB-10A and IB-10B were too badly shattered to obtain identifying clues.

The final discovery of the decade added two more to the CIL list. On October 24, 1949, Capt. William J. Daniel, Jr., the surgeon of the 30th Engineer Base Camp, found an isolated grave on a ridge along the Matanikau River. The remains of two individuals were unearthed. Among the usual debris of rotted shoes, rusted canteens, and pieces of field gear were a pair of ID tags for "C. A. Sauer, 315668." Cpl. Charles A. Sauer of Company "A," 2nd Marines, was killed on December 20, 1942, when a platoon patrol ran into a Japanese position. Heavy machine-gun fire drove off the Marines; they could not retrieve Sauer's body or extricate two wounded men, Pharmacist's Mate Second Class Robert B. Anderson and PFC William V. Wilkins. Anderson's remains were located by the AGRS expedition, and Sauer's identity was confirmed in November 1949. The second man in the grave was dubbed Isolated Burial 39; he may once have been William Wilkins, but without any teeth or facial bones to guide the CIL staff, he was doomed to be buried as an unknown.[56]

Not long after processing Sauer and IB-39, the Central Identification Laboratory reached the end of their queue. Having served its purpose to the "limits of science," the laboratory was deactivated.[57] During the lab's brief existence, CIL technicians examined thousands of remains from across the Pacific theater, and Dr. Mildred Trotter maintained that 94 percent of those remains were eventually identified.[58] Of those who were not, five were chosen as candidates for the Tomb of the Unknown Soldier in Arlington, Virginia; the rest joined their comrades in the National Memorial Cemetery of the Pacific.

The volcanic crater of Puowaina—often translated as "Hill of Sacrifice" and nicknamed "the Punchbowl"—was once an ancient Hawaiian religious site. The Army purchased the land in February 1948, and the first burials took place the following January. More than 2,000 citizens attended the public opening on July 19, 1949, "under a blue sky flecked with drifting clouds above the circling sea. A bright sun lit the trim greensward, with 10,000 small white crosses marking the graves of heroes." Famed newspaper correspondent Ernie Pyle was buried in the "brief and unpretentious" ceremony, alongside two Marines, one Army lieutenant, and an unknown warrior.[59] Among the 13,000 World War II servicemen buried in this beautiful spot are nearly 200 unknowns who lost their lives while serving in the Solomon Islands. Their graves may be found in almost every plot of the National Memorial Cemetery of the Pacific. Perhaps as many as thirty may be Marines who have been officially unaccounted for since the battle of Guadalcanal.

Half a world away, in yet another massive cemetery, their names are etched into tall limestone slabs. The Walls of the Missing at Manila American Cemetery, Philippines, bear the names of 36,286 servicemen who have no known grave. The Guadalcanal Marines are among those commemorated here. The names of Frank Goettge, Steven Custer, Ralph Cory, and the rest of the infamous patrol are inscribed on the Walls; a few yards away is the name of Raymond Rosalik, who died trying to find them. Leon McStine, and Mickey Boschert, Luther "Dusty" Rhodes and Tom Pilleri, Doyle Asher and Raymond Schulthies, Alvin Cockrell and Charmning Willie Rowe, Joseph Setzer and Albert "Whitey" Hermiston— hundreds of young men who gave their lives and left no physical trace of their existence. Some have headstones in hometown cemeteries; for many, the engraving on the Walls of the Missing is their only remembrance.

The Walls have stood mostly unchanged since the cemetery was dedicated in 1960. Very rarely, a bronze rosette appears next to a name, setting one individual apart from thousands of his fellows. The rosettes denote an individual who has been identified and repatriated; they also represent the closing of a painful chapter that has endured for generations. One need only to glance left or right, up or down, from a rosette to find a similar story that has not yet reached its conclusion—an open wound in a family far away.

The Case for Whitey Hermiston

Albert Laddce Hermiston was twenty-two years old when he landed on Guadalcanal. Intelligent, industrious, and morally upright, he joined the Marines in 1939 after graduating high school with honors and spending two years in the Civilian Conservation Corps. He witnessed the attack on Pearl Harbor; his desire for vengeance led him to volunteer for Carlson's Raiders in 1942. Cpl. Hermiston was one of the few applicants to pass the rigorous screening of Lt. Col. Evans Carlson and Maj. James Roosevelt, and he became an NCO in Company "D."[60]

Hermiston took part in Carlson's "Long Patrol" on Guadalcanal, a punishing four-week operation behind enemy lines, on temporary duty with Company "B" under Capt. Oscar Peatross. Upon his arrival on November 8, 1942, he was placed in charge of a fire group consisting of Privates Richard Clinton Farrar and Stuyvesant Van Buren. Their ten-man squad, led by Cpl. Orin Croft, included combat veterans like PFC Cyril Matelski, Pvt. Ben Carson, and Pvt. Keith Turner. Guadalcanal was Hermiston's first combat experience, but he acquitted himself well and toughed out the march as dozens of other men fell out sick, starved, or exhausted. Fellow Raider Walter V. Purcell said simply, "Al was a good Marine."[61]

On December 4, 1942, Col. Carlson gave orders to head for the perimeter. The Raiders were camped on top of Mount Austen and needed to reach safety fast. Three of their number were suffering from wounds sustained in a battle the previous day; doctors worried that 1Lt. Jack Miller would die if he did not reach a hospital. Capt. Peatross put Croft's squad in the lead, with Hermiston's team out front. Hermiston himself took the point. After only 50 yards, "Whitey" held up his hand to halt the column and fell dead with a Japanese bullet through his head. Farrar was killed in the same instant, and Van Buren wounded in the stomach. The ensuing firefight also claimed the life of Cyrill Matelski, who was shot between the eyes as he led his team around the flank of the Japanese machine gun. Due to the need for haste, the three dead Marines were buried along the trail. Lt. Miller died about an hour later—he was buried in a lone grave, the location of which was later lost—and Van Buren succumbed to his wounds the following day at the Division hospital.[62]

Although the occasional Army unit passed along the trail—a patrol from the 164th Infantry reported sighting the graves of three Marines near the summit of Mount Austen—no attempts were made to retrieve the remains for about eighteen months. On May 16, 1944, the 49th Quartermaster Graves Registration Company reported the reburial of three bodies found in an isolated grave. Dog tags identified "R. C. Farrar" and "C. A. Matelski," and the two Raiders were buried in Plot "C," Row 90, Graves 4 and 5, of the ANMC. The third man had nothing but a rotted pair of shoes. A Report of Interment was filled out: "Body disinterred from isolated burial 16 May 1944. No tags on cross or body.... Unknown body buried on the left of Matelski (346548 USMC). Body of R. C. Farrar was buried on the right of Matelski. All three graves in one row." A tooth chart was taken for future reference, but no further attempts at identification could be made. He became X-94 and was buried in Grave 6.[63]

The 604th Quartermaster Graves Registration Company investigated Corporal Hermiston as Case 7703 in August 1947. They hiked up Mount Austen, but it was another wild goose chase. "Due to the fact that no remains were found, it is possible that a previous search party picked them up and they are now buried in the Guadalcanal Cemetery as unknown," concluded the search report. The cases for Hermiston and Lt. Miller were recommended to be closed. Meanwhile, the remains of X-94 were exhumed from the ANMC, placed in a temporary casket, and shipped back for storage at Army Mausoleum No. 1, Schofield Barracks, Hawaii.

On March 23, 1948, the Central Identification Laboratory spread the bones of X-94 on a table. They pictured "a young man of average muscular build and of approximately 22 to 24 years of age," standing 5 feet 10 inches tall and weighing about 155 pounds. The teeth were charted yet again; a filling in an upper left molar was noted, and another was "believed extracted." One of X-94's four front teeth had been extracted. Others were missing posthumously; the same bullet that shattered parts of his jaw destroyed the facial bones before exiting near the right ear, making a description difficult. It took only one day for the lab to complete their report, and the results were not promising. One year later, on March 11, 1949, X-94 was buried as an unknown.

In my opinion, there is a very strong likelihood that X-94 is Albert Hermiston. Multiple Raider sources tell the story of the three men dying together. Lowell Bulger described the climax of the patrol in a detailed, multi-installment story for the *Raider Patch* newsletter. Walter Purcell, who served with Hermiston before the Raiders, told the *Patch* how the corporal "got his licks" at Mount Austen. Oscar Peatross, who later penned the definitive Raider history *Bless 'Em All*, had a soft spot for Van Buren and wrote movingly of his death. Unit muster rolls confirm the date, though only mention a burial "in the field." The degree of detail in the Report of Interment—and the exact correctness of identifying Farrar and Matelski down to their service numbers—is further confirmation of the veterans' memoirs.

The physical description of X-94 is a close match with Hermiston's as recorded in his Individual Deceased Personnel File and Official Military Personnel File. Hermiston was 5 feet 9 inches tall and weighed 153 pounds—within an inch and 2 pounds of the estimate for X-94. His age, twenty-two, is also a good match. Of course, this is not enough to make a complete case. Farrar and Matelski were also Caucasian males of similar stature (5 feet 8 inches and 165 lb.; 5 feet 7 inches and 140 lb., respectively), and both were twenty years old—within the range of error for technicians examining skeletal remains. It could be that the identification tags were placed with the wrong remains—as we know sometimes occurred with remains from the ANMC.

However, the technicians would have checked tooth charts to confirm Farrar and Matelski, and this is where the final piece of record-based evidence comes into play. The disinterment directive issued to the team who searched for Hermiston contains a rudimentary tooth chart with the following information where "X" means an extracted tooth; "F" indicates a filling. (To picture this view: 1s and 9s are the front center teeth, 8s and 16s are the rear molars.)

Upper Right								Upper Left							
X		X			X				X			X	F		X
8	7	6	5	4	3	2	1	1	2	3	4	5	6	7	8
X		X	X										X		X
16	15	14	13	12	11	10	9	9	10	11	12	13	14	15	16
Lower Right								Lower Left							

The dental chart for X-94 is strikingly similar. The maxilla and mandible were damaged, and some teeth were lost posthumously, causing some disarrangement and confusion indicated by asterisks:

Upper Right								Upper Left							
*		X				*	*	*	*			X	*	*	*
8	7	6	5	4	3	2	1	1	2	3	4	5	6	7	8
	X	X	X										X	X	*
16	15	14	13	12	11	10	9	9	10	11	12	13	14	15	16
Lower Right								Lower Left							

Most notably, the technician wrote that "either R1 or R2 is extracted, and the same for L1 and L2"—a close match to Hermiston's chart—and "there is one upper left molar present with an A-O filling. I feel that at least one upper left molar is extracted." This is almost an exact match with Hermiston's *antemortem* dental chart.

The similarities between the dental charts, physical descriptions, location of the remains, and the circumstances of death create the serious possibility that the remains buried in Plot "F," Grave 155, of the National Memorial Cemetery of the Pacific are those of Albert Hermiston. Perhaps someday soon, a rosette will appear next to his name, and one more Marine will be on his way home.[64]

10

Rosettes: 1970–2018

October 9, 1942, 2nd Battalion, 7th Marines, West of the Matanikau

The men of Lt. Col. Herman "Hard-Hearted" Hanneken's 2nd Battalion, 7th Marines, were feeling confident on the morning of October 9, 1942. Although the previous day had been a hard one—a difficult climb up the steep banks of the Matanikau River, an accidental grenade injury, and a skirmish over their bivouac that cost the life of Gunnery Sergeant Robert H. Ballew—this morning was marked by success. Company "F" spotted a party of Japanese soldiers installing a trio of machine guns that could have "swept the entire front of this battalion and the Third Battalion, 2nd Marines" and completely compromised their attack. Instead, the Japanese were ambushed and killed; two guns were destroyed, and the third became a battalion souvenir. The Marines jumped off as planned at 6:45 a.m., and for more than an hour, all was quiet.

At 8 a.m., another Japanese machine gun positioned on a ridge opened fire on the left flank squad of Company "E." Several Marines were killed outright; others were wounded, and the advance ground to a halt. Lt. Col. Lewis "Chesty" Puller's 1st Battalion, 7th Marines, was ordered to flank the troublesome gun and secure the ridge. Hanneken planned to have his own Company "G" "push through the area 'E' Company passed through and get out the Marines who had been killed or wounded in that area and their weapons"—but air-dropped orders received at 11:30 a.m. changed the battalion's objectives. The wounded were all evacuated, but the dead had to be buried where they fell.[1]

Eight Marines from Company "E" lost their lives on October 9 and were buried at coordinates (69.75–200.15). Three were found on August 23–24, 1944, and returned to their families:

PFC Rollen Mullins, buried ANMC Row 99, Grave 4
Corporal Edwin Mellor Langley, buried ANMC Row 99, Grave 6
PFC Alba William Jenkins, buried ANMC Row 99, Grave 7

The remaining five were investigated by the 604th AGRS as part of Case Number 716 but were not recovered.

Corporal John Frederick Suggs
PFC Godfrey Earl Hunter, Jr.
PFC David William Johns
Private Paul Emile Gagnon
Private Eugene Johnston

All five were declared non-recoverable in 1949, and their cases were closed.

1970

Retired Capt. Edwin C. Clarke of the 1st Marine Division Association received a letter from Guadalcanal. The sender was Mrs. Y. Timothy Kwaimani, the wife of a forestry official in Honiara. She told Clark she had found a human skeleton. This was not an uncommon occurrence, especially as Honiara was built upon the old battlefields of 1942. However, Mrs. Kwaimani had found identification tags around the skeleton's neck. The name, she said, was "G. E. Hunter."

Mrs. Kwaimani chose the right person to contact. Clarke, a former sergeant major of the 1st Raider Battalion, had lost many friends and comrades on Guadalcanal. He was also the officer whose name appeared on countless letters informing families that their loved ones had not been recovered. "That started a chain of events which led to the Australian government and Solomon Islands officials conducting a new search for grave sites on Guadalcanal," said a Marine Corps representative. Four more sets of remains were found in late 1971 and forwarded to the Smithsonian Institution in Washington, D.C. After five months of comparing dental records and archival files, the researchers announced the identification of Suggs, Hunter, Johns, Gagnon, and Johnston.

On June 28, 1972, the five Marines were laid to rest in a single grave at Arlington National Cemetery. "Marine officials said they could not recall another funeral held under similar circumstances," reported the Associated Press. "Wednesday's funeral services answered the plea of Mollie Johnston of Littleton, NC, mother of one of the Marines to bring her son's body home 'if it takes a hundred years to find him.' About 40 surviving relatives were expected to attend the funeral, but not Mrs. Johnston. She died a few years ago."[2]

John Suggs, Godfrey Hunter, David Johns, Paul Gagnon, and Eugene Johnston are buried in Arlington National Cemetery, Section 34, Site 5015.

September 14, 1942, 1st Raider Battalion, Edson's Ridge

In peacetime, Ed Shepard and Frank Whittlesey were as different as could be. Shepard, a small-town kid from coal country West Virginia, dropped out of high school to join the Marines and showed talent as a sniper. "Russ" Whittlesey grew up in the Park Avenue society of country clubs and New Hampshire prep schools; he left Yale to join up, following in the footsteps of his war hero uncle, Col. Charles Whittlesey, leader of the Lost Battalion at the Meuse-Argonne. By chance, the two wound up in Company "B" of the 1st Raider Battalion and became firm friends. On September 14, their platoon was deployed along the slope of a ridge just south of Henderson Field on Guadalcanal. A massive Japanese assault was anticipated; their platoon was little more than a "speed bump," which might delay, but could not stop, a determined onslaught.

Shortly after nightfall, the battle began. "The jungle was lit up like a stage," wrote Shepard, "battle cries broke out from both sides above the screams of wounded and dying men…. After about thirty minutes I was hit and dropped to the ground. Russ stood over me and fought like a madman. I asked him to leave me, and he only said, 'go to hell, Shep!'"

At the first break in the fighting, Whittlesey tore his shirt into pieces and used the strips to bandage Shepard's wounds. The two Marines realized they were now behind Japanese lines and began cautiously navigating along a narrow trail, hoping to reach friendly forces. An enemy patrol found them first. "Instead of getting away, [Russ] chose to die fighting and save my life," continued Shepard:

> He dropped me to the ground and stood with knife in hand…. With the cool art of a true Marine, he used certain tricks (we had often practiced together) to kill the first two [Japanese], and the third one stabbed him in the back with a bayonet…. He was hit several times in the stomach of which I was not aware. He said 'Well, Shep, I guess this is where we came in,' & smiled & began to try to hum his favorite tune, 'I'm Getting Tired So I Can Sleep.' Then he just went to sleep.[3]

After the battle, Pvt. Whittlesey's body was "buried 1,000 yards south of Airfield just forward of the front lines on Lunga Ridge." The location was not found during the war or by the AGRS search, and Whittlesey was declared non-recoverable in 1949.

1989

David Rockson was digging a hole when his shovel hit something hard. The Guadalcanal farmer discovered buttons, bones, and a dog tag tied to a twist of rusted barbed wire; the name "WHITTLESEY" was still clearly visible.

Rockson called the U.S. Embassy in Honiara. An investigating team arrived on October 13, 1989, and recovered the skeleton of "a Caucasoid male, approximately 71 inches tall, aged about 18 to 22 years." The remains were confirmed as Frank Whittlesey at CILHI on October 29, 1991. After an extensive search, genealogists located Susan Whittlesey Wolf, who invited her cousin's former comrades to his funeral on May 25, 1992.[4]

Frank Whittlesey is buried in the Walnut Hill plot of Pittsfield Cemetery, Pittsfield, Massachusetts.

August 19, 1942, 3rd Battalion, 5th Marines, First Battle of the Matanikau

Although the Goettge Patrol failed to accomplish any of its stated objectives before being wiped out on August 13, 1942, it did provide the 1st Marine Division with two crucial pieces of intelligence. The first was a preview to the nature of combat on Guadalcanal: gruesome, vicious, and without quarter. The second was even more important: the Japanese were concentrating forces west of the Matanikau and were prepared to defend that area. Having "found 'em" and "fixed 'em," the Marines prepared to "fight 'em" in a three-pronged assault aimed at the village of Horahi. They would also, orders said, attempt to locate the remains of the Goettge Patrol and recover them if practicable. In preparation for the attack, Company "L" of the 5th Marines crossed the Matanikau River and camped on a ridge overlooking the village.

On the morning of August 19, the attack began down the northern slope of Hill 73. The 2nd Platoon of Company "L" made the first contact when a Japanese sniper shot the acting platoon leader, Sgt. John H. Branic, straight through the heart. The company felt his loss keenly. "It didn't take much to put a smile on his face," said Company "L" veteran Ore Marion. "Though affable, Branic was quiet by nature, and extremely sensible.... [He was] a credit to the Corps." By necessity, Branic had to be buried where he fell, and this troubled his buddies. "Ben Selvitelle took it the hardest," continued Marion. "Even years later, he often said to me, 'I can't understand why we left John up there.' I had to dismiss Branic's death from my mind, but Ben couldn't forget it, couldn't stop feeling bad about it."[5]

1992

In February 1992, a construction crew breaking ground for an American war memorial uncovered skeletal remains on "Skyline Ridge" overlooking Honiara. A belt buckle found at the site suggested that they were those of a Marine. The following month, a team from the Joint POW/MIA Accounting Command (JPAC) arrived to take possession of the remains; further excavations turned up additional bone fragments and ammunition, but no more clues. The case quickly went cold.

A decade later, expert researcher John Innes learned that a Honiara resident possessed a gold ring that was found at the site. The ring was inscribed with the initials "JHB." Innes determined that the site of the American memorial was previously known as "Hill 73"—the same hill where Company "L" launched their attack on Horahi. Innes placed a phone call to Ore Marion, who described the last time he saw Branic's body. The location was a solid match.[6]

It took two more years to locate a blood relative, but eventually, the granddaughter of one of Branic's cousins was found living in New Jersey. Her DNA sample, along with the analysis of dental remains, confirmed the identity of Sgt. John Harold Branic on May 22, 2006. "I'm just so grateful we got him and gave him a proper burial after all these years," remarked Ben Branic, the Marine's first cousin. "It's just an amazing story."[7] Sadly, neither Ben Selvitelle nor Ore Marion lived to see their friend's remains recovered. Selvitelle died in 1993, Marion in 2003.

Sgt. John Branic is buried in Arlington National Cemetery, Section 69, Site 1532.

October 9, 1942, 1st Battalion, 7th Marines, West of the Matanikau

Lt. Col. Lewis "Chesty" Puller was chafing at his assignment. His battalion was designated the reserve for its task group during the Second Battle of the Matanikau; they had spent two days following behind the assault units and Division showed no inclination to change this mission for October 9. However, when a Japanese ambush inflicted heavy casualties on Company "E," 7th Marines, the 2nd Battalion commander called on the reserve for assistance. Puller sent Company "C" "across a ravine and up on a ridge on the left front" to assist, and they were quickly engaged by Japanese forces. A roiling firefight developed, and part of the company was cut off.

"We had to have more support, or we'd be out of luck, on top of that hill all by ourselves" recalled Cpl. Walter Bodt. "One of the fellows managed to go out around the crest of the hill, and the Japs machine-gunned him. They did that one, two, three. We were in a pretty bad fix."[8] Two Marines, PFCs Richard J. Kelly and Francis E. Drake, Jr., went running after a wounded man trapped 100 yards from friendly lines. They had almost returned safely when another burst of enemy fire killed PFC Drake. PFC Kelly hauled the wounded man to safety, then risked his life once again to retrieve Drake's body. Both Kelly and Drake received Silver Star medals for gallantry.

Meanwhile, Puller moved the rest of his battalion up to occupy the positions formerly held by the 2nd Battalion. "We were ordered to cross a narrow valley waist high in jungle grass," said Sgt. Joe Goble of Company "B." "Part of us had gotten across when two machine guns opened up, killing two of our men. We took the ridge but continued to receive heavy mortar fire."[9] PFC Harry C. Morrissey of Company "B" lost his life to machine gun fire; the other man was probably Pvt. Albert L. Bernes, a machine gunner from Company "D."

Puller's battalion inflicted heavy casualties on the enemy force before following the rest of their regiment north along the Matanikau. "During the fight, the casualties of the First Battalion were five killed and twenty-one wounded," reported Puller. "All casualties were either buried or brought back."[10] One Marine, PFC William A. Rust (Company "B") died of wounds while being evacuated; he and PFCs Andrew Martinchak and Leonard T. Novak (both Company "C") were buried in the First Marine Division Cemetery.

Drake, Morrissey, and Bernes were gathered together and buried in three separate graves beside a trail that led along the ridge. A careful sketch of the location was made. However, their bodies were not recovered during the war; the 604th QMGRC failed to locate the site during the 1947 expedition and recommended closing the case. The three Marines were declared non-recoverable in 1949.

2011–2013

While working on an outside kitchen for a building on Skyline Ridge, Honiara resident Mr. Yorick Tokuru uncovered "possible osseous remains"—in the form of a partial human skeleton. The remains changed hands several times, from the Royal Solomon Islands Police Force to a local archaeologist, then to historian John Innes, who contacted JPAC to take possession of the remains.

Almost seventy years to the day after Puller's battalion fought across the ridges west of the Matanikau, Radio Australia broke the news that suspected American remains had been found in Honiara. Michael Tokuru Junior was working on the very same kitchen when he unearthed more bones, and an American identification tag inscribed "F. E. Drake, Jr. 299871 USMC." Ewan Stevenson got word to JPAC, and an excavation of the site revealed a third set of remains.

In the four years that followed, JPAC was disbanded, and the Defense POW/MIA Accounting Agency (DPAA) took its place. On August 28, 2017, the remains of Francis Drake and Harry C. Morrissey were identified; formal announcements accounting for the two Marines soon followed. On May 28, 2018, Francis Drake was buried in Massachusetts Veterans Memorial Cemetery in Agawam, Massachusetts. Final burial details for Harry Morrssey are still pending as of early 2019.

The third individual, who may be Albert L. Bernes, is still officially unidentified.

August 24, 1942, VMF-223, Over Guadalcanal

The pilots of Marine Fighter Squadron (VMF) 223 waited on the alert at Henderson Field, ready to fight at a moment's notice. Although new to Guadalcanal, they were already picking up on the daily routine of morning and evening patrols—and in between, combat patrols, evening patrols, infantry support missions, sudden scrambles, and sector searches. On August 24, they would add another experience to their repertoire—fighting off a full-scale air raid.

At 2:25 p.m., a black flag shot up above the Pagoda, signaling Condition Red. The pilots raced for the flight line and clambered into cockpits. Second Lieutenant Elwood R. Bailey fired up F4F-4 Wildcat No. 02095. He first learned to fly while enrolled at Jackson Junior College, where he co-owned a small private plane with fellow students Zenneth Pond and Bill Maher. In 1941, Bailey and Pond signed up for naval aviation training; both became Marine pilots and were assigned to VMF-223. They arrived on Guadalcanal together on August 18, 1942, which happened to be Bailey's twenty-second birthday. Today, they would go into combat together.[12]

In a scramble, pilots of the "Cactus Air Force" joined up with the nearest friendly plane and went after the closest target. Lt. Bailey fell in with two fellow Wildcats and two Army P-400s for a fast and furious dogfight with six Imperial Navy pilots over Malaita Island. One of the Zeros went down in flames under the guns of 2Lt. Robert MacLeod, but the veteran Japanese pilots evened the score by riddling Bailey's Wildcat. The stricken plane dropped out of the fight and was last seen limping back towards Guadalcanal. An American parachute was seen opening over Tulagi; some believed this to be Bailey bailing out.[13]

The dogfight was a victory for the Cactus Air Force—Zenneth Pond claimed three of the fifteen reported victories himself—but resulted in the loss of three Marine pilots: Bailey, 2Lt. Lawrence R. Taylor, and 2Lt. Robert R. Read. The following day, Read was located, wounded but alive, on Tulagi. Bailey and Taylor never returned, and both pilots were declared dead on August 25, 1943.

Lt. Pond would fight on for another two weeks, claiming six Japanese aircraft and earning a Navy Cross before he was himself shot down over Guadalcanal on September 10, 1942. Like his childhood friend Elwood Bailey, he was declared dead and non-recoverable.

2012–2018

In 2012, Mr. Klement "Clay" Chulao was exploring in the jungles near his home in Mbarana Village, Guadalcanal when he stumbled across the rusting wreckage of an American fighter plane. He managed to pry loose a wing, which he sold to the proprietor of a museum in Honiara. The buyer alerted the Joint POW/MIA Accounting Command (JPAC), and a search team was dispatched in 2013. The site had been picked over, but significant debris remained – including the tail assembly, weather-bleached and rust-spotted, with the number "02095" still plainly visible.

Elwood Bailey's plane had not gone down at sea at all—instead, it had crashed to earth in the foothills of Mount Austen, significantly inland from Henderson Field. One mystery was solved, but the whereabouts of the pilot were still unknown. Had he bailed out, leaving the fighter to crash unmanned? Had the official records mistaken which plane he flew on the day he disappeared? Had he perhaps survived the crash, only to become lost in the jungles or caught by a Japanese patrol? Or were his remains somewhere nearby, hidden by years of jungle growth and disturbed by scavengers? The JPAC team recovered debris from the site, but nothing that could be identified as human remains.

Three more years passed before Mr. Chulao entered the picture once again. He had more items from the site of BuNo 02095. A pistol. An identification tag, bent and folded nearly in half as if hit by something hard. And, in the cautious language of the DPAA, "possible human remains." The tag, though damaged, was still plainly legible. It was of the early war style, acid etched instead of stamped, and bore the inscription "E. R. BAILEY 2nd Lt. USMCR." With a reasonable association thus confirmed, the DPAA contacted Elwood Bailey's family.

On 5 September 2017, just days after the seventy-second anniversary of his death, Elwood Ray Bailey was officially accounted for. His life and friendship with Zenneth Pond and Bill Maher become the subject of a documentary film produced by students at his alma mater. And on 13 October 2018, he was laid to rest beside his parents. "It's nice to finally think that their souls will be a little more at peace, knowing this whole thing had been brought to a conclusion," commented his nephew, Wayne Tompkins.

To this date, Lawrence Taylor and Zenneth Pond are still unaccounted for.

Epilogue:
He Is My Boy

Dear General
Sir:

I am writing this letter to you today in the hopes you may be able to help us.

First of all I am writing for myself: my feelings are very deep and very concerning. I am worried about my mom. Her health is declining, she is or rather will be 83 years old August 6th '79. She is a Gold Star mother and was dependent on my Brother Tommy as there were still 4 of us whom he supported, plus Mom made 5. I last saw my Brother Jan. 6 1942. Within a few days, Jan. 25, I would have been 12 years old. He promised me he would be back for my birthday, but he couldn't make it. I remember calling him and crying at the window, he blew kisses to me and Mom and waved – he yelled back, "I'll see you soon." We didn't, but he couldn't help it. It is 37 years now and still I remember. Oh yes, he did come back once and was called back, his leave was canceled. He left us again, but this time he never came back. I have had many birthdays since but always I remember Tommy in my prayers. If only he could come home, I would feel very happy knowing he is where he belongs. I have to think that way, otherwise I could become very sick.

You see, after Tommy left I developed rheumatic fever and got rheumatic heart condition from it. I did not have the strength to outgrow it, so, here I am trying to nurse Mom who cries constantly for Tommy.

As I said, Mom will be 83 years old. Now I am writing for her:

I want my son Tommy to come home. I cannot rest till we have him here. I dream of Tommy all the time. He don't want to be where he is. He want to come home. We must find a way to bring him home now. He is my boy. Tell them, I wanted my boy when they told me I could send for him, then I get another letter, they tell me the Japs bombed where the graves were and they said it would be hard to find him.

I want my boy and I must find him. I cannot rest till we bring him home.

My sisters (4) and brothers (3) those of us—the total 7 plus Tommy was 8. We lost a sister so now there are 6 of us left: oldest being in order Patsy, Josie, Rosie, Frankie, Mary and me Elvira—we all agree to be able to give Mom peace of mind to do what we can to bring Tommy home.

More than a month now, we wrote to Ted Kennedy and asked him to please help us. I sent him copies of all the papers we have—all that I could find pertaining to our loss.

What we want to know is did you or your office receive any requests from Ted Kennedy concerning this matter? Time is very important. Every day is a bonus as far as Mom is concerned. Could you please advise us on how to get a quick reply?

We wrote another letter to Ted and mailed it Saturday but still we hear nothing.

We realize that we are not the only ones needing help but someone, somewhere should be able to tell us something.

If you need any more information please let us know. We had another family meeting day before yesterday—we all agree as to what to expect. We know after 37 years—I don't want to go into that—I know. But if it will put my Mom at ease we must hide our thoughts and our feelings for her sake. We must believe as she believes. It is important now.

You see, Sir: I don't think any of us was really convinced Tommy was really dead.

God help us. God help him.

Please help us.

Tell me what to do next.

My mom wants us to get her a plot as close to where Tommy will be. It is sad. My Mom lives with my husband and me. She cannot do for herself, she needs care. We have done it these last 8 years and she is not better. She is worse and every day counts. She cries in the night.

So we have to do this. Our telephone number is [redacted]—if you could only call her and tell her you are doing what you can. It would help.

Sincerely,

Mrs. George Paula [*née* Elvira Christine Pilleri] for Mom

Mrs. Angela Pilleri

Thomas Stephen Pilleri was killed in action at a listening post at the Overland Trail action on Guadalcanal, September 14, 1942. His body was reportedly found and buried in the field by members of his company three days later.

The 604th Quartermaster Graves Registration Company investigated Pilleri as part of Case No. 7188 in 1947 and again in 1949. After interviews with Chief Jacob Vouza, British officials, plantation owners, the 30th Engineer Topographic Battalion, and a thorough search of the area failed to reveal the location of Pilleri's grave, his case was unanimously declared non-recoverable by an AGRS Board of Review.

In 2001, Thomas Pilleri was awarded a posthumous Silver Star for gallantry in action on the date of his death. His citation reads, in part:

Private First Class Pilleri was manning a machine gun for the all-volunteer, forward element listening post when a Japanese Battalion initiated a full scale assault to overrun the Marine control of Henderson Field. In the ensuing heavy fire fight, Private First Class Pilleri heroically remained at his station to cover the ordered withdrawal to the unit perimeter. Due to the lethal fire he provided against the enveloping enemy the other members of the post were able to withdraw, the Japanese surge was checked and the defensive positions were altered to maximum readiness. Private First Class Pilleri's actions ultimately cost him his life, but helped saved the lives of other members of his unit and also helped the 11th Marines to repulse the Japanese attack.

The last of Thomas' siblings, Rose, passed away in 2007.

His remains have still never been recovered or identified.

Endnotes

Prologue

1. Wukovits, J., *American Commando: Evans Carlson, His WWII Marine Raiders, and America's First Special Forces Mission* (New York: NAL Caliber, 2009), p. 156.
2. Purcell, W. V., letter to the editor, *Raider Patch,* January 1982, p. 11.
3. Wukovits, *op. cit.*, p. 235.

Chapter 1

1. Steere, E., *The Graves Registration Service in WWII* (Washington: United States Government Printing Office, 1951), p. 15.
2. Miller, J. Jr., *Guadalcanal: The First Offensive* (1949; reprint, Washington: U.S. Army Center of Military History, 1995), p. 350. Miller does not specify Army Air Corps losses.
3. Zimmerman, J. L., *The Guadalcanal Campaign* (Washington, D.C.: Historical Division, U.S. Marine Corps, 1949), p. 169.
4. Miller, *op. cit.*, p. 350.
5. Steere, *op. cit.*, p. 15.
6. *Ibid.*, p. 10. Steere is quoting Quartermaster General Marshall Ludington in 1899.
7. Total U.S. military fatalities are estimated at 407,316. This total does not include civilians who died in combat zones, or members of the Merchant Marine service. Figure from the National World War II Museum.
8. Steere, *op. cit.*, p. v.
9. A chaplain's duties included conducting military funerals on posts or in the field. In the absence of a trained Graves Registration officer, he would also need "to familiarize himself thoroughly with all current orders and bulletins dealing with the burial of the dead, the disposition of the effects of the dead, and graves registration." Office of the Chief of Chaplains, *Technical Manual No. 16-205: The Chaplain* (Washington: USGPO, 1941), p. 66. (Hereafter, TM 16-205).

10. Risch, E. and Kieffer, C. L., *The Quartermaster Corps: Organization, Supply and Services,* vol. 2, (Washington: USGPO, 1955), pp. 386–387.
11. Steere, *op. cit.*, p. v.
12. *Ibid.*, p. 43.
13. Sledge, M., *Soldier Dead: How We Recover, Identify, Bury & Honor Our Military Fallen* (New York: Columbia University Press, 2005), p. 31.
14. *Ibid.*, p. 44.
15. *Ibid.*, p. 51.
16. This grave belonged to PFC Barney S. Mikus (C/1/7) who was KIA on September 27, 1942. Somewhat unsurprisingly, his grave was never found.
17. Herman D. Avery, Individual Deceased Personnel File (IDPF), Records of the Office of the Quartermaster General, Washington National Records Center, Suitland, MD. The other six men were Army personnel: 2Lt. Charles Barkman, T/5 Leslie F. Davis, PFC John J. McGuire, PFC George Fulkerson, Pvt. Lloyd P. Tyler, and Pvt. Ted J. Slonina.
18. Sledge, *op. cit.*, p. 32.
19. *Ibid.*, p. 86.
20. All cases involving AEF servicemen unaccounted for in World War I were closed in 1934. Since that time, twenty-six of 4,422 cases have been resolved.
21. "World War II Accounting," Defense POW/MIA Accounting Agency, accessed February 11, 2019, www.dpaa.mil/Our-Missing/World-War-II/. Although the term once included those "officially buried at sea," these individuals are considered to have had a military funeral and are not counted on the DPAA's list.
22. DPAA figure as of February 11, 2019. This number changes frequently; readers are encouraged to obtain the most recent tally at www.dpaa.mil/Our-Missing/Past-Conflicts/.
23. Hinchey, K. "Forensic anthropologist says he can identify unknown dead on USS Oklahoma," *The Oklahoman,* August 4, 2013, newsok.com/article/3868823.
24. A third set of remains found with Drake and Morrissey likely belongs to Pvt. Albert L. Bernes, who was known to be buried nearby. Officially, Bernes has not yet been accounted for.

Chapter 2

1. Tregaskis, R., *Guadalcanal Diary* (New York: Random House, 1943), pp. 20–21.
2. New York National Guard records give Buchman's date of birth as April 19, 1921, or age eighteen at enlistment. However, his actual date of birth was August 25, 1923, meaning he was only fifteen when he joined. Marine Corps muster rolls indicate he enlisted December 19, 1940, the same day he was released from the Army—age seventeen. William F. Buchman, New York National Guard Service Card, New York State Archives.
3. Phillips, S., *You'll Be Sor-ree! A Guadalcanal Marine Remembers the Pacific War,* (New York: Berkley Caliber, 2010), p. 54. Phillips was a member of the mortar section of H/2/1, the same company to which Buchman was attached. The decision to land in khakis—not the more combat-friendly dungarees—was made the night before the landing, and "made everyone gripe and growl because we all preferred dungarees because of the large, spacious pockets.... The whole second battalion landed in khaki." Evidently, this was done to distinguish the regiment's three battalions from each other.

4. Leckie, R., *Helmet For My Pillow*, (New York: Bantam Books, 2010), p. 56.

5. Phillips, *op. cit.*, p. 54.

6. *Ibid.*, 55; Leckie, *op. cit.*, p. 59.

7. 1st Marine Division, Headquarters, "Division Commander's Final Report on Guadalcanal Operation, Phase II: From H Hour to Evening 9 August," June 28, 1943, (RG 127, NARA), 10. (Hereafter Phase II Report).

8. Frank, R. B., *Guadalcanal* (New York: Penguin Books, 1992), pp. 62–63.

9. Leckie, R., *Challenge for the Pacific* (New York: Bantam Books, 2010), p. 102.

10. William F. Buchman, Individual Deceased Personnel File (IDPF), Records of the Office of the Quartermaster General, Washington National Records Center, Suitland, MD. The reasons behind Buchman's unusual attire are as much as mystery as whom he was challenging; the "mask" may have been mosquito netting or rain gear.

11. A *communiqué* from May 1950 reveals that "medical company was bivouacked in in the upper region of the Ilu River 4,500 yards south of the airfield on the night of 7 August 1942." No more accurate information has become available since. Buchman IDPF.

12. Leckie, *op. cit.*, *Helmet*, pp. 62–63.

13. Ulbrich, D. J., *Preparing For Victory: Thomas Holcomb and the Making of the Modern Marine Corps, 1936–1943* (Annapolis: Naval Institute Press, 2011), p. 35.

14. Sledge, M. *Soldier Dead: How We Recover, Identify, Bury & Honor Our Military Fallen* (New York: Columbia University Press, 2005), p. 136.

15. Twining, M. B., *No Bended Knee: The Battle for Guadalcanal* (ed.) Neil G. Carey (New York: Presidio Press, 2004), pp. 4–5.

16. "Triphibious" warfare relies upon coordinated efforts between seagoing (transport, supply, gunnery & air support), amphibious assault (shock troops to seize a beachhead), and ground combat (long-term campaign and occupation) forces. In the American system, these roles were fulfilled by the Navy, Marines, and Army respectively. For further reading, the author recommends the introductory chapters of Twining's "No Bended Knee"— Twining was one of the co-authors of FTP-167.

17. Condit, K. W., Diamond, G., and Turnbladh, E. T., *Marine Corps Ground Training in World War II* (Washington: Headquarters, U.S. Marine Corps, 1956), p. 33.

18. *Ibid.*, p. 56.

19. Steere, *Graves Registration,* p. 43.

20. Twining, *op. cit.*, p. 35.

21. 1st Marine Division, Headquarters, "Division Commander's Final Report on Guadalcanal Operation, Phase I: Events Prior To H-Hour, 7 August 1942," May 24, 1943, (RG 127, NARA), pp. 1-2. (Hereafter Phase I Report.)

22. Twining, *op. cit.*, p. 36.

23. Hoffman, J. T., *Silk Chutes and Hard Fighting: US Marine Corps Parachute Units in World War II,* (Washington: History and Museums Division, Headquarters US Marine Corps, 1999), p. 6.

24. Twining, *op. cit.*, p. 40.

25. Steere, *op. cit.*, p. 43.

26. 1st Marine Division, "Division Circular 6a-42: Personnel Administration," July 10, 1942 (Marine Corps Archives, Quantico, VA). (Hereafter "Division Circular.")

27. War Department, *Technical Manual No. 10-630: Graves Registration* (Washington: USGPO, 1941), p. 1. (Hereafter TM 10-630.)

28. Headquarters, U.S. Marine Corps, *Marine Corps Manual,* (Washington: USGPO, 1940), p. 249.

29. *Ibid.,* p. 229.

30. *Ibid.,* p. 237.

31. Headquarters Company, 2nd Battalion, 1st Marines (HQ/2/1), August 1942 muster roll, microfilm (RG 127, NARA). Medical personnel were frequently carried on the rolls of their battalion headquarters rather than the company to which they were attached.

32. *Marine Corps Manual,* p. 229.

33. Company "F," 2nd Battalion, 1st Marines (F/2/1), August 1942 muster roll, microfilm (RG 127, NARA).

34. Whyte, W. H. III, *A Time Of War: Remembering Guadalcanal, A Battle Without Maps* (New York: Fordham University Press, 2000), p. 104.

35. Marion, O. J., *On the Canal: The Marines of L-3-5 on Guadalcanal, 1942* (Mechanicsburg, PA: Stackpole Books, 2004), p. 32.

36. Company "L," 3rd Battalion, 5th Marines (L/3/5), August 1942 muster roll, microfilm (RG 127, NARA).

37. Company "C," 1st Battalion, 5th Marines (C/1/5), August 1942 muster roll, microfilm (RG 127, NARA).

38. 1st Marine Raider Battalion, September 1942 muster roll, microfilm (RG 127, NARA.)

39. Company "C," 1st Battalion, 7th Marines (C/1/7), September 1942 muster roll, microfilm (RG 127, NARA).

40. Company "E," 2nd Battalion, 5th Marines (E/2/5), November 1942 muster roll, microfilm (RG 127, NARA).

41. Company "G," 2nd Battalion, 7th Marines (G/2/7), October 1942 muster roll, microfilm (RG 127, NARA).

42. Ladd, D., and Weingartner, S., *Faithful Warriors: A Combat Marine Remembers the Pacific War* (Annapolis: Naval Institute Press, 2009), pp. 71–72.

43. John P. Clayton, Jr., interview by Jan K. Herman, Navy Medical Department, January 17–18, 2006, transcript.

44. Marion, *op. cit.,* p. 144.

45. Miller, T. I., *Earned In Blood: My Journey from Old Breed Marine to the Most Dangerous Job in America* (New York: St. Martin's Press, 2013), eBook, pp. 143–145.

46. McEnery, J. and Sloan, B., *Hell in the Pacific: A Marine Rifleman's Journey from Guadalcanal to Peleliu* (New York: Simon & Schuster, 2012), ebook, p. 119.

47. Marion, *op. cit.,* p. 145; pp. 164–165.

48. Felber, A., Felber, F. S., and Bartsch, W. H., *The Old Breed Of Marine: A World War II Diary* (Jefferson, NC: McFarland & Company, 2003), pp. 114–115.

49. Bartsch, W. H., *Victory Fever on Guadalcanal: Japan's First Land Defeat of World War II* (College Station: Texas A&M University Press, 2014), pp. 121–122.

50. "Matawan Marine Died A Hero Trying To Get 'Buddies' Aid," *The Asbury Park Evening Press,* December 7, 1943, pp. 1–3.

51. Wolfert, I., *Battle for the Solomons* (Boston: Houghton Mifflin Company, 1943), pp. 139–140.

52. Alexander, J. H., *Edson's Raiders: The 1st Marine Raider Battalion in World War II* (Annapolis: Naval Institute Press, 2010), p. 159.

53. Rogal, W. W., *Guadalcanal, Tarawa, and Beyond: A Mud Marine's Memoir of the Pacific Island War* (Jefferson, NC: McFarland & Company, 2010), p. 13.

54. 1st Marine Division, Headquarters, "Division Commander's Final Report on Guadalcanal Operation, Phase IV: 20 August–18 September," (Hereafter Phase IV Report) Annex B: Medical, 1943, (RG 127, NARA), p. 5.

55. Jones, W. K., *A Brief History of the 6th Marines* (Washington: History and Museums Division, Headquarters US Marine Corps, 1987), p. 65.

56. Moore, F. R., "The Development of Medical Service with Marine Corps Forces In The Field, World War II" (Navy Bureau of Medicine, *c.* 1945), p. 5.

57. Clayton interview.

58. Partner, S., *Toshié: A Story Of Village Life In Twentieth Century Japan* (Berkeley: University of California Press, 2004), p. 95.

59. Stauffer, A. P., *The Quartermaster Corps: Operations In The War Against Japan* (1956; reprint, Washington: U.S. Army Center of Military History, 1990), p. 252.

60. *TM 10-630*, p. 6.

61. Stauffer, *op. cit.*, p. 252.

62. Clayton interview.

63. Clark, J. M., *Gunner's Glory: Untold Stories of Marine Machine Gunners* (New York: Ballantine Books, 2004), p. 107.

64. McEnery, *op. cit.*, p. 119.

65. Miller, T. I. *op. cit.*, p. 151.

66. Driscoll, J., "Guadalcanal Cemetery Arouses Thirst for Vengeance on Japs Among Americans on Island," *The St. Louis Post-Dispatch*, July 4, 1943, 3B.

67. American Graves Registration Service, "USAF Guadalcanal, Solomon Islands," Grave Plot Charts of American Dead, 1946–1951 (RG 92, NARA). (Hereafter FMC Burial Chart.) In fact, several of the POWs were likely captured at other locations in the Solomons and interned on Guadalcanal. There were twenty-two graves in this section when the battle officially ended on February 9, 1943.

68. *Marine Corps Manual*, p. 89.

69. Cyrill Anthony Matelski and Gerald Paul Hopkins, Official Military Personnel Files (OMPFs), Records of the Office of the Quartermaster General, Washington National Records Center, Suitland, MD. (Hereafter Matelski OMPF and Hopkins OMPF.)

70. Robert Joseph Budd and Thomas Walter Phillips, Official Military Personnel Files (OMPFs), Records of the Office of the Quartermaster General, Washington National Records Center, Suitland, MD. (Hereafter Budd OMPF and Phillips OMPF.)

71. Emil Stanislaus Student and Luther Leru Rhodes, Official Military Personnel Files (OMPFs), Records of the Office of the Quartermaster General, Washington National Records Center, Suitland, MD. (Hereafter Student OMPF and Rhodes OMPF.)

72. Raymond Joseph Schulthies, Official Military Personnel File (OMPF), Records of the Office of the Quartermaster General, Washington National Records Center, Suitland, MD. (Hereafter Schulthies OMPF.)

73. Miller, T. I., *op. cit.*, p. 111.

Chapter 3

1. Soule, T., *Shooting the Pacific War: Marine Corps Combat Photography in WWII* (Lexington: The University Press of Kentucky, 2000), p. 71.

2. Cameron, C., ed., "Frank Lowell Few, His WW2 Experience," (unpublished, 1983).

3. Tregaskis, *Guadalcanal Diary,* p. 95.

4. Hurlbut, J. W., untitled press release, August 14, 1942, U.S. Naval Institute collection. Hurlbut interviewed Few for this piece immediately after the patrol; this may have been a disapproved draft version of a later article entitled "Marine Sergeant Tells How Valiant Patrol Cut To Pieces In Solomons." Obviously, Hurlbut could not mention the names of the deceased in publication. Few is specific about Sgt. David Alvin Stauffer being the man whose ammunition belt caught fire; other histories state that it was Plat. Sgt. Denzil Ray Caltrider, or "a corporal."

5. Charles C. Arndt, USMC (ret.), interview by David Wollschlager, 2006, DVD recording in author's collection

6. Although he arrived in France in August 1918, Goettge (whose last name proved a clerk's nightmare; they frequently misspelled it "Geottge") spent most of his time at a training camp in Chatillon. He officially took command of the 43rd Company, 5th Marines, on November 11, 1918–Armistice Day.

7. "Goettge Crosses Goal," *Leatherneck Magazine,* December 1923, p. 5.

8. Dietrich, P., "Goettge's Glory Rivaled Thorpe," *The Akron Beacon Journal,* 25 October 1963, p. 34.

9. Tuttler, Z., "Gridiron Nonpareil," *Leatherneck Magazine,* October 1952, p. 39.

10. Staff assignments were divided into four numbered sections: Personnel (1), Intelligence (2), Operations (3), and Supply (4). These were prefixed by the size of the unit: battalion (Bn), regiment (R), or division (D). Hence the D-2 Section was division level intelligence. In conversation, these were usually abbreviated to "2 Section," while the officer in charge was called "the D-2".

11. This is not as unusual as it may seem. The function of an "intelligence" outfit was somewhat hazily understood and dimly regarded by many in the Marine Corps. As trained prior to World War II, the 2 Section was primarily responsible for keeping commanders informed about the disposition of his own unit, rather than actively collecting information about the enemy. The name "intelligence" conjured images of cloak-and-dagger operations, "rather unsporting and better suited to what we like to think of as less honest and altruistic nations." Doubly stigmatized as errand boys and spies, lacking dedicated training facilities, and with few opportunities for upward movement, 2 Sections were difficult to staff. Goettge's lack of familiarity with his subject matter was presumably not considered a major handicap; he was, after all, personally intelligent and hard-working, and learned the job as he went. For an excellent contemporary analysis of the evolution of the 2 Section, see A. B. Waters, "The Price of Intelligence," *Marine Corps Gazette* vol. 38, no. 7 (July 1954) and both parts of William H. Whyte's "Information Into Intelligence," *Marine Corps Gazette* vol. 30, no. 4 (April 1946) and vol. 30, no. 5 (May 1946).

12. Soule, *op. cit.,* p. 27.

13. Kerr, H. B., "Marines Fought Savagely To Avenge Death Of Colonel Goettge on Guadalcanal," *The Akron Beacon-Journal,* March 28, 1943, 5D.

14. Shapiro, A., and Robards, J., *The Unknown Soldier,* directed by Carol L. Fleischer, PBS, aired 11 November 1985, DVD; Carl Custer, email to the author, February 7, 2017.

15. Soule, *op. cit.,* p. 31.

16. For Custer's first hitch, he went by "Alexander Steven Custer."

17. "Uncle Sam's Youngest Marine Has Situation Under Control," *The Tennessean,* 25 November 1940, 10. Carl Steven Custer, born November 24,

1940, reports a family belief that his father was involved with the Corps of Intelligence Police in the 1930s; he would occasionally depart, tweed civilian clothes in hand, for a few days and return unable to divulge where he had been.

18. Abady, J. *Battle at the Overland Trail: One Night of Combat on Guadalcanal* (Lynchburg: Warwick House Publishers, 2013), 101-102.
19. Whyte, W. H. III, *A Time of War,* xii. Whyte thought his collegiate status challenged and confused McKelvy, who "never figured out quite what to do with me.... He believed [Ivy Leaguers] were different from other people."
20. In the 1932 Gloucester High School yearbook, Ringer's awards and accolades dwarf his picture. They range from the military (manager of the rifle team, Medal Best Pistol Shot, ROTC Lt. Col., Senior Haskell Medal) to the literary (Harvard Club Book Prize, senior play chairman, the Sawyer Prize). One wonders how many of Ringer's achievements were due to pressure from his father, who happened to be a school headmaster.
21. Charles C. Arndt, quoted in *Notes on Jungle Warfare from the U. S. Marines and U. S. Infantry on Guadalcanal Island,* edited by Russell P. Reeder, Jr. (Washington: United States War Department, 1942), 19. Arndt kept up this practice on Guadalcanal. "Some of the other NCOs laughed at me because I am always seeing how quietly I can walk around and because I go out and practice on my own," he said. "But they have stopped laughing because I have been on more patrols than any man in the Regiment, and I am still alive."
22. Arndt, 2006 interview.
23. Soule, *op. cit.,* p. 70.
24. Camp, D. "Star-Crossed Translator: 2dLt. Merle Ralph Cory, USMCR—KIA on Guadalcanal," *Leatherneck Magazine,* August 2004, p. 28. Cory stopped using his given first name "Merle" as a young man.
25. Phase I Report, p. 24.
26. Zimmerman, J. L., *The Guadalcanal Campaign,* p. 14.
27. Merillat, H. C. L., *Guadalcanal Remembered* (New York: Dodd, Mead & Company, 1982), pp. 21-31.
28. Whyte, *op. cit.,* p. 25.
29. Soule, *op. cit.,* p. 45.."Crude and inadequate though they were, they contained all the information we had," Soule continued. "Magnetic declination was far off from present readings. No topographic maps of land areas existed, but we made sketch maps from aerial photographs. Large blank areas showed were clouds obscured the land.... At the last minute, the Navy published a map of its own ... but it was on a different scale and, to make matters worse, used a different grid."
30. Phase II Report, Annex G, "Intelligence," pp. 2-3.
31. Whyte, *op. cit.,* p. 28.
32. 1st Marine Division, Fleet Marine Force "D-2 Journal Volume I, From 7 August 1942 to 31 August 1942," (Marine Corps Archives, Quantico, VA), p. 9. (Hereafter "D-2 Journal".)
33. Twining, M. B., *No Bended Knee,* p. 74.
34. Phase II Report, p. 54.
35. Abady, *op. cit.,* p. 101.
36. Soule, *op. cit.,* p. 69.
37. 1st Marine Division, Headquarters, "Division Commander's Final Report on Guadalcanal Operation, Phase III: Organization of the Lunga Point Defenses, 10 August–21 August," July 13, 1943, (RG 127, NARA), p. 5. (Hereafter Phase III Report.)

38. Tregaskis, *op. cit.,* p. 69.

39. Jersey, S. C., *Hell's Islands: The Untold Story of Guadalcanal* (College Station: Texas A&M University Press, 2008), p. 439. While most historians agree on Sakado's name—a detail omitted by most veterans' memoirs—there is some confusion about the rest of the details. His rank is variously given as an enlisted man, warrant officer, or lieutenant. Historian Dick Camp places Tsuneto Sakado in command of a platoon on Tulagi, not Guadalcanal *(Shadow Warriors, 102)* and Eric Hammel states that *two* sailors (one enlisted and one warrant officer) were captured on 12 August (*Starvation Island, 132*).

40. Phase III Report, p. 5. "Surly" is the most common phrase used to describe Sakado.

41. Twining, *op. cit.,* p. 97.

42. "I felt from the first that the colonel wanted to prove to himself and to the Japanese that Marines weren't scared of anybody, least of all a bunch of little brown men who hid in the woods." (Soule, *op. cit.,* p. 69.) "In addition [to gathering information] it appeared desirable for humanitarian reasons to take steps to bring in the remaining labor troops who were wandering in bands beyond our outpost line." (Phase III Report, 5.)

43. Jersey, *op. cit.,* p. 196.

44. Vandegrift, A. A. with Asprey, R. B., *Once a Marine: The Memoirs of General A. A. Vandegrift, Commandant of the U.S. Marines in WWII* (New York: Ballantine Books, Inc., 1966), p. 135.

45. Soule, *op. cit.,* p. 69.

46. Hammel, E. *Guadalcanal: Starvation Island* (Pacifica, CA: Pacifica Military History, 1987), p. 132.

47. Jersey, *op. cit.,* p. 197.

48. Selvitelle, B., untitled memoir, *The Lower Deck Newsletter of the Warships & Marine Corps Museum* (Franklin, AU), September 2002.

49. McMillan, G., *The Old Breed: A History of the First Marine Division in World War II* (1949; repr. Nashville: The Battery Press, Inc., 2001), p. 52; Arndt 2006 interview.

50. Jack Clark (USN), interview with Peter Flahavin, date and location unknown, transcript, www.pacificwrecks.com/people/veterans/clark.html.

51. Cameron, *op. cit.*

52. Arndt, 2006 interview.

53. "The humor of which is nullified by the vast toll of lives it occasioned." Waters, A. B., "The Price of Intelligence," *Marine Corps Gazette,* July 1954, p. 35.

54. Soule, *op. cit.,* p. 70. The D-2 journal notes: "1912 Telephone: Col. Goettge through Commander Dexter reports flare off Beach Red."

55. Arndt, 2006 interview.

56. Jersey, *op. cit.,* p. 198.

57. Arndt, 2006 interview.

58. Steven Alexander Custer, Official Military Personnel File (OMPF), Records of the Office of the Quartermaster General, Washington National Records Center, Suitland, MD. (Hereafter Custer OMPF.)

59. Hurlbut, *op. cit.*

60. Arndt, 2006 interview.

61. Jersey, *op. cit.,* p. 198. While the identity of who confirmed Goettge's death and removed his belongings changes from account to account, Few and Arndt are present in every version. In 1983, Frank Few stated that he was undoing the insignia when Sakurai attacked. In 2006, Ardnt stated adamantly that

nobody had removed Goettge's insignia: "We didn't take anything, we'd just found him and that's when Few was jumped."

62. Keene, R. R. "The Goettge Patrol: Searching For Answers," *Leatherneck Magazine*, August 1992, p. 29.

63. McMillan, *op. cit.*, p. 53.

64. In 1949, Monk Arndt mentioned "a corporal" firing the tracers; in 2006, he stated "I was trying to fire tracers to get somebody's attention back at Lunga Point, but I guess due to the distance they couldn't see the tracers or wasn't expecting anyone to be firing."

65. "D-2 Journal," 30-31.

66. Marion, *On The Canal*, p. 80.

67. Jersey, *op. cit.*, p. 198.

68. Custer OMPF.

69. McMillan, *op. cit.*, p. 53. The 5th Marines timetable reports that the patrol landed at 2200, Goettge was killed at 2215, and Arndt was dispatched back at 2230, showing some quick decision making on Ringer's part (Phase III Report, Annex J: Fifth Marines, 1-2). Ardnt corroborated this timeline in 1942, but after the war, he reappraised his departure time to 1 a.m. (1949, 2006).

70. Exactly when Bainbridge was ordered back is not known for certain, as he did not survive his mission. Most historical accounts agree that Ringer ordered three men back to the perimeter, but these are usually thought to be the three survivors. Few, however, escaped not on orders but as the last man standing. Bainbridge, therefore, was one of the three; in 2006, Charles Arndt mentioned "We found Bainbridge's body in the river and somebody said that he was sent out [as] the second man when they heard shots fired at me."

71. According to the D-2 journal, the daily password was "Lillian." Either Arndt misheard the sailors, or misremembered the word when giving his interview in 1949.

72. Hurlbut, J. W. "Only 3 of 25 Marines Live to Tell of Clash With Japs," *Philadelphia Inquirer*, 12 September 1942, pp. 1-2.

73. Shapiro and Robards, *The Unknown Soldier.*

74. Keene, *op. cit.*, p. 28.

75. Phase III Report, Annex J. Hammel's *Starvation Island,* suggests that Spaulding and Few hailed the Company A boats from the beach and were picked up there (Hammel, *op. cit.*, pp. 135-136), however this is not mentioned by the regimental report. Veteran testimony from Art Boston claims that Few returned through the lines of Third Platoon, L/3/5 (Marion, *op. cit.*, p. 80).

76. Capt. William P. Kaempfer to Mrs. Stella Rosalik, September 9, 1942, original in private collection.

77. Sundberg, E. "Letters To A Granddaughter," accessed 21 April 2018, edsundberg.weebly.com/us-marine.html.

78. Muster rolls report that Bainbridge was killed by a gunshot wound in the chest, and that he was "interred on beach at mouth of Matanikau River" on August 13, 1942. A map overlay included in his IDPF clarifies the location as "sandspit between river and sea." Hammel places Bainbridge's discovery on 18 August after the assault on Horahi. Headquarters and Service Company, 5th Marines (H&S/5), muster roll, microfilm (RG 127, NARA); William Bainbridge, Individual Deceased Personnel File (IDPF), Records of the Office of the Quartermaster General, Washington National Records Center, Suitland, MD; Hammel, *Starvation Island,* 143.

79. McMillan, *op. cit.*, p. 52.

80. Zimmerman, *op. cit.*, p. 60. Zimmerman cites a letter from Lt. Warren S. Sivertson of the First Pioneer Battalion for these details.

81. Vandegrift and Asprey, *op. cit.*, p. 135.

82. McEnery, J. *Hell In The Pacific*, p. 81.

83. Robert Richard Lyons, Official Military Personnel File (OMPF), Records of the Office of the Quartermaster General, Washington National Records Center, Suitland, MD. (Hereafter R. Lyons OMPF.)

84. Custer OMPF.

85. "Cpl. Stephen Serdula Is Missing; Brother Follows Him Into Marines," *The Evening Leader* (Corning, NY), September 8, 1942, 7.

86. McEnery, *op. cit.*, p. 79. The identity and fate of the flier, an F4F Wildcat pilot, isn't known. "We never found a trace of the plane or pilot, and after what we *did* find, we forgot all about them."

87. Miller, T. I. *Earned In Blood*, pp. 104-107; McEnery, *op. cit.*, p. 79-82. These veterans' descriptions of this horrible scene are recorded so vividly in their memoirs that no summation or combination can do them justice.

88. George W. Kohler, interview by Patrick Brown, date unknown, George W. Kohler Collection (AFC/2001/001/06119), Veterans History Project, American Folklife Center, Library of Congress.

89. Miller, T. I., *op. cit.*, pp. 106-108.

90. Don Langer to James Rube Garrett, Jr., December 22, 1996, email transcript, www.nettally.com/jrube/dlanger.htm.

91. Phase III Report, p. 7.

92. Excerpt from an interview with *The Los Angeles Evening Herald and Express*, July 27, 1943, as printed in Marion, *op. cit.*, p. 85.

93. "13, killed in action against the enemy at mouth of Matanikau River, Guadalcanal, B. S. I.... 19, remains interred near mouth of Matanikau River, Guadalcanal, B. S. I." Company "A," 5th Marines (A/1/5), muster roll, microfilm (RG 127, NARA).

94. Marion, *op. cit.*, p. 84. Branic was an acting platoon leader, possibly in place of 2Lt. Thomas "Fred" Guffin, Jr., who was hospitalized from August 18–20.

95. Hurlbut, J. W., "Systematic Marine Patrols Wipe Out Jap Stronghold," *Tucson Daily Citizen*, September 14, 1942, 5. George Houk Mead (of the Mead Paper family) was reportedly giving aid to a wounded private when hit; he returned fire with his sidearm and killed the Japanese sniper. He received a posthumous Navy Cross for his actions on 19 August 1942.

96. Marion, *op. cit.*, pp. 91-94.

97. "Members of 'L' Company estimated that they had the remains of 22 bodies" (Keene, *op. cit.*, p. 29); "The officers were about to get the troops started on exhuming the twenty-one bodies found in the area" (Hammel, *op. cit.*, p. 143). These figures may have their source in the total number of missing, with Hammel subtracting Bainbridge as an isolated burial. They do not account for the remains found unburied and scattered at the Matanikau sandbar, which McEnery thought to be "at least four … there may have been several others in some bushes a few yards in from the water." (McEnery, *op. cit.*, p. 80).

98. Marion, *op. cit.*, p. 88.

99. Ibid., 93, 274.

100. Keene, *op. cit.*, p. 29. Keene does not delve far into specifics: "Members of Co. 'B' (5th Marines) claimed to have seen the bodies of American Marines by the mouth of the Matanikau River. Co. K on a later patrol would also report finding a human torso tied to a tree and believed it to the remains of 1stSgt. Custer. As late as November, Marine Second Lieutenant John Davis found part of a body with part of a uniform with chevrons near the beach. Another patrol

radioed that they had found the remains and later stated they assumed that graves registration had taken care of them."

101. Gallant, T. G., *On Valor's Side,* (New York: Kensington Publishing Group, 1963), 297.
102. Jack Clark interview.
103. Merillat, *op. cit.,* p. 86.
104. Tregaskis, *op. cit.,* pp. 95-97. Tregaskis was not the sole originator of this story, but the widespread success of his book—and the subsequent film— certainly helped to spread the rumor.
105. Kerr, *op. cit.,* p. 5-D.
106. "Jap Treachery Responsible For Serdula's Death, Says Gullo, Home From Pacific," *The Evening Leader* (Corning, NY) September 7, 1943, p. 3. Gullo's 7th Marines arrived on Guadalcanal more than a month after the patrol; his rendition was itself a secondhand story.
107. Phase III Report, p. 7.
108. Johnson, W. B., *The Pacific Campaign in World War II: Pearl Harbor to Guadalcanal* (New York: Routledge, 2006), p. 219.
109. Sledge, E. B., *With The Old Breed at Peleliu and Okinawa* (New York: Presidio Press, 2007), pp. 33-34. Sledge does not mention the survivor by name, but it is certainly Frank Few, who was serving with the MP Company of the 1st Marine Division at the time. Spaulding and Arndt were at stateside posts.
110. Stephen Serdula, Individual Deceased Personnel File (IDPF), Records of the Office of the Quartermaster General, Washington National Records Center, Suitland, MD.
111. 604th Quartermaster Graves Registration Company, "Expedition No. 2 Summary of Cruise, 9 June 1948–16 April 1949" (RG 554, NARA), 16. (Hereafter 604th QMGRC, "Expedition No. 2.")
112. Keene, *op. cit.,* p. 29. Naturally, the Japanese refrained from mentioning any mutilation of the remains.
113. Bartlett, T., "In Search Of The Goettge Patrol," *Leatherneck Magazine,* August 1988, pp. 29-30.
114. Radford University, "RU Students Write From Guadalcanal About Their Search for WWII Marine Remains," *Office of University Relations,* last updated July 14, 2008, www.radford.edu/NewsPub/July08/0712guadalcanaltrip.html.
115. Bartlett, *op. cit.,* p. 29. The unknown gardener evidently treasured the dog tags and wore them for the rest of her life, and had them buried with her when she died.

Chapter 4

1. "Guadalcanal Street," *Dayton Herald,* July 3, 1943, 4.
2. Felber, *The Old Breed of Marine,* pp. 75-76.
3. Horan, J. D., and Frank, G., *Out In The Boondocks: 21 U. S. Marines Tell Their Stories* (New York: G. P. Putnam's Sons, 1943), p. 138.
4. *Marine Corps Manual,* p. 21.
5. Phase I Report, Annex M: Medical.
6. Christ, J. F., *Battalion of the Damned: The 1st Marine Paratroopers at Gavutu and Bloody Ridge* (Annapolis: Naval Institute Press, 2007), p. 24.
7. The first-known Marine officer to occupy this billet was Capt. Richard Tonis, who joined Division HQ from the 1st Service Battalion on September 23, 1942.

8. Division Circular.

9. Griffith, S. B. II, *The Battle for Guadalcanal* (Champaign, IL: University of Chicago Press, 2000), pp. 23-24.

10. Drury, C. M., *The History of the Chaplain Corps, United States Navy,* Vol 2: "1939–1949" (Washington: USGPO, 1948), p. 12.

11. *Marine Corps Manual,* p. 697. Peacetime protocols assumed that the remains of dead servicemen would speedily be returned to the United States, where final dispositions would be made. The Marine Corps Manual of 1940 stipulates "pay for services of a clergyman at burials of enlisted men may be allowed when the services of a Navy chaplain are not available." (This is also the only time that chaplains are mentioned in the entire 1,118 page volume.)

12. TM 10-630, 15-16.

13. Drury, *op. cit.,* p. 175.

14. The chaplains' regular assignments were as follows: Dittmar, 11th Marines and acting Division Chaplain; Olton, 1st Marines; Sovik, 2/1st Marines; Willard, 3/2nd Marines; Fitzgerald, Division Headquarters; Reardon, 5th Marines.

15. Christ, *op. cit.,* pp. 65-69.

16. *Ibid.,* p. 99.

17. Willard, W. W., *The Leathernecks Come Through* (New York: Revell, 1944) pp. 19-20.

18. *Ibid.,* pp. 26-29.

19. O'Donnell, P. K., *Into The Rising Sun: World War II's Pacific Veterans Reveal The Heart Of Combat* (New York: Simon & Schuster, 2010), p. 25.

20. Christ, *op. cit.,* pp. 126-127. Christ places the burial on the morning of August 8, however, Gavutu was not yet secure, and Willard (who arrived on the morning of August 8) does not mention this event at all. Willard and Moore's memoirs both mention a heavy rain the night before the burial, which would place the date as August 9. While some of the 2nd Marines are reported in their muster roll as buried on August 8, most Paramarines show a date of August 9, and the later date is thought to be more accurate.

21. Willard, *op. cit.,* pp. 29-31. Unfortunately, Willard does not record the names of his assistants, and any copies of their cemetery map have been lost.

22. Marston, G. D., "There've Been Some Changes Made," *Leatherneck Magazine,* April 1945, p. 21.

23. Willard, *op. cit.,* p. 43. The corpsmen in question were HA1c Don O. Woods and PhM2c William L. Vincent, both of 3/2nd Marines. They were reported buried on August 11 1942, along with Plat. Sgt. Russell Walker (I/3/2), who may have been "the wounded man."

24. Marston, *op. cit.,* p. 21.

25. "Unknown X-257, Solomon Islands, Guadalcanal," Washington National Records Center, Suitland, MD.

26. Robert Lee Liston, Official Military Personnel File (OMPF), Records of the Office of the Quartermaster General, Washington National Records Center, Suitland, MD.

27. 1st Marine Division, Headquarters, "Division Commander's Final Report on Guadalcanal Operation, Phase V: 18 September–5 December," July 1, 1943, (RG 127, NARA), 244. (Hereafter Phase V Report.) An addendum entitled "Killed In Action Or Died As Result Of Wounds First Marine Division Reinforced 7 August To 10 December 1942" includes the names and burial locations, if known, of confirmed KIAs from all branches. (Hereafter Phase V Report: Burial Addendum.)

28. Christ, *op. cit.,* p. 179.

29. "Marine Youth Is Lakehurst Hope At Penn," *Morning Herald* (Gloversville and Johnstown, NY) October 16, 1943, p. 10. Dudenake gained a great deal of notice for his football prowess on the Lakehurst Naval Air Station team.

30. Mason, J. T. Jr., ed., *The Pacific War Remembered: An Oral History Collection* (Annapolis: Naval Institute Press, 1986), p. 113.

31. Office of Naval Intelligence, *Solomon Islands Campaign I: The Landing In The Solomons, 7-8 August 1942* (Washington: ONI, 1943), p. 34.

32. Zimmerman, J. L., *The Guadalcanal Campaign,* p. 264.

33. Groft, M. and Alexander, L., *Bloody Ridge and Beyond: A World War II Marine's Memoir of Edson's Raiders in the Pacific* (New York: Berkeley Caliber, 2014), ebook, pp. 45-46.

34. Phase III Report, Annex H "Medical," p. 4.

35. Jersey, S. C., *Hell's Islands,* pp. 165-166; 185. In Jersey alone, "Native" reference attributed to John P. Lanigan (USCG), "Chinese" reference attributed to James Sorensen (A/1/2), "Japanese" reference attributed to Dallas Bennett (HQ/2/2).

36. Banning, B., ed., *Heritage Years: Second Marine Division Commemorative Anthology, 1940-1949* (Paducah, Turner Publishing, 1988), p. 66.

37. USS *Aaron Ward,* War Diary, November 13, 1942.

38. A discrepancy should be noted here. In the IDPF for X-1 (later designated as X-219 ANMC), McKelvy is buried on the left (grave 29) and Pvt. Donald L. Hart (G/2/5) is on the right (grave 31). "Names of adjacent deceased are taken from adjoining grave markers" reads the Report of Interment. However, this does not agree with other sources—and, as Hart was temporarily re-designated as an unknown (X-231), it seems there may have been a misplaced grave marker in the Tulagi cemetery. Hart's identification was confirmed in 1950.

39. Burri was shot in the head as he jumped out of his landing craft; the crew probably pulled him back on board without realizing he was already dead.

40. Jersey, *op. cit.,* p. 159. "About 2200 there was a rumbling and an upper part of a battle-scarred coconut tree came crashing down in our area. It killed Bresing [*sic*]. Joe had gone through the day without a scratch only to be killed by a falling tree."

41. USS *Neville,* "Report on Operations off Tulagi Area, Solomon Islands, August 7–8–9 1942," p. 6.

42. Clemens, M., *Alone on Guadalcanal: A Coastwatcher's Story* (Annapolis: Naval Institute Press, 2002), pp. 307-308; Rogal, W., *Mud Marine,* p. 64. Muster rolls of 1st Battalion, 2nd Marines place Sparks in Grave No. 28; the Division Burial Roster corrects this to No. 22. Stafford is buried in Grave #20. Occupant of No. 21 is not known.

43. Horan and Frank, *op. cit.,* p. 101. Nickel and Key were decorated with the Silver Star and Navy Cross, respectively, for their actions.

44. Phase V Report, Burial Addendum.

45. Company "F," 5th Marines (F/2/5), muster roll, microfilm (RG 127, NARA).

46. Jersey, *op. cit.,* p. 133.

47. George Alfred Johnson, Official Military Personnel File (OMPF), Records of the Office of the Quartermaster General, Washington National Records Center, Suitland, MD.

48. Larson, T. J., *Hell's Kitchen, Tulagi 1942–1943* (Bloomington: iUniverse, 2003), p. 20.

49. "Lieutenant (j.g.) James J. Fitzgerald joined us [December 11, 1942] as Regimental Chaplain. He is a Catholic. He is a much younger man than

Chaplain Dittmar (Protestant) and does not have the latter's suavity and charm." Felber, *op. cit.,* p. 156.

50. *Ibid.,* 68.
51. "'Guadalcanal Padre' Consoles Relatives Of U.S. War Victims," *Oakland Tribune,* March 31, 1943, C17.
52. Division Circular.
53. Felber, *op. cit.,* p. 69. A slight discrepancy arises with Felber's mention of "two occupied graves" implying two complete interments. Four Marines were buried on August 12: PFC Oscar J. Grover, Jr. (C/1/1), Pvt. John R. Brotherston (H&S/1st Pioneer Battalion), Sgt. James P. Casey (H&S/11th Marines) and Sgt. Nicholas R. Windisch (I/3/11th Marines). Felber witnessed one burial before Casey's, and one after, which ought to be Brotherston and Windisch. The author believes that Grover was completely buried in Grave No. 1 when Felber's group arrived, and that Brotherston was "occupying" the open Grave No. 2, awaiting the Chaplain's words.
54. Garrett, J. R., "A Marine Diary: My Experiences on Guadalcanal," online transcript last accessed April 21, 2018, www.nettally.com/jrube/@guadaug. html. "Rube" Garrett wrote on August 11: "Machine gunned again. Sgt. Windish [*sic*.], our Instrument Section sergeant, was killed accidentally by one of our officers. Went on two-hour patrol with Sgt. Voelker. To river to bathe and saw two prisoners. A friend of mine, Casey from Headquarters' Battery, was killed in the night, I think by friendly fire." He added: "Sgt. Windish was killed accidentally by his own officer, who was the Instrument Section Commander, with whom he was bunking. He had left the bunker and, on returning, frightened the man inside who shot him two times with a .45-caliber pistol. Both men were gone before daylight—we never saw nor heard of the officer again."
55. Felber, *op. cit.,* p. 69.
56. PFC Grover of C/1/1 was the victim of an "intramural," or an accidental firefight between two Marine units. "In my platoon, the first man who was killed was killed by our people, by excitement, you know? They heard something and the poor guy was killed.... Night in the jungle, I can still see it, it was a scary feeling. We thought they were all around us." James Wagner, interview by David Siry, July 18, 2015, video, West Point Center for Oral History.
57. Division Circular.
58. The notoriously inaccurate Marine maps misidentified the Ilu River as the Tenaru. While the problem was later rectified, the name of the battle stuck.
59. This action by A/1/1, called the "Brush Patrol" after their commander Capt. Charles Brush, is described in detail in William Bartsch's excellent *Victory Fever on Guadalcanal: Japan's First Land Defeat of World War II.* Brush's men ran into a reconnaissance party from the Ichiki Detachment and killed nearly thirty, including many officers. Among the items captured were Japanese maps of Marine positions, routes of attack, and high-powered radios. The dead Marines—PFC Jack H. Gardner, Pvt. John C. Buckhalt, and Pvt. George H. Grazier—were buried near the scene of the ambush with their boondockers sticking out to facilitate their rediscovery later. Bartsch indicates that Ichiki's men might have mistaken the Marine graves for Japanese and disinterred them mistakenly.
60. Makos, A. and Brotherton, M., *Voices Of The Pacific: Untold Stories From The Marine Heroes Of World War II* (New York: Penguin, 2014), p. 39.
61. Bartsch, *op. cit.,* p. 194. Saphier was buried in Row 2, Grave 5, First Marine Division Cemetery.

62. Makos and Brotherton, *op. cit.,* p. 41. Sterling and Atwood were buried in Row 4, Graves 1-2. "That was the beginning of the Marine cemetery on Guadalcanal."

63. Knowlton, D. S. (MC USN), "Activities Of Medical Unit On Guadalcanal," March 27, 1943, transcript, (RG38, NARA).

64. Helling, T., *Desperate Surgery in the Pacific War: Doctors and Damage Control for American Wounded, 1941-1945* (Jefferson, NC: McFarland & Company, 2017), p. 46.

65. Bartsch, *op. cit.,* p. 194.

66. Clark, L. W., *An Unlikely Arena* (New York: Vantage Press, 1989), p. 45.

67. "I found later that the actual count of Jap bodies in the Tenaru battle was 871" Tregaskis, R., *Guadalcanal Diary,* p. 146. 1st Marine Division estimates were even higher.

68. Leckie, R., *Helmet For My Pillow,* p. 86.

69. Tregaskis, *op. cit.,* p. 148.

70. War Department, *Field Manual No. 100-10: Field Service Regulations: Administration* (Washington: USGPO, 1940), 131. [Hereafter FM 100-10].

71. Felber, *op. cit.,* p. 71.

72. Jack Clark interview.

73. Division Circular.

74. "Fighting 5th Chaplain Tells Story Of Heroism," *Brooklyn Daily Eagle,* August 16, 1943, 2.

75. Dorsett, L. W., *Serving God and Country: U. S. Military Chaplains in World War II,* (New York: Penguin, 2012), p. 48.

76. Reardon was the inspiration for "Father Donnelly" in the film version of *Guadalcanal Diary.* The nickname "Guadalcanal Padre" is more famously associated with Father Frederic Gehring who arrived with a Naval Construction Battalion, or "Seabees" unit, in late September 1942. However, newspapers of the period applied it to Reardon first. Crosby, D. F., *Battlefield Chaplains: Catholic Priests in World War II* (Lawrence: University Press of Kansas, 1994), p. 43.

77. Donahue, J. A., "Guadalcanal Journal," transcript online: web.archive.org/web/20150814122233/ and guadalcanaljournal.com:80/the-guadalcanal-journal/.

78. Groft, *op. cit.,* p. 103.

79. Alexander, J. H., *Edson's Raiders,* pp. 159-160.

80. "Unknown X-8, Solomon Islands, Guadalcanal," Records of the Office of the Quartermaster General, Washington National Records Center, Suitland, MD.

81. Tonis, R., *I Joined The Cardinal's Army: Memories of a Massachusetts State Trooper and Pacific Combat Marine,* (Brockton, MA: self-published, date unknown), p. 121.

82. Walsh, E. L., "Guadalcanal Padre retired, but prayers for peace continue," *Asbury Park Press,* December 16, 1979, p. A20.

83. Tonis, *op. cit.,* p. 122.

84. Walsh, *op. cit.*

85. Tonis, *op. cit.,* p. 122.

86. Cogswell and Annetti signed off on a Report of Interment for Cpl. Rollie Andrick, 164th Infantry, on January 4, 1943. William Annetti would have a long career in the Graves Registration field, including directing the Army Casualty Disposition Program during and after the Vietnam War.

87. Steere, *Graves Registration,* p. 43.

88. Clark, *op. cit.,* p. 120.

89. Leckie, *op. cit.,* pp. 92-93.
90. Donahue, *op. cit.* Donahue does not record the date but mentions making the placard sometime in mid-September.
91. Crane, A., ed., *Marines At War* (New York: Hyperion Press, 1943), p. 59.
92. Walsh, *op. cit.*
93. Associated Press, "No, They Can't" *Palm Beach Post-Times,* 27 December 1942, p. 5.
94. Venn, R. H., "Memorial Service Held At Guadalcanal Cemetery," *Philadelphia Inquirer,* February 11, 1943, p. 3.
95. Richard Greer, interviewer unknown, 2015, National World War II Museum.
96. Clark, *op. cit.,* p. 120.
97. Makos and Brotherton, *op. cit.,* p. 41.

Chapter 5

1. Birkett, P. D., *Guadalcanal Legacy 50th Anniversary, 1942–1992,* ed. Gene Keller, Robert C. Muehrcke, Donald W. Peltier and Joseph Micek (Paducah: Turner Publishing, 1992), p. 45.
2. Robert Corwin, interview by Roger B. Wilson, 2002, transcript, Robert L. Corwin Collection (AFC/2001/001/10706), Veterans History Project, American Folklife Center, Library of Congress. (Hereafter Corwin 2002 interview.)
3. Morse, H., and Head, G., *"A"-1-1: Pearl Harbor to Peleliu,* (A-1-1 Book Committee, 1994), p. 35.
4. Phase IV Report, 3.
5. Morse and Head, *op. cit.,* p. 36.
6. Freeman B. Blair, Silver Star citation, *United States Marine Corps Headquarters Bulletin* No. 213 (15 July 1943). Of the thirty-seven Marines who were killed in action or died of wounds in the Tenaru battle, Blair is the only BNR case. Proximity to the newly-established cemetery was a major factor in the successful recovery of the other remains.
7. Morse and Head, *op. cit.,* pp. 36-37.
8. Corwin 2002 interview. "What we missed most was toilet paper and shoelaces. You know you wear the same shoes day in and day out. The shoes held up pretty good. They were quality shoes. But eventually the shoelaces gave out and we had no way of keeping the shoes tied together. Little things like that that never occurs to somebody, but that's what we missed, shoelaces and toilet paper."
9. Phase IV Report, Annex "G," "History of the First Marine Regiment," 5.
10. Phase IV Report, 7.
11. Phase IV Report, Annex "G," 7.
12. Company "K," 1st Marines (K/3/1), muster roll, microfilm (RG 127, NARA). This grave was never found after the war.
13. Balester, V. J., ed. "Letters to Mark: Reminiscences of a Marine Corps Scout, Cpl. Fred J. Balester," 1988–1995, transcript online, www.privateletters.net/stories_balester.html.
14. Whyte, W. H. III, *A Time Of War,* p. 54; Morse and Head, *op. cit.,* p.37.
15. Zimmerman, J. L., *The Guadalcanal Campaign,* p. 93.
16. Company "A," 1st Marines (A/1/1), muster roll, microfilm (RG 127, NARA).
17. Morse and Head, *op. cit.,* p. 144. Childers' burial location was marked on a map overlay, but not located after the war.
18. Phase IV Report, Annex "G," 6. Estimate included casualties from September 13–16.

19. Vandegrift, A. A. with Asprey, R. B., *Once A Marine*, p. 159.

20. Twining, M. B., *No Bended Knee*, p. 131. Twining refers to this as *"the fundamental tactical decision of the Guadalcanal Campaign and one that was to have a wide effect."* (emphasis in original)

21. Leckie, R., *Challenge for the Pacific*, pp. 227-229.

22. Balester, *op. cit.* Cpl. Balester participated in several operations supporting (and in front of) the 1st Marines, and commented "when we showed up as assigned no one seemed quite sure how to take us, so we usually ended up as point scouts since it was assumed that we knew the way."

23. Company "B," 1st Marines (B/1/1), muster roll, microfilm (RG 127, NARA). Armstrong and Williams essentially traded roles on August 24. The reasons for this decision are not known.

24. Leon Walter McStine, Official Military Personnel File (OMPF), Records of the Office of the Quartermaster General, Washington National Records Center, Suitland, MD.

25. "Shenandoah Boy Killed In War," *Mount Carmel Item* (Mount Carmel, PA), October 27, 1942, 1.

26. Corwin 2002 interview. Quartermaster Nat Corwin survived the sinking of the *Quincy* on August 9. Corwin's buddy was PFC Bernard J. McCarthy; at the time of the patrol he was the company's only combat fatality.

27. "Randolph Boy Killed While Serving Land," *Jamestown Post-Journal* (Jamestown NY), October 26, 1942, 1.

28. Ferguson, Mrs. W., "Pray For Me," *Pittsburgh Press*, November 6, 1942, p. 28.

29. "Kin of Marine, Navy Casualties Tearful But Proud Of Heroes," *Brooklyn Daily Eagle*, November 12, 1942, 4.

30. Corwin 2002 interview.

31. Zimmerman, *op. cit.*, p. 93.

32. Herman Shirley, interviewer unknown, 2013, TV15 Victoria, Texas. (Hereafter Shirley 2013 Interview.)

33. Birkett, *op. cit.*, p. 45.

34. "Matawan Marine Died A Hero Trying To Get 'Buddies' Aid," *Asbury Park Evening Press*, December 7, 1943, 1-3.

35. Birkett, *op. cit.*, p. 45.

36. "48 Hours in Hell" *Leatherneck Magazine*, November 1942, p. A23.

37. Merillat, H. C. L., *The Island: A History of the First Marine Division at Guadalcanal, August 7 – December 9, 1942* (Yardley, PA: Westholme Publishing, 2010), p. 117.

38. "Matawan Marine," 3.

39. Leckie, *op. cit.*, p. 229.

40. Birkett, *op. cit.*, p. 45.

41. Morse and Head, *op. cit.*, p. 37. The authors appear to combine the events of the two patrols, placing the Company "B" fracas and the Cresswell anecdote on September 14.

42. Hammel, E., *Starvation Island*, p. 235-236.

43. *Ibid.*

44. Birkett, *op. cit.*, p. 45.

45. Shirley 2013 interview. The patrol was heading south; thus "left side" would be the eastern bank and *vice versa*.

46. Debele is a prominent figure in both Corwin's and Shirley's memories of September 17. I have tried to use his presence in both narratives to connect the two when possible.

47. Shirley 2013 interview.

48. Birkett, *op. cit.*, p. 45.

49. "Bullet That Hit Marine Hero Killed Local Boy," *Jamestown Post-Journal* (Jamestown NY), June 28, 1943, 10. This article misidentifies Debele as Ingerson.

50. Birkett, *op. cit.*, p. 45.

51. *Ibid.*, p. 44.

52. 1st Battalion, 1st Marines, "War Journal 8 June 42–26 June 45," (RG 127, NARA). (Hereafter "1/1 War Diary.")

53. *Ibid.*

54. Harry Dunn, Navy Cross citation, transcribed by The Hall Of Valor Project, http://valor.militarytimes.com/hero/8114. Dunn was also cited for "killing or wounding three men while fighting off hostile detachments intent upon mopping up the field."

55. Donahue, J. A., "Guadalcanal Journal." Donahue refers to "a First Lieutenant who made Captain" serving with the 3rd Battalion; he may have misunderstood the story details (elsewhere he reports a rumor that Ingerson was killed "the first night ashore" which was also not accurate). Capt. Williams was sent back to a stateside billet, but not until January 15, 1943, sometime after the 1st Marines left the island.

56. Fawcett, Maj. M. A., "Patrol Report 26 September 1942," attached to 1/1 War Diary (RG 127, NARA).

57. "Matawan Marine."

58. Fawcett, *op. cit.*

59. 1/1 War Diary.

60. Frank, R. B., *Guadalcanal,* p. 264. "Weirdest characters" is the opinion of the Division operations officer, Col. Gerald Thomas.

61. McStine OMPF; Charles Frederick Debele, Official Military Personnel File (OMPF), Records of the Office of the Quartermaster General, Washington National Records Center, Suitland, MD. (Hereafter Debele OMPF.) These personal items were likely found on the bodies, as Capt. Williams signed the inventory lists.

62. "James Pierce Killed At Guadalcanal," *Berkshire Evening Eagle* (Pittsfield, MA), December 24, 1942, 9.

63. As a corpsman, Pierce was officially a member of the battalion headquarters company; records and muster rolls reflect this accurately. However, as corpsmen attached to line companies tended to identify more strongly with those units, I have counted Pierce among the Company "B" casualties.

64. An interesting but unverified account of discovering Pierce's remains was found during research for this book. The individual, posting on a treasure hunter's forum in 2010, claimed to be a Guadalcanal veteran. "I returned in 1944 and cut my way back behind Henderson about 4–5 miles to where there had been a Japanese ammo dump, with the idea of getting a few souvenirs. On the way, I dropped down into a small valley, perhaps 50 meters in diameter. There I found the remains of a US Marine squad that had been wiped out by the Japanese. They were still in their foxholes which were in a small circle, with dead Japanese surrounding them. I took the dog tags of one and later informed the grave locators. The dog tag that I took was for James Francis Pierce. Later, I asked about the site and was told that the bodies had been recovered, thanks to my information. They told me that James Francis Pierce was a hospital corpsman, 3rd class and was eventually buried at Arlington." Requests for additional information went unanswered.

65. Oddly, the B/1/1 men were not all buried sequentially. Curry was placed in Plot "A," Row 27, Grave 10; graves in this section were originally dug in February 1943, and he evidently displaced a Chinese laborer named Don Ken

Chow. Garrettson occupied Plot "B," Row 75, Grave 10, among graves dug in November 1943. Ingerson, Debele, and Gorczysky were in Plot "C," Row 102, Graves 1-3; X-117 (later identified as Corpsman Pierce), McElvaine, and Compton in Graves 5-7. This was the section being expanded in October 1944. Why they were so separated is not clear; all were included on the Weekly Report of Burials for October 6, 1944. The outlier, Jensen, appears in Plot "C," Row 107, Grave 8.

66. Fawcett, *op. cit.* Fawcett's career began as an enlisted man in 1926; he served aboard the battleship USS *California* before being invited to attend a preparatory course for the Naval Academy. He graduated with a commission in 1932, rose through the officer ranks, and was one of the top shots on the USMC marksmanship team. Commended for his performance on Guadalcanal, he retired at the end of his twenty years as a lieutenant colonel.

67. Shirley 2013 interview.

68. Corwin: "Perhaps half a mile south of our lines, our platoon was ordered to cross the Lunga to a small island in the river." (Birkett, *op. cit.*, p. 50). Merillat, speaking of evacuation from the ambush: "He [Dunn] carried his comrade about two and one half miles." (Merillat, *op. cit.*, p. 118.)

69. "Bullet That Hit Marine Hero Killed Local Boy," and Birkett, *op. cit.*, p. 45.

70. James Francis Pierce, Official Military Personnel File (OMPF), Records of the Office of the Quartermaster General, Washington National Records Center, Suitland, MD. (Hereafter Pierce OMPF.)

71. Merillat, *op. cit.*, p. 117.

72. Shirley, 2013 interview.

73. "48 Hours in Hell."

74. Shane, T., *Heroes of the Pacific* (New York: Julian Messner, Inc., 1944), pp. 252-253.

75. Shirley, 2013 interview.

76. "Bullet That Hit Marine Hero Killed Local Boy," and Birkett, *op. cit.*, p. 45.

77. Debele OMPF.

78. Pierce OMPF.

79. Frederick Lewis Secor, Official Military Personnel File (OMPF), Records of the Office of the Quartermaster General, Washington National Records Center, Suitland, MD.

80. "Matawan Man."

81. Mickey Aubrey Boschert, Individual Deceased Personnel File (IDPF), Records of the Office of the Quartermaster General, Washington National Records Center, Suitland, MD.

Chapter 6

1. Horan, J. D., and Frank, G., *Out In The Boondocks*, p. 186.

2. Hoffman, J. T., *Chesty: The Story Of Lieutenant General Lewis B. Puller, USMC* (New York: Random House, 2002), p. 161.

3. Hammel, E., *Starvation Island*, p. 253. Large portions of Map 104 are labeled "cloud"—indicating where clouds obscured the aerial photographs used to make the maps.

4. White, G. P., unpublished diary, Minnesota Historical Society Library collection.

5. Davis, B., *Marine! The Life Of Chesty Puller*, eBook, (New York: Open Road Media, 2016), p. 98.

6. Hoffman, *op. cit.*, p. 159.

7. White, *op. cit.*
8. Malanowski, J., "Andy Malanowski, USMC" *jamiemalanowski.com* (blog), March 9, 2010, jamiemalanowski.com/andy-malanowski-usmc.
9. Davis, *op. cit.*, p. 93.
10. Hoffman, *op. cit.*, pp. 146-147.
11. Charles M. Jacobs, interviewed by Michael Aikey, August 8, 2001, video, New York State Military Museum.
12. Alvin Chester Cockrell, Jr., Official Military Personnel File (OMPF), Records of the Office of the Quartermaster General, Washington National Records Center, Suitland, MD. (Hereafter Cockrell OMPF.)
13. White, *op. cit.*
14. Commander, Amphibious Force, South Pacific Force, "Report of operation for reinforcement of GUADALCANAL ISLAND by the Seventh Marines (Reinforced)," September 27, 1942, 9.
15. Twining, M. B., *No Bended Knee*, p. 130.
16. Goble, J., untitled memoir, *The Lower Deck Newsletter of the Warships & Marine Corps Museum* (Franklin, AU), September 2002, pp. 6-7.
17. White, *op. cit.*
18. Merillat, H. C. L., *Guadalcanal Remembered*, p. 147.
19. The destroyer escort *USS Leland E. Thomas* (DE-420) was later named for the fallen pilot.
20. Lundstrom, J. B., *First Team and the Guadalcanal Campaign: Naval Fighter Combat from August to November 1942* (Annapolis: Naval Institute Press, 1994), p. 260. Informed of the landings, the Japanese sent twenty-seven bombers and thirty-seven Zeros down from Rabaul. The Marines were saved by a storm front.
21. Vandegrift, A. A. with Asprey, R. B., *Once A Marine*, p. 159. "Day by day I watched my Marines deteriorate in the flesh. Although lean Marines are better than fat Marines, these troops were becoming too lean."
22. Jacobs interview. Jacobs is likely referring to Sgt. Ambrose Mihalek of C/1st Parachute Battalion. He got bum dope in this exchange: Mihalek was wounded on September 14, but ultimately survived.
23. Horan and Frank, *op. cit.*, p. 185; Charles Jacobs interview; White, *op. cit.*; Goble, *op. cit.*, p. 7; and Richard Greer interview.
24. Green, M. and Brown, J. D., *War Stories of the Infantry: Americans In Combat, 1918 to Today* (Minneapolis: Zenith Press, 2009), p. 45.
25. Davis, *op. cit.*, p. 97. Sprauge and Friedrichsen were buried in Graves 7 and 8, Row 19, First Marine Division Cemetery.
26. Green and Brown, *op. cit.*, p. 39.
27. Horan and Frank, *op. cit.*, p. 186. "Bayonne Bridge" and "Pioneer Bridge" are used interchangeably, both in accounts of this event and in the 1/7 muster rolls for September 1942. Presumably these two names for the same location. Bodt explained "We called [it] Bayonne Bridge because a lot of the fellows were from New Jersey and it made them feel good to call something after Bayonne."
28. White, *op. cit.*
29. Company "A," 7th Marines (A/1/7), muster roll, microfilm (RG 127, NARA). Beamer was buried in Grave 10, Row 19, First Marine Division Cemetery on September 22, 1942.
30. Horan, and Frank, *op. cit.*, p. 186; White, *op. cit.*
31. Hoffman, *op. cit.*, p. 177.
32. Several accounts, including Goble's memoir, Leckie's *Challenge For The Pacific* and Davis' *Marine!* report that Puller pinned Stafford's tongue to his collar

with a large safety pin, thus saving his life. Jon T. Hoffman's extensively-researched biography of Puller states "Others on the patrol interviewed later insisted that did not occur."

33. Goble, *op. cit.* "We rolled into some open fox holes that the Raider Battalion had dug during the week before when they had been in a fire fight there. I came out of that hole fast! I had sunk up to my knees into rotting Japanese bodies."

34. Charles Jacobs interview. Jacobs was speaking of Cpl. Beamer, whom he believed was killed by friendly fire.

35. United States Marine Corps, *Small Wars Manual* (Washington: GPO, 1940). The first edition of the *Small Wars Manual* dates to 1934.

36. Phase V Report, 15.

37. *Ibid.*, 17.

38. Green and Brown, *op. cit.*, p. 48. Ed Poppendick said, "Puller went to Vandegrift and started to beg him for action."

39. Hoffman, *op. cit.*, p. 158.

40. Phase V Report, 17. Several histories suggest that this patrol began on September 23, and that 1/7 fought several small engagements along the route. In examining the battalion's muster rolls, the regimental record of events, Gerald White's diary, and service summaries contained in OMPFs the author can find little indication that this is the case. One possible source is Goble, who recalled the entire event taking place on September 23, or the Final Report, which states "this operations [*sic.*] was to begin on 23 September and was to be completed by 26 September." The regiment's Record of Events refers to some local patrols taking place on September 23, but these are clearly distinct from Puller's expedition.

41. For a diagram of the original configuration, see Walraven, J. G., "Typical Combat Patrols in Nicaragua," *Marine Corps Gazette*, December 1929, pp. 243-244.

42. Reeder, R. P. Jr., ed. *Notes on Jungle Warfare from the U. S. Marines and U. S. Infantry on Guadalcanal Island* (Washington: United States War Department, 1942), pp. 25-26.

43. Smith, M. S., *Bloody Ridge: The Battle That Saved Guadalcanal* (Novato, CA: Presidio Press, 2000), eBook, p. 325. While the Maizuru Battalion would give its name to this trail for history, it is unknown if the term was in common usage with American forces at this time.

44. Twining, *op. cit.*, p. 156.

45. Goble, *op. cit.*, p. 9.

46. Hammel, *op. cit.*, p. 251.

47. Green and Brown, *op. cit.*, p. 49.

48. Goble, *op. cit.*, p. 10.

49. Green and Brown, *op. cit.*, p. 39.

50. Hammel, *op. cit.*, p. 253.

51. Goble, *op. cit.*, p. 10.

52. Jersey, *op. cit.*, p. 239.

53. This figure cited from Hammel, *op. cit.*, p. 271.

54. Davis, *op. cit.*, p. 100.

55. Green and Brown, *op. cit.*, p. 39.

56. Goble, *op. cit.*, pp. 9-10. Goble also reported the Japanese cooks: "The point crossed a ridge, and saw two Japs cooking rice on the stream bank. When the Japanese spotted our point, they moved back into the jungle and out of sight. 'B' Company and 'C' Company followed them." Eric Hammel interprets this as a different cooking party than the one encountered by Turner and Fuller.

However, Goble may be referring to Turner's squad as "the point" and relating a part of the story he did not personally witness.

57. Hammel, *op. cit.,* p. 271.
58. "A runner just behind Puller was hit in the throat and died quickly." (Davis, *op. cit.,* p. 100). "Chesty escaped the initial burst of fire … his runner and several other men were not so lucky." (Hoffman, *op. cit.,* p. 179). According to muster rolls, Wehr is the only KIA from HQ Company on this date and thus almost certainly Puller's runner. Headquarters Company, 1st Battalion, 7th Marines (HQ/1/7), muster roll, microfilm (RG 127, NARA).
59. Davis, *op. cit.,* p. 101.
60. "Two men of Haggerty's platoon were killed" (Davis, *op. cit.,* p. 98); "Five riflemen from the lead A Company platoon were felled" (Hammel, *op. cit.,* p. 271). A Company suffered three fatalities—one, Rowe, died of wounds later in the evening; ergo Edwinson and Pimentel were killed at the point.
61. White, *op. cit.*
62. Hoffman, *op. cit.,* p. 179.
63. Hammel, *op. cit.,* p. 255. Hammel describes the BARman's wound as "several rounds in the fleshy part of the leg just above the knee." Jarzynski was treated for "gunshot wounds, right thigh" on battalion muster rolls. The assistant is not named but was presumably KIA: there is no corresponding casualty on muster rolls and specific causes of death are not reported. He may have been PFC Erwin S. King, PFC James R. Walters, or Pvt. Joseph P. Karnaghon.
64. Goble, *op. cit.,* pp. 9-10.
65. Hoffman, *op. cit.,* p. 81. Hoffman states that the FO team attempted such a mission, but when the first round landed squarely on Marine lines, they understandably gave up.
66. Matthew Constantino, interview by Floyd Cox, October 7, 2015, transcript, National Museum of the Pacific War. [Note for researchers: the surname is misspelled "Constentino."]
67. Green and Brown, *op. cit.,* p. 40.
68. Hoffman, *op. cit.,* p. 180.
69. Green and Brown, *op. cit.,* p. 40.
70. Smith, *op. cit.,* p. 348.
71. White, *op. cit.*
72. Goble, *op. cit.,* p. 10.
73. Hammel, *op. cit.,* p. 256.
74. Historians Burke Davis and Michael S. Smith claim that the Marines managed to capture the Maizuru encampment and set up their night positions there, while Eric Hammel and Jon T. Hoffman state that Puller broke off the engagement and withdrew some 300 yards. Except for Poppendick (who does not mention either withdrawal or capturing an encampment), firsthand accounts support the withdrawal assessment. Walter Bodt tells of withdrawing to a hill to reorganize for the night, and capturing "Matanikau village" the following day. Gerald Smith references withdrawing to the main body when he was hit. Goble recalls "we pulled back through the jungle to an open hillside." Given this evidence, and the ensuing efforts to retrieve the fallen, this author finds the withdrawal version more plausible.
75. Hoffman, *op. cit.,* p. 181.
76. Goble mentions Chesty's promise to locate Cockrell, while Burke Davis quotes Chesty via an unnamed officer: "God, I hated that I had to curse at Cockrell out there tonight. He was a good, brave Marine—the fighting kind. It was something that had to be done." (Goble, *op. cit.,* p. 10; Davis, *op. cit.,* p. 102.)
77. Charles Jacobs interview.

78. White, *op. cit.*

79. Depending on the source, this was either 5 miles (Hoffman) or 8 miles (Goble).

80. Charles Jacobs interview.

81. Goble, *op. cit.*, pp. 10-11.

82. "The enemy losses were consequently indeterminate, but from a count of graves and unburied dead they greatly exceeded our own casualties." (Phase V Report, 17.)

83. Goble, *op. cit.*, p. 11.

84. Hoffman, *op. cit.*, pp. 181-182.

85. Goble, *op. cit.*, p. 11. Olliff survived, and the two men enjoyed "a great reunion" after the war.

86. Twining, *op. cit.*, p. 136.

87. Mason, J. T. Jr., e., *The Pacific War Remembered*, p. 116-117. Most of the Marines killed in this river crossing attempt were buried in the field; many remain unaccounted for.

88. *Ibid.*, 160.

89. Horan and Frank, *op. cit.*, pp. 186-187. Like many accounts in this volume, Bodt's account is so laden with press-ready 1940s machismo that one suspects creative editing on the part of the publishers. Even if his account is somewhat overblown, Company C likely took some fire—it would take only a single sniper or mortar round to kill Morris Canady.

90. Green and Brown, *op. cit.*, p. 41.

91. This number is variously reported. Zimmerman and Twining state seven Marines KIA; this number is based on Puller's first report to headquarters and does not account for three Marines who died of their wounds overnight. Davis relies on this figure in his history. Joe Goble claims thirteen KIA; Hammel follows Goble's figure. Battalion muster rolls name ten, as do final Marine Corps casualty figures and the burial maps included in OMPF files for Cockrell and Edwards.

92. Cockrell OMPF.

Chapter 7

1. Ladd, D. and Weingartner, S., *Faithful Warriors*, p. 26.

2. *Ibid.*, pp. 19-23.

3. The first Army unit to land on Guadalcanal, the 164th Infantry, Americal Division, arrived in mid-October. Additional artillery and support units arrived piecemeal over the following weeks.

4. Phase V Report, 45.

5. Ladd and Weingartner, *op. cit.*, p. 6.

6. William Albert Smith, Official Military Personnel File (OMPF), Records of the Office of the Quartermaster General, Washington National Records Center, Suitland, MD. (Hereafter William A. Smith OMPF.) The reasons for Bill's choice are not known; he may have been estranged from his mother around this time. Or he may simply have felt that, after six years on the chicken farm Artemecia Howard simply knew him better. He would eventually name Stella as his primary beneficiary.

7. *Ibid.*

8. Doyle Hugh Asher, Official Military Personnel File (OMPF), Records of the Office of the Quartermaster General, Washington National Records Center, Suitland, MD. (Hereafter Asher OMPF.)

9. Marshall P. Smith, interview by Jack Sigler, March 18, 2004, transcript, Marshall P. Smith Collection (AFC/2001/001/80079), Veterans History Project, American Folklife Center, Library of Congress. (Hereafter Marshall Smith interview.)

10. Raymond Joseph Schulthies, Official Military Personnel File (OMPF), Records of the Office of the Quartermaster General, Washington National Records Center, Suitland, MD. (Hereafter Schulthies OMPF.)

11. *Ibid.*

12. Ladd and Weingartner, *op. cit.*, p. 10.

13. Ross, B. and Shaffer, G. K., "Barney Ross On Guadalcanal," Installment 9, King Features Syndicate, March 1943.

14. Ladd, D., *Faithful Warriors: Memoirs of World War II in the Pacific* (Spokane: Teen-Aid, Inc., 1993), p. 26. This is an older version of Ladd's memoirs which provided some of the basis for his later work with Weingartner.

15. Ladd and Weingartner, *op. cit.*, p. 6.

16. Horan, J. D. and Frank, G., *Out In The Boondocks*, pp. 196-197.

17. Marshall Smith interview.

18. Horan and Frank, *op. cit.*, p. 197.

19. Marshall Smith interview.

20. Ladd and Weingartner, *op. cit.*, p. 14.

21. Ibid., 58.

22. K/3/8 lost Dressner, Cpl. Carl W. Brock, PFC William A. Price, and Pvt. William L. Berryman killed in action. Pvt. Lindesay Vance (K/3/8) and Sgt. Elmer G. Berg (L/3/8) were missing in action. None of these Marines are known to have been recovered. Company "K," 8th Marines (K/3/8) and Company "L," 8th Marines (L/3/8) muster rolls, microfilm (RG 127, NARA).

23. Ross and Shaffer, "Barney Ross On Guadalcanal," Installment 5, King Features Syndicate, March 1943.

24. Jeschke, Col. R. H., "Report of Operations of Eighth Marines while on Guadalcanal Island, 4 November 1942 to 9 February 1943," March 15, 1943, (RG 127, NARA), p. 12.

25. Ross and Shaffer, "Barney Ross On Guadalcanal," Installment 3, King Features Syndicate, March 1943.

26. Jeschke, *op. cit.*, p. 39. Emphasis in original.

27. Ross and Shaffer, "Barney Ross On Guadalcanal," Installment 5.

28. Terrain features were commonly named for their height in feet; ergo the summit of "Hill 66" was 66 feet above sea level.

29. Miller, J. Jr., *The First Offensive*, pp. 202-203.

30. Ross and Shaffer, "Barney Ross On Guadalcanal," Installment 5.

31. *Ibid.*

32. 1st Battalion, 8th Marines, "War Diary Record of Events, Vol. 1" (RG 127, NARA), 4. (Hereafter 1/8 War Diary.)

33. These locations are in modern-day Honiara. "Beach Ridge" is now called Vavaya Ridge, home to the Prime Minister's residence. "Beach Road" provided the foundation for commercial Mendana Avenue.

34. Marshall Smith interview.

35. Most of the 8th Marines wore the M1917A1 "Kelly Transitional Helmet," a slightly updated version of the iconic World War 1-era M1917 "Brodie" helmet. Smith was the proud owner of the only M1 "steel pot" helmet in his squad.

36. Company "B," 1st Battalion, 8th Marines, "Operations on November 18, 19, 20, 1942," November 21, 1942 (RG 127, NARA). (Hereafter B/1/8 Report.)

37. Marshall Smith interview.
38. Jeschke, *op. cit.*, p. 68.
39. Marshall Smith interview.
40. The 8th Marines seem to have been short on stretchers as mentions of "makeshift" measures (usually a dungaree shirt stretched between two sticks) appear in several accounts of this action. A regimental injunction forbade stretcher bearers from accompanying patrols below a certain size.
41. Smitty would even return to active duty in 1945, and left the service as a sergeant. He passed away in 2013, at the age of ninety.
42. Marshall Smith interview.
43. Ladd and Weingartner, *op. cit.*, p. 26.
44. *Ibid.* In describing the deaths of Smith, Asher, and Schlesinger, Ladd contradicts himself (and several military sources) in the two editions of his memoirs. In 1993, he wrote that "three men that I had served with in our 'B' Company weapons platoon were killed by an enemy machine gun ambush" on November 10, and that Spell's volunteers retrieved and buried the bodies "the following day." An appendix provides correct dates of death for Smith (November 18) and Schlesinger (November 19), without mentioning Asher. In 2011, he identified Smith, Asher, and Schlesinger as the ambush fatalities, again giving a date of November 10. None of the casualty reports, battalion records, or personnel files examined by this author mention B/1/8 casualties on November 10, 1942; all sources besides Ladd peg the date of the incident as November 18–19. For this reason, the author has chosen to respectfully diverge from Ladd's otherwise impeccable account of events.
45. 1/8 War Diary, p. 4. Evidently the scribe in charge of the journal confused the Sergeants Smith; he reported John Smith as KIA and noted that Marshall was "brother of Sergeant Smith." This notation was later crossed out and corrected.
46. Ross and Shaffer, "Barney Ross On Guadalcanal," Installment 5.
47. Ladd and Weingartner, *op. cit.*, pp. 31-32. Ladd was appointed to platoon leadership that morning when another officer failed in his duties. He could observe the other two platoons in action from his vantage point on Beach Ridge.
48. Horan and Frank, *op. cit.*, p. 261.
49. B/1/8 Report. Ladd recalls that the Marines stopped on the eastern side of Point Cruz.
50. Horan and Frank, *op. cit.*, p. 198.
51. Ross and Shaffer, "Barney Ross On Guadalcanal," Installment 1, King Features Syndicate, March 1943.
52. Ladd and Weingartner, *op. cit.*, p. 35.
53. Horan and Frank, *op. cit.*, p. 198.
54. Ross and Shaffer, "Barney Ross On Guadalcanal," Installment 1.
55. Horan and Frank, *op. cit.*, p. 199.
56. This epic tale was presented "as told to George K. Shaffer" and published by King Features Syndicate in March 1943.
57. Ladd and Weingartner, *op. cit.*, p. 39. This opinion was shared by "most of those who were in 'B' Company at the time." Washvillo and Guarnett were also awarded Silver Stars; their citations were identical to Ross'.
58. "0630. Two officers and eight litter bearers crossed river to evacuate casualties of preceding day. Two men wounded in action successfully evacuated, one man wounded in action not evacuated due to enemy machine gun fire, and is still unaccounted for as of [November 21] but we are aware of the fact that

we has wounded." B/1/8 Report. All three men survived their wounds. Atkins and Freeman received disability discharges. Monick returned to the company in time to participate in the invasion of Betio, he was killed in action one year to the day after his Guadalcanal adventure. Sadly, he is one of hundreds of Marines who were never identified at Tarawa.

59. Company "B," 8th Marines (B/1/8) muster rolls, microfilm (RG 127, NARA).
60. Ladd and Weingartner, *op. cit.*, p. 72.
61. Smith and Asher OMPFs.
62. Doyle Hugh Asher Individual Deceased Personnel File (IDPF), Records of the Office of the Quartermaster General, Washington National Records Center, Suitland, MD.
63. Schulthies, OMPF; John William George Onnen and Howard John Schlesinger, Official Military Personnel Files (OMPFs), Records of the Office of the Quartermaster General, Washington National Records Center, Suitland, MD. This notation, signed by Lt. Murdock, appears in each file.
64. Onnen OMPF.
65. Murdock may have created individual overlays for each burial site. Only Schlesinger's could be located for this book.
66. Second Lieutenant Chester E. Goodwin to Surgeon General, Washington, D.C., September 10, 1943, (RG92, NARA). The other three soldiers were PFC Barnet Klass, Pvt. Morris S. Kaplan, and Pvt. Frank A. Talokowski, all from C/182nd Infantry. Klass was initially misidentified as PFC Stanley Kondziolka; as of 2018, Kondziolka has not been recovered.
67. Ross and Shaffer, "Barney Ross On Guadalcanal," Installment 10, King Features Syndicate, March 1943. Ross does not provide context for this event in the timeline of his story.
68. B/1/8 Report.
69. Schulthies OMPF.

Chapter 8

1. Hurlbut, J. W., "Marine Landing & Subsequent Actions In Solomon Islands," recorded March 10, 1943, transcript (RG 38, NARA).
2. Merillat, H. C. L., *Guadalcanal Remembered*, p. 270.
3. Morison, S. E., *The Struggle for Guadalcanal, August 1942–February 1943* (1949; repr. Chicago: University of Illinois Press, 2001), pp. 371-372.
4. Merillat, *op. cit.*, p. 272.
5. Steere, *Graves Registration*, p. 45. Steere does not provide a date for the establishment of this section, though according to his notes it was some time prior to February 24, 1943.
6. Morison, *op. cit.*, p. 372. "Never to this day" was in 1949.
7. Zimmerman, J. L., *Guadalcanal Campaign*, p. 169.
8. The first known use of the formal name "Guadalcanal Army, Navy and Marine Cemetery" appears in quartermaster correspondence in January 1943. On the 22nd, reports read "No name yet for new cemetery. Will notify your office immediately upon decision." By the 24th, the new name was being used. Headquarters, Graves Registration Service, QMC, "Weekly Report of Burials Recorded," No. 7, January 17–23, 1943; and No. 8, January 24–31, 1943 (RG 92, NARA).
9. Steere, *op. cit.*, p. 45.
10. TM 10-630, 6.

11. Steere, *op. cit.*, p. 45.
12. "N. D. Soldiers Share Guadalcanal Glory With Marines," *Bismarck Tribune*, January 23, 1943, p. 3.
13. Steere, *op. cit.*, pp. 45-46.
14. Dr. Jeffrey Panosian, telephone interview by the author, May 6, 2018. Lt. Panosian's involvement with the Guadalcanal cemeteries was overlooked by history; his signature was discovered by chance on the Report of Interment for Pvt. Elmer A. Slaton, 161st Infantry, buried in Row 94, Grave 5 of the First Marine Division Cemetery on January 21, 1943. The exact dates of his tenure are not known, but other ROI files suggest that he was present from the end of January to early March 1943, during the first major reinterment period.
15. 2Lt. Kermit G. Sloulin, PFC Wenceslaus J. Novotny, Cpl. Louis D. Dibbert, PFC Joseph F. Kelly, and PFC Walter B. Montgomery. First Marine Division Cemetery, Row 94, Graves 6–10.
16. 2Lt. Lester R. Pfaff, T4 Joe A. Krawczyk, Cpl. Jack A. Sharrock, PFC Alex G. Sygulla, and Pvt. Harold C. Ruth were all killed in action on January 13, 1943, and have not been accounted for as of publication.
17. "Cullom Soldier Sees Buddy Buried Third Time," *Ford County Press* (Melvin, IL), April 2, 1948, 5.
18. Bergerud, E. M., *Touched with Fire: The Land War In The South Pacific* (New York: Penguin, 1996), pp. 467-468.
19. Steere, *op. cit.*, p. 33.
20. First Platoon, 45th Quartermaster Graves Registration Company, "Historical Record of Organization," August 9, 1943 (RG 407, NARA). (Hereafter 45th QMGRC History.)
21. Stauffer, A. P., *Quartermaster Corps*, p. 249.
22. Steere, E. and Boardman, T. M., *Final Disposition of World War II Dead, 1945–1951* (Washington, D.C.: Office of the Quartermaster General, 1957), p. 443.
23. 1st Raider Battalion, muster roll, September 1942, microfilm (RG 127, NARA). (Hereafter 1st Raiders Muster Roll.)
24. "Ashes Of War Dead Scattered," *The Arizona Republic* (Phoenix AZ), March 12, 1948, 16. It was eventually decided that Payne had died on January 12, 1943. The black mark of desertion was removed from his file. His family requested that Payne be buried at sea; his ashes, along with an army officer and a sailor, were scattered off Diamond Head, Hawaii, in March 1948.
25. McCarthy, F. L., "1,600 Graves in Solomons Under 24-Hour Guard," *Morning News* (Wilmington, DE) September 24, 1943, p. 16. Goodwin's gesture was appreciated: "To date [September 14, 1943] he has received 900 replies."
26. Stauffer, *op. cit.*, p. 249. The use of service troops as gravediggers and general labor is outlined in TM 10-630.
27. 45th QMGRC History.
28. Student OMPF. His name appears on a post-war grave chart of the First Marine Division Cemetery, which certainly seems to indicate that a new marker was put in place.
29. Morriss, M., *South Pacific Diary 1942–1943*, ed. Ronnie Day (Lexington: University Press of Kentucky, 1996), p. 147.
30. "Unknown Solomon Islands X-98 Guadalcanal," Washington National Records Center, Suitland, MD.
31. "Unknown Solomon Islands X-86 Guadalcanal," Washington National Records Center, Suitland, MD. The only W. L. Fleming on Marine casualty rolls, Sgt. William Louis Fleming of HQ/1/25, was killed in action at Iwo Jima on March 5, 1945.

32. 1st Raiders Muster Roll. Carney's body was brought to the Division cemetery and buried in Row 8, Grave No. 2.

33. Groft, M. and Alexander, L., *Bloody Ridge And Beyond,* p. 139. When recounting "the perfect raid," Groft mentions two Marine KIAs, and that "I helped to bury one man by a coconut tree." This must have been Smith, as Carney's body was brought to the Division cemetery almost immediately after the raid. How Smith's remains wound up uncovered and exposed will never be known.

34. 45th QMGRC History.

35. Second Platoon, 49th Quartermaster Graves Registration Company, "Record of Movement 10 May 1943–20 March 1944," (RG 407, NARA).

36. Steere, *op. cit.,* p. 47.

37. Berry, H., *Semper Fi, Mac* (New York: Harper, 1982), p. 66.

38. Headquarters Company, 1st Battalion, 11th Marines (HQ/1/11), muster roll, microfilm (RG 127, NARA). Notations for these men all read "Buried in Lunga area, North Coast, Guadalcanal." That they were field burials and not taken to the nearby cemetery suggests that they were not extricable from their shelter. Ironically, Seiden had just been recommended for a medal after helping to pull trapped men out of a collapsed dugout two days before his death.

39. Celipkas, T. A., ed., *We Did It: The Story of the 77th Naval Construction Battalion* (Baton Rouge: Army & Navy Pictorial Publishers, 1946), p. 33.

40. McCarthy, *op. cit.*

41. Johnson, W. B., *Pearl Harbor to Guadalcanal,* p. 293.

42. The Eleanor Roosevelt Papers Project, "South Pacific Travel Diary," 1943, excerpt, transcribed online (George Washington University, Columbian College of Arts & Sciences) erpapers.columbian.gwu.edu/eleanor-roosevelts-south-pacific-travel-diary-excerpts.

43. Roach was buried at Map 104 coordinates 71.99–199.30; McArdell at 73.30–199.30.

44. Lane, E., "Promise To The Dead Kept By Marine," *Marine Corps Chevron,* October 7, 1944, 6. Photograph by International News Service appears in *Portsmouth Herald* (Portsmouth, NH), September 26, 1944, p. 3.

45. 45th QMGRC History, July 13, 1944. Chester Goodwin, somewhat naturally, became a Graves Registration training officer at New Caledonia; he was succeeded by 2Lt. Simeon J. Larkins.

46. The exact date of this recovery is not known; the five recovered Marines were not listed on the Weekly Report of Burials. Possibly the new 49th QMGRC was not aware that field recoveries required reporting. The five are buried sequentially between graves dated April 16 and April 22, so the recovery date was likely in mid to late April.

47. "Unknown Solomon Islands X-94 Guadalcanal," Washington National Records Center, Suitland, MD. The author believes there is a strong possibility that X-94 is Cpl. Albert L. Hermiston of the 2nd (Carlson's) Raider Battalion.

48. Second Platoon, 49th Quartermaster Graves Registration Company, "Historical Record 1 July 1944–30 September 1944," (RG 407, NARA). A C-87 Liberator Express (Bureau Number 41-11706) "Consairways 706" ferrying high-ranking passengers to Australia crashed on Florida Island on July 26, 1944; fifteen bodies were recovered and twelve identified by the GRS platoon on August 13. An R4D-5 (BuNo 12405) evacuating soldiers from Munda crashed into a mountain on San Cristobal Island on July 29, 1943; nine bodies were retrieved and two identified by the GRS platoon on August 22, 1944.

49. Thiesen, W. H., "USS *Serpens*—the Coast Guard's Greatest Loss," *Cutter Of The Month* (blog), *US Coast Guard Alumni Association*, February 2018, www.cgaalumni.org/. The disaster remains the single greatest loss of life in Coast Guard history. The luckless man ashore may have been Cpl. Charles L. Campney of the 897th Quartermaster Laundry Company.

50. Headquarters, South Pacific Base Command "General Orders No. 9: Redesignation of 2d Platoon, 49th Quartermaster Graves Registration Company," January 24, 1945 (RG 407, NARA). The redesignation was ordered on January 24, 1945 and went into effect on February 1, 1945. No changes to personnel or assignment were required.

51. Hoover, W., "Mysterious Schofield plot filled with untold stories," *Honolulu Advertiser* April 22, 2001. Online. the.honoluluadvertiser.com/article/2001/Apr/22/ln/ln05a.html. A grave chart of the ANMC shows Pearson's lone grave in "Plot Z." Today, he is buried in the National Memorial Cemetery of the Pacific with six other dishonored servicemen in "Plot 9." Hoover mistakes Robert A. Pearson for Robert L. Pearson, who was coincidentally executed by American military authorities at Shepton Mallet Prison, Somerset, England, the very same week.

52. Lt. Joseph Dobler and AMM1c Vernon L. Petrick were members of VS-6 off the *USS Enterprise*, shot down on January 30, 1943.

53. "Unknown Solomon Islands X-182 Guadalcanal," Washington National Records Center, Suitland, MD.

54. Steere and Boardman, *op. cit.*, p. 395.

55. Steere, *op. cit.*, p. 193.

56. Steere and Boardman, *op. cit.*, p. 398.

57. *Ibid.*, pp. 395-398.

58. "Unknown Solomon Islands X-308, -311, -312, -313, -314, -320, Guadalcanal," Washington National Records Center, Suitland, MD.

59. Gleason, J. *Real Blood! Real Guts! US Marine Raiders and their Corpsmen in WWII* (Tampa: Raider Publishing, 2003), p. 118.

60. Company "G," 2nd Battalion, 8th Marines (G/2/8) and Company "C," 1st Battalion, 8th Marines (C/1/8), muster rolls, microfilm (RG 127, NARA); Jeschke, *op. cit.*, pp. 15-19.

Chapter 9

1. Pope, Q. "Finds Grave Of War Ace Son In Four Year Hunt: Father Reburies Body on Guadalcanal," *Chicago Sunday Tribune*, February 23, 1947, p. 12.

2. Office of the Quartermaster General, "Tell Me About My Boy," 1946, transcribed by Army Quartermaster Foundation, Inc., 2018, www.qmfound.com/article/tell-me-about-my-boy/.

3. Rhodes OMPF.

4. Bernes OMPF.

5. Steere and Boardman, *Final Disposition,* p. 468.

6. *Ibid.*, 468-469.

7. Quartermaster General, *Tell Me About My Boy.*

8. Steere and Boardman, *op. cit.*, p. 523.

9. *Ibid.*, 523-532.

10. "The result of the entire operation was that only 49% of the bodies said to be interred in Tarawa atoll was [*sic.*] actually located." Lt. H. H. Robinson to Chief Memorial Branch, Quartermaster Section, ARMFORMIDPAC, "Dental

Officer's Report on Identification Operation at Tarawa,
" May 31, 1946.

11. Steere and Boardman, *op. cit.,* p. 469.

12. Sledge, M., *Soldier Dead,* p. 158.

13. Trapp, Lt. R. I., "Summary of Cruise, Search & Recovery Expedition No. 1 on USAIT LST-711," (RG 407, NARA). Although he accompanied both missions, the mortician's name eluded the various scribes; he is reported as Dunman, Dunnam or Dumman. Unfortunately, his first name was not recorded.

14. *Ibid.*, pp. 1-3. Trapp seems to have fancied himself an amateur anthropologist, as his summary reads in places more like an explorer's travelogue than a military report. While he paints an interesting picture of Pacific life in the post-war era, details on the searches themselves are frustratingly few.

15. "Unknown Schofield Mausoleum #1, X-1," Washington National Records Center, Suitland, MD. Interestingly, Charles Wheeler "C. W." Iglehart was an American Methodist missionary who was an important figure in spreading Protestant Christianity in Japan, both before and after World War II.

16. Robert Herschel Ballew, Individual Deceased Personnel File (IDPF), Records of the Office of the Quartermaster General, Washington National Records Center, Suitland, MD.

17. Schulthies OMPF.

18. Cockrell OMPF.

19. Gerald Paul Hopkins, Official Military Personnel File (OMPF), Records of the Office of the Quartermaster General, Washington National Records Center, Suitland, MD.

20. John Carmen Buckhalt Individual Deceased Personnel File (IDPF), Records of the Office of the Quartermaster General, Washington National Records Center, Suitland, MD. The reader may remember the description of Buckhalt, Grazier, and Gardner as hasty graves with boondockers sticking out, not the manicured memorial described by the picture.

21. Trapp, *op. cit.,* pp. 14-15.

22. Steere and Boardman, *op. cit.,* p. 535.

23. "Graves Registration Units To Leave For South Pacific," *Honolulu Star-Bulletin*, October 29, 1947, 23.

24. Steere and Boardman, *op. cit.,* p. 536.

25. Trapp, *op. cit.,* p. 14.

26. Steere and Boardman, *op. cit.,* p. 537.

27. Martin, C. J., "The Aftermath of Hell: Graves Registration Policy and U. S. Marine Corps Losses in the Solomon Islands During World War II," *Marine Corps History* Vol. 2, No. 2 (Winter 2016), p. 63. Martin continues: "The majority of more than 3,000 remains processed by the 9105th TSU were skeletal and not casketed. Therefore, the possibility exists that a large number of these remains were unable to be identified and were later buried as unknown remains."

28. Steere and Boardman, *op. cit.,* pp. 536-539. The casketed remains, along with those exhumed from Australia, were returned to Hawaii aboard the *USAT Cardinal Victory*. Not so fortunate was the beleaguered 9105th TSU, which boarded the *Goucher Victory* and set off to disinter the cemeteries on Saipan.

29. *Ibid.*, pp. 471–473. 3,562 non-recovered remains were estimated in "Group E"—the Solomon Islands and Australia—in April 1948. Of these, only 454 were believed to be recoverable. While the exact breakdown between the two sub-regions is not known, the Solomons almost certainly accounted for the lion's share. The same report estimated that only 35 percent of the search in the Solomons was completed by the first expedition.

30. *Ibid.*, 473.

31. 604th QMGRC, "Expidition No. 2," p. 31.

32. Harold Gustave Dick, Individual Deceased Personnel File (IDPF), Records of the Office of the Quartermaster General, Washington National Records Center, Suitland, MD.

33. Malcolm Lewis Pratt, Individual Deceased Personnel File (IDPF), Records of the Office of the Quartermaster General, Washington National Records Center, Suitland, MD.

34. Cockrell, Edwards, and Rowe OMPFs.

35. Joseph Francis Setzer, Individual Deceased Personnel File (IDPF), Records of the Office of the Quartermaster General, Washington National Records Center, Suitland, MD.

36. Budd OMPF.

37. Peel, B., "Guadalcanal May Give Up His Brother's Lost Grave," *Syracuse Herald American*, October 8, 1989, p. J3.

38. 604th QMGRC, "Expidition No. 2," 31.

39. Steere and Boardman, *op. cit.*, p. 476.

40. *Ibid.*, 632.

41. Warren, M. W., Walsh-Haney, H. A., and Freas, L., eds., *The Forensic Anthropology Laboratory* (Boca Raton: CRC Press, 2008), pp. 48-49. The CIL was deactivated in 1949, then reactivated in 1976 as U.S. Army Central Identification Laboratory, Hawaii (CILHI) to process skeletal remains retrieved from Vietnam. Since 2003, CILHI has been administered by the Joint POW/MIA Accounting Command (JPAC) (2003–2015) and the Defense POW/MIA Accounting Agency (DPAA) (2015–present).

42. Martin, *op. cit.*, p. 63. A handful of X-files for Solomon Islands dead show CIL report dates in mid-December 1942; this may have been a typographical error, as the remains had not yet shipped from Guadalcanal at that time.

43. Steere and Boardman, *op. cit.*, p. 632.

44. Williams, R. C., *The Forensic Historian: Using Science to Reexamine the Past* (New York: Routledge, 2015), p. xi.

45. Onnen OMPF.

46. Heller ran away from home and lied his way into the Corps: he was just fifteen years old when killed in action on October 8, 1942, and likely the youngest Marine killed on Guadalcanal. Today he is buried in Gettysburg National Cemetery.

47. "Unknown Solomon Islands X-14 Guadalcanal," Washington National Records Center, Suitland, MD.

48. "Unknown Solomon Islands X-12 Guadalcanal," Washington National Records Center, Suitland, MD.

49. "Unknown Solomon Islands X-12C Guadalcanal," Washington National Records Center, Suitland, MD.

50. Thomas John Christie, Official Military Personnel File (OMPF), Washington National Records Center, Suitland, MD.

51. "Unknown Solomon Islands X-12C Guadalcanal."

52. Christie OMPF.

53. Bruce Bertram Bender, Official Military Personnel File (OMPF), Washington National Records Center, Suitland, MD.

54. A search of muster rolls does not disclose "N. L. Hamilton" anywhere in the Marine Corps during the time of the campaign. The cup in question may have been reissued, or acquired from a soldier or sailor. There was an Angelo M. Pepe serving with B/1/1st Marines on Guadalcanal; there is a chance, albeit

very remote, that the canteen was once his. Although wounded on Peleliu, Pepe ultimately survived the war.

55. "Unknown Schofield Mausoleum #1, Isolated Burial #10A–10B," Washington National Records Center, Suitland, MD. Lt. Pratz was a "mustang"—an officer promoted up from the enlisted ranks—and his ID tag still bore his enlisted serial number (281869). He scratched the letters "LT" onto the tag himself. Originally an artilleryman, Pratz was assigned to E/2/2nd Marines just one week before his death.

56. "Unknown Schofield Mausoleum #1, Isolated Burial #39," Washington National Records Center, Suitland, MD.

57. Warren *et al.*, *op. cit.*, p. 49.

58. Williams, *op. cit.*, p. xi.

59. "Ernie Pyle Rites Open Punchbowl Cemetery," *The Honolulu Star-Bulletin*, July 19, 1949. Pyle, who was killed in Ie Shima on April 18, 1945, is buried in Plot "D," Grave 109. Beside him, in D 110 is the unknown man; then PFC Francis A. Riese (21st Marines, killed on Iwo Jima on March 3, 1945), 1Lt. William G. Sylvester (97th Coast Artillery, killed at Hickam Airfield on December 7, 1941) and Pvt. Bruce A. Mitchell (1st Marines, killed on Okinawa June 15, 1945).

60. 2nd Raider Battalion, muster roll, microfilm, (RG 127, NARA).

61. Purcell, W. V., letter to the editor, *Raider Patch,* January 1982, p. 11.

62. Peatross, O. F., *Bless 'Em All: The Raider Marines of World War II* (Irvine, CA: ReView Publications, 1996), pp. 165-166.

63. "Unknown Solomon Islands X-94 Guadalcanal," Washington National Records Center, Suitland, MD.

64. Albert Laddce Hermiston, Official Military Personnel File and Individual Deceased Personnel File, Washington National Records Center, Suitland, MD; "Unknown Solomon Islands X-94 Guadalcanal."

Chapter 10

1. Hanneken, H. H., "Operations, October 7, 8, 9 1942," October 10, 1942, (RG 127, NARA).

2. Associated Press, "5 Marines Killed In WWII Get Arlington Burial," *Palladium Item* (Richmond, IN), June 29, 1972, 28.

3. Carroll, A., ed., *War Letters: Extraordinary Correspondence from American Wars* (New York: Scribner, 2001), p. 198.

4. Klose, K., "Lost Marine Comes Home," *The Washington Post*, May 25, 1992, online, www.washingtonpost.com/archive/politics/1992/05/25/lost-marine-comes-home/a81ed093-9fee-4a05-938f-6cc13d8771b1/?utm_term=.fb163775d975.

5. Marion, O.J., *On The Canal,* p. 274.

6. *Ibid.*, pp. 92-93.

7. "John Harold Branic," Arlington National Cemetery Website, August 25, 2006, last accessed April 29, 2018, www.arlingtoncemetery.net/jhbranic.htm.

8. Horan, J. B. and Frank, G., *Out In The Boondocks*, p. 188.

9. Goble, J., untitled memoir, pp. 15-16.

10. Puller, L. B., "Summary of operations of First Battalion, Seventh Marines, 7-9 October 1942," October 10, 1942 (RG 127, NARA).

11. Because of the distance between their bases at Rabaul and Guadalcanal, Japanese aircraft had to operate on a schedule in order to depart, strike, and

return under favorable conditions. This schedule put them over Henderson Field between 11:30 a.m. and 2:30 p.m. every day. The Americans nicknamed this window "Tojo Time" and quickly learned to have a combat air patrol aloft and waiting.

12. Peggy Maher, email to the author December 13, 2017.
13. Lundstrom, J. B., *First Team and the Guadalcanal Campaign*, p. 143.

Epilogue

1. Thomas Stephen Pilleri, Individual Deceased Personnel File, Individual Deceased Personnel File (IDPF), Records of the Office of the Quartermaster General, Washington National Records Center, Suitland, MD.

Bibliography

Books and Published Works

Abady, J., *Battle at the Overland Trail: One Night of Combat on Guadalcanal* (Lynchburg, VA: Warwick House Publishers, 2012)

Alexander, J. H., *Edson's Raiders: The 1st Marine Raider Battalion in World War II* (Annapolis: U.S. Naval Institute Press, 2001)

Ayling, K., *Semper Fidelis: The U. S. Marines in Action* (New York: Literary Classics Inc., 1943)

Bartsch, W. H., *Victory Fever on Guadalcanal: Japan's First Land Defeat of WWII* (College Station, TX: Texas A&M University Press, 2014)

Bartlett, T., "In Search of the Goettge Patrol," *Leatherneck* 71, no. 8 (August 1988): pp. 26-31.

Bergerud, E. M., *Touched with Fire: The Land War in the South Pacific* (New York: Penguin, 1996)

Berry, H., *Semper Fi, Mac: Living Memories of the U.S. Marines in World War II* (New York: Harper, 1982)

Birkett, P. D., *Guadalcanal Legacy 50th Anniversary, 1942–1992*, edited by Gene Keller, Robert C. Muehrcke, Donald W. Peltier, and Joseph Micek (Paducah: Turner Publishing, 1992)

Banning, B., (ed.), *Heritage Years: Second Marine Division Commemorative Anthology, 1940–1949* (Paducah: Turner Publishing, 1988)

Cameron, C. M., *American Samurai: Myth, Imagination, and the Conduct of Battle in the First Marine Division, 1941–1951* (Cambridge, UK: Cambridge University Press, 1994)

Camp, D., *Shadow Warriors: The Untold Stories of American Special Operations During WWII* (Minneapolis: Zenith Press, 2013); "Star-Crossed Translator: 2dLt. Merle Ralph Cory, USMCR—KIA on Guadalcanal," *Leatherneck* 87, no. 8 (August 2004): pp. 28-32

Carroll, A., (ed.), *War Letters: Extraordinary Correspondence from American Wars* (New York: Scribner, 2001)

Celipkas, T. A., (ed.), *We Did It: The Story of the 77th Naval Construction Battalion* (Baton Rouge: Army & Navy Pictorial Publishers, 1946)

Christ, J. F., *Battalion of the Damned: The 1st Marine Paratroopers at Gavutu and Bloody Ridge, 1942* (Annapolis: U. S. Naval Institute Press, 2007)

Clark, J. M., *Gunner's Glory: Untold Stories of Marine Machine Gunners* (New York: Presidio Press, 2004)

Clark, L., *An Unlikely Arena* (New York: Vantage Press, 1989)

Clemens, M., *Alone on Guadalcanal: A Coastwatcher's Story* (Annapolis: US Naval Institute Press, 1998)

Condit, K. W., Diamond, G., and Turnbladh, E. T., *Marine Corps Ground Training in World War II* (Washington, D.C.: Headquarters, U.S. Marine Corps, 1956)

Crane, A., (ed.), *Marines at War* (New York: Hyperion Press, 1943)

Davis, B., *Marine! The Life of Chesty Puller* (New York: Open Road Media, 2016. PDF e-book)

Dorsett, L. W., *Serving God and Country: U.S. Military Chaplains in World War II* (New York: Berkley Caliber, 2012. PDF e-book)

Drury, C. M., *The History of the Chaplain Corps, United States Navy, Volume II: 1939–1949* (Washington, D.C.: U. S. Government Printing Office, 1948)

Elrod, R. H., *We Were Going to Win, Or Die There: With the Marines at Guadalcanal, Tarawa, and Saipan*, edited by Fred H. Allison (Denton, TX: University of North Texas Press, 2017)

Evans, E. T., *Hold Your Head High, Marine: Stories from G-2-5 Marines who fought in the South Pacific Theater in World War II*, edited by Lisa Downey, Cherie Smith, and Sean MacLeod, second edition (California: Tom Evans, 2006)

Farrington, A. C., *The Leatherneck Boys: A PFC at the Battle for Guadalcanal* (Manhattan, KS: Sunflower University Press, 1995)

Felber, A. S., Felber, F. S., and Bartsch, W. H., *The Old Breed of Marine: A World War II Diary* (Jefferson, NC: McFarland & Company, 2003)

Frank, R., *Guadalcanal: The Definitive Account of the Landmark Battle* (New York: Penguin Books, 1992)

Gallant, T. G., *On Valor's Side* (New York: Kensington Publishing, 1963)

Gleason, J., *Real Blood! Real Guts! U.S. Marine Raiders and their Corpsmen in World War II*, edited by John McCarthy (Raider Publishing, 2003)

Goble, J., Untitled memoir. *Lower Deck Newsletter of the Warships and Marine Corps Museum* no. 30 (September 2002): pp. 6-16

Green, M., and Brown, J. D., *War Stories of the Infantry: Americans In Combat, 1918 to Today* (Minneapolis: Zenith Press, 2009)

Griffith, II, S. B., *The Battle for Guadalcanal* (Champaign: University of Illinois Press, 2000. First published 1963 by Lippincott)

Groft, M., and Alexander, L., *Bloody Ridge and Beyond: A World War II Marine's Memoir of Edson's Raiders in the Pacific* (New York: Berkley Caliber, 2014)

Hammel, E., *Guadalcanal: Starvation Island* (Pacifica, CA: Pacifica Military History, 1987)

Headquarters, U. S. Marine Corps. *Marine Corps Manual* (Washington, D.C.: U.S. Government Printing Office, 1940)

Helling, T., *Desperate Surgery in the Pacific War: Doctors and Damage Control for American Wounded, 1941–1945* (Jefferson, NC: McFarland & Company, 2017)

Hoffman, Col. J. T., *Chesty: The Story of Lieutenant General Lewis B. Puller, USMC*, paperback edition (New York: Random House, 2002); *Silk Chutes and Hard Fighting: U. S. Marine Corps Parachute Units in World War II* (Washington, D.C.: History and Museums Division, Headquarters, U.S. Marine Corps, 1999)

Horan, J. D., and Frank, G., *Out in the Boondocks: Marines in Action in The Pacific* (New York: G. P. Putnam's Sons, 1943)

Jersey, S. C., *Hell's Islands: The Untold Story of Guadalcanal* (College Station, TX: Texas A&M University Press, 2008)

Johnson, W. B., *The Pacific Campaign in World War II from Pearl Harbor to Guadalcanal* (New York: Routledge, 2006)

Johnston, R. W., *Follow Me! The Story of The Second Marine Division in World War II* (New York: Random House, 1948. Reprint, Nashville: The Battery Press, 1987)

Jones, W. K., *A Brief History of the 6th Marines* (Washington, D.C.: History and Museums Division, Headquarters, U.S. Marine Corps, 1987)

Keene, R. R., "The Goettge Patrol: Searching for Answers," *Leatherneck* 75, no. 8 (August 1992): pp. 27-29

Ladd, Lt. Col. D., *Faithful Warriors: The Second Marine Division in the Pacific War* (Spokane: Teen-Aid Inc., 1993)

Ladd, Lt. Col. D., and Weingartner, S., *Faithful Warriors: A Combat Marine Remembers the Pacific War* (Annapolis: US Naval Institute Press, 2009)

Laing, W. H., *The Unspoken Bond* (London, Ontario: Third Eye Publications, 1998)

Larson, T. J., *Hell's Kitchen, Tulagi 1942–1943* (Bloomington, IN: iUniverse, 2003)

Leckie, R., *Challenge for the Pacific: Guadalcanal, The Turning Point of the War* (New York, Bantam Books, 2010. First published 1965 by Random House); *Helmet For My Pillow: From Parris Island to the Pacific* (New York: Bantam Books, 2010. First published 1957 by Random House); *Strong Men Armed: The United States Marines Against Japan* (New York: Da Capo Press, 1997. First published 1962 by Random House)

Lundstrom, J. B., *The First Team and the Guadalcanal Campaign: Naval Fighter Combat from August to November 1942* (Annapolis: United States Naval Institute Press, 1994)

MacClanahan, G., *Tojo And Me* (West Conshohocken, PA: Infinity Publishing, 2007)

Makos, A., and Brotherton, M., *Voices of the Pacific: Untold Stories from the Marine Heroes of WWII* (New York: Berkley Caliber, 2013)

Marion, O. J., Cuddihy, T., and Cuddihy, E., *On The Canal: The Marines of L-3-5 on Guadalcanal, 1942* (Mechanicsburg, PA: Stackpole Books, 2004)

Marston, G. D., "There've Been Some Changes Made," *Leatherneck* 28, no. 4 (April 1945): pp. 21-23

Martin, C. J., "The Aftermath of Hell: Graves Registration Policy and U. S. Marine Corps Losses in the Solomon Islands During World War II," *Marine Corps History* 2, no. 2 (Winter 2016): pp. 56-64

Mason, Jr., J. T., (ed.), *The Pacific War Remembered: An Oral History Collection* (Annapolis: US Naval Institute Press, 1986)

McEnery, J., and Sloan, B., *Hell in the Pacific: A Marine Rifleman's Journey from Guadalcanal to Peleliu* (New York: Simon & Shuster, 2012. PDF e-book)

McMillan, G., *The Old Breed: A History of the First Marine Division in World War II* (Washington, D.C.: Infantry Journal Press, 1949. Reprint, Nashville: The Battery Press, 2001)

Merillat, H. C. L., *Guadalcanal Remembered* (New York: Dodd, Mead & Company, 1982); *The Island: A History of the First Marine Division at Guadalcanal, August 7–December 9, 1942* (Yardley, PA: Westholme Publishing, 2010. First printed by Houghton Mifflin Company, 1944)

Miller, Jr., J., *Guadalcanal: The First Offensive* (Washington: U. S. Army Center of Military History, 1995. First published 1949)

Miller, T. I., *Earned in Blood: My Journey from Old-Breed Marine to the Most Dangerous Job in America* (New York: St. Martin's Press, 2013. PDF e-book)

Morison, S. E., *The Struggle for Guadalcanal, August 1942–February 1943* (Chicago: University of Illinois Press, 2001. Originally published Boston: Little, Brown, 1947)

Morriss, M., *South Pacific Diary 1942–1943*, edited by Ronnie Day (Lexington, KY: The University Press of Kentucky, 1996)

Morse, H., and Head, G., *"A"-1-1: Pearl Harbor to Peleliu* (A-1-1 Book Committee, 1994)

Muehrcke, R. C., (ed.), *Orchids In The Mud: World War II in the Pacific—Pain, Boredom, Adventure* (Chicago: R. C. Muehrcke, 1985)

Niven, W. L., *Tarawa's Gravediggers* (Mustang, OK: Tate Publishing, 2015)

O'Donnell, P. K., *Into The Rising Sun: In Their Own Words, World War II Pacific Veterans Reveal the Heart of Combat* (New York: The Free Press, 2002)

Office of the Chief of Chaplains. *Technical Manual No. 16-205: The Chaplain* (Washington, D.C.: US Government Printing Office, 1941)

Partner, S., *Toshié: A Story of Village Life in Twentieth Century Japan* (Berkeley, CA: University of California Press, 2004)

Peatross, Maj. Gen. O. F., *Bless 'Em All: The Raider Marines of World War II* (Irvine, CA: ReView Publications, 1995)

Phillips, S., *You'll Be Sor-ree! A Guadalcanal Marine remembers the Pacific War* (New York: Berkley Caliber, 2010)

Reeder, R. P., (ed.), *Notes on Jungle Warfare from the U.S. Marines and U.S. Infantry on Guadalcanal* (Washington, D.C.: United States War Department, 1942)

Richmond, P., *My Father's War: A Son's Journey* (New York: Simon & Shuster, 1996)

Richter, D., *Where The Sun Stood Still! The Untold Story of Sir Jacob Vouza and the Guadalcanal Campaign* (Calabasas, CA: Toucan Publishing, 1992)

Risch, E., and Keiffer, C. L., *The Quartermaster Corps: Organization, Supply, and Services,* Volume II (Washington, D.C.: United States Government Printing Office, 1955)

Rogal, W. H., *Guadalcanal, Tarawa and Beyond: A Mud Marine's Memoir of the Pacific Island War* (Jefferson, NC: McFarland & Company, 2010)

Rokster, B., *Preparing for the Casualties of War: The American Experience Through World War II* (Santa Monica: RAND Corporation, 2013)

Rosenquist, R. G., Sexton, Col. M. J., and Burlein, R. A., *Our Kind of War: Illustrated Saga of the U.S. Marine Raiders of World War II* (Richmond: The American Historical Foundation, 1990)

Ross, B., and Shaffer, G. K., "Barney Ross on Guadalcanal," Installments 1-10 (King Features Syndicate, 1943)

Selvitelle, B., Untitled memoir, *Lower Deck Newsletter of the Warships and Marine Corps Museum* no. 30 (September 2002): pp. 4-6

Shane, T., *Heroes of the Pacific* (New York: Julian Messner, Inc., 1944)

Sharp, A., *Second Marine Division, 1940–1999* (Paducah: Turner Publishing, 1999)

Sledge, E. B., *With The Old Breed at Peleliu and Okinawa* (New York: Presidio Press, 2007. First printed by Presidio Press, 1981)

Sledge, M., *Soldier Dead: How We Recover, Identify, Bury, and Honor Our Military Fallen* (New York: Columbia University Press, 2005)

Smith, M. S., *Bloody Ridge, The Battle That Saved Guadalcanal* (San Marin, CA: Presidio Press, 2000)

Soule, T., *Shooting the Pacific War: Marine Corps Combat Photography in WWII* (Lexington, KY: The University Press of Kentucky, 2000)

Stauffer, A. P., *The Quartermaster Corps: Operations in the War Against Japan* (Washington, D.C.: United States Government Printing Office, 1956)

Steere, E., *The Graves Registration Service in WWII* (Washington: United States Government Printing Office, 1951)

Steere, E., and Boardman, T. M., *Final Disposition of World War II Dead* (Washington, D.C.: Office of the Quartermaster General, 1957)

Tonis, R., *I Joined The Cardinal's Army* (Brockton, MA: R. J. Tonis, date of publication unknown)

Thomas, L., *These Men Shall Never Die* (Philadelphia: The John C. Winston Company, 1943)

Tregaskis, R., *Guadalcanal Diary* (New York: Random House, 1943)

Twining, Gen. M. B., *No Bended Knee: The Battle for Guadalcanal*, edited by Neil G. Carey (New York: Presidio Press, 1996)

Ulbrich, D. J., *Preparing for Victory: Thomas Holcomb and the Making of the Modern Marine Corps* (Annapolis: U. S. Naval Institute Press, 2011)

Vandegrift, A. A., *Once A Marine: The Memoirs of General A. A. Vandegrift, United States Marine Corps*, edited by Robert B (Asprey. New York: Ballantine Books, 1966)

War Department. *Technical Manual No. 10-630: Graves Registration* (Washington, D.C.: U. S. Government Printing Office, 1940); *Field Manual No. 100-10: Field Service Regulations: Administration* (Washington, D.C.: U. S. Government Printing Office, 1940)

Warren, M. W., Walsh-Haney, H. A., and Freas, L., (eds.), *The Forensic Anthropology Laboratory* (Boca Raton: CRC Press, 2008)

Waters, A. B., "The Price of Intelligence," *Marine Corps Gazette* 38, no. 7 (July 1954): pp. 34-44

Whyte, W. H., *A Time of War: Remembering Guadalcanal, A Battle without Maps* (New York: Fordham University Press, 2000)

Williams, R. C., *The Forensic Historian: Using Science To Reexamine The Past* (New York: Routledge, 2015)

Willard, W. W., *The Leathernecks Come Through* (New York: Fleming H. Revell Company, 1944)

Wolfert, I., *Battle for the Solomons* (Boston: Houghton Mifflin Company, 1943)

Wukovits, J., *American Commando: Evans Carlson, His WWII Marine Raiders, and America's First Special Forces Mission* (New York: New American Library, 2009)

Zimmerman, J. L., *The Guadalcanal Campaign* (Washington, D.C.: Historical Division, U. S. Marine Corps, 1949)

Newspapers

The Akron Beacon-Journal (Akron, OH)
The Arizona Republic (Phoenix, AZ)
The Asbury Park Evening Press (Asbury Park, NJ)
The Berkshire Evening Eagle (Berkshire, MA)
The Bismarck Tribune (Bismarck, ND)
The Brooklyn Daily Eagle (Brooklyn, NY)
The Chicago Tribune (Chicago, IL)
The Dayton Herald (Dayton, OH)
The Evening Leader (Corning, NY)
The Ford County Press (Melvin, IL)
The Honolulu Advertiser (Honolulu, HI)
The Honolulu Star-Bulletin (Honolulu, HI)
The Jamestown Post-Journal (Jamestown, NY)
The Marine Corps Chevron (San Diego, CA)
The Morning Herald (Gloversville and Johnstown, NY)

The Morning News (Wilmington, DE)
The Mount Carmel Item (Mount Carmel, PA)
The Oakland Tribune (Oakland, CA)
The Oklahoman (Oklahoma City, OK)
The Palm Beach Post-Times (Palm Beach, FL)
The Palladium Item (Richmond, IN)
The Philadelphia Inquirer (Philadelphia, PA)
The Pittsburgh Press (Pittsburgh, PA)
The Portsmouth Herald (Portsmouth NH)
The St. Louis Post-Dispatch (St. Louis, MO)
The Tennessean (Nashville, TN)
The Tucson Daily Citizen (Tuczon, AZ)
The Washington Post (Washington, DC)

Archival and Unpublished Sources

Ardnt, C. C., Interview conducted by David Wollschlager, 2006. Author's collection.
Cameron, C., "Frank Lowell Few, His WW2 Experience," Unpublished manuscript, 1983.
Hurlbut, J. W. Untitled press release, 14 August 1942. U.S. Naval Institute collection.
White, G. P., Diary. Minnesota Historical Society Library collection.

Library of Congress, American Folklife Center, Veterans History Project

Allen Coolidge Troutman Collection (AFC/2001/001/55196)
George W. Kohler Collection (AFC/2001/001/06119)
James Joseph Messina Collection (AFC/2001/001/54346)
Joseph M. Barnes Collection (AFC/2001/001/76039)
Leonard Gadi Lawton Collection (AFC/2001/001/23602)
Marshall P. Smith Collection (AFC/2001/001/80079)
Norman R. Korsmeyer Collection (AFC/2001/001/99815)
Paul Green Collection (AFC/2001/001/92969)
Pete Arias Collection (AFC/2001/001/50203)
Robert L. Corwin Collection (AFC/2001/001/01706)
Theodore R. Cummings Collection (AFC/2001/001/78232)

Marine Corps History Division, Reference Branch, Quantico, VA

1st Marine Division: Division Circular 6a-42: Personnel Administration, 10 July 1942
1st Marine Division, Fleet Marine Force, D-2 [Intelligence] Journal; Volume I: From 7 August 1942 to 31 August 1943; Volume VII: From 22 November 1942 to 11 December 1942
1st Marine Division: Message: Disposition of Personal Effects In The Case Of Personnel Killed or Missing, 19 August 1942.

National Museum of the Pacific War, Nimitz Education & Research Center Digital Archive

Constentino, Matthew. Interview conducted by Floyd Cox, 7 October 2005.

National World War II Museum, Digital Collections

Greer, Richard. Interviewer unknown.

US National Archives and Records Administration, College Park, MD

Record Group 92: Records of the Office of the Quartermaster General, 1774-1985
Grave Plot Charts of American Dead, 1946–1951.
Headquarters, Graves Registration Service, Quartermaster Corps. Weekly Report of
Burials Recorded. 10 January 1943–30 December 1944; General Correspondence,
Miscellaneous Files. Box 276.
Maps of Temporary American Grave Sites Overseas, 1946-1951.

Record Group 127: Records of the U.S. Marine Corps, 1775-
Records of Ground Combat Units
1st Battalion, 1st Marines. War Journal, 8 June 1942–26 June 1945.
1st Battalion, 2nd Marines. Record of Events, November 1942–January 1943.
1st Battalion, 8th Marines. War Diary, 19 October 1942–7 September 1945.
2nd Marines. Record of Events, November 1942–January 1943.
7th Marines. Record of Events—Guadalcanal.
1st Marine Division, Headquarters. "Division Commander's Final Report on
Guadalcanal Operation."
24 May 1943. Box 39; Phase I: "Events Prior to H-Hour, 7 August 1842"; Phase
II: "From H Hour to Evening 9 August"; Phase III: "Organization of the Lunga
Point Defenses, 10 August–21 August"; Phase IV: "20 August–18 September";
Phase V: "18 September–5 December"
Company Muster Rolls, 1st Marine Division, July 1942–February 1943 (microfilm).
Company Muster Rolls, 1st Marine Raider Battalion, July 1942–October 1942
(microfilm).
Company Muster Rolls, 2nd Marine Division, November 1942–February 1943
(microfilm).
Company Muster Rolls, 2nd Marine Raider Battalion, July 1942–December 1942
(microfilm).
Company Muster Rolls, 2nd Marine Regiment, July 1942–February 1943
(microfilm)
Company Muster Rolls, 6th Marine Regiment, October 1942–February 1943
(microfilm)
Company Muster Rolls, 8th Marine Regiment, October 1942–February 1943
(microfilm)
Squadron Muster Rolls, Marine Aircraft Wings, Pacific, July 1942–February 1943
(microfilm)

Record Group 338: Records of U.S. Army Operational, Tactical, and Support
Organizations (World War II and Thereafter), 1917–1999.
604th Quartermaster Graves Registration Company: Unit Photo History

Record Group 407: Records of the Adjutant General's Office, 1905–1981.
1st Platoon, 45th Quartermaster Graves Registration Company. Historical Record.
1st Platoon, 49th Quartermaster Graves Registration Company. Historical Record.
2nd Platoon, 49th Quartermaster Graves Registration Company. Historical Record.

604th Quartermaster Graves Registration Company. Summary of Cruise, Search & Expedition No. 1, LST 711, 15 July 1947–17 February 1948; Summary of Cruise, Search & Expedition No. 2 Diary, June 1948–18 April 1949.

US National Archives and Records Administration, St. Louis, MO

Official Military Personnel Files: US Marine Corps
Asher, Doyle H.; Barber, Owen M.; Bernes, Albert L.; Budd, Robert J.; Christie, Thomas J.; Cockrell, Alvin C.; Custer, Steven A.; Debele, Charles F.; Drake, Francis F. Jr.; Edwards, Randolph R.; Farrar, Richard C.; Harrison, Joseph H.; Hermiston, Albert L.; Hopkins, Gerald P.; Johnson, George A.; Liston, Robert L.; Lyons, Robert R.; Matelski, Cyrill A.; McStine, Leon W.; Morrissey, Harry C.; Onnen, John W. G.; Phillips, Thomas W.; Rhodes, Luther L.; Schlesinger, Howard J.; Schulthies, Raymond J.; Secor, Frederick W.; Smith, William A.; Student, Emil S.; Treptow, George A.
Official Military Personnel Files: US Navy
Bender, Bruce B.; Pierce, James F.

US Navy Bureau of Medicine and Surgery Oral History Program

Clayton, John. Interview conducted by Jan K. Herman, 17–18 January 2006.
Ortega, Louis. Interview conducted by Jan K. Herman, 23 June 1995.

Washington National Records Center, Suitland, MD.

Records of the Office of the Quartermaster General
Individual Deceased Personnel Files: US Army
Albertson, Hallard D.; Andrick, Rollie A.; Bland, Leland S.; Cellini, John; Collalti, Robert F.; Dixon, Clifford C.; Doherty, Philip H.; Fiedler, William F. Jr.; Manyak, Joseph S.; Ross, Dale H.; Slaton, Elmer A.; Wood, Raymond S.

Individual Deceased Personnel Files: US Marine Corps
Anderson, Robert G.; Asher, Doyle H.; Bainbridge, William; Ballew, Robert H.; Beddla, Michael J.; Boschert, Mickey A.; Buckhalt, John C.; Bunch, Talmadge A.; Butland, Gerard M.; Copple, Julius W.; Custer, Steven A.; Dick, Harold G.; Durr, Leland N.; Fox, Havard G.; Gardner, Jack H.; Gill, Richard F. Goettge, Frank B.; Grazier, George H.; Hermiston, Albert L.; Johnson, Paul J.; Kowal, Henry L.; Lovelace, Robert W.; Lyons, Jack F.; Lyons, Robert R.; McCulloch, Gordon R.; Mead, George H.; Miglin, Charles W.; Miller, Clarence C.; Pilleri, Thomas S.; Rogers, Otho L.; Schuler, Larry J.; Serdula, Stephen; Setzer, Joseph W.; Walter, Blaine G.; Waltz, Forrest D.; Ward, Lloyd E.; Wilkins, William V.; Wise, Horace M.; Wisner, Ben B.

Individual Deceased Personnel Files: US Navy
Buchman, William F.; Pratt, Malcolm L.

Unknown (X) Files, Solomon Islands, Guadalcanal
X-8, -12, -14, -16, -19, -25, -27, -32, -33, -35, -36, -37, -38, -39, -40, -42, -42, -46, -47, -48, -52, -53, 54, -57, -62, -63, -67, -68, -69, -70, -71, -73, -74, -75, -77, -78, -81, -82, -83A, -83B, -86, -88, -89, -89A, -91A, -91B, -92, -94, -95A–G, -97, -98, -99, -104, -112, -112A, -113, 114A–C, -115, -118, -176, -177, -178, -179, -182, -183, -190, -195, -206, -208, -209, -210, -211, -212, -214, -215, -216, -218,

-219, -220, -221, -225, -226, -227, -228, -229, -230, -232, -233, -234, -235, -237, -239, -240, -241, -242, -245, -248, -249, -250, -251, -252, -254, -255, -256, -257, -277, -280A–B, -281, -282, -283, -284, -285, -286, -287, -288, -289, -290, -291, -292A–B, -293, -294, -295, -296, -297, -298, -301, -302, -303, -304, -308, -311, -312, -313, -314, -320, -323, -324, -325, -338, -339, -340, -341, -342, -343, -344, -346, -347

Unknown (X) Files, Schofield Mausoleum #1 (Guadalcanal)
X-1, X-9, X-10A-B, X-12C, X-16, X-30, X-31, X-254

Unknown (X) Files, Schofield Mausoleum #2 (Guadalcanal)
X-2, X-7, X-25, X-26, X-27, X-29, X-39, X-40, X-41, X-42

Cross Reference for Positive Identification, X-1 thru X-322.

West Point Center for Oral History

Wagner, James. Interview conducted by David Siry, 18 July 2015.

Online Sources

Ancestry.com. US Military Collection, US Marine Corps Muster Rolls, 1798–1958, www.ancestry.com
Balester, V. J., (ed.), "Letters to Mark: Reminiscences of a Marine Corps Scout, Cpl. Fred J. Balester," 1988–1995, transcript online, www.privateletters.net/stories_balester.html
Clark, J. E., "Personal Log," www.sibconline.com.sb/wp-content/uploads/2014/02/Jack-Clark-Diary.pdf
Defense POW/MIA Accounting Agency, www.dpaa.mil
Donahue, Jr., J., (ed.), "Guadalcanal Journal: A Personal History of the Battle for Guadalcanal," web.archive.org/web/20150814122233/http://guadalcanaljournal.com:80/the-guadalcanal-journal/
Fold3.com. WWII War Diaries, www.fold3.com
Garrett, J. R., "A Marine Diary: My Experiences on Guadalcanal," www.nettally.com/jrube/@guadaug.html
Malanowski, J., "Andy Malanowski, USMC," Blog entry, 9 March 2010, jamiemalanowski.com/andy-malanowski-usmc/
Newspapers.com. Historical Newspapers, www.newspapers.com
Office of the Quartermaster General, "Tell Me About My Boy," 1946; transcribed by Army Quartermaster Foundation, Inc., 2018, www.qmfound.com/article/tell-me-about-my-boy/
Radford University Office of University Relations, "RU Students Write From Guadalcanal About Their Search for WWII Marine Remains," www.radford.edu/NewsPub/July08/0712guadalcanaltrip.html
Roosevelt, E., "South Pacific Travel Diary," 1943. Collection of George Washington University, Columbian College of Arts & Sciences. Transcribed online, erpapers.columbian.gwu.edu/eleanor-roosevelts-south-pacific-travel-diary-excerpts
Taylan, J., (ed.) "Jack Clark: USN Lunga Boat Patrol & Beachmaster." Transcript of interview conducted by Peter Flahavin, www.pacificwrecks.com/people/veterans/clark.html

Thiesen, W. H., "USS *Serpens*—the Coast Guard's Greatest Loss," *Cutter of the Month* (blog), *US Coast Guard Alumni Association* (February 2018), www.cgaalumni.org/

Sundberg, E., "Letters to a Granddaughter," edsundberg.weebly.com/us-marine.html

Victoria Texas Videos, "WWII Marine Veteran Herman Shirley Discusses Guadalcanal," 22 January 2013, www.youtube.com/watch?v=qT9sjMePzF4&t=108s